Introduction to
Community
Development

Introduction to
Community
Development

Theory, Practice, and Service-Learning

Edited by

Jerry W. Robinson, Jr.
Delta State University and University of Illinois at Urbana-Champaign

Gary Paul Green
University of Wisconsin-Madison

Los Angeles | London | New Delhi
Singapore | Washington DC

For information:

SAGE Publications, Inc.
2455 Teller Road
Thousand Oaks, California 91320
E-mail: order@sagepub.com

SAGE Publications Ltd.
1 Oliver's Yard
55 City Road
London EC1Y 1SP
United Kingdom

SAGE Publications India Pvt. Ltd.
B 1/I 1 Mohan Cooperative Industrial Area
Mathura Road, New Delhi 110 044
India

SAGE Publications Asia-Pacific Pte. Ltd.
33 Pekin Street #02-01
Far East Square
Singapore 048763

Printed in the United States of America

Library of Congress Cataloging-in-Publication Data

Introduction to community development: theory, practice, and service-learning / Jerry W. Robinson, Jr., Gary Paul Green.
   p. cm.
Includes bibliographical references and index.
ISBN 978-1-4129-7462-2 (pbk.)
   1. Community development. 2. Economic development. I. Robinson, Jerry W., 1932- II. Green, Gary P.

HN49.C6I588 2011
307.1′4—dc22   2009037028

This book is printed on acid-free paper.

10   11   12   13   10   9   8   7   6   5   4   3   2   1

Acquisitions Editor:	Lisa Cuevas Shaw
Editorial Assistant:	MaryAnn Vail
Production Editor:	Catherine M. Chilton
Copy Editor:	Liann Lech
Typesetter:	C&M Digitals (P) Ltd.
Proofreader:	Annette R. Van Deusen
Indexer:	Gary Paul Green
Cover Designer:	Edgar Abarca
Marketing Manager:	Christy Guilbault

Contents

Acknowledgments ────

Several of our colleagues contributed to this project by reviewing chapters for us. We would like to thank Alan Barton (Delta State University), John Green (Delta State University), Albert Nylander (Delta State University), William Harris (MIT), Margaret Holt (University of Georgia), Ron Hustedde (University of Kentucky), Anne Silvis (University of Illinois), Greg Wise (University of Wisconsin–Extension), Bill Rizzo (University of Wisconsin–Extension), Anna Haines (University of Wisconsin–Stevens Point), Tim Borich (Iowa State University), John Allen (Utah State University), Ellen Taylor Powell (University of Wisconsin–Extension), Mark Harvey (Florida Atlantic University), and Matt Carroll (Washington State University).

Elizabeth Gering, Ellie Jessup, and Evan Armstrong helped identify the service-learning case studies and the supporting material for service-learning that is available online. Elizabeth also meticulously reviewed each chapter of the manuscript.

Our editor at Sage, Lisa Shaw, has been a great supporter. Lisa helped us refocus our proposal and identify its potential contribution. She kept us moving, and we appreciate all her encouragement throughout this project.

Finally, it was a joy working with all of the authors in this volume. We appreciate all of their contributions and support.

SAGE Publications would also like to thank the following reviewers: Steven Soifer, University of Maryland; Tim Chapin, Florida State University; Sammy L. Comer, Tennessee State University; Demetrius Latridis, Boston University; Robert Mark Silverman, University at Buffalo; and Anne Statham, University of Southern Indiana.

1

Developing Communities

*Jerry W. Robinson, Jr.,
and Gary Paul Green*

BEHAVIOR OBJECTIVES

After studying this chapter and completing the online learning activities, students should be able to

1. Understand the criticism of the concept of "community."
2. Define community of place.
3. Differentiate between community development and economic development.
4. Describe the social forces that led to the rise of the community development field.
5. Differentiate between development "of" community and development "in" community.
6. Identify issues that influence the interests of residents in specific localities.
7. Understand the role of participation in the community development process.
8. Distinguish between community service-learning and volunteering/community service.

Introduction

Much has been written in recent years about the loss of community and the implications for civil society (Putnam, 2000). Globalization has restructured economic, political, and social relationships at the local level. Technological and social changes have opened new paths for sharing collective interests, such as social networking sites on the Internet and mass media that link individuals to a common culture. Corporations and financial institutions shift capital around the globe to seek out more profitable locations for doing business. Workers increasingly move to places where they can find better job opportunities. All of these factors undermine the sense of community in places.

Although our social relationships and interests are no longer limited to local communities, the power of place remains. Local issues, such as education, housing, health, and jobs, are critical concerns for most residents. There continues to be interest in mobilizing local residents to build assets that improve their quality of life (Green & Haines, 2007; Kretzmann & McKnight, 1993). Although communities are tightly integrated into the global economy and culture, local relationships and issues continue to play an essential role in the daily life of residents.

This idea that community is a valid concept today is often criticized by social analysts. Much of this analysis emphasizes the individualistic nature of many modern societies (Bellah, Madsen, Sullivan, Swidler, & Tipton, 1985). Although it is true that many cultures today are more individualistic, there are many issues that encourage people to look for common interests and concerns at the local level. Other critics charge that the concept of community is laden with assumptions about a common set of values and norms. This assumption tends to ignore the divisions in a locality (such as race, gender, and class) that may produce different values and interests. Our use of the concept of community does not assume that residents hold the same values or adhere to the same norms. It does presuppose that there are issues that are imposed on or common to many people who live in a certain area. So, for example, factors influencing the value of homes in a neighborhood might be an issue that is a source of collective action. Residents may work together to fight crime or improve the quality of education in the area. Similarly, environmental problems (such as illegal dumping of trash or hazardous waste sites) may contribute to local responses by residents. This is not to say that all residents will act on some of these common interests. These issues, however, provide opportunities and incentives for residents to act on a local basis. This view of community, then, does not require consensus. And it does not imply that residing in a specific geographic location constitutes a community. Instead, community is constituted when residents in a specific geographic place are mobilized to act on locality-oriented collective interests. Kenneth Wilkinson (1991) adds a third criterion (in addition to territory and collective action) to the definition of community—local institutions. Local institutions are important because they produce regular social interactions.

This book examines the theory and practice of community development. Community development can be defined as networks of actors engaged in activities through associations in a place (Wilkinson, 1991). There are a couple of key points to emphasize in this definition. First, this definition is limited to "communities of place" rather than "communities of interest." It focuses on social relationships that are defined by territory rather than simply by interests. Examples of a "community of interest" would be a group of people who have common hobbies or interests. A community of place includes a group of residents who have common interest related to territory or place. An example would be factors that influence the local quality of life, such as education, environmental conditions, or jobs.

Second, community development is a social process involving residents in activities designed to improve their quality of life. An implicit value of community development is that this involvement should be inclusive, with and by residents from all walks of life in the community, not to and for them. In many respects, the process of development is just as important as the outcomes.

Community development is often confused with economic development. What is the relationship between community and economic development? Most people view community development as a set of activities that must precede economic development. Communities need to provide a good social and physical infrastructure, including housing and schools, in order to generate jobs and income. Many community development activities, however, are more directly related to economic development, such as job training and business management. The concept of community development, then, is broader than economic development and may include many activities that are economic in nature.

Community development can be traced to the Progressive Era at the turn of the 20th century, when Progressives sought to address the major problems facing cities, such as rising crimes rates and juvenile delinquency. Their view was that these urban problems were caused by the social conditions in local neighborhoods. Progressives also emphasized the need to engage local citizens and experts in identifying strategies to address these problems. Their interventions to address these issues were at the community rather than the individual level.

The Progressives provided a rich conceptual framework for community development, but it was the social activists of the 1960s that broadened the basis of community intervention and institutionalized it in national policy. The War on Poverty directed several programs at the problems of concentrated poverty. These programs required the "maximum feasible participation" of the poor in the design and implementation of programs.

Community development has evolved to include a much broader focus than just poverty. Affordable housing, job training, and social services continue to be the "meat and potatoes" of community development programs. Community development, however, has expanded to include local issues such as education, health care, and the environment. Thus, community development is a field composed of many disciplines. For example, individuals from any of the following disciplines may become involved in community development—anthropology, business, education, economics, geography, organizational behavior, sociology, or social work. The common thread that runs through various disciplines and issues is the continuing importance of place and the value (necessity) of public participation in decisions that affect local people.

The community development literature is filled with contradictory notions about the field. The literature is often divided among those who promote "development-in-the-community" and those who advocate "development-of-the-community" (Shaffer & Summers, 1989). This distinction is often characterized as process versus outcomes. Is community development about increasing civic participation in local matters, or is it about generating tangible outcomes, such as jobs, businesses, and affordable homes? This is probably a false choice because most community development practitioners do both. But the outcomes can be contradictory as practitioners may emphasize outcomes at the expense of the process of community engagement.

Inherent in this definition is another contradiction. Community development is often viewed as a normative science, advocating public participation and civic engagement. By normative science, we mean that it is not objective and value-free but is shaped by values and norms. It also may mean that community development is more of an "art" than a "science." There is no conceptual map for how to work with all communities. Community development, however, can be considered a positive science, focusing on identifying the most effective ways to promote development in communities. This view of community development sees the importance of basing local programs on empirical evidence and not just on the desires and preferences of local residents.

The Practice of Community Development

Community development practitioners are engaged in a variety of activities, including economic development, housing, job training, and others (Brophy & Shabecoff, 2001). To a large extent, the field has been shaped by community practice rather than guided by theory. Many of the institutional innovations that have become basic tools, such as community land trusts and community development financial institutions, were developed through local experiments. Methods of community organizing and facilitation have evolved as well through practice and social learning.

This is not to suggest that research has not made important contributions to community development. Several examples illustrate this link. There has been a plethora of recent research on the concept of social capital. This concept, which is discussed more fully in some of the later chapters, focuses on the role of social networks and relationships in generating or inhibiting collective action. Although the research has been widely debated, the empirical work on this topic has some immediate implications for community development. Strategies for establishing social ties across groups within the community and with outside organizations and institutions are essential to the development process.

Another example is the research on workforce development, which documents the role that community-based organizations can play in linking employers, workers, and training institutions (Melendez, 2004). Workforce development networks can be structured so as to provide employers with incentives to invest in training of low-wage workers (Green, 2007).

Although the context for community development varies widely, most practitioners would prefer to base their activities on research-based ideas and concepts. This book brings these disparate pieces (theory and practice) together in an integrative fashion that summarizes the current state of the field. The goal is to more fully integrate the insights from research and practice to advance both. One additional dimension—service-learning—is introduced. Recently, there has been increased interest in the concept of community service-learning.

Service-learning provides students with an opportunity to integrate the concepts and theories that are based in research with an actual community experience.

————— Service-Learning and Community Development

Service-learning has been widely acclaimed as an important pedagogical tool. The basic premise of this concept is that experiential learning enhances classroom knowledge. Service-learning can be defined as a teaching methodology that integrates the goals of academic learning with a community experience to produce a community service. Service-learning has several characteristics that distinguish it from traditional community service or volunteering. First, service-learning involves experiences that meet community needs. Rather than just fulfilling a course requirement, service-learning serves the needs of local residents and organizations. This element can be challenging because many service-learning activities are oriented toward students rather than the needs of communities (Stoecker & Tryon, 2009).

Second, it requires reflection and academic learning on the topic related to the service. Service-learning provides students with practical learning experiences that allow them to apply theories and concepts learned in the classroom. This community experience enriches the student's classroom knowledge as well by providing concrete activities that demonstrate the value (or weaknesses) of the conceptual material discussed in class.

Third, the experience contributes to the student's understanding of community life. Students gain an appreciation for how and why the local context matters. Much of what is taught in the classroom focuses on general principles and theories. Service-learning provides a more nuanced understanding of how these general principles and theories work in different community settings.

In the remaining chapters of this text, examples of community service-learning are provided. These case studies demonstrate the value of service-learning for enhancing understanding of community development. Additional material on service-learning is also available on the course Web site. Service-learning activities offer students an opportunity to take the concepts and theories discussed in this book and apply them in a real-world setting. Our goal is to introduce these concepts in the book and provide exercises and activities that will enhance the opportunities for students to use them in their community.

————— A Few Words on Pedagogy—Learning and Teaching

This book offers a unique approach to the study of community development. Rather than just summarizing and defining theories and concepts, the book provides exercises, most of which are online, that allow students and practitioners to apply the central ideas presented in each chapter. In addition, it provides a series of community service-learning activities. Learning activities are conceptualized on three levels.

1. **LARK:** The first or most basic level of learning is cognitive, or "Learning And Repeating Knowledge." For each chapter, a series of online action learning or LARK activities is provided that students will complete to ensure that they grasp the full meaning and understanding of all fundamental and basic theoretical concepts presented in the chapter. Batteries of multiple-choice and short essay questions are included online for each chapter.

2. **SOAR:** The next basic level of learning is synthesis, which involves "Searching Out And Relating" knowledge. For each chapter, we offer a series of action learning and research exercises online, or SOAR activities. SOAR activities ensure that students grasp the full meaning of all fundamental concepts and basic skills presented in the chapter by relating their new knowledge to the practice of community development. SOAR activities include case studies, demonstration, role-plays, and action research projects. Thus, batteries of case studies, essay questions, team learning exercises, and action research projects are included for each chapter.

3. **LIFE:** The highest level of learning is creativity, which involves "Learning In Field Experiences," or the laboratory of life. Each chapter will have a series of LIFE activities that require students to (a) apply what they have learned to the practice of community development in real-world or on-the-job tasks; (b) analyze and interpret outcomes; and (c) suggest new, creative approaches for understanding and practicing community development. For example, exercises will be included that enable students to interpret situations that they encounter in real-world community development challenges for a practical and theoretical approach, and to provide suggestions to colleagues, instructors, and the authors of chapters in this book that will enrich the community development field. In addition, many chapters will provide instructors with information on community service-learning activities that can be integrated into the course.

Theory and Practice of Community Development ————

As we already have suggested, the field of community development has been shaped more by practice than by theory. Over the past 50 years, however, experience in the field has accumulated to the point where there are a growing number of general principles and theories about community intervention. In Chapter 2, Lorraine Garkovich provides a brief history of the community development field and identifies the major trends in theory and practice. In this first section of the book, the history of the field is reviewed and basic theories of community development are outlined. These theories tend to be very general guidelines about how practitioners intervene in communities and the goals of social action.

Several different theoretical/methodological approaches are discussed. In Chapter 3, Barton and Selfa discuss the complex and multifaceted ways in which communities are linked to their landscape. They discuss strategies in which community development helps people to share meaningfully in the natural elements that surround their community. In Chapter 4, Robinson and Fear outline some of the premises and types of technical assistance provided to communities. In addition, they outline the basic contradictions involved in this approach. The self-help approach to community development (Chapter 5) is in many respects the polar opposite of the technical assistance approach. Rather than providing technical support, practitioners facilitate the process so as to build the capacity of communities to address future issues. In Chapter 6, Bridger, Brennan, and Luloff discuss the interactional approach to community development. Rather than focusing on the structure of communities, interactional theory stresses the central roles that local interaction and capacity play in the emergence of community among people who share a common territory. They emphasize that community is not taken as a given, but is a contingent phenomenon that develops through social interaction. Finally, in Chapter 7, Robinson and Smutko sketch out the basic elements of the conflict approach. Based on the work of Saul Alinsky, the conflict approach holds an important place in the field of community development.

Community Development Issues

In the second section, several common issues facing community development practitioners are discussed. The list of potential issues facing communities is endless, so we have chosen some of the most common issues that practitioners face in the field. Increasingly, community development practitioners are being asked to evaluate their efforts and demonstrate the impact of their programs. In Chapter 8, Green and Kleiner discuss some of the basic elements to conducting evaluation research in communities. A common issue and challenge for community development programs is leadership. In Chapter 9, Stovall and his colleagues identify strategies for building leadership skills in communities. Successful community development usually involves collaboration that brings together individuals who normally do not work together. Ayres and Silvis (Chapter 10) provide a discussion of the issues related to building partnerships across organizations, institutions, and communities.

Although rural and urban areas face some common issues, they also have some unique challenges. Distance and scale are two of the most obvious obstacles. Beaulieu and Israel (Chapter 11) describe some of the special obstacles and issues facing small, rural places and offer some strategies for community development in these places. In Chapter 12, Lowe and Harris evaluate some of the obstacles that inner cities, especially concentrated poverty neighborhoods, face today.

The final section of the book focuses on several substantive issues facing communities. In Chapter 13, Wheeler and Thomas examine programs directed toward engaging youth in communities and provide examples of different approaches toward delivering youth programs. In Chapter 14, Morton and Glasgow explore how health has become a major community development issue. They also examine some of the models for implementing health programs in communities. Schafft and Harmon (Chapter 15) focus on the unique role that educational institutions can play in the community development process. They see schools as a significant resource that can provide the basis for collective action in communities. There is a growing recognition that sustainability is one of the major challenges that communities face today. Hembd and Silberstein (Chapter 16) provide an overview of different approaches that localities are taking toward developing more sustainable communities. In Chapter 17, Meikle and Green discuss some of the obstacles communities face through globalization. Globalization presents new obstacles to communities, especially in developing countries. Rather than completely constraining the efforts of local governments and organizations, globalization does offer some opportunities to relocalize the economy. And the last chapter (Chapter 18) presents some of the editors' opinions about the emerging issues in the field of community development.

Conclusion

This book is intended as an introduction to the field of community development for students and practitioners. The approach is somewhat different in that we explore the linkages between community theory, community development practice, and service-learning. Community development practitioners and students need a strong conceptual base for understanding local development issues. They need the ability and skills to understand the social, economic, and political dynamics at the local level, as well as a means of understanding how local communities are shaped and constrained by external forces. This text will help students develop the abilities and skills needed to be more effective as a community developer.

References

Bellah, R. N., Madsen, R., Sullivan, W. M., Swidler, A., & Tipton, S. M. (1985). *Habits of the heart: Individualism and commitment in American life*. Berkeley: University of California Press.

Brophy, P. C., & Shabecoff, A. (2001). *Careers in community development*. Washington, DC: Island Press.

Green, G. P. (2007). *Workforce development networks in rural areas: Building the high road.* Northhampton, MA: Edward Elgar.

Green, G. P., & Haines, A. (2007). *Asset building and community development* (2nd ed.). Thousand Oaks, CA: Sage.

Kretzmann, J., & McKnight, J. (1993). *Building communities from the inside out: A path toward finding and mobilizing a community's assets.* Evanston, IL: Center for Urban Affairs and Policy Research, Northwestern University.

Melendez, E. (Ed.). (2004). *Communities and workforce development.* Kalamazoo, MI: W. E. Upjohn Institute for Employment Research.

Putnam, R. D. (2000). *Bowing alone: The collapse and revival of American community.* New York: Simon & Schuster.

Shaffer, R., & Summers, G. F. (1989). Community economic development. In J. A. Christenson & J. W. Robinson (Eds.), *Community development in perspective* (pp. 173–195). Ames: Iowa State University Press.

Stoecker, R., & Tryon, E. A. (Eds.). (2009). *The unheard voices: Community organizations and service learning.* Philadelphia: Temple University Press.

Wilkinson, K. P. (1991). *The community in rural America.* New York: Greenwood.

2   A Historical View of Community Development

Lorraine E. Garkovich

BEHAVIOR OBJECTIVES

After studying this chapter and completing the online learning activities, students should be able to

1. Explain the historical relationship between community studies and community development.

2. Provide at least three different definitions or views of community development.

3. Explain the different core approaches to community development.

4. Explain the roles of key players in the history of community development in America.

5. Explain how community organizing and community development might be considered contradictory activities.

6. Identify the role or function that the federal government has played in community development.

7. Describe the changing role of foundations in community development.

8. Define similarities and differences in international and U.S. community development efforts.

Introduction

We have been engaged in community development (CD) from the beginning of human society. Social groups have always sought ways to modify their natural and built environments; create new opportunities; or alter the nature of social relationships, power, or decision making. The purpose of this chapter is to situate contemporary community development as both a substantive knowledge base and a field of practice in a historical context. With literally hundreds of years to cover, this task is greater than a single chapter. More in-depth explorations of the history of community development are available (Cary, 1970; Christenson & Robinson, 1980, 1989; Fear & Schwarzweller, 1985a, 1985b; Summers, 1986; Summers & Branch, 1984; Vidal, 1992). So this review will use five topics to provide a context for understanding the roots of contemporary community development:

- The diverse meanings of community development
- The knowledge base of community development
- Core approaches (technical assistance, self-help, conflict) to community development
- The policies and the players
- International community development

Case Study 2.1   Fashion Design and Service-Learning

Students in the Fashion Design and Merchandising program at Virginia Commonwealth University (VCU) participate in a service-learning course in Guatemala to apply their skills in design, production, and merchandising to women's clothing cooperatives. Led by Professor Linda Lee, students participate in the 2½-week course that includes a pre-trip workshop on the VCU campus, 11 days immersed in the cultural and economic world of garment design and production in Guatemala, and a wrap-up session on the VCU campus after the international service-learning experience. While in Guatemala, the students focus their knowledge and skills in local workshops and cooperatives run by Mayan women, learning traditional production and design styles and gaining insight into the economic impact of international markets. The trip is coordinated through the Highland Support Project (HSP), a Virginia nonprofit organization that promotes cultural awareness and empowerment through fair trade markets. HSP provides the student group with connections and support while in Guatemala as the students of VCU and the Mayan women's cooperatives work together to create a line of apparel and accessories that can be sold through fair trade markets in North America. Through this collaboration, the students gain an understanding of the cultural and economic importance of their studies. Their Mayan partners gain resources to participate in fair trade markets that will help them maintain a stable income and outlet for their traditional work. After such an intensive experience, the student group returns to its Richmond, Virginia, campus and shares what the students have learned. In the past, students have presented their experience formally to a panel of VCU faculty and administrators as well as featured their designs in an exhibition that is open and free to the public.

For more information, contact

- VCU Education Abroad, abroad@vcu.edu; http://www.international.vcu.edu/abroad/

———— The Diverse Meanings of Community Development

What is community development? To begin, we need to define two key concepts: community and development. *Community* has a multitude of meanings—from a geographically bounded physical place with people living together and meeting their livelihood and social interaction needs (e.g., urban neighborhoods, small towns, cities) to groups of people whose interaction is based not on physical proximity but on common interests (e.g., the community of buyers and sellers on eBay) (McMillan & Chavis, 1986; Theodori, 2005). In this chapter, the focus will be on the concept of community as a geographically defined place where people interact with each other and have psychological ties with each other and the place in which they live.

Development also has several meanings, including modernization, urbanization, industrialization, social or political transformation, technological improvement, and economic growth. Implicit in all of these is the idea that development involves change directed toward some particular social or economic goal. Shaw (2008) reminds us why definitions are important:

> How community is constructed politically provides the discourses and practices which frame the parameters of community development at any given time; its possibilities and its limitations. Politics expresses the totality of interrelationships, involving power, authority and influence. Clearly community does not exist within a political vacuum, but reflects and reinforces the dynamics of power within particular contexts and times. The same is true for community development. (p. 34)

Christenson, Fendley, and Robinson (1989) catalogue many different definitions of community development, with the essential meanings captured by this one: "A group of people in a locality initiating a social action process (i.e., a planned intervention) to change their economic, social, cultural and/or environmental situation" (p. 14). Essentially, then, community development is planned change.

Summers (1986) offers a somewhat different definition:

> Rural community development is planned intervention to stimulate social change for the explicit purpose of the "betterment of the people" and so development is ultimately a normative activity based on someone's "vision of what might be or ought to be." (p. 360)

This definition asserts that the planned change is the basis for "progress" or an enhanced quality of life and that there is some agreement on what we mean by an enhanced quality of life, who decides this, and how it is achieved. In practice, these may be points of dispute depending on the particular perspective on CD brought by the practitioners and held by those in the community where it happens.

Underlying the diversity of definitions are contrasting frameworks for understanding the meaning of CD and its practice. These are community development:

- As a *process* (a method of implementing change) such as technical assistance, self-help, or conflict approaches;
- As a *program* of specified activities such as housing construction, adoption of agricultural innovations, or implementation of recreational programs;
- As an *outcome* (the desired end result of a change) such as more employment, housing, access to health care, or civic engagement; or
- As an *ideology* of action "to restructure the social, normative and economic order for desired ends" (modified from Christenson & Robinson, 1989, p. 13).

Thus, there are many possible definitions and conceptual frameworks of community development, but one idea threads through all—a change in some aspect of community structure or life. But the degree of change, how it occurs, or who bears the burden of the change or benefits from it are questions whose answers, although shaped by our definitions, play out in the context of policies, ideologies, and practitioners' perspectives.

The Knowledge Base of Community Development ———————

The CD knowledge base is grounded in research on the nature of community processes and social change. Fear and Schwarzweller (1985a) argue that to understand the emergence of CD in America, you must look to the history of rural sociology because

> so rich has been the contribution of rural sociology to community development, that the roots of community development as a professional activity and field of competence are deeply embedded in, if not closely intertwined with, the profession and field of rural sociology. (pp. xx–xxi)

Rural sociologists in particular have a long history of linking both community research and engagement in community development.

Research is a factor in understanding the history of community development for two reasons. First, research provides the intellectual underpinning for the focus of CD programs. Research draws our attention to aspects of community life that may shape the design, implementation, and effectiveness of CD programs. Second, what we discover through the practice of community development or in evaluation research of programs of change can shape how we conceptualize and understand the nature of community. Topics that have influenced community development as a process and a program include studies of power and leadership, voluntary associations and social participation, and theories and models of community change (see Fear & Schwarzweller, 1985b;

Goe & Noonan, 2007; Sanders & Lewis, 1976; Summers, 1986; and Summers & Branch, 1984, for reviews of community research).

These community research topics hint at why there has always been a tension within academia and mainstream politics/organizations about community development. Community studies often point to the structural characteristics of places that create unequal life conditions that become the focus of community change/development efforts, and these can be unsettling for the existing leadership. To achieve its community-building goals, CD efforts often must challenge the political and/or economic position of community or national leaders.

Three examples illustrate this relationship between research and practice. First, a social systems approach to community has informed community development practice through its focus on the ways in which community beliefs shape community dynamics and how communities maintain their boundaries (Loomis & Beegle, 1950; Sampson, 1991; Sanders, 1958). Second, research on the community as an interactional field has informed community development practice through its focus on the systematic interactions of people and organizations as they succeed (or fail) in mobilizing people for collective action toward a shared goal, or to strengthen the community (Kaufman, 1959; Theodori, 2005; Wilkinson, 1970, 1972). Third, planned change has been the focus of many community studies. A review of this research would show that there has always been disagreement as to the most effective approach to planned change, as well as concern about the outcomes of different approaches (Castells, 1983). Summers (1986) outlines these differing views as follows:

Reform versus revolution—focuses on whether planned change can occur by simply modifying the existing social system or by replacing it.

Populist versus elitist—focuses on who should decide the path and method of planned change, the people or experts such as scientists, technicians, professional planners or elected leaders.

Structural versus individualistic—focuses on whether change efforts should be focused on institutions and social structures or individuals and their behaviors and capacities.

Outcome versus process—focuses on whether change should be directed at "immediate improvements in material well-being or toward developing new social, economic, and political processes" that eventually will lead to a better quality of life. (p. 361)

Newman and Lake (2006) illustrate these contrasting perspectives on planned change in a review of the politics of community development in U.S. urban areas since 1968. They argue that inner-city neighborhoods are now "viewed by entrepreneurial municipal regimes as material inputs for building livable cities and are being reintegrated into urban circuits as 'underutilized assets' for development capital" (p. 57), resulting in the elimination of entire low-income neighborhoods, replaced by upscale commercial and residential projects. From one perspective, this is community development even though the residents of these transformed neighborhoods are displaced, dispersed, and disempowered by the process. In other words, in the process of community development, "community" is destroyed. Newman and Lake (2006, p. 57) argue that the original focus of community development on enabling racially or culturally based neighborhoods to define their own identity and build local opportunities has shifted to an emphasis on the development of physical places, regardless of the effects on people. As a result, community organizing and community development have different goals.

Community studies provide knowledge on community dynamics that influence if, when, and how development may occur. Thus, community studies enable us to design strategies of development based on an understanding of community structures and processes. From this research, three major approaches to community development have emerged.

Core Approaches to Community Development ————————

Nearly all historical reviews of community development note that there are basically three approaches to its practice: technical assistance, self-help, and conflict. Briefly, a technical assistance approach focuses on the use of technical (e.g., agricultural, health, education, industrial) knowledge to design and implement a targeted program of change (see Chapter 4). In this approach, a technical expert performs a needs assessment of a community situation and designs a focused intervention project. Typically, these are "hard" projects such as the building of a bridge or industrial park, the adoption of ordinances, or the introduction of new or enhanced services (e.g., educational, health). Technical assistance is a typical approach of governments, public agencies (e.g., TVA), and foundations. It also has dominated international development efforts for decades.

Self-help approaches emphasize people in a community coming together and learning how to address their problems as they define them so as to improve their own situation (see Chapter 5). Typically, the self-help approach engages professionals and businesspersons in the community to become more active in their community through projects that address their interests and concerns. In this approach, the CD practitioner provides information as requested and facilitates the development of skills and knowledge in local people so that they can define alternatives and act in their own interests. This approach is more typical of community or regional development agencies, some foundations, and the Cooperative Extension Service.

Conflict approaches also emphasize local people working together to identify their own needs, nurture their own leadership skills and knowledge, and organize their own action strategies (Chapter 7). But practitioners using a conflict approach assume that the primary challenges facing those with whom they work are their poverty and powerlessness. So this approach assumes that addressing the issues or needs of clients will inevitably lead to confrontation with those who have more wealth or power. The CD practitioner, then, is an organizer who helps people discover that they have power because of their numbers and the justice inherent in their demands (Korten, 1980). As a form of a conflict approach to CD, community organizing has an explicit ideological perspective: The "commitment, first and foremost, is to the expansion of democracy" (Stoecker, 2009, p. 23). This approach is more typical of neighborhood or community agencies, especially those in urban areas (Gittell & Vidal, 1998), as well as regional and national advocacy groups (e.g., environmental justice groups).

Historically, the importance of each of these approaches has shifted with changing policies, programs, and resources. But particular approaches have been more commonly used in certain situations than others. For example, in rural America, self-help and technical assistance have been the most common approaches, and the efficacy of these approaches documented most often by rural sociologists. In rural communities, CD has tended to be a community-based process for creating change, often because the size, geographic isolation, and limited resources of these communities make a primary reliance on technical assistance more difficult. On the other hand, in urban areas, technical assistance and conflict have been the most common approaches, and the efficacy of these approaches documented most often by political scientists, economists, urban geographers, and urban studies researchers. In urban areas, CD has tended to be driven by a diversity of community-based agencies, organizations, and foundations with a strong focus on housing and economic development. Research suggests that community organizing has been a major factor influencing both neighborhood associations and urban development (Orr, 2007; Rubin & Rubin, 2007; Smock, 2003).

Some would argue that there are inherent tensions among each of these approaches to community development. For example, Stoecker (2003) argues that there is a fundamental dialectic between community development and community organizing that makes it difficult for any one organization to engage in both processes. For Stoecker (2003), community development is

> supposed to engage in comprehensive development, attempting to create jobs, housing, crime reductions, and a host of other changes in dis-empowered and disinvested neighborhoods . . . [and] they are supposed to accomplish all this within the existing political economic system, bringing historically marginalized people into the economic mainstream. (p. 494)

Moreover, community organizing assumes that there are no common interests between the "haves and have nots," whereas community development depends on the identification of common interests because these become the basis for development partnerships (see also Fisher & Shragge, 2000).

Thus, throughout the history of community development, there has been both a sense of complimentarity as well as tension among the dominant approaches to the practice of CD. As we will see in the next section, whether there is co-existence or tension among these different approaches has sometimes depended on national policies that allocate resources for different types of community development.

The Policies and the Players

Who is involved in the practice of community development, and which approach is most emphasized, has grown more complex over the past century. Why? Because public policies on CD ebb and flow, as do the resources available for it, and as a result, the availability of funding often influences the approaches to CD. For example, if you don't have a lot of money for development, you focus on building relationships within the community to gain access to the resources to make development possible.

Research by the Urban Institute identifies four key components of the national community development system that began to solidify by 2001:

1. Community development corporations (CDCs);

2. Production systems that "mobilize, allocate, and regulate the use of land and capital for community development purposes";

3. Capacity-building systems that accumulate and allocate resources in support of community development activities; and

4. Leadership systems that "mobilize political support and resources for a community development agenda." (Walker, 2002, p. 3)

Frisch and Servon (2006) assert that there is now a "community development system" that "consists of a range of new actors, strategies, policy tools and best practices" (p. 89). In general, the players in this system include the federal government, state and local governments, national intermediaries, community development financial institutions, community development corporations, community-based development organizations, nonprofit organizations, private foundations, for-profit organizations, professional associations, and universities. What follows is a brief explanation of the role and focus of each.

Federal Government

Federal government agencies and federal policies have always been central to community development efforts. For example, westward expansion was fueled by a decision to "spend" federal lands in support of the development of a railroad infrastructure. Over time, an alphabet soup of federal community development programs has emerged.[1] Federal funding

---

[1]See the following sources for more information: http://www.rurdev.usda.gov/rbs/ezec/; DHHS programs—http://www.policyalmanac.org/social_welfare/archive/community_development.shtml; USDA programs—http://www.rurdev.usda.gov/; HUD programs—http://www.hud.gov/offices/cpd/communitydevelopment/programs/; other federal programs—http://www.nemw.org/Biz&EconDev_NEMW%20FedComm RevitProgs2006.pdf.

of development programs has been a critical source of financial support that has also encouraged the inflow of private funds and the emergence of new community development organizations (Phifer, List, & Faulkner, 1989; Summers, 1986). Table 2.1 provides an overview of federal community development programs, illustrating the diversity of approaches and goals within these programs.

Table 2.1 Sampling of Federal Community Development Programs

Date	Program	Agency	Purpose
1926	Community facilities loans and grants	USDA, Rural Development	To construct, enlarge, improve community facilities providing services to rural residents
1932	Business and industry loans	USDA, Rural Business, Cooperative Service	To help private and nonprofit organization to obtain quality loans for business development or to improve the climate for economic growth
1949	• Rural housing site loans and self-help housing development loans • Rural rental housing loans	USDA, Rural Development, Rural Housing Programs	• To assist public or nonprofit entities to acquire and prepare land for building sites for low income families • To provide economically designed and constructed rental housing
1961	Area Redevelopment Act	Economic Development Administration	Low cost loans to industries and loans or grants to local government for infrastructure development in support of industrialization
1963	Community Resource Development	USDA—Cooperative Extension Service	Funding to states to hire regional agents to provide direction to help rural communities build the capacity to organize and act for themselves
1964	Office of Economic Opportunity	Independent agency	Funded establishment of community action agencies
1965	Appalachian Regional Commission	Independent agency	Infrastructure and industrial development as well as poverty mitigation programs in geographic areas identified as having serious economic challenges

(Continued)

Table 2.1 (Continued)

Date	Program	Agency	Purpose
1965	• Investments for Public Works and Economic Development Facilities • Economic Development—Technical Assistance • Economic Adjustment Assistance	Department of Commerce, Economic Development Administration	A set of program initiatives to promote economic competitiveness in regions with severe economic distress
1972	Rural Development Act	US Department of Agriculture	Authorized new loans for commercial and industrial development and infrastructure; authorized cost-sharing provisions related to improving water quality and conserving natural resources; gave first priority to the location of new offices and other facilities in rural areas
1974	Community Development Block Grants	Department of Housing and Urban Development	A set of programs that fund infrastructure, housing, and economic development in poor primarily urban communities
1977	Community Reinvestment Act	Federal financial regulatory agencies	Mandates that banks address the credit needs of all segments of their service area
1980	Rural Development Policy Act	US Department of Agriculture	Created an Office of Under Secretary of Agriculture for Small Community and Rural Development; authorized grants of $15 million a year through the Farmers Home Administration for planning and technical assistance
1981	Intermediary Relending Program	USDA, Rural Business, Cooperative Service	To finance business facilities and community development
1986	Low Income Housing Tax Credit	Internal Revenue Service, tax credit	Provide incentives for use of private equity to build affordable housing
1989	Rural Business Enterprise Grants	USDA, Rural Business, Cooperative Service	To facilitate the development of small and emerging businesses and industries in rural areas

Date	Program	Agency	Purpose
1990	• National Affordable Housing Act • HOME Investment Partnerships Program	Department of Housing and Urban Development	A set of programs to expand the supply of affordable housing, particularly rental housing, for low and very low income Americans
1991	National Community Development Initiative	Consortium of national corporations, foundations, and U.S. Dept of Housing and Urban Development	In 2001 incorporated as a nonprofit as Living Cities: The National Community Development Initiative
1993	Empowerment Zone/Enterprise Community (EZ/EC)	Multiple federal agencies had control over components of this program	Uses tax incentives and other strategies to encourage comprehensive planning for economic development and infrastructure improvements in individual or clusters of distressed communities
1993	Brownfields Economic Development Initiative	Department of Housing and Urban Development, Community Planning and Development	To return brownfields to productive use
1993	Capacity Building for Community Housing and Community Development	Department of Housing and Urban Development, Community Planning and Development	To help improve the capacity of community organizations to develop affordable housing and other community development projects (amended 2007)
1994	Community Development and Regulatory Improvement Act	Federal bank and thrift regulatory agencies	• In Title 1, subpart A, establishes the Community Development Financial Institutions Fund • To increase the availability of affordable capital in underserved markets by fostering and certifying new financing entities and providing them capital
1995	Community Reinvestment Act revised (originally enacted, 1977)	Federal financial regulatory agencies	Banks judged more on actual lending and investment performance in low income and minority communities in service area than on their outreach efforts

(Continued)

Table 2.1   (Continued)

Date	Program	Agency	Purpose
1996	Rural Business Opportunity Grants	USDA, Rural Business, Cooperative Service	To promote sustainable economic development in rural areas with exceptional needs
1998	Rural Housing and Economic Development	Department of Housing and Urban Development	To expand the supply of affordable housing and access to economic opportunities in rural areas
1998	Community Services Block Grant Act	Department of Health and Human Services	Provide assistance to states and local communities, through community action agencies and other neighborhood-based organizations, for the reduction of poverty, the revitalization of low-income communities, and the empowerment of low-income families and individuals in rural and urban areas to become fully self-sufficient
1998	Urban and Rural Community Economic Development Programs (DHHS) (amended in 1998; originally part of Community Services Block Grant Act)	Department of Health and Human Services	Self-help and mobilization of the community-at-large through projects that provide employment and ownership opportunities for low-income people through business, physical, or commercial development in economically depressed areas
2002	Brownfields Assessment and Clean-up Cooperative Agreements	Office of Brownfields and Land Revitalization, Office of Solid Waste and Emergency Response, Environmental Protection Agency	To capitalize a revolving loan fund for cleanup of brownfields real property
2007	National Affordable Housing Trust Fund Act	Department of Housing and Urban Development	To establish the National Affordable Housing Trust Fund in the Treasury of the United States to provide for the construction, rehabilitation, and preservation of decent, safe, and affordable housing for low-income families

What is most noteworthy about federal involvement in community development is the way it waxes and wanes with crises and the influence of interest groups. Generally, federal approaches

- Have been directive rather than self-initiated;
- Have been project based not integrative—that is, have not taken a holistic approach wherein projects are integrated into an overall vision for community development;
- Have often imposed requirements (e.g., regional collaboration, a strategic plan) as preconditions for funding;
- Have not been consistently funded or supported;
- Have been based on the asserted "needs" not "assets" of communities; and
- Have been limited in scope (i.e., primarily economic development—industrial recruitment, job creation—or agricultural development in rural areas, or housing development in urban areas).

Phifer et al. (1989, p. 275) argue that there are two consequences of this proliferation of federal programs. The availability of federal funds has led to a distortion in local government decision making, shifting action from priority needs as defined by the community to program areas where federal funds are available. Second, local initiative has been undermined as communities have come to rely on federal largesse to support local action. In some places, this has provided a convenient excuse for not solving local problems, indicated by the comment "Well, we didn't get (or qualify for) that grant, so we can't do this project."

This is not to say that all federal community development efforts are seriously flawed. Sometimes, jumping through the hoops of requirements for federal programs can force communities to engage in behavior (e.g., strategic planning, multi-community collaboration) that produces positive outcomes. Finally, federal programs "created an elaborate and extremely complex matrix of interdependencies among state and federal governments, the private sector and communities" that has continued to shape CD efforts at all levels (Summers, 1986, p. 366).

State/Local Government

State/local governments create policies and programs (e.g., state economic and housing development initiatives), control access to federal funds (e.g., community development block grants), and in many other ways influence if and how community development occurs (Bonds, 2004). State economic development programs, especially their focus and how incentives are used, can create the conditions for growth or decline and often put communities into competition with each other or create conditions of winners and losers. For example, studies on environmental justice (Bullard, 2000; Carruthers, 2007; Pellow, 2004) suggest that state/local governments may inadvertently create conditions that concentrate hazardous economic development projects in low-income and minority communities.

National Intermediaries

National intermediaries provide local CDCs with financial resources, investments, information, advocacy, training, and technical assistance (McDermott, 2004). There are about a dozen national intermediaries, with the three largest being Local Initiatives Support Corporation, Enterprise Foundation, and the Neighborhood Reinvestment Corporation. Intermediaries "are able to access national funding sources, including the federal government, national foundations or national super-banks and bring that funding to the local level in a rational way" (McDermott, 2004, p. 172). According to McDermott (2004), national intermediaries provide

- Funders with "a coordinated administration and monitoring system";
- Guidance in the establishment of "performance standards for CDC operations and development" that legitimize "CDCs as viable and effective agents of community development";
- Financial and technical support for local community development funding collaboratives;
- Creative financing and investment tools for local development;
- Advocates for national policies to address fundamental economic, social, and political inequities in our nation;
- Information on best practices; and
- Opportunities to bring new partners into the arena of community development. (p. 172)

Community Development Financial Institutions

Community development financial institutions (CDFIs) have several forms: community development credit unions, banks, venture capital funds, business development loan funds, and microloan funds (Benjamin, Rubin, & Zielenbach, 2004). In 2009, there were approximately 819 certified community development loan funds in the United States (http://www.cdfi.org/).

The CDFI Fund makes available credit, investment capital, and financial services in distressed urban and rural communities. The fund supports the creation and expansion of CDFIs that serve challenged communities and low-income individuals, and offers incentives to traditional banks for investment, lending, and services in distressed areas.

Community development loan funds "provide financing and technical assistance for businesses; for-profit and nonprofit real estate and housing developers; and nonprofit organizations looking for facility or operating capital" (Rubin, 2008, p. 192). CDFIs also provide financial assistance to low-income individuals to purchase or rehabilitate their homes or to start new microbusinesses. Finally, CDFIs and their national association have also influenced the development of state and national CD policies (e.g., the establishment of the CDFI Fund, the New Markets Tax Credit, and the New Markets Venture Capital program in the 1990s).

Community Development Corporations

CDCs (e.g., Corporation for Enterprise Development, National Association of Development Organizations, Association for Enterprise Opportunity) are nonprofit organizations involved in supporting the development of housing, businesses, commercial real estate, child care and other community facilities, or other components that enhance the quality of life in the communities in which they operate (Bratt & Rohe, 2004; Vidal, 1992; Walker, 2002). Vidal's 1992 study, *Rebuilding Communities,* "was the first major study to focus squarely on the urban community development field" and concluded that CDCs were "models for urban neighborhood revitalization" (Frisch & Servon, 2006, p. 88).

CDCs have shifted from largely independent, grassroots organizations to a model of development built upon key relationships with government, philanthropy, and churches. By building these relationships, CDCs create and insert themselves into networks that are critical to their ability to build capacity (Glickman & Servon, 1998). The emergence of the CD system has led to an emphasis on capacity building within CDCs, often facilitated by other system actors such as intermediaries (Frisch & Servon, 2006, p. 90).

Walker's 2002 study examined the activities of CDCs in 23 cities from 1991 to 2001 and concluded that during this decade,

> they increased their ability to influence neighborhood markets and to respond to neighborhood problems. They expanded their physical revitalization activities and began to pursue more comprehensive approaches to community improvement. These advances were largely the result of an institutional revolution with most major U.S. cities. Support for CDC initiatives had been largely ad hoc and poorly coordinated before 1990. By decade's end, support for CDCs had become more rational, entrenched, and effective. (Walker, 2002, p. i)

During the 1990s, CDCs expanded their efforts to include "commercial development, workforce and youth development, and community facilities programs" (Walker, 2002, p. i) and thus sought a more comprehensive approach to neighborhood revitalization.

Community-Based Development Organizations

Community-based development organizations (CBDOs) tend to have a strong focus on a conflict approach and community organizing with an emphasis on empowerment, social and economic justice, and building neighborhood or community capacity. Some examples include Industrial Areas Foundation (established by Saul Alinsky), the Gamaliel Foundation, the Direct Action Research and Training Center, the Midwest Academy, and ACORN. What drives the work of CBDOs is the interests and needs of local people, so the influence of other sectors of the CD system is primarily through access to financial resources and partnerships.

Nonprofit Organizations

Nonprofit organizations encompass a diverse group of organizations and associations with an interest and role in community development. Since the late 1990s, for example, churches have seen their roles increased through faith-based initiatives (Vidal, Freiberg, Otchere-Agyei, & Saunders, 1999). Nonprofits provide funding, land, and other resources as well as administrative and client-based services in support of CD efforts. Through partnerships with CDCs, nonprofit organizations can broaden and deepen the impact of CD efforts in communities. For example, neighborhood associations can be the springboard for community organizing and mobilizing local people into action.

Private Foundations

Private foundations have played a major role in community development through research and targeted funding initiatives. In the early 1990s, several private foundations collaborated to set up the Comprehensive Community Initiative. This program encouraged community development corporations to develop partnerships with other locality-based organizations that shared overlapping missions in order to deepen the impact of CD efforts (Frisch & Servon, 2006, p. 96).

Community foundations are a particular type of private foundation and date back to the early 1900s when businesses used these organizational entities to invest in enhancing the lives of the people and communities where they operated (Lowe, 2004). The oldest are located in the major urban areas of the Northeast and Midwest. For example, the Cleveland Foundation was established in 1914, and within a year, several other cities (Chicago, Detroit, Milwaukee, Minneapolis, and Boston) had community foundations. Lowe (2004) provides an overview of key CD initiatives by major foundations (e.g., the Charles Stewart Mott Foundation's Community Foundations and Neighborhoods Small Grants program, the Ford Foundation's Community Development Collaborative Model, and the Cleveland Foundation's Neighborhood Progress, Inc.).

During the 1950s and 1960s, community foundations shifted their focus to provide the major funding for addressing local social service needs. The Tax Reform Act of 1969 provided significant tax advantages to investment in community foundations, and as a result, both the number and assets of community foundations grew significantly. The focus of their work also expanded beyond social service needs to housing, commercial, and economic development. By 2000, there were more than 300 community foundations, and this is counting only those with assets over $5 million (Foundation Center, 2002).

For-Profit Firms

For-profit firms such as banks, retirement funds, and commercial developers are key players who can fund, encourage, lead, divert, or diminish CD initiatives. For example, banks have a role to play through the Community Reinvestment Act, which requires banks to reinvest a portion of their profits back into the communities in the forms of low-interest loans, grants, and other programs. The private sector has also contributed to the history of community development through community improvement programs and funding, and in the case of some (e.g., TVA, rural electric cooperatives), the hiring of staff whose job is to assist communities in their service area with CD initiatives. Obviously, many of these CD efforts also created conditions that led to greater demand for power from utilities and created more customers for banks and local businesses.

Professional Associations

Professional associations have emerged to provide training, certification, and coordination for the efforts of those engaged in community development. Sociologists will tell you that two indicators of the maturation of an institutional sector are the emergence of professional or trade associations and the professionalization of practitioners. The Community Development Society was established in 1970 and might be viewed as a bridge between the private and nonprofit sectors and academia. The National Congress for Community Economic Development, formed in 1988, is the trade association for community development corporations. The Society for Community Research and Action is the professional association for community psychologists.

Universities

Community development as an academic discipline probably began with the work of William Biddle at Earlham College, Indiana, in 1947 (Christenson & Robinson, 1980, p. 13). Within academia, disciplines (e.g., economics, sociology, political science, social work, education) have defined community development and change differently, and incorporated these concepts into their own theories and approaches in ways that reflect their orientations.

Although disciplinary perspectives emphasize different concepts, methods, or goals, the divisions are porous. For example, a social work press published Bonds's (2004) study on how the politics of race in Milwaukee, Wisconsin, influenced the distribution of a quarter billion dollars in community development block grants over a 25-year period. In the *Journal of the American Planning Association,* Carr and Servon (2009) explore how to integrate local cultural assets into decisions on urban economic development so as to sustain unique neighborhood qualities. The *Professional Geographer* published Martin's (2004) study that explores the role of foundation grants in enabling community organizations to participate in urban governance. The *Journal of the Community Development Society* published a study of psychological and behavioral factors in understanding "participation in particular settings, how to maintain participation, and how these various motivations and behaviors interact with various settings and organizational characteristics" (Perkins, Hughey, & Speer, 2002, p. 34). The *Annual Review of Public Health* published a study of public health concerns, especially as influenced by environmental conditions, as well as the relationship between health and economic development (Israel, Schulz, Parker, & Becker, 1998).

Other university-based players include the four regional rural development centers, which seek to build capacity within the land grant system (Agricultural Experiment Stations, Cooperative Extension Service) in support of community development; and community development research and action centers at universities (e.g., the Rural Policy Research Institute, the National Community Development Policy Analysis Network).

In summary, the field of CD players and policies is as complex as the playbook of an NFL team. The diversity of players and the complexity of their relationships reflect both the importance attached to community development as well as the persistence of fundamental differences in our understanding of what it is and how to do it. As we shall see in the next section, this situation would also describe international CD efforts.

International Community Development

You cannot separate community development at the international level from the history of colonialism, the emergence of new states, the Cold War, modernization efforts, social justice movements, or the emergence of the global economy (Popple, 2006; Voth & Brewster, 1989). International community development is marked by a diversity of CD practices arising from different ideologies, desired outcomes, and traditions. Building on an earlier review of international community development by Voth and Brewster (1989), this section will briefly explore what Arce (2003) calls international CD policy orientations, or "the set of ideas, assumptions and methodologies that orients policy-makers and practitioners when addressing specific development problems" (p. 200).

The meaning of international CD has included everything from a process for improving the infrastructure of colonies for their economic value, to a strategy of building grassroots democratic institutions to combat the spread of communism, to a means for jump-starting the modernization of nonindustrial economies, to a way of incorporating the resource and consumer base of nations into a global economic system. As in the United States, technical assistance, self-help, and conflict approaches have been used in international CD efforts, but with important distinctions that reflect cultural and ideological differences. For example, European countries and their former colonies have tended to approach CD from a modified self-help perspective that simultaneously emphasizes grassroots efforts (i.e., local participation in decision making) but directed toward central government goals. On the other hand, international aid organizations and some national governments tend to emphasize technical assistance but often focus on goals determined by the foundations or the governments themselves.

Voth and Brewster (1989) point out that there is a pattern to CD in non-Western nations. A brief overview (see also Berger & Weber, 2007; Uvin, 2007) of the relationship between historic eras, ideologies, and CD practice illustrates this point in Table 2.2. In addition, the *Directory of Development Organizations* (http://www.devdir.org/) provides a listing of 53,750 organizations engaged in community development worldwide.

Discussions about the meaning and purpose of development in an international context continue. Sen (1999) argues that development is the expansion of "substantive human freedoms" to lead the kind of life one values. This, Sen suggests, requires the elimination of those things that limit freedom, such as poverty, limited "economic opportunities as well as systematic social deprivation, [and] neglect of public facilities" (p. 1). What Sen and others (e.g., United Nations Development Programme, 2000; Uvin, 2007) are suggesting is that development is intertwined with human rights, political freedoms, and economic opportunities. Sengupta (2000) reinforces this by stating that development from a human rights perspective must be "participatory, accountable, and transparent, with equity in decision-making" so that the process of development institutionalizes the involvement of those it claims to help (Uvin, 2007, p. 603). Geoghegan and Powell (2008) assert that the practice of international CD today continues to reflect differing ideologies and traditions. They state that today, there are three dominant practices of community development:

> a neoliberal version where civil society is subservient to the needs of economic development; a corporatist version that advocates a partnership between the state, market and civil society; and an activist version, where community development is envisaged as local, nodal and global resistance to neoliberalism. (p. 1)

If this interpretation is correct, the meaning and practice of international CD continues to adapt to changing economic, political, and social conditions.

Table 2.2 Examples of Changing International Community Development Strategies

Era	Program Focus	General Purpose	Method/Practice Emphasis
1950s to mid-1960s	• Centralized national infrastructure development (dams, electricity, telephone systems) • Public health programs (e.g., public water systems, immunizations)	• Modernization • Economic development • Community development as a bulwark against communism, Soviet expansion • Overcoming resistance to modernization	• Technical assistance through the coordinated actions of all specialized bureaucracies within national and subnational government • Village-level workers providing technical assistance to supplement self-help
Mid-1960s to early 1970s	• Family planning • Agricultural development projects	• Modernization • Addressing food shortages to stabilize populations and nation states	• Technical assistance • National development programs
Mid-1970s to early 1980s	• Population planning and public health • Infrastructure development • Rural development	• General community development • US New Directions mandate • Right to development[a]	• Locality-based participatory development as a form of self-help • Technical assistance
Mid- to late 1980s	• Agricultural development • Social welfare • Public health (e.g., AIDS, infectious disease) • Focus on addressing individual social problems	• General community development • Economic modernization and incorporation into global economic and communication systems • Human rights	• Technical assistance • Participatory development but typically within technical services

a. In 1986, the U.N. General Assembly passed a resolution affirming that "the right to development is an inalienable human right by virtue of which every human person and all peoples are entitled to participate in, contribute to, and enjoy economic, social, cultural and political development, in which all human rights and fundamental freedoms can be fully realized" (www.unhch.ch/html/menu3/b/74.htm).

Summary

Some have argued that international CD efforts failed, but others say that its successes were not what proponents intended. Increasingly, the conceptualization of international CD has come to mean the empowerment of marginalized groups, the challenging of oppressive political power structures, and the equalization of economic life conditions.

The same might be argued for community development efforts in the United States. Despite a half-century of public and private efforts, the issues that have driven community development—poverty, limited economic opportunities, poor living conditions, and minimal ability to influence life conditions—remain in too many neighborhoods and communities. Yet, as with international efforts, perhaps the issue is more complex, reflecting the impact of inappropriate and contradictory expectations, scale of operations, different emphases, and different evaluation measures.

From the beginning, locality-based participatory development efforts have been most successful in producing changes that reflect the expectations and interests of residents, even though these may not be the goals intended by those providing resources to support the effort. Although communities or neighborhoods may focus on empowerment to control their own destiny, funders may be more interested in physical or countable outcomes, or vice versa.

Within the field of community development, there has always been a struggle between a generalist and a technical/specialist approach. The complexity of funding for community development activities—grants, loans, and donations from governmental, nongovernmental, foundation, and individual sources—often creates contradictory expectations, competing evaluation measures, and unclear goals. For community development organizations, the need to fund not only programs but also administrative operations often leads to grant-chasing that is more reflective of donor interests than community needs. For donors, the fact that they are providing the support for development efforts leads to an expectation of influence, if not control, over the project. Projects and development strategies that work on a small scale in a particular sociocultural setting may not transfer to another. Or, locality-based programs may not work as expected if "scaled up" to national or state-level initiatives. Finally, governments and other formal organizations typically operate on a short time line with an expectation of quick results or returns on investments, but participatory development strategies are typically slow and uncertain.

Still, throughout the United States and the world, people in neighborhoods and communities continue to come together, sometimes on their own, sometimes encouraged by a specific program, to work together to improve their lives and living conditions. Participatory community development strategies, fueled by the desire to improve opportunities and the places where people live, cut through the restraints of limited resources, program guidelines, and bureaucratic obstacles. Community development efforts have encouraged public/private partnerships and moved the issue of human rights onto the main agenda of national and international politics. Over the decades, community development has seen a persistence of certain designs—participatory decision making, locally initiated actions, use of technical expertise to address challenges, an emphasis on rights and empowerment—as well as the introduction of new ones—innovative financing, the emergence of new players, a greater emphasis on human rights—that continue to create a unique tapestry of planned social change.

References

Arce, A. (2003). Value contestations in development interventions: Community development and sustainable livelihoods approaches. *Community Development Journal, 38*, 199–212.

Benjamin, L., Rubin, J. S., & Zielenbach, S. (2004). Community development financial institutions: Current issues and future prospects. *Journal of Urban Affairs, 26*, 177–195.

Berger, M. T., & Weber, H. (2007). Introduction: Beyond international development. *Globalizations, 4*, 423–428.

Bonds, M. (2004). *Race, politics, and community development funding: The discolor of money*. New York: Haworth Social Work Practice Press.

Bratt, R. G., & Rohe, W. (2004). Organizational changes among CDCs: Assessing the impacts and navigating the challenges. *Journal of Urban Affairs, 26*, 197–220.

Bullard, R. D. (2000). *Dumping in Dixie: Race, class and environmental quality* (3rd ed.). Boulder, CO: Westview.

Carr, J. H., & Servon, L. J. (2009). Vernacular culture and urban economic development: Thinking outside the (big) box. *Journal of the American Planning Association, 75*, 28–40.

Carruthers, D. V. (2007). Environmental justice and the politics of energy on the US-Mexico border. *Environmental Politics, 16*, 394–413.

Cary, L. J. (Ed.). (1970). *Community development as a process*. Columbia: University of Missouri Press.

Castells, M. (1983). *The city and the grassroots: A cross cultural theory of urban social movements*. Berkeley: University of California Press.

Christenson, J. A., Fendley, K., & Robinson, J. (1989). Community development. In J. A. Christenson & J. Robinson (Eds.), *Community development in perspective* (pp. 3–25). Ames: Iowa State University Press.

Christenson, J. A., & Robinson, J. (Eds.). (1980). *Community development in America*. Ames: Iowa State University Press.

Christenson, J. A., & Robinson, J. (Eds.). (1989). *Community development in perspective*. Ames: Iowa State University Press.

Fear, F. A., & Schwarzweller, H. K. (1985a). Introduction: Rural sociology, community and community development. In F. A. Fear & H. K. Schwarzweller (Eds.), *Research in rural sociology and development: A research annual: Focus on community* (pp. xi–xxxvi). Greenwich, CT: JAI.

Fear, F. A., & Schwarzweller, H. K. (Eds.). (1985b). *Research in rural sociology and development: A research annual: Focus on community*. Greenwich, CT: JAI.

Fisher, R., & Shragge, E. (2000). Challenging community organizing: Facing the 21st century. *Journal of Community Practice, 8*, 1–19.

Foundation Center. (2002). *The foundation directory, 2002 edition*. New York: Author.

Frisch, M., & Servon, L. J. (2006). CDCs and the changing context for urban community development: A review of the field and the environment. *Community Development: Journal of the Community Development Society, 37*, 88–108.

Geoghegan, M., & Powell, F. (2008). Community development and the contested politics of the late modern *agora*: Of, alongside or against neoliberalism? *Community Development Journal*, doi:10.1093/cdj/bsn020

Gittell, R., & Vidal, A. (1998). *Community organizing: Building social capital as a development strategy*. Thousand Oaks, CA: Sage.

Glickman, N. J., & Servon, L. J. (1998). More than bricks and sticks: Five components of community development capacity. *Housing Policy Debate, 9*, 497–539.

Goe, W. R., & Noonan, S. (2007). The sociology of community. In C. D. Bryant & D. L. Peck (Eds.), *21st century sociology: A reference handbook* (pp. 455–464). Thousand Oaks, CA: Sage.

Israel, B. A., Schulz, A. J., Parker, E. A., & Becker, A. B. (1998). Review of community-based research: Assessing partnership approaches to improve public health. *Annual Review of Public Health, 19*, 173–202.

Kaufman, H. F. (1959). Toward an interactional conception of community. *Social Forces, 38*, 8–17.

Korten, D. C. (1980). Community organization and rural development. *Public Administration Review, 40*, 480–511.

Loomis, C. P., & Beegle, J. A. (1950). *Rural social system: A textbook in rural sociology and anthropology*. New York: Prentice Hall.

Lowe, J. S. (2004). Community foundations: What do they offer community development? *Journal of Urban Affairs, 26*, 221–240.

Martin, D. (2004). Nonprofit foundations and grassroots organizing: Reshaping urban governance. *Professional Geographer, 56*, 394–405.

McDermott, M. (2004). National intermediaries and local community development corporation networks: A view from Cleveland. *Journal of Urban Affairs, 26*, 171–176.

McMillan, D. W., & Chavis, D. M. (1986). Sense of community: A definition and theory. *Journal of Community Psychology, 14*, 6–23.

Newman, K., & Lake, R. W. (2006). Democracy, bureaucracy and difference in US community development policies since 1968. *Progress in Human Geography, 30*, 44–61.

Orr, M. (Ed.). (2007). *Transforming the city: Community organizing and the challenge of political change*. Lawrence: University Press of Kansas.

Pellow, D. (2004). The politics of illegal dumping: An environmental justice framework. *Qualitative Sociology, 27*, 511–525.

Perkins, D. D., Hughey, J., & Speer, P. W. (2002). Community psychology perspectives on social capital theory and community development practice. *Journal of the Community Development Society, 33*, 33–52.

Phifer, B., List, F., & Faulkner, B. (1989). An overview of community development in America. In J. A. Christenson & J. Robinson (Eds.), *Community development in perspective* (pp. 253–279). Ames: Iowa State University Press.

Popple, K. (2006). The first forty years: The history of the *Community Development Journal*. *Community Development Journal, 43*, 6–23.

Rubin, J. (2008). Adaptation or extinction? Community development loan funds at a crossroads. *Journal of Urban Affairs, 30*, 191–220.

Rubin, H. J., & Rubin, I. S. (2007). *Community organizing and development* (4th ed.). Boston: Allyn & Bacon.

Sampson, R. J. (1991). Linking the micro- and macrolevel dimensions of community social organization. *Social Forces, 70*, 43–64.

Sanders, I. T. (1958). *Community: An introduction to a social system*. New York: Ronald Press.

Sanders, I. T., & Lewis, G. F. (1976). Rural community studies in the United States. *Annual Review of Sociology, 2,* 35–53.

Sen, A. K. (1999). *Development as freedom*. New York: Knopf.

Sengupta, A. (2000). Realizing the right to development. *Development and Change, 31,* 553–578.

Shaw, M. (2008). Community development and the politics of community. *Community Development Journal, 43,* 24–36.

Smock, K. (2003). *Democracy in action: Community organizing and urban change*. New York: Columbia University Press.

Stoecker, R. (2003). Understanding the development-organizing dialectic. *Journal of Urban Affairs, 25,* 493–512.

Stoecker, R. (2009). Community organizing and social change. *Contexts, 8,* 20–25.

Summers, G. (1986). Rural community development. *Annual Review of Sociology, 12,* 347–371.

Summers, G., & Branch, K. (1984). Economic development and community social change. *Annual Review of Sociology, 10,* 141–166.

Theodori, G. (2005). Community and community development in resource-based areas: Operational definitions rooted in an interactional perspective. *Society and Natural Resources, 18,* 661–669.

United Nations Development Programme. (2000). *Human development report 2000: Human rights and human development*. New York: Oxford University Press.

Uvin, P. (2007). From the right to development to the rights-based approach: How human rights entered development. *Development in Practice, 17,* 597–606.

Vidal, A. C. (1992). *Rebuilding communities*. New York: Community Development Research Center, New School for Social Research.

Vidal, A. C., Freiberg, S., Otchere-Agyei, E., & Saunders, M. (1999). *Faith-based organizations in community development*. Washington, DC: Urban Institute.

Voth, D., & Brewster, M. (1989). An overview of international community development. In J. A. Christenson & J. Robinson (Eds.), *Community development in perspective* (pp. 280–306). Ames: Iowa State University Press.

Walker, C. (2002). *Community development corporations and their changing support systems*. Washington, DC: Urban Institute. Retrieved May 5, 2009, from http://www.urban.org/url.cfm?ID=410638

Wilkinson, K. P. (1970). The community as a social field. *Social Forces, 48,* 311–322.

Wilkinson, K. P. (1972). A field theory perspective for community development research. *Rural Sociology, 37,* 43–52.

3

Community Development and Natural Landscapes

Alan W. Barton and Theresa Selfa

BEHAVIOR OBJECTIVES

After studying this chapter and completing the online learning activities, students should be able to

1. Describe ways in which community development is influenced by the natural environment.

2. Define "landscape."

3. Explain how landscapes shape and reinforce the characteristics of the culture of the people who use them.

4. Explain how a landscape becomes a commodity, and identify some of the ramifications of this process.

5. Explain how a landscape can reinforce stratification in a community.

6. Explain what it means to say that landscapes are historically produced, and provide examples of how this process operates.

7. Explain how landscapes can be used to bring community factions together.

8. Explain how the values of a landscape can be marketed as an economic development tool.

Introduction

Social scientists have long debated the extent to which nature and society interact. One line of thought, proposed by Émile Durkheim (1895/1982), suggests that social consequences have social causes. According to this view, to understand how humans interact in a community context, only social factors offer a valid explanation. So, for example, to understand why some people in a community are suspicious of individual achievement, it is more valid to argue that a relative lack of differentiation in social roles leads people to value homogeneity, rather than to suggest that living in a hot climate suppresses people's desire to achieve.

Those who believe that social behavior is best explained by social causes generally pay little attention to the natural context. Others, however, argue that human behavior is always embedded in nature (Burch, 1971/1997; Buttel & Humphrey, 2002; Firey, 1960/1999; Wilson, 1978). Humans are, after all, biological beings whose behavior is controlled at least in part by genetic codes and chemical reactions. Furthermore, human groups live in a natural context, within ecosystems that establish boundaries within which people must operate to construct and reproduce social systems. Humans frequently find meaning in the natural environment and use natural elements in processes of social construction. Under this approach, humans cannot escape nature, even analytically, and social scientists should consider the natural environment when studying social behavior.

Theory Is an Essential Ingredient to Community Development

Community developers often look to social theory to help guide their actions, but community development is a more applied enterprise. Community developers are not limited by the rules of social science methodology. Theories of social behavior can help community developers set goals and perhaps predict with some accuracy the consequences of decisions and actions. But community developers also must take into account the real-world circumstances of their own communities. At any given time, the unique historical trajectory of each community creates a set of circumstances that includes economic opportunity, political feasibility, and social capacity, which combine to produce a limited set of options. Sometimes ignored, but always important, are the natural conditions as well. In this chapter, we examine some of the ways in which natural ecosystems and landscapes interact with community structure and culture to create opportunities and constraints for community developers.

Natural Resources and Community Development ———

How do natural conditions play a role in communities? For one thing, communities draw on natural resources to sustain themselves economically. Indeed, the term *resource* is commonly used to describe the plants, animals, minerals, and water that make up natural communities, particularly those that humans use to satisfy their needs and wants. This approach suggests that nature is separate from human communities, and its primary function is to provide for humans as inputs in a productive process.

Also, natural resources serve communities in other ways. They shape community development by opening up opportunities for some community groups, and imposing constraints on other groups. Sometimes overlooked are the characteristics of the resources themselves, such as the frequency of harvest, whether the resource is stationary or mobile, whether it is renewable or nonrenewable, and the endowment of a resource in a particular area. All of these directly influence how individual communities interact with resources. Soil quality and structure, topography, and vulnerability to natural disasters vary by location and shape the opportunities and worldviews available to people and communities. The social institutions that emerge can organize and control social relations with resources. For example, some institutions allocate property rights and control access, use, and disposal to specific plots of land and the trees, soil, water, wildlife, minerals, and buildings on the land.

In some cases, natural resources come to define communities. Farming towns, ranching towns, logging towns, fishing villages, mining towns, hunting camps, and resort towns are closely tied to one dominant industry, and each type of community brings to mind particular cultural markers, such as the architecture, apparel, cuisine, political preferences, and organizational proclivities typical of each. These cultural elements support and sustain the local industry by shaping the worldviews and identities of residents and ensuring that at least some members of each generation will choose to pursue their livelihoods in the community's industry. Understanding the cultural functions of resources broadens the relationship between human communities and nature, but resources are still conceptualized as individual entities that function primarily to service humans.

Landscape: A New Vision of Communities and Nature

In recent years, a new vision has emerged that offers a different conception of how nature and communities are related. Rather than focusing on specific resources and their role in production, today many analysts use the concept of *landscape* to highlight that communities and nature are linked in complex and multifaceted ways (Greider & Garkovich, 1994; Hinrichs, 1996; Petrzelka, 2004; Walker & Fortmann, 2003). Landscapes are extensive tracts of land and all that is on them—trees, rivers, beaches, mountains, crops, wildlife, buildings, roads, and, of course, people. The concepts of community and landscape have commonalities in that both are emergent properties. Communities are more than aggregates of people—they have their own reality that forms a community identity that may reflect the individual identities of community members, but that has its own essence as well. Likewise, landscapes are more than aggregates of natural elements. They also have their own reality and identity. Landscapes are composed of physical and biological components, but fundamentally, they are social and cultural constructs (Greider & Garkovich, 1994). They take on meaning as people interact with them, and that meaning becomes part of how people see themselves, as attached to and shaped by a particular place.

As social and cultural constructs, landscapes contribute to the creation of meaning, the foundation and development of communities, the construction and reproduction of social institutions, and the formation and internalization of social hierarchies. As humans interact, they assign social meaning to places and use these meanings as symbolic markers that facilitate mutual understanding through shared interpretation of worldly settings and events. Over time, these meanings become ingrained and take on their own independent form; as sociologists like to say, they take on "a life of their own." They begin to shape how people view themselves and others around them. People also contest these meanings and try to shape them to enhance their own individual well-being. Thus, even as these institutional forms facilitate social interaction, they also produce conflict between social groups, each of which interprets the meaning assigned to nature and landscape differently.

Community developers contribute to these processes by helping communities develop these shared markers, and community developers that work with landscapes in particular aim to construct and convey institutions that allow people to share meaningfully in the natural elements that surround and comprise the places where their communities are located. The natural characteristics of a particular place influence how community developers might approach the process of constructing meaning on landscapes.

The Landscape as Commodity

The way in which people shape landscapes often reflects the dominant culture. In a highly commercialized setting such as the United States, it is not surprising that many landscapes are seen as commodities. In other words, they are valued because of their market potential. Residents develop an identity in part based on how the landscape can generate income for the community (Silver, 1993). This process involves more than the conversion of the natural elements into commodities (Shepherd, 2002). The landscape itself, including the people and their sense of self, take on the form of a commodity. Over time, the landscape identity can evolve into a sort of "logo" that can be used to sell the stories of the landscape. Thus, California's "wine country," Florida's "sun coast," or South Dakota's "badlands" shape how both outsiders and residents perceive a place, and these labels build a set of expectations associated with the culture of those who live there.

Tourism Is Derived From Some Landscapes. A significant motivator for viewing landscapes as commodities is the establishment of tourism, a community development strategy that many rural areas are adopting. The narratives that people create to understand their landscapes come to be viewed as marketable entities and a source of income for residents. Landscapes with a strong place identity have an advantage in marketing to tourists, as it is relatively easy to compartmentalize and market their narratives. Such places may have disadvantages as well, however (Krannich & Petrzelka, 2003). If place identity is tied to a particular industry, local residents may feel strongly attached to the definitions of place that stem from involvement in that industry, and they may resist losing that identity in favor of one based on a tourism industry (Walker & Fortmann, 2003). People rooted in landscape may feel close ties to other community members and may resent the incursion of outsiders whom they believe are different and challenge their common identity. Finally, local residents may feel that this process reduces their identities to mere commercial transactions, and they may believe they sacrifice what is unique and special about their place.

Constructing Landscapes

How do landscapes become commodities? We examine two case studies that illustrate these processes. First, we consider the case of the Mississippi Delta, a region that has been characterized by internal divisions over racial identity. These divisions have produced very different perceptions of the meaning of the landscape. For many white residents, the land is a source of wealth. For many black residents, it represents oppression. An emerging tourism industry has the potential to unite these groups. We then examine the construction of landscape identity in the Flint Hills region of Kansas, a case that shows how interaction with outside forces can galvanize community action and reshape a region's identity. In Kansas, opposition to the federal government united local residents, but then efforts to reshape the landscape brought about an alliance with the government and a new sense of meaning to local residents. Finally, we describe a service-learning project in the Delta that aimed to reshape perceptions of the landscape and bring about racial reconciliation.

The Mississippi Delta: Race and Landscape

Landscapes take on different meanings for different groups, meanings that are historically produced. Community developers generally can work more effectively if they understand the historical conditions in the communities they serve. For example, in places with strong cultural divides, the meaning that competing groups assign to the landscape can serve to accentuate the differences between the groups.

The Mississippi Delta is a 7,000-square-mile floodplain in the northwest corner of the state of Mississippi. The Delta's culture is rooted in cotton production and plantation agriculture (Cobb, 1992). This was, perhaps, inevitable, given the region's natural history and the level of technology available at the time the land was first settled. For millennia, the waters of the Mississippi River spread out across the Delta landscape during its periodic flood phase, depositing rich and extraordinarily deep alluvial topsoils and carving the unusually flat landscape. The floods shaped the vegetative cover, consisting of bottomland hardwood forests dominated by species such as oak, sweet gum, cottonwood, willow, and bald cypress, and thick patches of bamboo-like plants known as cane breaks (Eyre, 1980). The dense vegetation inhibited human settlement, as did the threat of diseases such as malaria and yellow fever, and the dangers posed by wild animals. Most difficult, however, was the frequent flooding (Saikku, 2005). As Asch (2008) described it,

> Clearing the land required excruciating, time-consuming labor with handsaws and axes (not until the 1940s did gas-powered chain saws come into use). Teams of men and mules struggled to drain the bogs, saw down centuries-old cypress trees, and burn the remaining stumps to prepare the land for cotton cultivation. (p. 67)

It was hard to get a foothold and survive at a level above hunting and gathering in this swampy landscape.

As a result, farming arrived to the Delta late in the country's history. After the cotton gin was introduced in 1793, cotton production became highly profitable and expanded rapidly around the South. The plantation system was firmly entrenched at this point, although most farms were still small, family-run efforts. But planters, who had slaves to do the hard labor of clearing the Delta's forest, moved into the region in the 1820s and 1830s, first settling the high lands near the Mississippi River (Tompkins, 1901). They expanded across the landscape and organized to build an increasingly sophisticated series of levies to hold the river's floodwaters at bay beginning around the middle of the 19th century. African American labor was crucial to clearing the forests and building and maintaining the levees. Even after slavery was abolished, forest clearing and levee building continued, and African American tenants continued to supply the labor to carry out these rigorous tasks.

The plantation system shaped not only the region's demographics, but also its distribution of status, wealth, and power. The African descendants formed the majority of the population from the beginning. The plantations established a rigid system of polarized stratification, in which the vast majority of the fruits of the slave labor went to the white planters. Each plantation operated as a small empire, outside the system of rational law and administration that was developing elsewhere. Following emancipation and a brief period of reconstruction, a long period of repression ensued to maintain the rigid race-based hierarchy in the Delta, which supported the local system of production (Blackmon, 2008; Cobb, 1992). Black residents were relegated to sharecropping or tenant farming, and Jim Crow law and politics ensured that African Americans stayed on the plantations as cheap labor. The Jim Crow system was enforced by the white elite, using a mixture of paternalism, violence, and a rigged legal system, which invariably ceded to the will of the planters (Asch, 2008). The plantations served to concentrate substantial power and influence in the hands of the landowners, and consistently marginalized the black labor force by systematically denying rights and opportunities.

The conditions produced by this system shaped perceptions of the land and nature in the Delta. Today, race relations remain strained. A report on the region prepared by the Housing Assistance Council (2002) described the situation:

> The experience of enslaved Africans and of generations of African Americans in the region is in many ways the defining characteristic of the Delta. Wealthy landowners bought African slaves to cultivate the land in order to make a fortune in the cotton industry. For enslaved Africans, the Delta was notoriously the worst place in America to be a slave. . . . White landowners . . . were forced to coexist with a people they both feared and depended on for their wealth. This uneasy situation, racial animosity combined with forced proximity, set the tone for tense race relations in the Delta. (p. 84)

Although the civil rights movement has made many gains, and today African Americans hold most of the local and county political offices around the Delta, racial stratification and racial bigotry remain. Wealth is highly polarized, and the region has one of the highest rates of poverty in the United States, with African Americans at high risk of poverty. Substantial power is still concentrated in land ownership, and perceptions and beliefs about the landscape continue to reflect the region's history in many ways. The challenging natural landscape shaped the course of history in the Delta, leading to the polarizing parallel racial cultures found in the Delta today (Duncan, 1999). The service-learning case study discussed later illustrates how racial identity is embedded in the landscape and shapes people's interactions, and highlights how nature tourism could serve as a uniting force in the Delta.

Tourism in the Delta. In the early 21st century, the Delta is in the process of building a tourism industry. This may seem strange for an area that is poor, isolated, and rural, as these characteristics are probably not what most tourists are looking for. But the Delta's unusual and at times tragic history has produced a number of compelling stories of triumph over adversity, as well as highly marketable commodities. Most significant is the region's reputation as the "birthplace of the blues," a musical form that recounted many of the hardships that African Americans experienced in the plantation system. Blues stories shaped the identity of the Delta and today resonate with many potential tourists, who also are willing to visit blues clubs and purchase blues recordings. The State of Mississippi has embraced blues tourism with a series of special historic markers along a Blues Heritage Trail, and with a number of blues-oriented museums and events throughout the year.

Blues stories are intimately woven into the cultural fabric of the Delta and provide a unique opportunity to attract tourists to the region. But the blues stories in many ways derive directly from the landscape, which spurred the plantation system. Other natural features in the landscape are ripe for tourism development as well. The Mississippi River along the western boundary of the Delta is a substantial draw and closely tied to the regional identity. The Delta also provides world-class hunting and fishing experiences, and the story of cotton cultivation provides many opportunities for agricultural tourism. All relate directly to the landscape and the identity of the residents, a fact that community developers can build on in cultivating a tourism industry in the region.

The Flint Hills: Constructing a Common Landscape

As in the Mississippi Delta, the population of most rural counties in the state of Kansas has been declining steadily throughout the 20th century. Since the 1980s farm crisis, low prices for agricultural commodities have furthered ongoing farm loss, farm consolidation, and economic decline. In addition, resource extractive industries (especially oil) have been in decline, contributing to dramatic population losses across the Great Plains (Johnson & Rathge, 2006). As a result, many rural communities in Kansas face school consolidation, inadequate access to health and social services, and loss of local businesses (Hamilton, Hamilton, Duncan, & Colocousis, 2008).

Many of these communities are eager to reinvigorate their local economies, and some are trying to capitalize on the unique cultural and natural amenities their region offers. The Flint Hills landscape in north central Kansas offers an instructive case study of one such effort at revitalization. Historically, the prairies of the Flint Hills region were valued for their productive qualities, but more recently, changing values have converted the Flint Hills into an object of visual "consumption" and made the region into an object for tourism and local economic development.

This transition cannot be understood without reviewing the context that produced the current conditions (Table 3.1). The region first became known as the Flint Hills in the early 19th century, named for the flint-like chert stones that glinted through the tall prairie grasses. In this nearly treeless region, big bluestem grass nourished by minerals in the limestone grew so tall as to obscure the horizon (Middendorf, Cline, & Bloomquist, 2008). The lush grass drew herds of buffalo that the native hunters followed, but beginning in the mid-1800s, cattle rapidly replaced the buffalo and homesteaders displaced the Indians. Because its rocky soil made plowing difficult but cattle grazing was viable, the Flint Hills region retained much of its original character (Middendorf et al., 2008).

Ecologists have had a long-standing interest in the Flint Hills because they contain the largest contiguous tract of tall-grass prairie left in North America. Recently, others have taken notice as well. In April 2007, *National Geographic* magazine featured the Flint Hills in a cover story titled "Splendor of the Grass" (Klinkenborg, 2007). Soon thereafter, an article in the *New York Times* travel section described the region as follows: "Seemingly endless, the landscape offers up isolated images—a wind-whipped cottonwood tree, a

Table 3.1	Time Line of Important Dates in Flint Hills	
Date	*Event*	*Principal Actors*
1920s–1950s	Ongoing modest efforts to establish a prairie park	Conservationists, ecologists
1960s	Opposition to national prairie park due to antigovernment sentiments	Local Flint Hills residents, especially those who were displaced by earlier federal projects
1970s	Proposal for legislation to create a prairie park is opposed	Governor of Kansas, environmental groups support prairie park; Kansas Livestock Association opposes it
1970s	Manhattan Citizens for Tallgrass National Park is formed and lobbies for a landmark commemorating ranching heritage and preserving area for conservation	Environmentalists, local citizens
1970s	Kansas Grassroots Association (KGA) is formed to oppose any park idea	Ranchers and landowners
1975	Kansas legislature passes bill requesting U.S. Congress to reject authorization of a Tallgrass Prairie Park in Flint Hills, while support among conservationists grows	Kansas legislature, with support of KGA, continues to express antigovernment involvement
1988	Private conservation organization offers to buy ranch in Flint Hills to establish a park, with National Park Service (NPS) as manager; locals agree to private ownership; National Park Trust (public-private entity) is formed	Audubon Society; National Park Service
1996	Tallgrass Prairie Preserve is designated; National Park Trust created	National Park Service and conservation organization
2004	The Nature Conservancy (TNC) purchases land; management will be joint public-private	TNC owns land; TNC, NPS, and KS Park Trust jointly manage land
2005	Flint Hills Scenic Byway created; Scottish Power proposes industrial wind farm; "Protect the Flint Hills" campaign and Flint Hills tourism begins	Flint Hills Tourism Coalition, along with KS Department of Transportation; 22 counties in Flint Hills
2009	Flint Hills Heritage Conference is held; local organizations come together to promote the Flint Hills landscape as international tourist destination	Many local governments and tourism groups

rusted cattle pen, a spindly windmill, an abandoned limestone schoolhouse, the metal-gated entrance to a hilltop cemetery" (Rubiner, 2007). *National Geographic* photographer and local booster Jim Richardson proclaimed, "The Flint Hills should never play second fiddle to our nation's most recognized landmark landscapes" (Kansas Department of Commerce, 2008).

Local interest in preserving and promoting the Flint Hills landscape would have been unpredictable based on past history. Battles between local residents, between conservation and agriculture interests, and between state and federal agencies were ongoing throughout the 20th century over the costs and benefits of preserving the prairie. The battle lines were drawn between those who wanted the Flint Hills to remain in private ownership for productive uses versus those who wanted to preserve it as a public good. In short, the cleavages divided agriculture and environmental interests, and local and national interests. How these groups came together and now are jointly promoting the landscape provides an interesting case study in community development.

Starting in the 1920s, natural scientists expressed alarm at how quickly the ecologically important prairie ecosystem was disappearing. Their concerns were overshadowed by the more pressing issues of the Great Depression and the Dust Bowl, however, and efforts to establish a "prairie park" were thwarted (Conard, 1998). Modest efforts continued in the subsequent decades but again were sidelined by more important issues, such as World War II. Between the 1930s and the 1950s, advocates focused their attention on tallgrass prairie—what they viewed as "true prairie"—and considered various sites across the Great Plains to establish a prairie national park.

By 1960, the National Park Service recommended developing a large park near Manhattan, Kansas, based on several criteria: acreage; the topography, drainage systems, vegetation, and wildlife species were typical of a prairie ecosystem; the site was free of intrusions; and the site had sufficiently scenic qualities. Even at this early stage, local residents began to take sides for or against the establishment of the prairie park. The opposition was shaped in part by an earlier flood control dam project, which some locals perceived as a federal land grab. Ranchers and farmers also felt the National Park Service had excluded them from the planning process for the dam. Thus, the dam project pitted many locals against the federal government in general. Over the ensuing years, several park proposal bills were defeated in subcommittees by opposition from local landowners and congressmen from western states. Although public interest in the prairie park was growing, no further federal legislation was introduced in the 1960s.

In 1970, the governor of Kansas appointed an advisory committee, which brought environmental groups, the Prairie National Park Natural History Association, universities, newspapers, and many individuals together to ask for the introduction of legislation to create a prairie park. The Kansas Livestock Association led the opposition and instead proposed a 600-mile "prairie parkway" driving tour along existing highways in the Flint Hills. In an effort to unite agriculturalists and environmentalists, the Manhattan Citizens for

Tallgrass National Park was formed and lobbied for creating a landmark commemorating the ranching heritage of the region along with a prairie ecosystem preserve. An alternate proposal of an "integrated park system" was put forth by a Kansas representative who thought that a large expanse of prairie park alone would not attract enough tourists to offset the loss of property tax revenue. This idea further polarized the opposing sides, with environmentalists favoring the park while ranchers and landowners organized against it, forming a group they called the Kansas Grassroots Association (KGA).

Throughout the 1970s, Kansas remained divided over the issue, and in 1975, the Kansas legislature overwhelmingly passed a bill requesting that Congress reject authorization of a tallgrass prairie park in the Flint Hills. Again, there was a strong antigovernment rationale for opposing the park; opponents claimed that the federal government already controlled large amounts of property in the state (apparently military reservations and reservoirs) and that a national park would remove too much land from property tax collection. Meanwhile, support for a prairie park was growing throughout the rest of the country, as national environmental and conservation organizations began to galvanize around the idea. In a major concession to agriculture interests, the legislation proposed creation of a "tourway-parkway" that the federal government would not acquire directly, but would jointly manage with state and local government and private conservation organizations. These proposals were still rejected by the KGA, whose members stated: "Preserve, reserve or whatever it's called, it's a park. We oppose a national park in Kansas," and "the Flint Hills would either become an 'uninhabited no-man's land' or a 'tourist trap complete with curio shops and hot dog stands' if H.R. 5592 passed" (Conard, 1998, p. 28). They continued to express serious reservations about additional federal land ownership in the state.

In 1988, the idea of a prairie park resurfaced with proposals that highlighted public-private management partnerships. The National Audubon Society offered to purchase a 10,000-acre historic ranch in the Flint Hills and share management responsibilities with the National Park Service. Ranchers agreed to private ownership of the land but were still wary of federal involvement. A spokesperson for the Kansas Livestock Association stated, "There is just a deep-seated philosophy in the Flint Hills that the government should not own land" (Conard, 1998, p. 33). Over the next few years, as the National Park Service funded a feasibility study, the KGA, the Kansas Livestock Association, and the Farm Bureau escalated opposition to federal landownership. The National Parks and Conservation Organization entered the arena by creating the National Park Trust, a nonprofit land trust that would keep the ranch in private ownership but enter into a relationship to have the National Park Service manage the property. But to do so, the federal government needed to own a minimum of 180 acres, so in 1996, the 180-acre Tallgrass Prairie Preserve was designated. Various interest groups were organized into an advisory committee to make recommendations concerning the management and development of the Tallgrass Preserve. In 2004, the Nature Conservancy purchased the land and assumed ownership of the preserve, with the National Park Service maintaining management control. This unique public-private partnership coordinates land management responsibilities between the Nature Conservancy, the National Park Service, and the Kansas Park Trust (The Nature Conservancy, 2009).

Since the Tallgrass National Preserve was finally established in 1996, the growth in the number of organizations devoted to the preservation and commoditization of the Flint Hills landscape has been phenomenal. The Flint Hills Scenic Byway was designated in 2005. Then, a proposal in 2005 by Scottish Power to install industrial-scale wind farms in the Flint Hills was fought vociferously by locals, national environmental organizations (especially the Nature Conservancy), and the state government, and galvanized them to form the "Protect the Flint Hills" campaign. The proposal was withdrawn, and opposition remains strong to any development of wind farms in the Flint Hills. Maintaining an undeveloped Flint Hills landscape for its scenic value and the public good has become the dominant objective in this region that was long dominated by commercial interests and the value of private property rights.

In 2005, the Flint Hills Tourism Coalition began with a mission of increasing "the economic base of the region and the state through the promotion and marketing of the Kansas Flint Hills" (Flint Hills Tourism Coalition, 2008, p. 48). The organization promotes the Flint Hills as "one of the few places left in the world that hasn't changed since [the dawn of time]" and "an unblemished experience of nature's magnificence" (Flint Hills Tourism Coalition, 2008, pp. 16–17). The organization is now working with the Kansas Department of Transportation in the design and creation of gateway monuments, and is exploring the feasibility of establishing a visitor's center and a national heritage site. A Flint Hills Heritage Conference was held in 2009 to bring together local groups to "identify the common threads of our shared heritage" (Flint Hills Tourism Coalition, 2009, p. 1). The Flint Hills Tourism Council has branded the Kansas Flint Hills as "The Grassroots of America," placing large markers along highways to signal you have entered the region. Twenty-two counties in central Kansas now claim to be located in the Flint Hills region and are attempting, through the Flint Hills Tourism Coalition, to promote the Kansas Flint Hills as an "international tourism destination as a means of economic development of our region" (Flint Hills Tourism Coalition, 2009, p. 4).

The Flint Hills case illustrates how conflicting visions of development can be drawn together by focusing on landscape. Historically, the region was divided between advocates of productive versus consumptive uses, public versus private ownership, or local versus federal control, but the designation of a national prairie preserve offers a new conception of landscape as a conservation area that highlights the ranching heritage of the region. By shifting focus to a landscape that incorporated a variety of resources, organizers were able to craft a partnership that included public and private interests and national and local voices, which afforded a compromise between long-standing opposing interests. Now residents are able to capitalize on the landscape for local economic development.

Service-Learning

Both the Flint Hills of Kansas and the Delta region of Mississippi are creating tourism industries, but efforts have been complicated by conflicting interpretations of local heritage and differing visions of how to best develop local resources. Both have settled on public-private partnerships—the Tallgrass Prairie National Preserve, created in 1996, and the Mississippi Delta National Heritage Area, another federal public-private format, designated in early 2009. In the Delta, small-scale tourism development efforts focusing on the blues and civil rights have incorporated racial reconciliation as a key goal. Here we illustrate how racial differences in attitudes are shaped by the natural landscape, using a case study of three communities near a small national wildlife refuge in the northwestern Delta. Insights about race and landscape were generated from a service-learning project carried out by graduate students studying sustainable development at a nearby university. Service-learning involves using community service to provide learners with practical experience, engage them in active learning, illustrate important concepts, and bring particular learning objectives to life. As Simons and Cleary (2006) note, service-learning is distinguished from community service, volunteerism, and other forms of experiential learning by the intention to benefit learners and service recipients equally. The case illustrates how race becomes acculturated and shapes interactions with the landscape.

The service-learning project was carried out in conjunction with the Dahomey National Wildlife Refuge (NWR) and a nonprofit "friends group" that collaborates with the refuge on educational projects. This federally protected sanctuary conserves 9,691 acres of forest and wetland ecosystems, including the largest remaining tract of bottomland hardwood forest in the northern Mississippi Delta (U.S. Fish & Wildlife Service, 2009). The refuge provides habitat for migratory waterfowl species and other wildlife, and opportunities for day hikes, hunting, fishing, wildlife observation, and photography. The refuge manager periodically engages students and teachers in educational activities and has a variety of materials that are available to local teachers (Barton & Atchison, 2007).

Dahomey NWR was designated in 1990, and prior to this, the land was occupied by the Benoit Hunting Club, a private facility that was widely known by residents in the area. Like many facilities in the Mississippi Delta in the past, the Benoit Hunting Club admitted only whites to hunt on its lands, even though 63% of the county population was African American in 1990 (U.S. Census Bureau, 2009). White residents still recall the hunt club fondly; one said, "you can't believe the amount of money [the hunt club] brought into this area. People from all over came here to hunt!" (Barton &

Atchison, 2007, p. 4). Before the Benoit Hunting Club, the area belonged to the Dahomey Plantation, originally established in the 1830s. A portion of the Dahomey Plantation still exists today. The image of the plantation serves as a reminder to local black residents of an oppressive past.

The project was conducted in three communities surrounding Dahomey NWR. Partnering groups included the refuge manager, a friends group dedicated to the refuge, and the campus geospatial information technologies (GIT) lab. Each student worked with classmates in one of the three communities, but within each community, each student had a unique role, and students also worked with those who had the same role in the two other communities. The community coordinator established ties with community leaders and developed a strategy to collect data in the community, including demographic data. The goal was to assess how community members perceived Dahomey NWR, although specific research questions were left up to the three community coordinators working together. The community coordinators used focus group interviews to gather information from community members. The education coordinator contacted teachers and school personnel to assess the potential for collaboration between schools and Dahomey NWR. Education coordinators in the three communities worked together to identify common themes and collect a common set of data. The environment coordinator collaborated with the refuge manager at Dahomey NWR and with the Friends of Dahomey to identify areas of concern and opportunities for local communities at the refuge. Dahomey refuge is small, so it was important to understand how much interaction between the refuge and surrounding communities was possible and desirable. The geographic information systems (GIS) coordinators were responsible for pulling together the information from the other group members, organizing it into a GIS database, and developing ways of communicating findings to communities and to refuge personnel. A GIS course was set up to provide access to the GIT lab and the instructors, and it was recommended that the GIS coordinators sign up for this course. Students also had the opportunity to sign up for a regular GIS instructional course to learn more about using geospatial information technologies.

Findings from the service-learning project revealed a substantial amount of resentment toward the wildlife refuge among community residents. This is not unusual, as protected areas frequently provoke strong feelings in nearby communities. What was interesting was how attitudes about the refuge carried racial meaning. Recent research suggests that African Americans visit federal protected areas less than other racial and ethnic groups (Johnson, Bowker, Green, & Cordell, 2007; Mangun, Degia, & Davenport, 2009). This finding also holds true generally for the Mississippi Delta (Barton, 2007), as shown in Table 3.2. In a 2005 telephone survey of randomly selected residents of 11 Delta counties, black respondents reported visiting both state and federal protected areas at a significantly lower rate than white respondents. The same result held for private hunting clubs, as well as for one type of cultural site, those related to literature and authors. There was no significant racial difference in visits to other

| Table 3.2 | Percent of Residents of 11 Delta Counties Who Have Visited Various Heritage Tourism Sites at Least Once in the Past Year |

	Blues Club or Blues Festival	Blues Museum or Other Blues Site	Literary Museum or Literary Site	Civil Rights Museum or Site	Historic Church	Private Hunting Club	National Park, Forest, or Wildlife Refuge	State Park, Forest, or Wildlife Management Area
All Respondents	32.0	22.6	17.9	26.4	22.8	15.1	30.3	52.9
White	32.6	23.4	22.7	19.9	20.9	33.3	37.3	66.9
Black	31.3	21.6	15.2	30.3	23.4	4.4	25.3	44.4

SOURCE: From a telephone survey conducted in February 2005 (Barton, 2007).

heritage tourism sites, such as historic churches, or blues-related sites such as clubs, festivals, and museums. African American respondents reported visiting civil rights sites at a significantly higher rate than whites.

In the communities near Dahomey, almost all of the community leaders, residents, and educators who were interviewed were aware of the refuge, but knowledge of the refuge's purpose varied. A common perception was that the refuge continued to exclude African Americans and other minorities. As one informant expressed, "I've always thought it was a private hunting club where just white guys could go" (Barton & Atchison, 2007, p. 4). Historic patterns of exclusion persisted in residents' minds, even more than a decade and a half after the refuge was established. The federal government certainly bears some responsibility for this. Naming the refuge after a local plantation certainly did not show sensitivity to the area's majority population. In addition, as one informant noted, "When you drive through and see the no trespassing signs posted, it's obvious they don't want you there" (Barton & Atchison, 2007, p. 5). The refuge manager and friends group have taken up this challenge and are coordinating community outreach efforts to include more local residents, particularly schoolchildren, in the refuge's activities. In addition, the results from this project motivated a service-learning project in another class that aimed to increase environmental education in one of the study communities. Continued efforts like this are necessary to build a climate that is conducive to nature-based tourism in the region.

Preparing Students for Community Development

Activities carried out in university classes are often overlooked as community development, yet how instructors prepare students is perhaps one of the strongest forms of community development. More and more, students are seeking opportunities to engage in service, and instructors can encourage this by incorporating service activities into their courses (Rimer, 2008). As illustrated here, service-learning provides opportunities to better understand the linkages between landscape and community, and can also serve to strengthen those linkages. The results of this service-learning project were presented at a public meeting held on campus at the end of the semester. Students also collaborated to prepare a report detailing the results to distribute to the schools, communities, and the refuge. The professor organized the results into a poster, which has shown at regional conferences. The instructor has also used this project as a case study in conference presentations on the scholarship of teaching and learning. Educational projects like this can serve a broader community development agenda if results are distributed to participants and others.

Conclusions

Community development is fundamentally a process of building relationships, institutions, and culture, which shapes the personalities, worldviews, and identities of community members. But communities are located in places and are influenced by the specific characteristics of the landscape on which the community is embedded. Landscapes both shape and reflect the local culture, as illustrated in the case studies on Kansas's Flint Hills and the Mississippi Delta. The meaning that groups assign to landscapes can serve to produce conflict and suppress efforts at community development, or landscapes can serve as uniting features and produce a sense of shared meaning and community among various groups. Community developers can enhance opportunities and possibilities if they recognize that landscapes unite diverse resources and take on their own meaning, and work to produce common meanings that unite landscape and community.

Public officials have many tools that they can use to shape people's understanding and perception of landscapes, but traditional tools such as legislation and regulation are coercive in nature. When a public entity designates a park, wildlife reserve, or conservation area, they not only affect the natural resources in the area, they also affect local residents and communities. Protected areas have economic impacts, but also alter how residents think about their home. Community developers who work for public agencies must use these tools carefully, as shown in the Kansas case study, because they risk alienating local populations and eroding the legitimacy of government if their actions are perceived as abusive. Partnering with local private organizations has made federal interventions more palatable in both the Kansas and Mississippi cases.

Community developers who work for private organizations face different issues. Local businesses and nonprofit groups often enjoy support from residents as they are seen as representing and defending local interests. But they may only represent the interests of the dominant group, at the expense of marginalized groups, as the Delta case illustrates. The Benoit Hunting Club and Dahomey Plantation enjoyed substantial support among the region's white residents, but because these groups were built on fundamentally unfair principles that systematically excluded most of the area's residents based on the color of their skin, they engendered a deep and long-standing resentment that has carried over to the federal agency that now manages the same land. Private organizations by their nature represent the interests of specific groups, but exist in broader communities and must recognize the broader implications of their activities. Community developers in private organizations must be aware of the larger context and incorporate these insights into the decisions and activities of their organizations.

Landscapes can serve important functions as the basis of community identity, which can be marketed to tourists. The development of a tourism industry can offer many economic development opportunities, but as the case studies reviewed here emphasize, tourism also brings opportunities for community development. Tourism frequently relies on an identification with landscape, which motivates people to look beyond historic conflicts and draw together based on both their own and their community's interests. In designing community development strategies, organizers can enhance their efforts by constructing new visions of the local landscape.

References

Asch, C. M. (2008). *The senator and the sharecropper: The freedom struggles of James O. Eastland and Fannie Lou Hamer.* New York: New Press.

Barton, A. W. (2007). *Visitation to heritage tourism sites by residents of the Mississippi Delta.* Delta Rural Poll Policy Brief No. 07-01. Cleveland, MS: Delta State University, Center for Community and Economic Development.

Barton, A. W., & Atchison, E. (2007). *Constructing sustainable development in Bolivar County, MS: Linking communities and Dahomey National Wildlife Refuge.* Unpublished manuscript, Delta State University, Cleveland, MS.

Blackmon, D. A. (2008). *Slavery by another name: The re-enslavement of Black Americans from the Civil War to World War II.* New York: Anchor Books.

Burch, W. R., Jr. (1997). *Daydreams and nightmares: A sociological essay on the American environment.* Middleton, WI: Social Ecology Press. (Original work published 1971)

Buttel, F. H., & Humphrey, C. R. (2002). Sociological theory and the natural environment. In R. E. Dunlap & W. Michelson (Eds.), *Handbook of environmental sociology* (pp. 33–69). Westport, CT: Greenwood.

Cobb, J. C. (1992). *The most southern place on earth: The Mississippi Delta and the roots of regional identity.* New York: Oxford University Press.

Conard, R. (1998). *Tallgrass Prairie National Preserve legislative history, 1920–1996.* Iowa City, IA: Tallgrass Historians L.C. Retrieved June 30, 2009, from http://www.nps.gov/history/history/online_books/tapr/tapr_7.htm

Duncan, C. M. (1999). *Worlds apart: Why poverty persists in rural America.* New Haven, CT: Yale University Press.

Durkheim, E. (1982). *The rules of sociological method*. New York: Free Press. (Original work published 1895)

Eyre, F. H. (1980). *Forest cover types of the United States and Canada*. Washington, DC: Society of American Foresters.

Firey, W. (1999). *Man, mind and land: A theory of resource use*. Middleton, WI: Social Ecology Press. (Original work published 1960)

Flint Hills Tourism Coalition. (2008). *Kansas Flint Hills travel guide*. Retrieved July 30, 2009, from http://www.newbostoncreative.com/files/FHG-2008_lowres.pdf

Flint Hills Tourism Coalition. (2009, Winter). *Flint Hills heritage newsletter, 3*(1). Retrieved July 30, 2009, from http://kansasflinthills.travel/newsletters/HNWinter2009.pdf

Greider, T., & Garkovich, L. (1994). Landscapes: The social construction of nature and the environment. *Rural Sociology, 59*, 1–24.

Hamilton, L. C., Hamilton, L. R., Duncan, C. M., & Colocousis, C. R. (2008). *Place matters: Challenges and opportunities in four rural Americas*. Durham: University of New Hampshire, Carsey Institute, Reports on Rural America. Retrieved July 30, 2009, from http://www.carseyinstitute.unh.edu/publications/Report_PlaceMatters.pdf

Hinrichs, C. C. (1996). Consuming images: Making and marketing Vermont as distinctive rural place. In E. M. Dupuis & P. Vandergeest (Eds.), *Creating the countryside: The politics of rural and environmental discourse* (pp. 259–278). Philadelphia, PA: Temple University Press.

Housing Assistance Council. (2002). *Taking stock: Rural people, poverty and housing at the turn of the 21st century*. Washington, DC: Author. Retrieved May 30, 2009, from http://www.ruralhome.org/pubs/hsganalysis/ts2000/index.htm

Johnson, K. M., & Rathge, R. W. (2006). Agricultural dependence and changing population in the Great Plains. In W. A. Kandel & D. L. Brown (Eds.), *Population change and rural society* (pp. 197–218). New York: Springer.

Johnson, C. Y., Bowker, J., Green, G., & Cordell, H. (2007). Provide it . . . but will they come? A look at African American and Hispanic visits to federal recreation areas. *Journal of Forestry, 105*, 257–265.

Kansas Department of Commerce. (2008). Kansas Flint Hills featured in April issue of *National Geographic*. Retrieved June 30, 2009, from http://www.travelks.com/s/index.cfm?aid=107

Klinkenborg, V. (2007, April). Splendor of the grass. *National Geographic*. Retrieved July 30, 2009, from http://ngm.nationalgeographic.com/2007/04/tallgrass-prairie/klinkenborg-text/2

Krannich, R. S., & Petrzelka, P. (2003). Tourism and natural amenity development: Real opportunities? In D. L. Brown & L. E. Swanson (Eds.), *Challenges for rural America in the twenty-first century* (pp. 190–199). University Park: Pennsylvania State University Press.

Mangun, J. C., Degia, C. A., & Davenport, M. A. (2009). Neighbors yet strangers: Local people's awareness of Cypress Creek National Wildlife Refuge, Southern Illinois, USA. *Society & Natural Resources, 22*, 295–307.

Middendorf, G., Cline, D., & Bloomquist, L. (2008). Agrarian landscape transition in the Flint Hills of Kansas: Legacies and resilience. In C. Redman & D. Foster (Eds.), *Agrarian landscapes in transition: Comparisons of long term ecological & cultural change* (pp. 206–237). New York: Oxford University Press.

The Nature Conservancy. (2009). *Tallgrass Prairie National Preserve*. Retrieved July 30, 2009, from http://www.nature.org/wherewework/northamerica/states/kansas/preserves/art15403.html

Petrzelka, P. (2004). The new landform's here! The new landform's here! We're somebody now!! The role of discursive practices on place identity. *Rural Sociology, 69,* 386–404.

Rimer, S. (2008, June 23). Big paycheck or service? Students are put to test. *New York Times*. Retrieved June 23, 2008, from http://www.nytimes.com/2008/06/23/world/americas/23iht-23careers.13901489.html

Rubiner, B. (2007, May 7). Old Kansas: Still growing tall. *New York Times*. Retrieved June 2009 from http://travel.nytimes.com/2007/05/04/travel/escapes/04American.html

Saikku, M. (2005). *This Delta, this land: An environmental history of the Yazoo-Mississippi floodplain*. Athens: University of Georgia Press.

Shepherd, R. (2002). Commodification, culture and tourism. *Tourist Studies, 2,* 183–201.

Silver, I. (1993). Marketing authenticity in third world countries. *Annals of Tourism Research, 20,* 302–318.

Simons, L., & Cleary, B. (2006). The influence of service learning on students' personal and social development. *College Teaching, 54,* 307–319.

Tompkins, F. H. (1901). *Riparian lands of the Mississippi River: Past, present, prospective*. Chicago: A. L. Swift & Co.

U.S. Census Bureau. (2009). *American factfinder, 1990 summary tape file 1*. Retrieved April 2009 from http://factfinder.census.gov

U.S. Fish & Wildlife Service. (2009). *Dahomey National Wildlife Refuge: Refuge facts*. Retrieved April 4, 2009, from http://www.fws.gov/southeast/pubs/facts/dahcon.pdf

Walker, P., & Fortmann, L. (2003). Whose landscape? A political ecology of the "exurban" Sierra. *Cultural Geographies, 10,* 469–491.

Wilson, E. O. (1978). *On human nature*. New York: Bantam.

4

The Technical Assistance Approach

Jerry W. Robinson, Jr., and Frank Fear

BEHAVIOR OBJECTIVES

After studying this chapter and completing the online learning activities, students should be able to

1. Define technical assistance in simple terms.

2. Explain how the technical assistance approach can be used in planned change.

3. Describe the difference between the self-help approach, the technical assistance approach, and the conflict approach.

4. List and explain three approaches to providing technical assistance.

5. List and describe how different institutional actors use power to achieve their objectives in community change.

6. Describe three basic assumptions undergirding technical assistance.

7. Describe the differences between the nondevelopmental and developmental approaches to planned change.

8. Describe how technical assistance can be used to co-opt a community.

9. Prepare a short essay on the appropriate use of technical assistance in democratic society.

10. List and describe at least five criteria advocated for by the U.S. Agency for International Development for leaders of technical assistance teams.

11. Describe how changes in technology may affect the need for and use of technical assistance.

AUTHORS' NOTE: Some of the material in this chapter is drawn from Fear, Gamm, and Fisher (1989).

Introduction

Technical assistance is intended to help communities define their problems, needs, and potential solutions. It may allow for some degree of community autonomy or ownership of problem definition and solution. Technical assistance is broadly defined as the provision of "programs, activities, and services . . . to strengthen the capacity of recipients to improve their performance with respect to an inherent or assigned function" (Wright, 1978, p. 343). A key ingredient in this definition is the application of expertise to aid the recipients (Poats, 1972).

This chapter reviews the basic elements of the technical assistance approach to community development and identifies a variety of issues that practitioners and communities should consider in adopting this approach. We also provide some comparison of this approach with others in the field of community development. Technical assistance has been a popular approach in international development. The experience with technical assistance in this context is discussed and analyzed. Finally, we consider some of the conditions in which technical assistance works best in community development.

Perhaps more than other community development approaches, technical assistance raises numerous ethical and professional issues for practitioners. Technical assistance providers need to guard against maintaining the power structure in communities and undermining the capacity of communities to solve their own problems. These challenges are discussed and proposals for handling these dilemmas are reviewed.

Case Study 4.1 Engineering Projects in Service-Learning

The Engineering Projects in Community Service program was created at Purdue University to allow students to gain experience in communicating and working with people of varying social backgrounds. Students are given long-term design goals and are allowed to participate in the program for multiple semesters. Projects are multidisciplinary, and teams are large and diverse in terms of age and experience. This results in high gains for participants in skills like teamwork, communication, resourcefulness, and professionalism. When a project partner is initially found, a team is organized around it and must first come up with the long-term project goals. After a proposal is approved, the project moves forward for as many semesters as are necessary until completion, with a final goal of supplying a successful system to the project partner. Successful systems include a modified telephone for children with disabilities, thermal imaging of houses to determine energy efficiency for Habitat for Humanity, and an improved computer network for a local health care service.

SOURCE: Tsang, E. (Ed.). (1999). *Projects that matter: Concepts and models for service-learning in engineering.* Washington, DC: American Association for Higher Education.

———— Understanding the Technical Assistance Approach

From a technical assistance position, the scientific method is highly valued, advances in technology are considered signs of progress, and rational planning in the decision-making process is a corollary of the scientific method. Indeed, planning is a prized process, and the collection and analysis of data are important elements in that process. It is assumed that all situations can be analyzed objectively and that bad decisions are frequently a result of poor planning.

In the technical assistance approach, technical know-how is assumed to be good because efficiency is a valued end. New technology may be uncritically accepted as a better way of doing things. Technology transfer is often defined as the process of effectively communicating or marketing the technology's benefits to potential users. However, full attention may not be given to the technology's fit to the sociocultural context and the dysfunctional consequences that may come about because of its introduction.

A community's official power structure is usually the employer or sponsor of technical assistance work. Economic growth or improvement of the physical infrastructure is typically the focus of attention; advancing community-based capacity may or may not be a central concern. Local resources—physical and human—may or may not be drawn upon during the assistance episode.

Comparisons of Technical Assistance, Self-Help, and Conflict Approaches

The three major themes of community development—technical assistance, self-help, and conflict—generally parallel the approaches to planned change. For example, in comparing schools of thought about planned change, Crowfoot and Chesler (1976) discuss the countercultural (self-help) perspective, the professional-technical (technical assistance) perspective, and political (conflict) perspective. In a discussion of the primary areas of community organization in social work, Rothman (1974b) identifies three approaches: locality development (self-help), social planning (technical assistance), and social action (conflict). Chin and Benne (1976) consider three strategies of planned change: the normative-re-educative (self-help), the empirical-rational (technical assistance), and the power coercive (conflict).

A unifying theme of the approaches (or perspectives) is that they differ in a number of fundamental areas. Crowfoot and Chesler (1976), for instance, emphasize ideological distinctions by showing how the approaches vary in their response to very basic, value-laden questions: What are their general images of society? What are their general images of the individual? What are their diagnoses of contemporary society? What are their priorities with regard to change? Rothman focuses on selected practice variables, including salient practitioner roles; differential conception of the client's role, tactics, and techniques; and orientation toward the community power structure. A comparative analysis of the approaches is presented in Table 4.1.

Table 4.1 Self-Help, Technical Assistance, and Conflict as Planned Approaches

Planned Change Approaches			
Factor	*Self-Help*	*Technical Assistance*	*Conflict*
Image of society	• Dehumanized • Mechanical	Bureaucratic organizations with authority figures	Groups constantly struggle to maintain or add to their power base
Image of individual	Inherently good but goodness is suppressed	System-defined players and roles	Oppressed
Assumption examples	People have the right and ability to identify and solve collective problems	Science provides means to solve problems	Power is the most basic of all resources
Core problem to be addressed	Capacity of people to take collective action	Capacity to harness science to solve human problems	Concentration of power in the hands of a few persons
Examples of action goals	Community capacity building	Technical problem solving	Redistribution of power

SOURCE: Adapted from Rothman (1974b), Chin and Benne (1976), and Crowfoot and Chesler (1976).

The differences described by these authors are worthy of note, especially for students and practitioners of technical assistance. For our purposes, a useful distinction may be drawn between self-help and conflict, on one hand, and technical assistance on the other hand. Both the self-help and conflict approaches fix attention on human and collective development. Community residents are expected to come together, identify problems through mutual agreement, and mobilize change that is fundamental to technical assistance. Collective action is just as important—perhaps more important—than the products derived from the change episode. That is, the process of collective action represents a literal learning laboratory where persons can expand their repertories of community change skills. Self-help and conflict practitioners are successful (other things being equal) to the extent that they possess well-developed process skills—something emphasized in the literature on practice roles (Bennett, 1973).

Indeed, the differences between the technical assistance approach and self-help and conflict approaches are often more than superficial. For example, because the power structure is the employer or sponsor of technical assistance efforts, citizens are frequently not seen as consumers or end users. The concept of residents as consumers or clients is also frequently eschewed in the self-help approach. In the conflict literature, residents are often described as the victims of social inequalities and injustices. Similarly, members of the local power structure are collaborators, at best, and "blockers," at worst, in the self-help approach; they are oppressors to those who espouse the conflict approach.

Types of Technical Assistance

Is it possible to classify technical assistance by type? We believe it is, and two classifications will be discussed here: (a) use of power actors to achieve goals; or (b) as a strategy used by consultants or volunteer leaders as developmental activity.

Technical Assistance and Power Actors. Technical assistance relationships—and decisions to enter into them—may vary according to the auspices under which they are organized and the impetuses for undertaking technical assistance. The power sources under which technical assistance is provided can be categorized as (a) *legislation*—having the powers to create, legislate, and appropriate; (b) *administration*—having the power to manipulate resources, knowledge, and information; (c) *education*—having the knowledge, skills, and processes of a specialized nature associated largely with educational and research institutions; (d) *collaborators*—creating mechanisms, often mutually, for the specified purpose of providing or enhancing technical assistance in the recipient's domain; and (e) *consultants*—generally, performing specific tasks by private consultants.

The sources for offering technical assistance—how it finds its way into a recipient's domain—can be categorized in the following ways: (a) imposed (i.e., thrust on the recipient unilaterally from the outside); (b) negotiated (i.e., reached by mutual consent); or (c) most importantly, a community activity initiated by those who perceive that there is such a need.

Nondevelopmental and Developmental Technical Assistance

Although technical assistance essentially involves the acquisition of problem-solving resources, the rationale for the resource exchange and the nature of the relationship between the provider and the recipient are critically important issues if we are to view technical assistance as a theme of community development. Contemporary technical assistance efforts are predominantly associated with the desire of the provider to enable recipients to do what they are incapable of doing or unwilling to do on their own. That is, the provider is committed to some goal that, if it is to be attained, requires an adoption of particular skills or technologies by the recipient. Additionally, the provider is unwilling to wait for "natural" (communication, travel) means of transfer to reach the recipient and is unwilling or unable to directly take over the recipient's responsibilities.

These points are essentially captured in the basic assumptions of technical assistance:

1. Someone knows something about the issues that another does not know.

2. Someone decides that the potential recipient needs assistance.

3. A provider-recipient relationship can be established.

4. The provider provides and the receiver receives.

Given this backdrop, it can be argued that technical assistance, although an important approach to planned change, may or may not be an approach (or theme) of community development. Technical assistance as a nondevelopment approach to change is generally described by Batten (1975) in his discussion of the directive approach to group and community work as follows:

> The directive approach means that the agency . . . decides whatever . . . it thinks people need or ought to value or ought to do for their own good, and sometimes how they ought to behave. These decisions become the agency's goal for people. The agency will then provide whatever staff, equipment, premises, and programmes it thinks are needed to meet the needs or interest of the people it wishes to help, in the hope that they will avail themselves of the services or activities it provides. This will bring them into contact with the agency's workers who will then try to influence people in relation to the agency's ideas of betterment for them. . . . The agency and its workers think, decide, plan, organize, administer, and provide for people. Always the main initiative, and the final say, remain with them. (p. 5)

Christenson and Robinson's (1980) widely quoted definition describes community development as the shared decision by community residents to initiate a planned change process. When conceptualized through this filter, technical assistance involves the residents' desire to accept assistance because of its fundamental importance for improving the locale's social, economic, and/or physical environment. Outside assistance is therefore necessary and appropriate. In addition, legitimate representatives of the community collaborate with the external change agents (i.e., those providing the assistance) as change agents on the "planning change team." This collaboration is based on a mutually agreeable set of role relationships. If these elements are in place, then it is possible for technical assistance to be compatible with the Oberle, Stowers, and Darby (1974) definition of development as the "process in which increasingly more members of a given area or environment make and implement socially responsible decisions" (p. 61). This approach to technical assistance can be classified as the developmental approach.

Perhaps the basic difference between technical assistance as a nondevelopmental and developmental approach to planned change rests with values. In reviewing the definition and assumptions associated with technical assistance, a development ethician such as Goulet (1977) might pose the question: Who decides what assistance will be provided to whom, how, and when? In this realm, value-oriented questions may be raised—questions that surround the issues of goal selection, problem definition, means selection, and assessment of consequences (Kelman & Warwick, 1978):

1. Whose values are to be served by the intervention?

2. To what extent do the recipients have an opportunity to participate in the choice of the goals?

3. To what extent does the process enhance the power of the target population to solve problems?

4. To what extent is the provider engaging in a self-serving activity?

5. Whose problem(s) is (are) being primarily addressed in the technical assistance episode: the provider's or the recipient's?

6. Is a reasonable set of alternatives available to the recipient? Does the recipient have the power of choice? If so, does the provider assist the recipient in making informed choices?

7. Is incomplete or distorted information presented about the effects of assistance? Or, are only the probable benefits emphasized? Indeed, does the provider know, understand, and communicate the probable sociocultural, economic, environmental, and psychological impacts?

8. Will the assistance create a dependency relationship between the donor and receiver?

For example, if assistance is knowledge-induced (knowledge in search of an application) or profit-induced (knowledge primarily or exclusively transferred with a profit motive in mind), then development is not likely to be served. To the extent that the recipient fully participates—indeed, is at least a co-owner—of the assistance process, developmental technical assistance is possible. The fundamental importance of these questions and shaping the process leading to the answers need to be emphasized because technology transfer characterizes much of what we know as technical assistance. Technology transfer, according to Glaser, Abelson, and Garrison (1983), is the application of knowledge or technology by a new user.

From our perspective, technology transfer may or may not be a means of development. Technology of itself is equivocal, according to Glaser and his colleagues. The reasons for its application, and the consequences of its use, typically define the relative goodness and badness of the transfer in development terms. That is why different evaluators can advance very different—sometimes incompatible—criteria to evaluate the process and its effects. Glaser et al. (1983) emphasize the need to consider the impacts from a developmental point of view:

> Technology is defined as more than technique—that is, more than science and engineering. It encompasses the totality of specialized means, including those of management, administration, and public policy, used to develop goods or services for human sustenance and comfort. Technology also has deeper anthropological meaning. It is a key element of culture; it determines the relationship of a community with its natural environment, and is the most concrete expression of values (Wenk, 1979). Sooner or later, each society that strives to upgrade its technical capability discovers that it is both unfeasible and socially counterproductive simply to paste a veneer of technology onto indigenous culture. Hence, transfers of technology require a high sensitivity to match technical resources congenially not only with social goals but also with infrastructural, or cultural/social, foundations. (p. 383)

Using Technical Assistance as a Community Development Activity

Given this background, we believe that technical assistance exists at both ends of a continuum: It exists at both nondevelopmental and developmental modes of planned change. At one extreme, technical assistance involves imposing assistance, technology, information, or ways of thinking on a community. Community involvement exists at best for appearances or legitimation. At worst, it serves the purpose of the co-optation. Conversely, as a developmental model, it is a vital and necessary approach to community development: recipients need assistance, donors are able and willing to provide it, and recipients regulate the assistance process in self-protective ways. The challenge to community development scholars and practitioners rests not in debating whether technical assistance is community development; our argument is that it is not. In our opinion, the field is better served by uncovering (a) when technical assistance is an appropriate approach to community development, and (b) how the community developer may effectively implement the developmental mode of technical assistance.

Technical Assistance as an Appropriate Approach to Community Development

The concept of appropriateness occupies a central place in the vocabulary of community development. Being able to analyze a situation and determine how to proceed appropriately are essential community development skills.

What this means is that technical assistance has its place as an approach to community development. Where? The concept of reliance on local resources and indigenous capacity is stressed again and again in the community development literature. However, the notion of complementing these resources (when necessary) with outside resources and assistance is also emphasized in the literature. It is naïve to believe that all of the resources necessary for all successful community actions are available within the local setting. Community leaders often need resources (e.g., money, technology, advice, person power) that exist outside the locale.

Technical Assistance as Community Development

The developmental question that looms large is this: How is it possible to acquire, direct, and control outside resources in ways that are consistent with local values and preferences? The tail-wagging-the-dog scenario in technical assistance comes to pass when the cost of external resource mobilization is such that it subverts the residents' ability to build capacity. The challenge to technical assistance as community development is that it takes place within a *process* whereby local people have an opportunity to enhance their individual and collective problem-solving abilities. This is the same challenge facing self-help and conflict as community development. The basic difference is that both of these latter approaches are inherently absent in the technical assistance approach, but they must be added to the approach if community development is to occur.

The collective capacity-building notion is equivalent to the opportunity to enhance the sense of community in the locale. Frequently in community development, we naively assume—sometimes with disastrous consequences— that sufficient levels of community exist, in the psychological and socio-logical senses, so that all practitioners need to do is focus attention on the substantive problem(s) at hand. In the developmental sense, levels of community vary with the extent that people socially and psychologically identify with the locale and aspire to strengthen its capacity to solve problems (Cottrell, 1977).

In self-help community development, the fundamental task of people wanting to come together to deal with common problems assumes that sufficient levels of community exist. We know from experience that people often do not participate in self-help opportunities because of their belief that an alternative means of action can provide needed resources more quickly and effectively (Rothman, 1974a; Rothman, Erlich, & Teresa, 1976). Similarly, lower levels of community may exist in precisely those environments where community organizing (the conflict approach) would seem most appropriate. This may be primarily because feelings of collective powerlessness—frequently expressed as fatalism and apathy—are often ubiquitous in disadvantaged environments. Much of Alinsky's work focused on describing tactics that organizers can use to bring people together effectively and enhance the sense of community for the purpose of taking collective action (Alinsky, 1971). This often involved using local institutions (e.g., faith-based organizations) as a medium to broaden the sense of community.

Nondevelopmental technical assistance does not require the existence of high levels of community. Outside change agents can "do for" the community because community capacity building is not a goal. At times, community members even request such a structure. External assistance, in this case, is not viewed as a means to capacity-building, but as an end in itself. This is precisely when technical assistance is not community development but simply an approach to planned change.

In technical assistance as community development, practitioners must resist playing a service delivery role only. Recognition of the existing socio-cultural environment and the leadership structure, and an understanding of the consequences of extending assistance, are imperative (Truman, Grether, Vandenberg, & Fear, 1985). For example, are the potential dysfunctions of the technical assistance considered prior to the initiation of the assistance process? To what extent will the leadership structure be affected by the assistance process?

To further enhance technical assistance as community development, we recommend that greater attention be given to (a) increasing the instances where technical assistance is subsumed under one of the other approaches to community development, and (b) considering how technical assistance can be serially joined with other approaches.

In the first case, this would mean delivering technical assistance as part of a larger self-help or conflict process. Opportunities exist to accomplish this goal, although they are often missed. On the other hand, political realities of agency agendas may preclude this, especially with respect to linking technical assistance with conflict. A recent experience of one of the authors comes to mind. Research services (to be offered by a publicly funded university) were requested by a community group to document the supposed unjust and arbitrary decision by a local school district to close its neighborhood elementary school. The researcher providing the assistance quickly found himself in several confrontational sessions with representatives of the city power structure, most notably the superintendent of schools.

The serial linking of technical assistance with other approaches to community development appears to be a more politically reasonable option, especially for organizations involved in longer-term development efforts within specific community settings. The experience of nongovernmental organizations that provide assistance in the developing world is that they constantly struggle with choices between relief and development. Faith-based organizations are ideologically drawn to the self-help notion of community development as a medium for holistic development, but also search for ways to break out of the seemingly vicious cycle of providing relief with development even though technical assistance is very much needed. This suggests that technical assistance is being viewed only as a nondevelopmental approach. The temporal sequencing of developmental technical assistance (first) with self-help (later) would seem to be a strategy for providing emergency services within a long-term developmental thrust.

Alliband (1983), a developmental writer, argues that both nondevelopmental *and* developmental technical assistance are needed in the developing world because "each one works to solve different problems and to address the problems of different socio-economic groups" (p. 3). On one hand, when considering Third World agricultural development, he believes that many larger farmers stand ready to adopt new production technology imported from Europe and the United States. On the other hand, he feels that the purpose of the developmental approach is "to generate community-based, community-wide, problem-solving capacity" (Alliband, 1983, p. 5). The relevance of this approach is to encourage the cooperative pooling of internal resources (mental, material, and financial) so that optimal change can occur when these resources are commingled with scarce outside assistance.

——— Helping Others Use Technical Assistance Effectively

In developmental technical assistance, the *process* by which the assistance is carried out is as important as the content of the assistance. Increasing concern is being directed toward including nonproduct and process criteria in the determination of development effectiveness. Consider these effectiveness criteria advanced by the U.S. Agency for International Development (USAID) in 1973 for leaders of technical assistance teams. Note that the criteria pertain to issues of competence (Items 1, 2, and 3), morality (Items 4, 5, and 6), and development orientation (Items 7 and 8):

1. Are the technical assistance givers technically qualified?

2. Can they administer what will probably be a complex process?

3. Will they be perceptive and politically astute in picking up undercurrents and tension in interpersonal and interagency relations?

4. Do they exhibit decency, sensibility, and interpersonal skills?

5. Will they understand and accept their responsibility for the attainment of stated objectives?

6. Will they be able to defend convictions under stress?

7. Can they be relaxed about their own status in the community and be willing to share credit for success openly and freely?

8. Will they accept the challenge of development and institution building as primary tools so as to leave behind local skills and resources to carry on?

Perhaps the most impressive movement designed to bring developmental thinking to technical assistance involves appropriate technology. Appropriate technology may be defined as

> a way of thinking about technological change, recognizing that tools and techniques can evolve along different paths and toward different ends. It includes the belief that human communities can have a hand in deciding what their future will be like, and that the choice of tools and techniques is an important part of this. It also includes the recognition that technologies can embody cultural biases and sometimes have political and distributional effects that go far beyond a strictly economic evaluation. Appropriate technology therefore involves a search for technologies that have, for example, beneficial effects on income distribution, human development, environmental quality, and the distribution of political power—in the context of particular communities and nations. (Darrow, Keller, & Pam, 1981, p. 326)

The paradigm statement associated with the appropriate technology movement was published in 1973 by Schumacher in *Small Is Beautiful: Economics as if People Mattered*. Schumacher extolled the virtues of "small scaleness" as a development alternative and emphasized the importance of such concepts as local autonomy, consumer participation in decision making, and the optimal use of local resources in the problem-solving process (Alliband, 1979, p. 136). Development does not start with goods, "it starts with people and their education, organization and discipline" (Schumacher, 1973, p. 159).

> If you want to go places, start from where you are. If you are poor, start with something cheap. If you are uneducated, start with something relatively simple. If you live in a poor environment, and poverty makes the market small, start with something small. If you are unemployed, start using your labor power because any productive use of it is better than letting it lie idle. In other words, we must learn to recognize our boundaries. A project that does not fit, educationally and organizationally into an environment, will be a failure and a cause of disruption. (as quoted in Dunn, 1979, p. 1)

Dunn (1979) conceptualizes appropriate technology as technology that is community-based, is small to moderate in scale, and includes the following characteristics: (a) is labor-intensive, (b) is amenable to management by its users, (c) encourages local innovativeness, (d) is compatible with local values and customs, (e) helps meet local needs, (f) contributes to local self-sufficiency, and (g) relies on local human and natural resources.

Even those who advocate appropriate technology as an approach to technical assistance might agree that the more we attempt to impose technical assistance from the outside, the more we come to realize it does not work as often or as well as those involved had hoped it would. The World Bank

(Cernea, 1985) and other international development assistance groups are finding this to be the case, and they are realizing the importance of defining projects from the points of view of the clients, rather than from the points of view of the technical assistance teams who assess the situations. The international experiences are equally germane to the United States.

This suggests—and, indeed, there is evidence—that developmental thinking is creeping into the writing and practice of those who would classify neither themselves as community developers nor their work as community development. The reason is that experience has revealed that developmental thinking is vitally important for "effective" (i.e., putting into place) technical assistance whether it be embodied (artifact-based) or disembodied (conceptual) in nature (cf. Egea, 1975).

From this point of view, the considerable research that has been conducted on the factors that are associated with planned change must be reviewed carefully. Zaltman (1983) believes that consensus is beginning to emerge from research and that the successful practice of planned change can be described in a compact set of concepts and guidelines. A convergent validity seems to exist, according to Zaltman, because the work in diverse disciplines seems to be pointing to the same general conclusions about what works in the field.

Among the numerous to summarize what is known about the successful practice of change is the well-known and frequently cited work of Davis and Salasin (1975). Based on their work in the mental health field, these authors have developed an eight-factor framework, arranged as an acronym: "A V-I-C-T-O-R-Y." Each letter represents a factor that change agents should consider when designing and implementing planned change projects. Note that literally every element in the framework addresses one or more of the developmental aspects discussed in this chapter.

A V-I-C-T-O-R-Y

Ability: The ability of members of the target system to understand and evaluate the assistance being offered.

Values: The degree of fit between the assistance party and the target system's philosophy and operating style.

Information: The adequacy of the target system's knowledge and understanding of the assistance process to be used.

Circumstances: The extent to which those offering the assistance understand the target system's sociocultural context.

Timing: The ability of the party offering assistance to consider the optimal timing for structuring the change process.

Obligation: The need for the assistance party to consider the change from the target system's point of view, particularly in terms of whether or not the change relates to one or more of their felt needs.

Resistance: The assistance party should understand and appreciate the myriad of forces—cultural, social, organizational, and psychological—that may lead to change resistance.

Yield: The benefits and payoffs to the end user(s) if the change is implemented.

Zaltman (1983) has extended the utility of the framework by creating a set of principles and propositions that fine-tunes the requirements associated with successful planned change. With respect to ability, for example, planners are advised that it is important for them to distinguish between client inabilities that can be altered and those that are relatively fixed and to which they must adapt. The more unalterable a client's inability is, Zaltman counsels, the more change agents should focus on innovation-related alterations and less on client-related alterations.

Concluding Observations

We have argued that technical assistance is the only theme or approach to community development that is not inherently developmental in nature. In some places, technical assistance has been used inappropriately in the name of community development. To be community development, technical assistance activities must conform to the underlying tenets expressed earlier in this chapter and volume, namely, that it take place within a larger process where community residents make a shared decision to initiate a planned change process—a process that is based on a mutually agreeable set of role relationships between community members and outside providers.

Contemporary emphasis on the "people component" of development is reflected in literature and practice (Korten & Klauss, 1984; Pulver & Dodson, 1992). It suggests the timeliness of the developmental approach to technical assistance. To take advantage of this situation, community development must use its value-oriented, normative base as the foundation for "sciencing" the technical assistance process. This means carefully documenting processes and results as well as testing process alternatives. In many fields, this recognition that technical assistance should be grounded in community participation is widely accepted. Most professionals in the community planning field now recognize the value and importance of this dimension. In other professions, however, there is less value placed on the role of community participation in technical assistance. Part of the problem may be that many professions do not have adequate models for how they may engage the community in this respect.

What this all signifies, at least to us, is that community development professionals who provide technical assistance must prove themselves to be worthy colleagues in the community development arena. The potential of technical assistance has already been recognized; the community development way of thinking is being increasingly viewed as relevant, appropriate, and necessary. Now the challenge becomes one of "delivering the goods," that is, producing efficient and effective results. Brokensha's (1968) assertions that community development is known for its "murky banalities and half-truths" must be invalidated. The very future of technical assistance in the community arena as an objective scholarly enterprise hinges on disproving its murky banalities and half-truths.

References

Alinsky, S. D. (1971). *Rules for radicals*. New York: Random House.

Alliband, T. (1979). Community development and the search for appropriate change: A book review essay. *Journal of the Community Development Society, 10*, 135–139.

Alliband, T. (1983). *Catalysts of development: Voluntary agencies in India*. West Hartford, CT: Kumarian.

Batten, T. R., with Batten, M. (1975). *The non-directive approach in group and community work*. London: Oxford University Press.

Bennett, A. (1973). Professional staff members' contributions to CD. *Journal of the Community Development Society, 4*, 58–68.

Brokensha, D. (1968). Comments. *Human Organization, 27*, 78.

Cernea, M. M. (Ed.). (1985). *Putting people first: Sociological variables in rural development*. New York: Oxford University Press.

Chin, R., & Benne, K. D. (1976). General strategies for effective changes in human systems. In W. G. Bennis, K. D. Benne, R. Chin, & K. E. Corey (Eds.), *The planning of change* (pp. 22–45). New York: Holt, Rinehart and Winston.

Christenson, J. A., & Robinson, J. W., Jr. (1980). In search of community development. In J. A. Christenson & J. W. Robinson, Jr. (Eds.), *Community development in America* (pp. 3–17). Ames: Iowa State University Press.

Cottrell, L. S., Jr. (1977). The competent community. In R. L. Warren (Ed.), *New perspectives on the American community: A book of readings* (pp. 546–560). Chicago: Rand McNally.

Crowfoot, J. E., & Chesler, M. A. (1976). Contemporary perspectives on planned social change: A comparison. In W. G. Bennis, K. D. Benne, R. Chin, & K. E. Corey (Eds.), *The planning of change* (pp. 188–204). New York: Holt, Rinehart and Winston.

Darrow, K., Keller, K., & Pam, R. (1981). *Appropriate technology sourcebook, Vol. 2*. Stanford, CA: Volunteers in Asia, Inc.

Davis, H. R., & Salasin, S. E. (1975). The utilization of evaluation. In E. L. Struening & M. Guttentag (Eds.), *Handbook of evaluation research, Vol. 1* (pp. 621–666). Beverly Hills, CA: Sage.

Dunn, P. D. (1979). *Appropiate technology with a human face*. New York: Schocken.

Egea, A. N. (1975). Multinational corporations in the operation and ideology of international transfer of technology. *Studies in Comparative International Development, 10*, 11–29.

Fear, F. A., Gamm, L., & Fisher, F. (1989). The technical assistance approach. In J. A. Christenson & J. W. Robinson, Jr. (Eds.), *Community development in America* (pp. 69–88). Ames: Iowa State University Press.

Glaser, E. M., Abelson, H. H., & Garrison, K. N. (1983). *Putting knowledge to use.* San Francisco: Jossey-Bass.

Goulet, D. (1977). *The uncertain promise: Value conflicts in technology transfer.* New York: IDOC/North America.

Kelman, H. C., & Warwick, D. P. (1978). The ethics of social intervention: Goals, means, and consequences. In G. Bermant & D. P. Warwick (Eds.), *The ethics of social intervention* (pp. 3–33). Washington, DC: Wiley.

Korten, D. C., & Klauss, R. (Eds.). (1984). *People-centered development: Contributions toward theory and planning frameworks.* West Hartford, CT: Kumarian.

Oberle, W. H., Stowers, K. R., & Darby, J. P. (1974). A definition of development. *Journal of the Community Development Society, 5,* 61–71.

Poats, R. M. (1972). *Technology for developing nations.* Washington, DC: Brookings Institution.

Pulver, G., & Dodson, D. (1992). *Designing development strategies in small towns.* Washington, DC: Aspen Institute.

Rothman, J. (1974a). *Planning and organizing for social change.* New York: Columbia University Press.

Rothman, J. (1974b). Three models of community organization practice. In F. M. Cox, J. L. Erlich, J. Rothman, & J. E. Tropman (Eds.), *Strategies of community organization* (2nd ed.). Itasca, IL: Peacock.

Rothman, J., Erlich, J. L., & Teresa, J. G. (1976). Fostering participation. In J. Rothman, J. L. Erlich, & J. G. Teresa, *Promoting innovation and change in organizations and communities* (pp. 96–133). New York: Wiley.

Schumacher, E. F. (1973). *Small is beautiful: Economics as if people mattered.* New York: Harper Colophon.

Truman, B., Grether, C. H., Vandenberg, L., & Fear, F. A. (1985). When the tire hits the pavement: A case study of the dilemmas associated with conducting action research. *Journal of the Community Development Society, 16,* 105–116.

Tsang, E. (Ed.). (1999). *Projects that matter: Concepts and models for service-learning in engineering.* Washington, DC: American Association for Higher Education.

U.S. Agency for International Development. (1973). *Selecting effective leaders of technical assistance teams.* Washington, DC: Bureau of Technical Assistance.

Wenk, E., Jr. (1979). *Margins for survival: Overcoming political limits in steering technology.* Oxford, UK: Pergamon.

Wright, D. S. (1978). *Understanding intergovernmental relations.* North Scituate, MA: Duxbury.

Zaltman, G. (1983). Theory in use among change agents. In E. Seidman (Ed.), *Handbook of social intervention* (pp. 289–312). Beverly Hills, CA: Sage.

5 The Self-Help Approach to Community Development

Gary Paul Green

BEHAVIOR OBJECTIVES

After studying this chapter and completing the online learning activities, students should be able to

1. Define the self-help approach to community development.

2. Describe how self-help differs from other community development approaches.

3. Identify the community settings in which self-help might work best.

4. Identify the contexts in which the self-help approach would be less effective.

5. Define asset-based development. Illustrate how it differs from needs assessments.

6. Explain the general process of mapping community assets.

7. Define social capital and give three examples of how community development practitioners can promote social capital.

8. Compare and contrast bonding and bridging social capital.

9. Discuss some of the obstacles and issues that community developers face in promoting self-help in communities.

10. Identify three key responsibilities of facilitators in implementing self-help projects.

Introduction

Self-help is a key concept in community development. The central idea of self-help is that by working together, people can improve their quality of life (Christenson, 1989). Self-help is less concerned with achieving immediate outcomes and impacts, but more interested in bringing residents together to identify common goals. Through this process, communities strengthen their capacity to solve problems, not simply those encountered at this time, but also those they might face in the future. This approach is employed by a variety of organizations, including the U.S. Agency for International Development and the U.S. Cooperative Extension Service, as well as many federal agencies during the War on Poverty.

Although self-help has been widely adopted as a community development strategy, there has been little theory or empirical research to guide this approach in the past. There have been a few case studies in the literature that demonstrate the importance of self-help (Medoff & Sklar, 1994), but there has been very little conceptual development of the concept. In many respects, this approach is based on the value many practitioners place on local democracy and community building.

Over the past decade, the self-help approach has developed a much stronger conceptual base. This chapter reviews some of the major work in this area and discusses how it has contributed to the practice of self-help in community development. The focus is on two somewhat related concepts: asset-based community development and social capital theory. Asset-based community development has emerged as a widely acclaimed approach to community building that focuses on using the resources available in communities (Green & Haines, 2007). It contrasts in ways with technical assistance approaches (Chapter 4) that are perceived to create dependency between communities and technical assistance providers. Although asset building is not a social theory, it does provide some important guideposts for practitioners. Asset-based development offers a positive outlook, and also identifies key resources that can be mobilized and leveraged.

Social capital is a much more theoretical concept, but provides a less specific framework or guidelines for community development practitioners. This theory stresses the importance of social relationships and networks in making possible collective behavior in communities. The emphasis in social capital is on how social relationships establish trust, norms, and reciprocity among community members. These social relationships emerge through participation in formal and informal community organizations. Involvement in these organizations also builds experience and skills in democratic decision making.

Understanding the Concept of Self-Help

Self-help assumes that residents possess the potential for improving the quality of life in their communities. The role of community development practitioners is to facilitate, rather than to guide or direct, a process that helps achieve this goal. The facilitator organizes community efforts and processes that will enable residents to come together and identify strategies for accomplishing their collective goals. In addition, facilitators often help identify potential resources that will enhance the capacity of communities to address their opportunities.

Many communities look to external resources to address their challenges. These resources might include financial assistance, investments by businesses, or technical expertise. Outside resources are attractive because of a perceived local deficiency, such as expertise or financial support. Dependence on external resources, however, presents obstacles to capacity building. Communities can become dependent on external resources and never develop the ability to solve the issues and challenges facing them. John McKnight (1995) argues that technical assistance from professionals (or experts) creates dependency. Technical assistance is usually premised on the assumption that the community has a problem and the professional has the solution. Professionalized service, then, creates clients who are in need of continued care. This relationship, McKnight argues, works against community capacity building. Foundations and government agencies also can create dependency by not encouraging community control over the services and projects they are supporting. Bureaucrats and public officials often view community control and participation as too time-consuming or even idealistic.

Looking to outside resources and assistance can create additional problems. Technical assistance may not match the needs in the local setting. Providers of technical assistance frequently have a generic response to community issues. They have little, if any, local knowledge or understanding of the local context. Professional training focuses on learning general processes and concepts that need to be interpreted and translated at the local level. It takes time to understand the community context and the social dynamics that might influence the success of community interventions. Technical assistance providers usually lack the time and resources to adequately study how the local context may influence the intervention process. So, many times, the reports and recommendations of technical assistance providers sit on a shelf and are never implemented by the community.

Technical assistance providers seldom are able to offer follow-up support. Continual attention is critical to the success of community development. The professional model of technical assistance typically lacks this element. Technical assistance is usually characterized by delivery of a product or service that is limited in time. Most community projects take much more time and commitment than outside experts are able to provide or communities are able to afford. Typically, experts do not live in the community and spend little time with implementing and monitoring interventions.

Finally, technical assistance providers may not make much of an effort to build community control over the projects that are proposed. Residents may not feel they have had adequate input into the design, implementation, or evaluation of the program. Lacking a sense of ownership, communities are less likely to commit to the programs or projects, which ultimately undermines their ability to succeed.

The goal of facilitators should be to avoid some of the typical traps of consultants by taking seriously the role of local knowledge and building a process that allows residents to take full ownership in the intervention. Hopefully, if residents see the process as theirs, they will commit to implementing and monitoring the interventions that are proposed.

Facilitators who implement self-help projects, however, do face two somewhat contradictory demands. On one hand, community groups want results. Many residents become frustrated if the process takes too long or loses focus. Thus, the facilitator needs to continually push the process forward. On the other hand, self-help as a style of planning can take a lot of time because the process is developing skills and collaboration that can contribute to broad community objectives. Change agents employing a self-help process need to recognize these tensions and prepare residents for these challenges. Thus, facilitators need to understand when to let residents struggle with issues and when to help them through the process.

Two different ways of conceptualizing these approaches are discussed below. Asset-based development is a fairly broad approach to mapping and mobilizing local resources. It involves engaging residents in identifying their underutilized resources that could contribute to the development process. Social capital theory is a much richer conceptual approach that focuses more narrowly on social resources. This approach focuses on the important role of social relationships in managing information and resources in the community development process.

Case Study 5.1	**Organizational Development and Service-Learning**

The College of Business Administration at Notre Dame has offered a course called Corporate Strategy. The goal of this course is to give students experience in analyzing and evaluating an organization, then coming up with strategies to meet the organization's goals. Students are taught theory and models in lecture, then connected with outside organizations to aid them in an objective. For example, one class was asked to determine why a local religious charitable organization was facing an aging population of volunteers. The student team's analysis was that the organization was failing to recruit new members at the local church level, and that potential new members were not joining due to fear of interacting directly with the poor and needy without guidance. The team proposed new recruiting techniques at the church to attract interest among young people, as well as adopting a mentoring program that would place experienced volunteers with newcomers to make them feel more comfortable.

SOURCE: Godfrey, P.C., & Grasso, E.T. (Eds.). (2000). *Working for the common good: Concepts and models for service learning in management.* Grand Rapids, MI: Stylus.

Asset-Based Community Development

Jody Kretzmann and John McKnight (1993) are considered the architects of the asset-based community development approach, which was outlined in their publication, *Building Communities From the Inside Out: A Path Toward*

Finding and Mobilizing a Community's Assets. Based on this approach, numerous organizations and communities have sought to build communities through enhancing and leveraging local resources. The central premise of asset-based community development is that most communities have individual, organizational, and institutional resources that are often overlooked and can be used to enhance the quality of life. By contrast, when communities focus on their problems, or needs, they tend to look to outside assistance to solve them.

Asset-based development is an exemplary approach to self-help for several reasons. Asset building assumes that significantly relying on technical assistance and external resources does not build community capacity. Instead, it creates dependencies that constrain the ability of community residents to solve their social and economic problems (McKnight, 1995). The strength of asset-based development is that it emphasizes processes that enhance community control, as well as problem-solving capacity, and that solutions exist from within the community.

Asset-based development typically starts with a mapping process that identifies individual, organizational, and institutional resources in communities. Individual resources might include education and training, experiences, and skills that are frequently overlooked. In expert-based community initiatives, youth, the elderly, and the disabled are overlooked as potential contributors. Yet these individuals may have a variety of gifts that contribute to community well-being.

Local organizations also are important assets. Many residents continue to belong to community organizations, although there has been a long-term decline in membership in voluntary organizations (Putnam, 2000). These organizations are important because of the social resources they hold. These social resources can be mobilized to contribute to community initiatives. The organizations themselves can be visible and important actors in the community as well. They also provide important opportunities for residents to come face-to-face and deliberate over issues that they have in common. They are the arenas in which residents learn how to participate in the democratic process. Part of the mapping process might include identifying both the formal and informal organizations in the community. Formal organizations are often emphasized in the literature because they typically have a long-term presence in the community. But informal organizations have increasingly become an important way for residents to collectively work toward common interests.

Finally, the mapping process usually examines community institutions and evaluates their resources and how they can better serve local residents. For example, local libraries, hospitals, and schools hold many key resources that can be mobilized. They have facilities and equipment that can be used for community purposes. These institutions all have purchasing power that could be directed toward local businesses. They can hire workers from the local community. The mapping process reveals the potential of these institutions for the development of the community.

The mapping process is an important first step for mobilizing communities. An assessment of these assets needs to be placed in the context of community goals or vision. Communities need to identify their common goals and aspirations so they can develop strategies that build on local resources to achieve them. A visioning process attempts to develop a consensus regarding the preferred future of the community. These goals provide the framework for the asset-building process.

It is important to understand the relationship between asset building and external resources and technical assistance. Asset-based community development is frequently portrayed as ignoring the larger social and economic forces that shape localities. It is true that asset-building strategies are shaped by the resources that are available, but these resources are often leveraged as part of a strategy for enhancing the quality of life. Communities may seek financial assistance, for example, but the resources are managed to benefit local residents. Technical assistance may be helpful, but it must be provided in a way that enhances local capacity rather than simply providing a service to residents. The main issue is community control. Can these resources be managed by local residents? Will external agencies and organizations relinquish control of these resources? Will the community be in a position to address future situations without relying on expert support?

This issue of how asset building manages external resources raises larger questions about how self-help relates to other community development approaches, especially technical assistance and conflict. Asset-based development is often criticized for relying too heavily on consensus and avoiding issues of power and conflict that exist in communities. A more accurate characterization might be that asset-based development assumes that the use of conflict or consensus is dependent on the context or situation. It does not assume that conflict or consensus should be used in all situations. In many cases, practitioners may use a process to identify common concerns among residents to develop strategies and goals. This may ultimately require conflict with local officials or other individuals in powerful positions. John Perkins (1993), summarizing the evolution of community development, suggested that

> the motto of community development in the 1960s could have been this: "Give people a fish and they'll eat for a day." The 1970s motto could have been: "Teach people to fish and they'll eat for a lifetime." The 1990s (and beyond) approach to development needs to ask the question: "Who owns the pond?" (p. 119)

So, asset-based development may begin by helping individuals help themselves, but may need to ultimately address broader issues, especially power relations.

Asset-based development also may overlap with the technical assistance approach in some cases. It is obvious that many local issues may involve some complexity or require technical expertise that may not exist in the community. One example could be the difficulty in monitoring environmental problems at the local level. Residents often struggle with documenting the extent of problems, such as air pollution or nonpoint pollution. One appropriate role for technical assistance providers in this case might be to help residents learn how to monitor pollution. Rather than conducting the research *for* the community, technical assistance providers can build capacity by enhancing the skills of residents to address these issues. The key element here is that the process does not generate dependency, but instead increases community power.

In summary, asset-based development offers an exemplary model for the self-help approach. The central feature of this approach is that communities begin with the individual, organizational, and institutional resources that already exist. Rather than focusing on the problems or needs facing the community, asset-based development identifies the local strengths that can provide opportunities. Thus, asset-based development can be combined with other community development approaches (conflict and technical assistance) to provide a richer, more sustainable intervention.

Social Capital

One of the most controversial concepts in the social sciences over the past two decades or so has been the idea of social capital. Social capital has been fiercely debated in sociology, economics, political science, and other disciplines. Social capital is most often defined as trust, norms, and social networks that facilitate collective action (Coleman, 1988). The concept has been applied to a variety of issues, such as job markets, health, regional development, and others. This section explains how social capital has been applied to the field of community development. The concept of social capital can provide a strong conceptual basis for a self-help approach to community development. But we also must understand that social capital can serve as a constraint to collective action at the local level in some instances.

The central premise of social capital is that the structure of social networks influences the capacity of communities to act collectively. Social networks can play an especially important role in providing information and social support to residents. In addition, social networks establish trust and norms that are essential to the development process. Social networks can be produced in a variety of ways. Robert Putnam (2000) focuses on voluntary organizations as a critical source for building social capital. In this view, voluntary organizations bring together people in a neighborhood or locality and create social bonds and relationships that can be leveraged for other social activities. For example, members of a voluntary organization may turn to other members to organize the community to address some social need. Voluntary organizations also provide unique opportunities for residents to learn how to be citizens. They learn how to debate, compromise, and organize. It is through these experiences that residents can learn to trust one another and to count on one another to provide support. Putnam demonstrates that the number of individuals participating in formal voluntary organizations has declined dramatically over the past 50 years. Social capital, however, can be generated in other ways, such as informal associations, the workplace, churches, and schools. It is safe to say, however, that once social capital declines, it is very difficult to rebuild it.

The literature on social networks distinguishes between bonding and bridging social capital. Bonding capital is defined as strong relationships among individuals who know each other very well. Bridging capital is based on weak relationships (acquaintances) among people who do not have a great deal of contact with one another. Both bonding and bridging capital can contribute to the community development process. Bonding capital establishes trust and facilitates cooperation. These relationships can be mobilized to organize residents. Bridging capital provides different types of information and resources than would be available through bonding capital. Bonding capital is often found in poor communities where individuals must rely on family and friends for most of their social resources (Saegert, Thompson, & Warren, 2001). Bridging capital is most likely to exist in more affluent neighborhoods where residents have a broader set of contacts.

What role can community development practitioners play in promoting social capital? How does social capital enhance community capacity? Most communities continue to be segregated by race, ethnicity, and/or social class. Many issues cut across an entire community, such as education, housing, and transportation. Yet many times, the issues are taken on by a single group at the exclusion of others. One role for facilitators is to ensure that a diverse set of interests and voices is represented in the deliberation. It is especially important not to simply round up the usual suspects of community leaders. Failure to recruit a cross-section of the community can undermine the success of the project. The intervention may not be perceived as legitimate, and important perspectives and information will not be included. Social capital can also be supported through social gatherings. Community events, such as potlucks and social gatherings, can provide important venues for increasing social interaction and trust.

Social institutions, such as schools and churches, are important organizations in most communities and are potentially important sources of social capital. Most of these institutions, however, can be characterized as primarily consisting of bonding capital. These institutions are typically segregated by class and race, which adds to the difficulty in mobilizing multiple institutions with a common purpose. Community development practitioners can help bridge residents in these different organizations and institutions so as to generate new social relationships and potential sources of resources.

The concept of social capital is not without its critics. Some practitioners suggest that social capital cannot compensate for the lack of other key resources, especially financial and political capital. Building social relationships may have little impact on providing affordable housing or providing start-up capital to new businesses. It is possible that social capital can improve access to information and possibly access to resources that would not be available without these relationships. It also may help build power among the disadvantaged who lack these other resources. Social capital is often strongly linked to other forms of capital (especially financial and political capital) that is so important to development.

Other critics argue that poor residents do not lack social ties and contacts that they can count on for support. Rather, what they lack is the power to change the economic and political system that disadvantages them. Again, this is obviously a problem for residents in poor neighborhoods. It is possible, however, to build on existing social relationships to organize for power that will challenge the broader system. In this regard, social capital can become an important element to gain control over community institutions and resources.

Finally, some critics charge that social capital tends to reinforce in-group behavior that discriminates against other groups. By promoting social capital, according to this view, practitioners may be creating divisions within the community. This criticism really focuses on some of the negative effects of bonding capital. This critique is directed at efforts to strengthen social bonds within a racial or ethnic group rather than across groups. Yet there are some positive benefits to group members of this type of support. One example would be the informal credit that is often available to immigrant entrepreneurs based on nationality or ethnicity. Although they are restricted to residents based on these social characteristics, they offer important forms of support that are essential for immigrants.

Social capital theory, and, more broadly, the self-help approach to community development, does not argue that communities have all the necessary resources to address their challenges. It does argue, however, that social relationships are a key element and that external resources can be accessed and managed through these local ties.

Implementing Self-Help Projects

The principal role of community development practitioners in the self-help approach is facilitation. The most basic task of facilitators is to promote participatory decision making. As discussed earlier, it is essential to involve a representative group of participants. This means that the facilitator needs to ensure that individuals from various groups in the community are recruited to avoid relying on the usual leaders.

Beyond representation, facilitators need to promote a free-flow exchange of ideas and, in many instances, manage the discussion process to create a safe environment for participants. This may involve developing processes that increase the opportunities for all participants to have a voice and to limit or constrain those participants who would otherwise dominate the process. This is a delicate balance for facilitators. They need to maintain community ownership and control in the process, while preventing the process from being shaped by specific interests or individuals.

The following are major steps involved in implementing a community self-help project. It should be noted that the stimulus for a community effort may not align with an otherwise orderly beginning-middle-end process. The facilitator needs to be true to this impetus and respect the community's starting point while also guiding the process back to a logical sequence that will ultimately result in a more holistic and sustainable effort. Although each community may approach this process differently, there are some common elements that most will follow.

Getting Started. Probably the first step in any community intervention process is to establish a local advisory committee that can guide decision making. There are a variety of operational issues that an advisory committee needs to address. One of the critical issues is to define the boundaries of the community. Who is to be included? In some cases, it may be obvious that it includes all residents in a specific territory marked by political boundaries. Often, however, the task is more difficult.

Second, it is important to determine the expected outcomes of the process at the start. What is the group trying to accomplish, and how will it know when it has been successful? As is discussed below, most communities establish some benchmarks that provide an indication of how well the effort has fulfilled these objectives.

Third, the community needs to plan for the resources that will be needed and the time frame for completing the project. Obtaining commitments from various leaders, organizations, and institutions is important not only in providing the necessary resources, but also building some "buy-in" to the process. This support may be necessary to implement the project successfully later.

Finally, the advisory committee needs to identify the process that will be used to achieve its objectives. How will decisions be made? What role will the advisory committee play in the process? Will the self-help process engage elected leaders?

The advisory group must be seen as representative of the neighborhood or community. At the same time, it is beneficial to use this opportunity to build new leadership rather than relying on the existing leaders who are most likely to be called upon to serve the community. There is often a trade-off here between accessing power through key individuals and opening up the process to new leaders.

Action Planning. Many communities begin an action process by identifying the vision or long-term goals of the community. The action-planning portion of the process then focuses on the specific projects or programs that the community can implement to achieve these goals. Participants are asked to identify the current state of the issue and which groups are currently working on this issue in the community. A common approach is to evaluate the hindering and helping forces on the projects that are identified (a force field analysis). Similarly, it is important to identify groups that will be potential opponents to the project and groups that will be potential allies. It is also important to identify resources needed for the project and set a time line for completing the project.

Many communities want to start with the solutions rather than studying and analyzing the issues they face. Facilitators need to help communities resist this temptation and provide a thorough understanding of the issues they face. Some communities can do this in a few weeks, whereas others may take months to understand the various dimensions of the issue.

Maintaining Momentum. Communities often experience a point where they lose momentum in the process. There are several possible problems (see Green et al., 2001, for a broader discussion of these issues). The project may encounter some conflict or controversy. There may be insufficient resources. The project may suffer from a lack of leadership or direction.

If the project has lost momentum because of resources, it may require some effort to leverage new resources. If the problem is conflict, it may be necessary to confront the issue directly and attempt to mediate between the different sides. Leadership can be a more fundamental problem that will challenge momentum. Building leadership skills can take too much time for a community development project. It may be necessary to find existing leaders who can step in and contribute to the project.

Monitoring and Evaluation. Beyond expected outcomes of the process, communities need to develop a system for assessing the planning process. Monitoring requires an assessment of whether the resources are adequate, how well participants are working, and whether changes need to be made. This information is useful to decide if the programs that are being implemented are the right ones.

Evaluation is essentially an assessment of the success of the project. The specific impacts or outcomes need to be identified by participants. Impacts usually refer to the immediate consequences of the programs and processes, and outcomes are the long-term effects. An example could be economic development. Although the immediate goal might be to create new jobs and increase income, the long-term outcomes could be reduced poverty and increased income mobility for residents. Clear indicators should be developed so the community can judge the success of its effort.

Conclusion

The self-help approach to community development has been widely adopted in a variety of organizational and institutional settings. The idea of self-help is attractive because it assumes that communities can build the capacity to solve their own problems and take advantage of opportunities that are presented to them. It does not depend on large subsidies by federal and state governments. It is consistent with our democratic principles. It supports our notions about the importance of community. Finally, self-help supports some of our belief in social mobility and bootstrapping.

Self-help may work best in middle-class neighborhoods where residents have experience and capacity in this type of process (Christenson, 1989). An implicit assumption of self-help approaches is that community residents are interested and motivated to participate in efforts to discuss local issues and develop plans of action (Littrell & Hobbs, 1989). Most practitioners would admit that these conditions are often not present in poor (and other) neighborhoods. Residents in poor neighborhoods may face more powerful obstacles because of their lack of political power. They may have very little experience with democratic participation in organizations and institutions. The lack of power and experience can generate a sense of hopelessness and alienation.

Self-help also may not work as well for all community issues. Some issues may be more conducive to a conflict approach. Issues with organized opposing factions may not lend themselves to the self-help approach. If a community lacks access to social services or public transportation, it may be necessary to organize the community to exert influence on public officials.

Practitioners also struggle with the tendency for community groups to define issues as technical ones in need of expertise. When problems are defined in this manner, it is more difficult for practitioners to convince residents of the benefits to a self-help approach. They are ready to get the answers to their problems.

Even 20 years ago, Littrell and Hobbs (1989) discussed the greater interdependency of communities that is created through social, political, and economic forces over which they have little control. But they suggested that

> it is possibly more important than ever for communities to orient themselves toward achieving a greater degree of self-determination and adopting the self-help procedures and principles that will allow the idea of community to retain its meaning in coming years. (p. 67)

Interdependency has accelerated even more over the past decades through economic and cultural globalization and the growth of the Internet. The desire for self-determination, however, continues to grow in response to these processes.

References

Christenson, J. A. (1989). Themes of community development. In J. A. Christenson & J. Robinson (Eds.), *Community development in perspective* (pp. 26–47). Ames: Iowa State University Press.

Coleman, J. S. (1988). Social capital in the creation of human capital. *American Journal of Sociology, 94*(Suppl.), S95–S120.

Godfrey, P. C., & Grasso, E. T. (Eds.). (2000). *Working for the common good: Concepts and models for service learning in management.* Grand Rapids, MI: Stylus.

Green, G. P., Borich, T. O., Cole, R. D., Darling, D. L., Hancock, C., Huntington, S. H., Leuci, M. S., McMaster, B., Patton, D. B., Schmidt, F., Silvis, A. H., Steinberg, R., Teel, D., Wade, J., Walzer, N., & Stewart, J. (2001). *Vision to action: Take charge too* (Report No. RRD 182). Ames, IA: North Central Regional Center for Rural Development.

Green, G. P., & Haines, A. (2007). *Asset building and community development* (2nd ed.). Thousand Oaks, CA: Sage.

Kretzmann, J., & McKnight, J. (1993). *Building communities from the inside out: A path toward finding and mobilizing a community's assets.* Evanston, IL: Northwestern University, Center for Urban Affairs and Policy Research.

Littrell, D. W., & Hobbs, D. (1989). The self-help approach. In J. A. Christenson & J. Robinson (Eds.), *Community development in perspective* (pp. 48–68). Ames: Iowa State University Press.

McKnight, J. (1995). *The careless society: Community and its counterfeits.* New York: Basic Books.

Medoff, P., & Sklar, H. (1994). *Streets of hope.* Boston: South End Press.

Perkins, J. (1993). *Beyond charity: The call to Christian community development.* Grand Rapids, MI: Baker Publishing Group.

Putnam, R. D. (2000). *Bowling alone: The collapse and revival of American community.* New York: Simon & Schuster.

Saegert, S., Thompson, J. P., & Warren, M. R. (Eds.). (2001). *Social capital and poor communities.* New York: Russell Sage Foundation.

6

The Interactional Approach to Community

J. C. Bridger, M. A. Brennan, and A. E. Luloff

BEHAVIOR OBJECTIVES

After studying this chapter and completing the online learning activities, students should be able to

1. Explain the origins of community sociology.

2. Define community agency.

3. Understand the origins of field theory.

4. Define community development within the interactional approach.

5. Identify the key challenges to the interactional approach to community development.

6. Describe the community action process.

7. Define the "community field."

8. Identify some of the uses of the interactional approach since the 1980s.

Introduction

Most theories of community revolve around structure. *The interactional approach, on the other hand, is tied to process.* It focuses on local citizen interaction, mobilization, and residents working together as they address place-relevant matters. How this process, fueled by interaction, transcends divisions, self-interests, and local divides is central to interactional theory. This does not happen in some utopian context of harmonious agreement, but rather in normal, day-to-day settings characterized by conflicting interests. The key is the recognition of overarching, common needs and goals that serve as the basis for collective action. In our opinion, the interactional approach provides a particularly useful conceptualization of community for understanding local social change. We believe interactional factors explaining the emergence and development of community are the same in most settings and are at least as important as the routine structural and ecological factors typically studied.

Building on the seminal contributions of Kaufman (1959) and Wilkinson (1991), the interactional perspective has been applied to a wide range of substantive areas, conditions, problems, and issues. More importantly, it has generated consistent findings in diverse national and international settings, underscoring its usefulness in helping us understand community processes and social change. The theory's application in outreach and community-based programming has also been widespread, again indicating a measure of its utility.

This chapter has three nested goals: (a) Provide an overview of interactional theory highlighting its origins and logic, (b) discuss the advances and applications of this perspective in the professional literature over the past 20 years, and (c) explore areas for future advancement and theoretical development. By addressing these objectives, this chapter provides a better understanding of the field theoretical perspective and its use in the practice of community development.

Case Study 6.1 — Food Security

Students began this coalition as part of the Local Knowledge program, a set of courses related under that heading that focuses on local collaboration as a way to empower and sustain communities. It became a stand-alone nonprofit addressing local food issues. The initial project idea seemed to be to start an affordable local foods cafe. This doesn't seem to have been achieved, but the group does work through food banks, meal programs, shelters, and advocacy organizations to increase area food security.

SOURCE: The Gleaners Coalition (Evergreen State University) http://academic.evergreen .edu/curricular/localknowledge/home.html; http://www.gleanerscoalition.org/index .php?option=com_frontpage&Itemid=1

Origins of Field Theory: The Historical Context

For the first half of the 20th century, community sociology was dominated by approaches that emphasized the structural features of local life and the stability of local institutions and organizations. Standard definitions described community as a social system composed of enduring patterns of interaction between two or more units (Bates & Bacon, 1972; Hillery, 1968; Loomis, 1960; Parsons, 1960; Sanders, 1958; Warren, 1978). Whether it was the systems approach of Roland Warren (1978) or the human ecological tradition exemplified in the work of Amos Hawley (1950), most scholars of community focused their attention on the factors creating and maintaining structure and order in local life.

By the 1950s and 1960s, it was apparent—at least to some observers—that this emphasis on order and predictability did not reflect life in many communities. The economic, social, cultural, and technological changes following World War II rapidly transformed life at the local level. Suburban sprawl, which began with the construction of housing for returning veterans and their families in Levittown, Long Island, blurred the boundaries between previously well-defined settlements. With the construction of the Interstate Highway System, suburban housing developments were becoming the dominant settlement pattern in many parts of the country, displacing traditional neighborhoods and community centers. The rise of television, computers, and other forms of telecommunications flattened regional cultural distinctions. When coupled with advances in transportation, they made possible "the easy maintenance of dispersed primary ties" (Wellman, 1979, p. 1206). People could now participate in multiple communities. The community in which they slept each night was no longer the inclusive, inescapable fact of existence it had been for most of human history.

As these changes accelerated, many scholars turned their attention to better understanding those forces altering community life. Early analyses focused on how such changes were affecting the community as a social system or as an enduring pattern of relationships. Gradually, many students of community concluded that the systems model was no longer relevant, and what was needed was a conception of community capable of reflecting the complexity characterizing life in most settlements. The interactional approach emerged as one of the most cogent alternatives to the community as a social system. As we explain in more detail in the next section, the interactional approach takes as a given that the community is no longer the Mother Hubbard it once was assumed to be (Wilkinson, 1991). At the same time, however, one central feature of local life persists—people who share a common territory interact with one another on place-relevant matters even as they participate in far-flung social networks and relationships. In short, social interaction continues to be the key element of community. For this reason, it is the primary focus of the interactional approach.

Theoretical Framework

The field theoretical/interactional perspective emphasizes the central roles that local interaction and capacity play in the emergence of community among people who share a common territory. In contrast to ecological and systems theory, which emphasize the stable and predictable aspects of local life, the interactional perspective underscores the complexity characteristic of the places where most of us live. As Wilkinson (1991) put it:

> What the sociology of community expresses mainly is a conception of community relevant to the Middle Ages and a lament that community thus conceived is being destroyed by long-distance communications,

multisite organizations, rationality of culture, and other modern trends. What is needed is a conception of community that recognizes its complexity. (p. 7)

Seen from this angle, community is best thought of in dynamic terms; it represents a complex social, economic, and psychological entity reflective of a place, its people, and their myriad relationships (Bridger, Luloff, & Krannich, 2003; Christenson & Robinson, 1989; Kaufman, 1959; Wilkinson, 1979, 1991). As a field of social interactions, community emerges from the collective actions of its members. This collective capacity allows citizens to participate purposively in the creation, articulation, and maintenance of efforts designed to support and/or change social structures. From this perspective, citizen participation and action are the basis for the development *of* community, as an interactional phenomenon.

What is most unique about the interactional approach is its emphasis on the emergence of community. Unlike other theories of community organization, community is not taken as a given. Instead, it is developed, created, and recreated through social interaction. As described by Wilkinson (1991), "Social interaction delineates a territory as the community local; it provides the associations that comprise the local society; it gives direction to processes of collective action; and it is the source of collective identity" (p. 13).

In this process, the collection of individuals creates an entity whose whole is greater than the sum of its parts. The emergence of community depends on unsuppressed interaction. People interact in all sorts of ways. Even when involved in the most rational exchanges, we are simultaneously engaged in cooperative and affectionate relationships. Community depends on all types of interaction; when there are barriers to interaction, the emergence of community is retarded (Luloff & Swanson, 1995; Wilkinson, 1970, 1979, 1991).

The Community Field

In every community, groups exist that are organized around various interests and goals. Instead of these entities being described as well-defined systems or subsystems, they are viewed as relatively unbounded fields of interaction from the field theoretical perspective. For instance, in most communities, it is possible to identify a social field focusing on economic growth and development. This field typically consists of groups like the chamber of commerce; a workforce development board; a local economic development agency; and other, similarly dedicated entities. There are also many other social fields addressing issues such as social services, health care, and parks and recreation.

For a place to "hang together" as a local society, there must be a mechanism or process capable of connecting the acts occurring in the special interest fields into a discernible whole. According to the interactional perspective, this is accomplished by the broader community field. Like other social fields, the community field is made up of actors, agencies, and associations. However, unlike these more narrow fields, the community field does not pursue a single set of interests. Instead, it creates linkages and channels of communication between and among the actions and interests of other social fields:

> The community field cuts across organized groups and across other interaction fields in a local population. It abstracts and combines the locality-relevant aspects of the specialized interest fields, and integrates the other fields into a generalized whole. It does this by creating and maintaining linkages among fields that are otherwise directed toward more limited interests. As this community field arises out of the various special interest fields in a locality, it in turn influences those special interest fields and asserts the community interest in the various spheres of local social activity. (Wilkinson, 1991, p. 36)

Through this process of interaction, an awareness of common interests emerges, as do opportunities for involvement in activities for meeting common needs. In the course of this process, the community field creates a larger whole—one that is unbounded, dynamic, and emergent. As it builds linkages across class, race, and ethnic lines; organized groups and associations; and other entities within a local population, the community field provides the interactional context supportive of individual and social well-being (Bridger & Alter, 2008). As these relationships are strengthened, they simultaneously increase local capacity to address the many problems and issues that inevitably cut across special-interest fields.

Because the community field plays such an important role in fostering general well-being, it is the primary focus of community development efforts. Obviously, the interactional processes giving rise to and shaped by the community field are in a continuous state of change. As a result, the strength of the community field can vary greatly over time, reflecting shifts in local social, cultural, and political structures. Depending upon the strength of the community field, local actions can significantly enhance and improve local well-being. Efforts that do not contribute to the community field, or enhance the well-being of only select groups, do little to contribute to the emergence of community. That is, actions contribute to the development *of* community only when they represent purposive efforts to create and strengthen the community field. In short, the main goal of development is to strengthen and institutionalize the community field by finding points of intersection between and among other social fields. This includes the establishment and maintenance of communication channels and other efforts cutting across typically diverse social and community divides. As a result of establishing new and creative relationships through interaction, the adaptive capacity of local people is enhanced.

Describing the community field in these terms should not be taken to mean that structural or system-level characteristics are unimportant. Nor does it presuppose a utopian view of community—one devoid of conflict and self-interest. Indeed, sociodemographics, the local economy, organizations, natural resources, institutions (both apart and together), *and* conflict are vital to the makeup of a community and its residents (Brennan, 2007; Brennan & Israel, 2008; Brown & Swanson, 2003; Luloff & Bridger, 2003). However, such distinctive pieces of the local society serve only as the backdrop for local participation and action. They reveal little about the motivations and ability of local people to work together to meet common goals. It is in this very important sense we come to fully understand how community emerges from the conscious efforts of local citizens coming together to address widely felt and recognized needs.

Community Agency

From an interactional perspective, the community is a constantly changing environment characterized by community action and social interaction (Swanson, 2001; Wilkinson, 1991). As the various social fields adapt to and act in response to a constantly changing environment, groups and organizations take on the quality of agency, which reflects not only the motives of people to act, but also their capability to do so (Luloff & Swanson, 1995; Swanson, 2001; Wilkinson, 1991). This adaptive capacity is reflected in the ability of people to manage, utilize, and enhance those resources available to them in addressing local issues (Brennan & Luloff, 2007; Bridger & Luloff, 1999; Wilkinson, 1991).

The existence of community agency directs attention to the fact that local people, through interacting, often have the power to transform and change society (Gaventa, Morrissey, & Edwards, 1995; Giddens, 1984; Luloff & Swanson, 1995; Swanson, 2001). Community agency reflects the creation of local relationships capable of increasing the adaptive capacity of people within a common territory. The key component to this process is found in the creation and maintenance of linkages and channels of interaction across local social fields that otherwise are directed toward more limited interests (Brennan, Flint, & Luloff, 2009; Luloff & Bridger, 2003; Theodori, 2005).

Community agency and corresponding development can be seen as the process of building relationships that increase the capacity of local people to come together to act. As long as people care about each other and the place in which they live, there is potential for agency and the development of community. The ability to engage this action creates a distinction between simple aggregations of people and what interactional perspectives call community. Through interaction and agency, common needs and the means to address them are identified. As a result, local people are linked more inclusively and are able to focus on a wider range of community issues. The culmination of this process is the emergence of community.

Community Action and Development

The emergence of community involves both interaction and community action. Community action refers to the process of building social relationships in pursuit of common community interests and maintaining local life (Kaufman, 1959; Wilkinson, 1991). Wilkinson (1991) identified several characteristics of community action. In order to achieve change, community action must be purposive (Kaufman, 1959; Wilkinson, 1991). Community development and action always have a positive purpose (Kaufman, 1959; Wilkinson, 1979, 1991). From a field theoretical perspective, community action is the foundation of the community development process because it encompasses purposive and positive efforts designed to meet the common needs of the locality.

It is important to note that from this perspective, community development is not judged by objective measures of success. Here, attention is given to local effort—that is, merely attempting to accomplish a goal counts as development. To require success not only ignores the fact that many forces other than purposive actions contribute to change, it also misses the point that "development is process rather than an outcome of interaction. . . . Development exists in the action that is undertaken with positive purpose" (Wilkinson, 1991, p. 94). Indeed, the simple fact that people have taken an action to improve local life contributes to local capacity and enhances well-being because the action itself helps to build the linkages upon which the community field depends.

To have an impact on social well-being, community action must seek the development of community as an interactional phenomenon. This means community action processes contain far more than simple individual actions and efforts (Wilkinson, 1991). The "communityness" of any action depends on the degree of locality orientation (Brennan, 2007; Luloff & Swanson, 1995; Wilkinson, 1986, 1991). Kaufman (1959) suggested that *community* action requires three conditions: (a) the principal actors must be local actors, (b) the goals must represent collective community interests, and (c) the action must be oriented toward the improvement of the local area and collective. These requirements indicate that all actions can be placed on a continuum ranging from private to those addressing the interests of the larger community. The former actions are more typical of social fields, whereas the latter actions emerge out of the community field. That is, actions that address the needs and interests of a wide range of local groups, and the communication networks arising from this process, provide the foundation for continued efforts to improve local well-being (Bridger & Alter, 2008; Luloff & Swanson, 1995; Wilkinson, 1991).

Interactional Theory Since 1990

Since the publication of Wilkinson's *The Community in Rural America* in 1991, the interactional approach has figured prominently in a wide range of research and programmatic activities. All share a common focus on improving well-being at the local level through local efforts. A methodical review of the extant literature, including online databases and subject matter experts, identified nearly 350 peer-reviewed articles and book chapters using this perspective. Despite this number, the review cannot be considered complete and is seen as representing only a fraction of the body of knowledge in its entirety. We recognize the absence of much gray literature; nonetheless, this review speaks to the vast impact and adoption of interactional theory in a variety of disciplines.

Interactional theory has been well represented in leading journals focusing on small towns and communities, community development, and rural and small-town community development-related issues. Such breadth of use demonstrates the utility of this perspective as a logical basis for explaining community-level responses to a host of conditions. This includes important continuing work in traditional areas of inquiry such as community/community development (Bridger & Luloff, 1999; Bridger et al., 2003; Korsching & Allen, 2004; Robinson, 1997; Theodori, 2008), community agency (Brennan & Luloff, 2007; Bridger et al., 2003; Matarrita et al., 2006, 2008; Swanson, 2001; Zekeri, 1994), attachment (Brehm, Eisenhauer, & Krannich, 2006; Petrzelka, 2004; Theodori, 2004; Theodori & Luloff, 2000), community theory (Allen, 2001; Brennan & Israel, 2008; Bridger & Luloff, 2001; Korsching & Allen, 2004), rural development (Farmer, Lauder, Richards, & Sharkey, 2003; Humphrey & Wilkinson, 1993; Jacob & Luloff, 1995; Schafft, Alter, & Bridger, 2006), and community/individual well-being (Brehm, Eisenhauer, & Krannich, 2004; Claude, Bridger, & Luloff, 2000; Jacob, Bourke, & Luloff, 1997; Jacob, Luloff, & Bridger, 2005; Kassab, Luloff, & Schmidt, 1995).

The interactional approach has increasingly become the basis for pioneering work linking community with topics such as natural resource management (Field, Luloff, & Krannich, 2002; Flint & Luloff, 2005; Humphrey & Wilkinson, 1993; Jagnow et al., 2006; Krannich & Albrecht, 1995; Luloff, Albrecht, & Bourke, 1998; Luloff, Bridger, & Brennan, 2006), criminology (Hunter, Krannich, & Smith, 2002), culture (Brennan et al., 2009), demography (Liao, 2001), economic development (Beck, 2001; Zekeri, 1999), disaster mitigation (Brennan & Flint, 2007; Carroll, Higgins, Cohn, & Burchfield, 2006; Flint & Haynes, 2006; Flint & Luloff, 2005), health care (Bourke et al., 2004), international development (Bourke, 2003; Brennan, 2007; Brennan & Luloff, 2007; Cheers & O'Toole, 2000), leadership (Bourke & Luloff, 1997; Pigg, 1999), and youth development (Bourke, 2003; Brennan, 2008; McGrath, Brennan, Dolan, & Barnett, in press).

All of these highlight the important roles and processes of the local community in meeting a variety of personal, social, and structural needs. They all share a perspective that views these interactional processes as leading to the emergence of community, while at the same time helping to serve the needs of the various social fields within it. In this setting, the focus or topics of community actions are not as important as the process of bringing together a diverse and representative locality to meet the unique and ever-changing needs of the place.

The interactional perspective has served as the basis for a wide and deep body of knowledge. Yet in the study of an entity as complex as community and the issues present within it, the need for substantial theoretical development remains. Differences in the community development process in response to different stimuli need to be explored, as do additional theoretical explorations of various aspects of the process.

Future Directions and Challenges

Although interactional theory has provided important insights into the processes by which community and collective actions emerge, many issues remain unexplored. For example, interactional theory is being used to explore the continuing impacts of technology on community, changing territorial dimensions of community, community power's role and place, the processes behind effective community-based leadership, as well as the role interactional theory can play in building transdisciplinary frameworks for studying the ever-expanding relationships between natural resources and community.

Technology and Changing Territorial Dimensions

The impacts of changing territorial dimensions coupled with the materialization of new technology on community has been an important area of concern for decades (Bender, 1978; Bridger & Alter, 2008; Hillery, 1968; Konig, 1968; Wilkinson, 1986) and continues to be central to students of community. Expansion of geographic boundaries, growth in use and development of technology, and increased migration patterns have each raised concerns about the potential demise of community—at least in a territorial setting. Many technologies that were virtually nonexistent during the early work of Kaufman and Wilkinson now profoundly affect patterns of interaction. The Internet, email, cellular phones, text messaging, and social networking Web sites broadened our channels of frequent and routine interaction to a seemingly limitless extent. These tools have greatly expanded our local and extralocal interactions, and further blurred their distinction. At the same time, however, these technologies have the potential to contribute to interactions capable of building and sustaining community in local settings. On one hand, it can be argued that electronically mediated interaction—especially across great distances—is more superficial than the face-to-face interactions we associate with the local community. On the other hand, as experiments like the Blacksburg Electronic Village and the Starksboro, Vermont Virtual Front Porch Forum demonstrate, new forms of communication technology can actually work to strengthen lines of communication across social fields. The challenge for interactional theory is to both conceptualize and empirically investigate the relationship between communication technology and the emergence of community. A related challenge is to develop a better understanding of how new communications technologies can be used to promote collaboration across communities to address regional concerns and problems.

The broadening of social networks beyond localities coupled with expanding geographic ranges for meeting our daily needs has made it much more difficult to understand how local citizens can come together in collective action. This is compounded by the fact our workweeks have increased and we generally have much longer commutes, both of which dictate that much of our lives exists outside our home localities. As locality becomes more difficult to define and the connections among people more challenging to conceptualize, the ability of people to come together for broad-based collective action becomes more problematic. Although community may not have been lost, its environment is much different from that in the past. According to Bridger and Alter (2008), "The relationship between place and community has become increasingly contingent" (p. 104). In many places, daily life has become more regional in nature. As a result, research and practice must adapt to this changing geography of the community.

Two key challenges arise for the interactional approach in this area. First, we must better understand the possibility for the emergence of community in the increasingly turbulent settings where many of us live. The second, and closely related, challenge concerns the extent to which effective collective action occurs within places and regions.

Community Power

Of all the factors affecting the quality and quantity of local social interaction, the exercise of power is probably the most important. However, it has not been a central theoretical or empirical focus of the interactional perspective (Brennan & Israel, 2008). For instance, although Wilkinson (1991) acknowledged that the appearance of community solidarity in some cases "suppresses the expression of real interest of classes other than the local elite" and that according to this line of thought, "community mobilization tends to be class action" (p. 19), he did not explore how power affected patterns of social interaction.

This gap in the interactional literature raises two challenges. First, we must develop a better theoretical and empirical understanding of how the exercise of power affects patterns of social interaction (both positively and negatively) and how these in turn affect the development of the community field. Second, we must use this knowledge to create practical development strategies specifically incorporating power and the central role it plays in shaping community life.

Community Leadership

An understanding of the processes leading to the emergence of effective local leadership remains somewhat elusive in the field theoretical literature. This shortcoming reflects in part the failure to clearly distinguish between leadership and power. We know, for instance, leadership is rarely distributed equally among different segments of the community. Instead, it is often monopolized by a select few who pursue narrow interests. A key challenge in better understanding community leadership is the identification of structural and interactional characteristics that promote diffuse versus concentrated leadership. A closely related challenge is developing a better understanding of how different leadership styles and structures affect the emergence of the community field and the ability of local residents to effectively address common issues and problems.

Apathy, Disaffection, and Free Riders

The active participation and engagement of diverse local citizens is essential to the development of community and collective capacity building. However, such comprehensive involvement is often, and some would argue increasingly, unlikely. Marked by apathy, disaffection, and a lack of understanding of their potential role in social change, many citizens remain complacent and uninvolved in the actions shaping local life.

Other citizens, although aware of the significant positive impacts of community action, remain uninvolved yet reap the benefits of such actions. These people represent an untapped resource—one that can potentially bring new human capital, ideas, and diversity to the community development process. Even small efforts to include their participation on a limited basis could prove valuable.

The key challenge arising from these conditions is how to link interactional theory to practice. To be specific, we need to develop strategies capable of educating citizens about the common interest they have in the place they live and how their participation can build a stronger and more vibrant community.

Diversity and Inequality

Over the past several decades, both our rural and urban communities have become increasingly diverse. This diversity has created new challenges and possibilities for community development. In many places, diversity has truncated social interaction and therefore has been a barrier to the emergence of community. These increasingly diverse settings are also marked by increasing social inequality, which also has direct effects on the extent and quality of local social interaction. Indeed, growing inequality can often block the emergence of community and hamper the ability of local residents to take coordinated action, despite the fact their lives are in many ways interrelated. Inequality can also distort and shape the types of interaction that take place within and outside of the locality.

As field theory grapples with the intertwined issues of diversity and inequality, two key challenges must be addressed. First, we must develop a better understanding of how diversity and inequality affect the emergence of community and the community field. Second, we must use this understanding to develop practical approaches that can facilitate the development of community in settings characterized by diversity and inequality.

Final Thoughts: Bridging Across Areas of Interest and Study

According to the agency and social participation literature, a variety of factors influence community action and shape the context in which community emerges. Levels of attachment, social interaction, social networks/ties, and individual sociodemographic characteristics have been used to explain community agency and social participation. However, these findings lack a unifying framework capable of both synthesizing them and linking them together. Interactional theory provides such a linkage. From a field theoretical perspective, each conceptual area outlined above shapes and/or is shaped by interaction and directly contributes to community agency. And the same case can be made for other topics such as natural resource management, child and family issues, and/or international development. By applying field theory to diverse settings and subjects, we will be better able to understand the substance that ties groups, associations, people, and interests together despite their many differences.

The instability and insecurity characterizing many modern communities has given rise to a sense of urgency around how to create places capable of providing us with a touchstone in our turbulent times. As Harvey (1996) puts it, "We worry about the meaning of place in general and of our place in particular when the security of actual places becomes generally threatened" (p. 297). And as we try to create meaningful communities in this environment, it is important to have a conceptual framework that allows us to analyze and understand the myriad forces affecting the local societies where most of us still live out our lives. We believe the interactional perspective, as outlined in this chapter, provides a basic toolkit needed to create healthy communities in the 21st century. At the same time, however, the challenges we have identified for interactional theory must also be addressed if we hope to remain abreast of a rapidly changing world.

References

Allen, J. C. (2001). Community conflict resolution: The development of social capital within an interactional field. *Journal of Socio-Economics, 30,* 119–121.

Bates, F., & Bacon, L. (1972). The community as a social system. *Social Forces, 50,* 371–379.

Beck, F. D. (2001). Do state-designated enterprise zones promote economic growth? *Sociological Inquiry, 71,* 508–532.

Bender, T. (1978). *Community and social change in America.* New Brunswick, NJ: Rutgers University Press.

Bourke, L. (2003). Toward understanding youth suicide in an Australian rural community. *Social Science & Medicine, 57,* 2355–2365.

Bourke, L., & Luloff, A. E. (1997). Women and leadership in rural areas. *Women & Politics, 17,* 1–23.

Bourke, L., Sheridan, C., Russell, U., Jones, G., DeWitt, D., & Liaw, S. (2004). Developing a conceptual understanding of rural health practice. *Australian Journal of Rural Health, 12,* 181–186.

Brehm, J. M., Eisenhauer, B. W., & Krannich, R. S. (2004). Dimensions of community attachment and their relationship to well-being in the amenity-rich rural West. *Rural Sociology, 69,* 405–429.

Brehm, J. M., Eisenhauer, B. W., & Krannich, R. S. (2006). Community attachments as predictors of local environmental concern: The case for multiple dimensions of attachment. *American Behavioral Scientist, 50,* 142–165.

Brennan, M. A. (2007). The development of community in the West of Ireland: A return to Killala twenty years on. *Community Development Journal, 42,* 330–374.

Brennan, M. A. (2008). Conceptualizing resiliency: An interactional perspective for community and youth development. *Child Care in Practice, 14,* 55–64.

Brennan, M. A., & Flint, C. (2007). Uncovering the hidden dimensions of rural disaster mitigation: Capacity building through community emergency response teams. *Southern Rural Sociology, 22,* 104–118.

Brennan, M. A., Flint, C., & Luloff, A. E. (2009). Bringing together local culture and rural development: Findings from Ireland, Pennsylvania, and Alaska. *Sociologia Ruralis, 49,* 97–112.

Brennan, M. A., & Israel, G. (2008). The power of community: Advancing community theory by understanding community power. *Journal of the Community Development Society, 39,* 82–98.

Brennan, M. A., & Luloff, A. E. (2007). Exploring rural community agency differences in Ireland and Pennsylvania. *Journal of Rural Studies, 23,* 52–61.

Bridger, J. C., & Alter, T. R. (2008). An interactional approach to place-based development. *Community Development: Journal of the Community Development Society, 39,* 99–111.

Bridger, J. C., & Luloff, A. E. (1999). Toward an interactional approach to sustainable community development. *Journal of Rural Studies, 15,* 377–387.

Bridger, J. C., & Luloff, A. E. (2001). Building the sustainable community: Is social capital the answer? *Sociological Inquiry, 71,* 458–472.

Bridger, J. C., Luloff, A. E., & Krannich, R. S. (2003). Community change and community theory. In A. E. Luloff & R. S. Krannich (Eds.), *Persistence and change in rural communities: A 50-year follow-up to six classic studies* (pp. 9–21). London: CABI.

Brown, D., & Swanson, L. (2003). *Challenges for rural America in the twenty-first century.* University Park: Pennsylvania State University Press.

Carroll, M. S., Higgins, L. L., Cohn, P. J., & Burchfield, J. (2006). Community wildfire events as a source of social conflict. *Rural Sociology, 71,* 261–280.

Cheers, B., & O'Toole, K. (2000). Untangling the mess: Community strength in rural Australia. Retrieved June 22, 2009, from http://www.lgcsaa.org.au/docs/568462.pdf

Christenson, J., & Robinson, J. (1989). *Community development in perspective.* Ames: Iowa State University Press.

Claude, L., Bridger, J. C., & Luloff, A. E. (2000). Community well-being and local activeness. In P. Schaeffer & S. Loveridge (Eds.), *Small town and rural economic development: A case studies approach* (pp. 38–45). Westport, CT: Praeger.

Farmer, J., Lauder, W., Richards, H., & Sharkey, S. (2003). Dr. John has gone: Assessing health professionals' contribution to remote rural community sustainability in the UK. *Social Science and Medicine, 57,* 673–686.

Field, D. R., Luloff, A. E., & Krannich, R. S. (2002). Revisiting the origins of and distinctions between natural resource sociology and environmental sociology. *Society and Natural Resources, 15,* 213–227.

Flint, C. G., & Haynes, R. (2006). Managing forest disturbances and community responses: Lessons from the Kenai Peninsula, Alaska. *Journal of Forestry, 104,* 269–275.

Flint, C. G., & Luloff, A. E. (2005). Natural resource-based communities, risk, and disaster: An intersection of theories. *Society & Natural Resources, 18,* 399–412.

Gaventa, J., Morrissey, J., & Edwards, W. (1995). Empowering people: Goals and realities. *Forum for Applied Research and Public Policy, 10,* 116–121.

Giddens, A. (1984). *The constitution of society: Outline of the theory of structuration.* Oxford, UK: Oxford University Press.

Harvey, D. (1996). *Justice, nature & the geography of difference.* Malden, MA: Blackwell.

Hawley, A. H. (1950). *Human ecology: A theory of community structure.* New York: Ronald Press.

Hillery, G. (1968). *Communal organizations: A study of local societies.* Chicago: University of Chicago Press.

Humphrey, C. R., & Wilkinson, K. P. (1993). Growth promotion activities in rural areas: Do they make a difference? *Rural Sociology, 58,* 175–189.

Hunter, L. M., Krannich, R. S., & Smith, M. D. (2002). Rural migration, rapid growth, and fear of crime. *Rural Sociology, 67,* 71–89.

Jacob, S., & Luloff, A. E. (1995). Exploring the meaning of rural through cognitive maps. *Rural Sociology, 60,* 260–273.

Jacob, S., Bourke, L., & Luloff, A. E. (1997). Rural community stress, distress, and well-being in Pennsylvania. *Journal of Rural Studies, 13,* 275–288.

Jacob, S., Luloff, A. E., & Bridger, J. C. (2005). Pennsylvania rural communities and individual mental health. *Journal of Rural Community Psychology, 8,* 1–24.

Jagnow, C. P., Stedman, R. C., Luloff, A. E., San Julian, G. J., Finley, J. C., & Steele, J. (2006). Why landowners in Pennsylvania post their property against hunting. *Human Dimensions of Wildlife, 11,* 15–26.

Kassab, C., Luloff, A. E., & Schmidt, F. (1995). The changing impact of industry, household structure, and residence on household well-being. *Rural Sociology, 60,* 67–90.

Kaufman, H. F. (1959). Toward an interactional conception of community. *Social Forces, 38,* 8–17.

Konig, R. (1968). *The community.* New York: Schocken.

Korsching, P. F., & Allen, J. C. (2004). Locality based entrepreneurship: A strategy for community economic vitality. *Community Development Journal, 39,* 385–400.

Krannich, R. S., & Albrecht, S. L. (1995). Opportunity threat responses to nuclear waste-disposal facilities. *Rural Sociology, 60,* 435–453.

Liao, P. S. (2001). Contextual analysis of rural migration intention: A comparison of Taiwanese and Pennsylvania data. *International Journal of Comparative Sociology, 42,* 435–460.

Loomis, C. (1960). *Social systems: Essays on their persistence and change*. Princeton, NJ: Van Nostrand.

Luloff, A. E., Albrecht, S. L., & Bourke, L. (1998). NIMBY and the hazardous and toxic waste siting dilemma: The need for concept clarification. *Society & Natural Resources, 11*, 81–89.

Luloff, A. E., & Bridger, J. C. (2003). Community agency and local development. In D. L. Brown & L. E. Swanson (Eds.), *Challenges for rural America in the twenty-first century* (pp. 203–213). University Park: Pennsylvania State University Press.

Luloff, A. E., Bridger, J. C., & Brennan, M. A. (2006). Achieving sustainable communities. In R. B. McKinstry, Jr., C. M. Ripp, & E. Lisy (Eds.), *Biodiversity conservation handbook: State, local, and private protection of biological diversity* (pp. 393–416). Washington, DC: Environmental Law Institute.

Luloff, A. E., & Swanson, L. (1995). Community agency and disaffection: Enhancing collective resources. In L. J. Beaulieu & D. L. Mulkey (Eds.), *Investing in people: The human capital needs of rural America* (pp. 351–372). Boulder, CO: Westview.

Matarrita-Cascante, D., & Luloff, A. E. (2008). Profiling participative residents in western communities. *Rural Sociology, 73*(1), 44–61.

Matarrita-Cascante, D., Luloff, A. E., Krannich, R., & Field, D. (2006). Community participation in rapidly growing communities. *Community Development: Journal of the Community Development Society, 37*(4), 71–87.

McGrath, B., Brennan, M. A., Dolan, P., & Barnett, R. (in press). Adolescent well-being and supporting contexts: A comparison of rural adolescents in Ireland and Florida. *Journal of Community and Applied Social Psychology*.

Parsons, T. (1960). *Structure and process in modern societies*. Glencoe, IL: Free Press.

Petrzelka, P. (2004). The new landform's here! The new landform's here! We're somebody now!! The role of discursive practices on place identity. *Rural Sociology, 69*, 386–404.

Pigg, K. E. (1999). Community leadership and community theory: A practical synthesis. *Journal of the Community Development Society, 30*, 196–212.

Robinson, G. M. (1997). Community-based planning: Canada's Atlantic Coastal Action Program. *Geographical Journal, 163*, 25–37.

Sanders, I. (1958). *The community*. New York: Ronald Press.

Schafft, K. A., Alter, T. R., & Bridger, J. C. (2006). Bringing the community along: A case study of a school district's information technology rural development initiative. *Journal of Research in Rural Education, 21*, 1–10.

Swanson, L. (2001). Rural policy and direct local participation: Democracy, inclusiveness, collective agency, and locality-based policy. *Rural Sociology, 66*, 1–21.

Theodori, G. L. (2004). Community attachment, satisfaction, and action. *Journal of the Community Development Society, 35*, 73–86.

Theodori, G. L. (2005). Community and community development in resource-based areas: Operational definitions rooted in an interactional perspective. *Society & Natural Resources, 18*, 661–669.

Theodori, G. L. (2008). Constraints to the development of community. *Journal of the Community Development Society, 39*, 91–110.

Theodori, G. L., & Luloff, A. E. (2000). Urbanization and community attachment in rural areas. *Society and Natural Resources, 13*, 399–420.

Warren, R. (1978). *The community in America*. Chicago: Rand McNally.

Wellman, B. (1979). The community question: The intimate networks of East Yorkers. *American Journal of Sociology, 84,* 1201–1231.

Wilkinson, K. (1970). Phases and roles in community action. *Rural Sociology, 35,* 54–68.

Wilkinson, K. (1979). Social well-being and community. *Journal of the Community Development Society, 10,* 5–16.

Wilkinson, K. (1986). In search of the community in the changing countryside. *Rural Sociology, 51,* 1–17.

Wilkinson, K. (1991). *The community in rural America*. New York: Greenwood.

Zekeri, A. A. (1994). Adoption of economic development strategies in small towns and rural areas: Effects of past community action. *Journal of Rural Studies, 10,* 185–195.

Zekeri, A. A. (1999). Community-ness of a major economic development effort in a biracial community of Alabama. *Journal of Rural Studies, 15,* 159–169.

7

The Role of Conflict in Community Development

Jerry W. Robinson, Jr., and L. Steven Smutko

BEHAVIOR OBJECTIVES

After studying this chapter and completing the online learning activities, students should be able to

1. Define conflict in terms of behavior threats and territory.

2. Give examples of conflicts over physical, social, and psychological territory.

3. List and explain how community conflict can occur in five arenas.

4. List and explain six sources of conflict, and describe each source in the context of a community development conflict.

5. List and describe the three basic steps or stages of conflict management.

6. Describe the advantages and limitations of five behavioral styles, illustrated in Pruitt and Rubin's Dual Concern Model, that community leaders can use in conflict situations.

7. Give an example of a community conflict and describe the positions held by the parties in conflict in terms of interests that underlie the position of each stakeholder.

8. Devise ways to reframe community conflicts that lead to problems that invite collaboration.

9. Explain the advantages and disadvantages of each dispute resolution as described in Table 7.2.

Introduction

Community development is a social process that involves people with different interests, values, and communication styles working to effect social change in a place. Because community residents have different opinions about development, interaction often leads to conflict. Conflict is natural and inevitable. Some view conflict, however, with fear and disdain. In workshops on conflict management, we ask our participants—mostly mid-career professionals in the public, private,

AUTHORS' NOTE: Much of this chapter is drawn from Robinson (1989).

and nonprofit sectors—what metaphors they associate with the word *conflict.* They respond with words such as "threat," "fear," "aggression," and "win/lose." But when we ask them to associate words with the term *managed conflict,* we hear words and terms such as "relief," "agreement," "communication," "satis- faction," and "better decisions." Conflict is inherently neither negative nor pos- itive, but it has the potential to be both. The defining difference from this perspective is whether and how the conflict can be managed.

Case Study 7.1	Environmental Policy and Service-Learning

Dartmouth has used an environmental studies course that gives students the opportunity to play an active role in addressing local policy on the environment. Students work in groups to learn about an environment-related issue and come up with a plan of action to be recommended to a citizenship or group. The intent is to simulate a consulting service that has been hired to address a local issue. Students are given a large degree of autonomy in this class, nearly to the degree of an independent study. In the most effective implementation of the course, community groups request the course to investigate an issue they find important, in all purposes making the student's work tangible and real. An example project involved providing a recommendation on what to do with a dam that had been replaced; students worked through options from repairing the dam and creating a park, to destroying the dam and building a shopping mall in its place. Other examples include assessing the impact of a pulp mill in a rural area, determining the feasibility of electric cars in a nearby city, and auditing the environmental impact of local schools. Although the goal of the class is not to take sides on a divisive local issue, effort is made to ensure that the projects involve more than simple data collection, instead focusing on evaluating options to provide novel contributions to public discussion.

SOURCE: Ward, H. (Ed.). (1999). *Acting locally: Concepts and models for service-learning in environmental studies.* Washington, DC: American Association for Higher Education.

Understanding the Concept of Conflict and Its Role in Community

Conflict is an expression of incompatible actions between two or more people (Deutsch, 1973). It exists when the actions of one person or group interfere with or prevent the actions of another person or group. The notion of perceived incompatibility in interests, goals, and aspirations is a critical determinant of conflict. The perception of incompatibility plays out in cognitive, emotional, and behavioral actions (Mayer, 2000). As a cognitive perception, conflict is a belief or understanding that one's own needs, interests, wants, or values are incompatible with someone else's. In the cognitive domain, not all parties need to share the same perception of conflict, but a conflict exists if at least one person perceives it and acts on it. Conflict also involves an emotional outcome to an interaction that signals disagreement. If we experience fear, bitterness, or anger as a result of some interaction, then we feel that we are in conflict.

Conflict and Territory

Conflict is most obvious in its behavioral manifestations, when a person acts on perceptions and emotions to meet needs in a way that prevents others from getting their needs met. It is a behavior threat by one person or group directed at the territory—rights, interests, or privileges—of another party (Robinson, 1989). We can identify the major dimensions of a conflict by describing different territorial components. Territory may be physical, social, or psychological. We are all territorial stakeholders to some degree, and we usually try to protect our territory. Our world is characterized by boundaries and boundary maintenance. Nations have borders, states and counties have lines, cities have limits, and China and Berlin have remnants of walls. Even spaces in buildings have special territorial status; the boss usually has the corner office and the best furniture. Many individuals are sensitive about others invading their territories, be it their home, office, or computer hard drive. Conflict over territory, however, is much more than a conflict over physical space. Physical territory itself often represents other values, such as power or control. Thus, community conflicts can result from behavior threats to three kinds of territory: physical, social, and psychological.

Physical Territory. Consider the contemporary conflict between farmers and urban dwellers in California and Arizona over who has rights to use water. Or, consider the controversy that has developed in many communities over the use of property for a landfill. These conflicts threaten physical territory or resources. One party's use of the physical territory or resource threatens another party's access to or use of the same or a neighboring resource or property. Although these conflicts are primarily over physical territory, social and psychological territory may also be involved.

Social Territory. Social territory is made up of all the rights assigned to you in a particular role. These can be manifested formally, through social institutions, or more informally, through social norms. Social territory is defined through written and unwritten rules. Rules are "prescriptions that define what actions (or outcomes) are required, prohibited or permitted, and the sanctions authorized if the rules are not followed" (Ostrom, 1999, p. 38). In the workplace, rules specified in a policy manual formally define work territory. A written job description defines the social territory of every employee. In other situations, the boundaries of social territory may be unwritten, but still very clear. Unwritten social norms govern much of our social territory.

Offering our seats to elderly riders on a crowded bus, and tipping waiters at a restaurant are examples of some social norms. Unwritten institutional rules or boundaries are also common. Referred to as "rules in use," we use them to govern many of our formal and informal interactions. For instance, in modern American culture, some rules-in-use are "first come, first served," and acceptance of the will of the majority as the basis for important collective decisions. When one party in a relationship decides it is time to change the arrangement of social territory, a conflict may result.

Psychological Territory. Psychological territory is made up of our beliefs and values. People can hold on to their beliefs and values as tenaciously as they hold on to physical and social territory. We own our beliefs and values, just as we may own property. When something challenges a stakeholder's beliefs and values, it becomes a conflict involving psychological territory. A stakeholder is any person who believes that he or she has an interest in the conflict, whether he or she does or not.

For example, one person may believe that jobs should be assigned without regard to age or sex, and another may not. There has been conflict over the roles of men and women in our workforce, especially in the armed forces. Although such a conflict may appear to be over physical resources (higher pay) or social territory (higher status), this issue also involves psychological territory—values about appropriate and inappropriate roles for men and women. Similarly, a group of farmers may wish to stop an economic development project because it will take valuable farmland out of production and give special tax breaks to industry. Although they have economic interests at stake regarding the use of the physical territory, these farmers may also be fighting to preserve a way of life they value. Thus, the conflict also involves psychological territory.

As these last examples indicate, community conflicts usually involve more than one aspect of territory. The territorial aspect of social conflict helps the conflict manager identify the stakeholders (owners of territory) and note all of the salient aspects of a dispute. It helps one analyze and understand stakeholders' attachments. When conflicts over space or physical territory happen, remember there are likely to be political, social, and psychological issues at stake, too. The social and psychological dimensions tend to complicate the situation.

Conflict Arenas

Conflicts can occur in five arenas—interpersonal, intergroup, interorganizational, intercultural, and international (Daniels & Walker, 2001; Putnam & Poole, 1987). Conflict arenas are a function of the parties involved in the conflict. Parties are "entities, individuals, groups, organizations, and governments capable of making decisions directly or indirectly related to the conflict" (Daniels & Walker, 2001, p. 30). Conflict in a community development context can take place in any of these five arenas, although intergroup, interorganizational, and intercultural conflicts are most typical and create the greatest community impact.

1. *Interpersonal conflicts* are conflicts between individuals that are consequential at the community level; are manifested between people with influence or authority within a community (a conflict between a mayor and a city council member, for instance); or have their roots at the interpersonal level but expand to the intergroup, organizational, or intercultural levels.

2. *Intergroup conflict* results from communication barriers and breakdowns in networks linked to organizational structures (Putnam & Poole, 1987). Groups that are not necessarily enduring over time can form and dissolve as issues and needs change. Also, groups may have a multiplicity of members, each of whom is an independent actor. An example of conflicting groups in a community might be a neighborhood that is opposing a City Parks Department proposal to construct a pedestrian/bicycle greenway along an undeveloped sewer easement. Although many people in the neighborhood might be in general opposition to the greenway, some neighborhood residents might favor a greenway under specific conditions, whereas others will never be satisfied with any form of development in the right-of-way.

3. *Interorganizational conflict* has many of the same characteristics as intergroup conflict, but the institutional environment shapes the context and defines the arena in which these conflicts play out (Van de Ven, 1976). Conflict between organizations occurs primarily in those times and places where organizations work to establish and maintain niches or domains and where they are likely to interact or compete (Putnam & Poole, 1987). Interorganizational conflict is quite common in community development. Conflicts can exist among government agencies, nonprofit organizations, and for-profit firms even as they work toward the same general goals.

4. *Intercultural conflict* is commonly considered to be centered on differences among people of different nations, nationalities, or ethnicities. The term *culture* can be defined as the enduring norms, values, customs, and behavioral patterns common to a particular group of people (Mayer, 2000). Cultural characteristics also differ among people of different professions, religions, places of residence or upbringing (rural/urban), economic strata, and even politics. Intercultural differentiation can occur between people with respect to the ways they view and accept power differences, their views toward individualism versus collectivism, their desire for long-term versus short-term results or gratification, and their acceptance or avoidance of risk and uncertainty (Hofstede, 2001).

5. *International conflict* involves conflicts across nations. Banishment and internment of Japanese Americans during World War II, and prejudicial acts perpetrated on American Muslims during the Iraq War, are two examples of how international conflict can be manifested at the community level.

Summarizing the Parties and Roles in Conflicts

Parties in a conflict are individuals, groups, or organizations (including governments) who have a stake in the outcome and are capable of making decisions directly or indirectly related to the conflict (Daniels & Walker, 2001). Parties in conflict can be considered either primary or secondary parties.

Primary parties are central to the conflict. Their interests, aspirations, or needs are being directly affected by and are incompatible with the interests, aspirations, or needs of other parties. Primary parties interact directly with one another to either intensify or de-escalate/resolve the conflict. They may also interact *indirectly* with one another through agents (e.g., attorneys).

Secondary parties have a vested interest in the conflict, but are not interacting with other parties either directly or through an agent. Rather, secondary parties are represented in the conflict by primary parties (or their agents). Parties may be secondary to a conflict for many reasons, including lack of resources, low intensity of disagreement, or perceptions of inappropriateness. For example, in a conflict between developers and conservationists around the location and intensity of a planned shopping area, the individuals representing the development company are primary to the conflict. Local builders and contractors are certainly affected by the outcome of the conflict but may defer to the developers in negotiations with conservation organizations.

Examples of Sources of Conflict

The causes of conflict can be characterized by source of incompatibility (Daniels & Walker, 2001; Mayer, 2000; Moore, 1986; Wehr, 1979). The forces at the root of most conflicts are value differences, conflicting interests, structural forces or impediments, imperfect communication, damaging relationships, and history. These are described in Table 7.1.

Conflict Scale, Setting, and Venues

Conflicts are contextual. In a community development setting, the scale of conflict can be localized to two parties over a single issue or all encompassing. It can involve any number of public and private institutions, and can be played out in a variety of venues.

The scale of conflict is defined by two measures: the number of parties and the complexity of the issues. At its simplest scale, a community conflict can involve just two people in conflict over a single issue, such as a dispute between two city council members over the placement of a community center. Community conflicts typically include multiple parties and complex, overlapping issues. For example, a conflict over a downtown redevelopment proposal may involve the developer, adjacent neighborhoods, the planning

Table 7.1	Sources of Conflict: Causes and Characteristics	
Conflict Source	*Cause*	*Key Characteristics*
Values	Differences in the criteria we use for evaluating ideas or behavior[a]	Conflicts that are predominantly determined in terms of values are usually significantly charged and often intractable.
Interests	Perceived or actual competition around substantive issues	Interests can be tangible (dollars or water) or intangible (control or respect). Interest-based conflicts lend themselves to negotiated outcomes.
Structures	The external frameworks in which interaction takes place[b]	Structural forces can include differentials in power, knowledge, and resources among parties; geographic, physical, time, or environmental factors that hinder communication; and laws and institutions that define rights and confer power to parties.[a]
Communication	Poor communication, miscommunication, or lack of communication	Communication-based conflict is more prevalent around complex issues and in situations where emotions run high.
Relationships	Incompatible styles of interaction, idiosyncratic behavior, repetitive negative behavior, or misperceptions and stereotypes	Disputing parties may have difficulty separating potentially resolvable, substantive issues from their feelings about others.
Past events or interactions	Historical experiences that define the present-day conflict	Complicated systems of interaction that develop over time, and the degree to which the conflict itself becomes part of the disputants' identity, can affect the degree and intractability of history-based conflict.[b]

a. Moore (1986).

b. Mayer (2000).

board, the economic development board, and other downtown business owners. The issues in contention may include environmental impacts, fiscal impacts and taxes, aesthetics, as well as equity and class issues.

Often, settings relevant to community development are within the sphere of public policy. These types of conflicts cover a wide ground and can include health care, environment, land use, transportation, education, economic development, immigration, and welfare.

Community development conflicts play out in a number of venues, both official and unofficial. Unofficial venues include predevelopment conferences between planners and builders, stakeholder meetings convened by government agencies, and mediated forums organized by community groups. Official venues include planning boards, city councils, county commissions, state legislatures, and the courts. Conflicts often cut across venues, such as starting in a predevelopment conference, moving to a city council meeting, and finally ending up in district court. Parties in a dispute often work to ensure that the conflict is settled in the venue in which they have more influence.

Managing Conflict in Community Organizations

Costatino and Merchant (1996) identify conflict as a *process* rather than an event. Viewed as a process, conflict is not amenable to resolution per se, so it can only be managed. Disputes, however, are the outcomes or manifestations of conflict, and they *can* be resolved. Community development conflicts are typically complex and large scale with social, political, cultural, economic, and scientific aspects. Complex conflict situations may never be resolved in the sense that the parties settle the core incompatibilities that gave rise to the conflict.

Resolution of long-standing or deep-seated conflict may be an unrealistic goal. As Lippitt, Lippitt, and Lafferty (1984) state, "Conflict is a predictable social phenomenon and it should be channeled to useful purposes. The goal of organizational leadership is not to eliminate conflict, but to use it" (p. 60).

Conflict management is inevitable. For example, situations arise where one can be a negotiator—a party with a stake in a conflict—or a mediator—a third party in a conflict.

We present the following five principles for managing conflict:

- Focus and negotiate on unacceptable behavior, not bad attitudes.
- Understand attitudes and values that support behavior.
- You can respect the feelings, attitudes, and values that undergird a conflict without agreeing with either of its stakeholders or adversaries. People have a right to disagree.
- In conflicts over major values, long periods of time are often required for values and rewards to support change to occur. The greater the value, the more time and greater the reward must be.
- A conflict manager must exhibit behavior consistent with the higher order or ideal values.

Community leaders should strive to keep conflicts from becoming destructive or detrimental to other community goals. Benefits to communities that successfully manage conflict are as follows:

- Communities are able to address problems and take action.
- Citizens realize welfare gains.
- People establish better long-term relationships.
- People and ideas come together and stimulate creativity.
- People grow personally and professionally.
- Leaders emerge. (Hustedde, Smutko, & Kapsa, 2000)

When is it appropriate to use conflict? Conflict is most appropriate if it gives power, justice, or freedom to a group whose rights are being challenged (Berman, Kelman, & Warwick, 1976). Yet it can be difficult to separate personal issues from these conditions.

Conflict Management Frameworks

Practitioners of conflict management offer a number of frameworks for working through conflict (Bush & Folger, 1994; Carpenter, 1990; Carpenter & Kennedy, 1991; Daniels & Walker, 2001; Raiffa, 2002; Susskind & Cruikshank, 1987, 2006). Most frameworks have three basic steps or stages in common: assessment, deliberation/problem solving, and implementation/ follow through.

Assessment of a conflict begins as issues are clearly identified and characterized. The assessment can be conducted by the parties in conflict or a neutral third party. A conflict assessment examines the history of the conflict; parties' perceptions, values, interests, and goals; the issues underlying the conflict; and processes or venues for working through it. The assessment forms a basis for the parties to determine whether there is sufficient commonality of interest and incentives among them to work toward the next step—negotiation and problem solving. The assessment also provides information to help the parties plan the logistics of the problem-solving process and settle on a negotiation agenda.

The deliberation/problem-solving phase spans the time from when the parties first come together and adopt procedures for working through the issues until they reach agreement or impasse. Successful negotiation of complex community issues requires parties to take the time necessary to share their perspectives, needs, concerns, and interests. This information forms the basis from which the parties can develop options for meeting each others' needs and interests. In addition to negotiating the substantive issues, the parties may also be negotiating the data that will be used for informing their decisions, and other criteria to be used for evaluating and selecting the best solution.

Once an acceptable solution has been identified, it must be approved and implemented by all parties. In the implementation/follow-through stage, the parties have to ratify the agreement, work out the details in carrying it out, develop processes for reopening negotiations if needed, and agree on methods of enforcing agreements.

Strategies for Managing Conflict

People exhibit a range of behavior styles—patterns or a collection of behaviors that they act out—while communicating with others. When people are in conflict, communication behaviors can be predictable and intentional or uncertain and unpredictable as situations become more complex or ambiguous. The ways that people intentionally respond to conflict can be considered strategic choices.

If you are attempting to manage a conflict, think in interactive or behavioral terms because it is easier to manage and negotiate behaviors than it is values. Adversaries are concerned for their own needs and interests, and to some degree or another, they are concerned about the needs and interests of the people with whom they are in conflict. This concept of dual concerns, developed by Blake and Mouton (1964) and refined by Thomas and Kilmann (1974) and Pruitt and Rubin (1986), can be represented graphically on x and y axes in Figure 7.1.

Figure 7.1   The Dual Concerns Model of Conflict Management

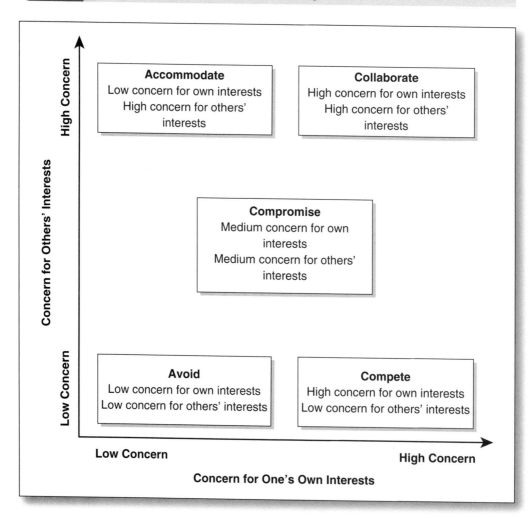

1. Avoid

In the bottom left quadrant of the graph labeled *Avoid*, each party shows low concern for his or her own interests and the interests of the other. Hence, they avoid interacting and gain or lose little.

Uses:

- When the issue is trivial or of passing importance, or more important issues are pressing
- When one perceives oneself to have very little power, or when confrontation has high potential for damage
- Allows time for emotions to cool, or allows others to resolve the conflict more effectively

Limitations:

- Coordination with other people suffers.
- Important issues may not get the attention they deserve.
- One's own input is never considered in decisions about the issue.

2. Compete

People in conflict can take a competitive strategy in an effort to maximize their gains. In the dual concerns model, the competitor focuses on his or her own needs and interests and has little regard for the needs of others.

Uses:

- When basic rights are at stake
- When the outcome sets a precedent for the resolution of similar disputes in the future

Limitations:

- Parties often close themselves off from information, or use information as a deceptive tactic resulting in suboptimal outcomes.
- Competition may cause a conflict to escalate, and losers will likely want to retaliate.

3. Accommodate

Accommodation is a response to conflict characterized by a low concern for one's own interests combined with a high concern for the interests of other parties.

Uses:

- When an issue is more important to others than to you
- Commonly perceived a gesture of good will

- Allows for legitimate exceptions to rules
- When you are outmatched and losing to a competitor

Limitations:

- One's own ideas and concerns don't get attention.
- Loss of respect, influence, or recognition may occur.

4. Compromise

The parties can agree to compromise and divide the pie equally among themselves. This is often achieved through the "negotiation dance" where each negotiator slowly works inward, each having started from an extreme position. When two offers are on the table, the natural focal point for further bargaining is the midpoint. Compromise is a response to conflict characterized by an intermediate concern for one's own interests coupled with an intermediate concern for the interests of the other parties.

Uses:

- Can reduce stress and potential for reaching consensus
- Enables participants to reach consensus with alienating others

Limitations:

- One can lose sight of one's own values or objectives.
- Compromise can distract from the merits of the issues as parties shift their resolution strategy from seeking the "right" solution to seeking any solution.

5. Collaborate

Collaboration is a response to conflict characterized by a high concern for one's own interests, paired with a high concern for the interests of other parties. Collaborators view each other as problem solvers and negotiators. Collaboration emphasizes direct communication of interests, aspirations, expectations, beliefs, and visions of the future, which produces opportunities for developing creative solutions. Negotiators can invent new strategies, create new alternatives, and develop new ways of implementing agreements.

Uses:

- When concerns are too critical to be compromised
- Helps one learn, test assumptions, see others' views, and merge different people's perspectives
- To gain commitment, and to work through hard feelings

Limitations:

- Collaboration requires time and energy.
- Collaboration requires exploratory overtures that may easily be disregarded.
- One's demonstrated trust and openness can be abused easily.

Satisfaction of Interests: A Summary

Effectively managing conflict and resolving disputes requires that the disputing parties deal with more than the subject matter around which the conflict centers. Substantive, procedural, and psychological interests must be satisfied if the parties hope to achieve a durable agreement to a dispute (Moore, 1986). Like a three-legged stool, the three types of interests form the basis of a negotiated outcome. If any one of the interest types is not fully satisfied, the agreement may very well collapse under future pressure.

Substantive interests. Most parties enter a mediation to "get" something. Although their ideas about their interests may change over the course of the negotiation, they need to come away with some sense of substantive satisfaction—a sense that they got what they came for.

Procedural interests. Even if they get what they want, parties will not be satisfied if they think the process was not fair. This is a subjective assessment, but a powerful one. In particular, if a party thinks the procedure was irregular, the party may distrust others and work against implementation of the agreement.

Psychological interests. Everyone needs to feel heard and respected. Should a party feel he or she was not adequately heard during the discussions, the agreement may not endure. Poor relationships that develop in the negotiation will overshadow otherwise acceptable results.

Formal Methods for Managing Conflict

People and organizations can use a variety of formal means of resolving their disputes. Each method differs with respect to the process, the people involved, the degree of formality, and the degree of control over the final decisions. Each also varies in how well the parties are able to satisfy their substantive, procedural, and psychological interests. The four most common methods for managing community conflict in the United States are negotiation, mediation, arbitration, and court litigation. These methods are compared in Table 7.2, which was provided by the American Arbitration Association.

| Table 7.2 | A Comparison of Dispute Resolution Processes |

Negotiation	Mediation	Arbitration	Court Litigation
Usually consensual; sometimes required by law	By agreement or contract	By agreement or contract	Voluntary as to plaintiff; involuntary as to defendant
No requirement to reach agreement; agreement, if reached, may be a contract	Recommendation of mediator not binding	Decision of arbitrator binding and enforceable in court	Court's decision binding but appealable
No third party involved	Third party involved as facilitator	Third-party decision maker	Third-party fact finder and decision maker
Informal unless procedure has been agreed to	Usually informal and unstructured	Relatively formal procedural rules	Rigid, formal procedures apply
Parties begin with facts	Mediator advises parties during negotiation	Parties present evidence and argument	Parties present evidence and argument
Mutually acceptable agreement sought	Mutually acceptable agreement sought	Win/lose results	Win/lose results unless settled
Agreement usually embodied in contract	Agreement embodied in contract	Reasons for decision may or may not be stated	Reasons for decision usually stated
Emphasis primarily on relationship and attitudes of parties	Emphasis primarily on relationship and attitudes of parties	Decision making emphasizes logic and some precedent	Decision making controlled by precedent and consistency
Private proceedings	Private proceedings	Private proceedings unless publicized	Public process, matter of record unless sealed by court

SOURCE: American Arbitration Association.

Helping Others Manage Conflict

Often when debating an issue, individuals focus their attention on a limited set of alternatives or positions, and the focus of the debate has limited alternatives. Communication takes the form of persuasion as each side attempts to expand the support for its chosen position and reduce opposition. Because each side is concentrated on defending its preferred position, no effort is made to truly understand why each stakeholder so adamantly favors or opposes each position.

By focusing on positions, parties in conflict see only a predetermined way to solve a problem. They spend time staking and defending extreme positions rather than dealing with the heart of the matter. Because their communication is focused on influencing and persuading, they limit opportunities for seeking creative solutions. The result is that they emerge from the debate with a win/lose outcome, an impasse, or a compromise rather than getting what they really need, and they risk damaging ongoing relationships.

In contrast, a discussion that allows for an understanding of the interests—the needs, concerns, and aspirations—that cause people to stake out one position or another moves people away from contending positions and allows a cooperative atmosphere to develop. Sharing information about interests encourages the generation of multiple options and permits the search for a creative solution (Fisher & Ury, 1991).

Identifying Interests

Positions tend to be fixed, tangible, and easily expressed. Underlying interests may well be intangible, difficult to put into words, and even inconsistent. How do you go about helping each stakeholder reveal his or her interests and position?

Ask "Why?" Put yourself in their shoes and think about why others may hold a particular position. Ask direct, but unbiased, questions. Make it clear that you are asking not for a justification of the position, but for an understanding of the needs, concerns, fears, and aspirations that led the individual to the particular position. Acknowledge others' interests as part of the problem to be solved.

Ask "Why not?" Think about why they have not taken another position. What interests of theirs stand in their way? Realize that people have multiple interests. Moreover, public issues often involve coalitions of interests, some of which coincide and some of which do not. One needs to understand the variety of interests that may shape positions.

Realize that the most powerful interests are basic human needs. Look first for the fundamental interests that motivate most people. These include personal security, economic well-being, a sense of control over one's life, and personal recognition. Help stakeholders articulate their interests in clear and understandable language. Draw them out. Have stakeholders tell their story. Remind them to be as specific as possible and use details.

State your reasoning before you answer. When people state what they want, and then why they want it, others may be too busy formulating a defensive retort to the stated position and don't hear the underlying interests. Stating the interests first, followed by a suggested option, will help others hear the interests.

Keep the discussion moving forward, not backward. When stakeholders argue, they often look backward to a cause. When they problem solve, they look forward to a solution. In backward-looking arguing, interests become rationale for causes. In forward-looking problem solving, interests become the foundation for solutions.

Issue Framing

In conflict management, the term *framing* or *reframing* refers to the action of directing the parties' attention away from positions toward the task of identifying interests, inventing options, and discussing criteria for selecting an option.

Reframing is used in two ways. In a broad context, issues can be reframed to increase the level of abstraction and bring diverse interests to the table. Issues framed in an either/or context often attract only those people who hold polar positions. The second use of reframing relates to the context of deliberating a particular issue. Reframing an issue or a statement can move people off a position and get them refocused on interests. Framing in this sense involves active listening skills, asking questions to probe for interests, and other techniques for producing win-win outcomes.

How an issue is initially framed will greatly affect the parties' problem-solving perspectives and level of conflict. Many community issues are initially framed as a debate. One of the most powerful ways of redirecting perspectives is to frame or reframe the initial issue. Consider the following example in which the parties are forced into polar perspectives: *"Should we consolidate all school systems in the county to improve the quality of education?"*

Reframing Invites Solutions

The statement above invites conflict because it presupposes a solution to a problem that has many facets for all of the stakeholders. Parents, teachers, and others passionate about the school consolidation issue may have very different interests, and school consolidation satisfies only some of those interests. If you asked the parents on the two sides of the consolidation issue why they are opposed to consolidation or why they advocate consolidation, you might discover reasoning behind positions similar to the information in Table 7.3.

Once interests are known, the issue may be reframed to reflect the parties' key interests, thus helping to move attention away from the two positions. Reframing the issue involves finding a common definition of the issue that is acceptable to all parties. Reframing is achieved by substituting the initial closed-ended question with an open-ended question. It also must reflect the key interests of the parties who are affected by or can affect the issue. By substituting a "How do we . . . ?" question for a "Should we . . . ?" question, the disputants are moved from debating the relative merits of their positions to focusing on a collaborative problem-solving venture.

| Table 7.3 | Examples of Reasons Supporting or Opposing School Consolidation |

Consolidation Opponents	Consolidation Proponents
• Our school is a source of community pride.	• We want our school system to be cost efficient.
• The school building is a historic structure.	• We need to maintain high education standards.
• We need to maintain support for our school.	• Our resources are stretched to the limit.

Conclusion

All communities have conflicts. And as communities become more diverse, it's normal for residents to have conflicting interests. Thus, conflict is not always bad! Community conflict may have positive or negative outcomes. After working through a conflict, social networks within the community may be strengthened. The goal of this chapter and its series of learning activities has been to help you learn more about conflict and enable you to develop behavioral skills that will empower you to understand and manage conflict situations in your community. We hope you will develop understandings and skills that will enable you to become a more productive participant in the community where you live and work.

References

Berman, G., Kelman, H., & Warwick, D. (1976). *The ethics of social intervention.* New York: Wiley.

Blake, R. R., & Mouton, J. S. (1964). *The managerial grid.* Houston, TX: Gulf Publications.

Bush, R. A., & Folger, J. P. (1994). *The promise of mediation: Responding to conflict through empowerment and recognition.* San Francisco: Jossey-Bass.

Carpenter, S. L. (1990). *Solving community problems by consensus.* Washington, DC: Program for Community Problem Solving.

Carpenter, S. L., & Kennedy, W. J. D. (1991). *Managing public disputes: A practical guide to handling conflict and reaching agreements.* San Francisco: Jossey-Bass.

Costatino, C. A., & Merchant, S. (1996). *Designing conflict management systems.* San Francisco: Jossey-Bass.

Daniels, S. E., & Walker, G. B. (2001). *Working through environmental conflict: The collaborative learning approach.* Westport, CT: Praeger.

Deutsch, M. (1973). *The resolution of conflict: Constructive and deconstructive processes.* New Haven, CT: Yale University Press.

Fisher, R., & Ury, W. (1991). *Getting to yes: Negotiating agreement without giving in* (2nd ed.). New York: Penguin.

Hofstede, G. (2001). *Culture's consequences: Comparing values, behaviors, institutions, and organizations across nations* (2nd ed.). Thousand Oaks, CA: Sage.

Hustedde, R., Smutko, S., & Kapsa, J. (2000). *Addressing public conflict: Turning lemons into lemonade.* Retrieved May 15, 2009, from http://srdc.msstate.edu/publications/lemons/221.htm

Lippitt, G., Lippitt, R., & Lafferty, C. (1984). Cutting edge trends in organization development. *Training and Development Journal, 38,* 59–62.

Mayer, B. (2000). *The dynamics of conflict resolution: A practitioner's guide.* San Francisco: Jossey-Bass.

Moore, C. W. (1986). *The mediation process: Practical strategies for resolving conflict.* San Francisco: Jossey-Bass.

Ostrom, E. (1999). Institutional rational choice: An assessment of the institutional analysis and development framework. In P. A. Sabatier (Ed.), *Theories of the policy process* (pp. 21–64). Boulder, CO: Westview.

Pruitt, D. G., & Rubin, J. Z. (1986). *Social conflict.* New York: Random House.

Putnam, L. L., & Poole, M. S. (1987). Conflict and negotiation. In F. M. Jablin, L. L. Putnam, K. H. Roberts, & L. W. Porter (Eds.), *Handbook of organizational communication* (pp. 549–599). Newbury Park, CA: Sage.

Raiffa, H. (2002). *Negotiation analysis: The science and art of collaborative decision making.* Cambridge, MA: Harvard University Press.

Robinson, J. W. (1989). The conflict approach. In J. A. Christenson & J. W. Robinson (Eds.), *Community development in perspective* (pp. 89–116). Ames: Iowa State University Press.

Susskind, L. E., & Cruikshank, J. L. (1987). *Breaking the impasse: Consensual approaches to resolving public disputes.* New York: Basic Books.

Susskind, L. E., & Cruikshank, J. L. (2006). *Breaking Robert's Rules: The new way to run your meeting, build consensus and get results.* New York: Oxford University Press.

Thomas, K. W., & Kilmann, R. W. (1974). *The Thomas-Kilmann conflict mode instrument.* Tuxedo, NY: Xicom.

Van de Ven, A. H. (1976). On the nature, formation, and maintenance of relations among organizations. *Academy of Management Review, 1*(4), 24–36.

Wehr, P. (1979). *Conflict regulation.* Boulder, CO: Westview.

8

Action Research and Evaluation in Community Development

John J. Green and Anna M. Kleiner

BEHAVIOR OBJECTIVES

After studying this chapter and completing the online learning activities, students should be able to

1. Assemble and use a "tool box" of the components needed for action research and evaluation.

2. Articulate frameworks of action research and evaluation relevant to community development.

3. Understand the importance of logic models and theories of change for evaluation.

4. Identify and discuss the different types of evaluation.

5. Describe a project-driven approach to evaluation.

6. Understand and differentiate between research methods, and determine the most appropriate research methods for a project.

7. Apply the concepts of triangulation to research methods and analysis.

8. Assess the credibility and ethics of evaluation research.

> *The two most important questions of evaluation in project-based research are: (1) whether your project is making a difference; and (2) why or why not.*
>
> —Stoecker (2005, p. 184)

Introduction

There are numerous community development frameworks, strategies, and techniques for practitioners to use. As a field of inquiry and practice, it is important for people working in the field of community development to learn what works and what does not in particular contexts. As Voth (1979) states,

> We need to know whether or not community development efforts have any of the effects they are purported to have, we need to know how these effects are brought about, and we need to know why they are not brought about if they are unsuccessful. (p. 154)

The point is that community developers, community residents, and organizations should take an informed, evidence-based approach to their work, and doing so requires serious attention to action research and evaluation. The idea that research is part of the community development process is emphasized in many community development texts (e.g., see Green & Haines, 2008; Hardina, 2002). This chapter presents an overview of evaluation as a form of action research for community development, providing the reader with a tool box and set of tools for planning, conducting, and using research.

Case Study 8.1 Action Research

When many people think of service-learning, they think of the most common examples of its practice: tutoring for younger students, volunteering at a homeless shelter, and so on. But service-learning can incorporate a wide range of public service. A program at the University of Richmond provides an example of action research, where the goal of the course is to help students identify actions that a community or organization should take on an issue. This research methods course gives students the opportunity to practice their skills of survey design and execution in a real-world environment. Undergraduates in the course work in groups to design surveys for local community service organizations. They administer the survey, analyze data, and write a paper interpreting the results for presentation to the program director. Although the students' knowledge makes them capable of only basic survey design, the results of the surveys are eagerly awaited by the local organizations. One example of a project undertaken is a study of check-cashing policies of stores and banks in poor neighborhoods. This research revealed data that pointed to unfairness in the check-cashing system that needed to be addressed. With this model, students are able to apply what they learn about research methods to a real, valuable organization, legitimizing the worthiness of learning how to survey properly. The total time of this project is about one month out of a semester.

SOURCE: Battistoni, R. M., & Hudson, W. E. (Eds.). (1997). *Experiencing citizenship concepts and models for service-learning in political science*. Washington, DC: American Association for Higher Education.

Although there are numerous concepts and terms among scholars of evaluation that often mystify nonspecialists, evaluation is basically a form of applied research focused on a specific project, program, or policy. Research entails systematic collection and analysis of data, and cannot be approached in a haphazard manner. Instead, it must be well planned and executed if results are to be treated credibly and used to develop knowledge and inform decision making. Action research is conducted with the purpose of taking action and achieving social change, using approaches that are conducive to this motive.

Different vocabularies are often used, but assessment and evaluation are two parts of an overall problem-solving process. Using a health problem as an example metaphor, a nurse would conduct an assessment of a person's health status. Later, after some type of intervention, he or she might meet with the patient again to evaluate whether the intervention had any influence on the person's health, relative to the original assessment. At this point, the treatment might be altered or different actions taken. This same logic and structure may be applied to community initiatives. Recognizing that assessment and evaluation may occur at different stages in the life cycle of a project, it is still critical to understand their interdependence. Conducting assessment prior to developing and implementing a community project is important if it is to respond to people's needs and interests. Additionally, assessment provides a basis for future comparisons in evaluation efforts. Given their connections, and for brevity, the term *evaluation* is used in this chapter in a general, holistic sense, which includes initial assessment.

Evaluation is often conducted because it is required by a funding organization, such as a government agency or private foundation. In these cases, an organization secures a grant to do some type of community project, such as increase access to health care services, provide safer housing, or advocate for greater access to healthy foods, and one stipulation of the contract is that a formal evaluation be conducted. This is an important motivation for doing evaluation, and what is learned from the effort has the potential to benefit the community organization and the funder. However, it is also likely that organizational staff, volunteers, and community residents will view evaluation as a necessary evil imposed from the outside.

As an alternative approach, the momentum for action-oriented evaluation research would ideally begin with community residents, organizational volunteers, staff, and leaders ascending from the grassroots level up through specific projects, programs, and policies. The primary focus in this scenario is on informing collective action at the organizational and community levels. The use of evaluation results to help funders and policymakers is of secondary concern. From this perspective, there are a variety of reasons for evaluating community development work, including to

- engage diverse people in the research process to better understand and take action on issues important to them;
- document and amplify people's experiences, concerns, and interests;

- learn about and improve a specific initiative;
- make decisions about priorities, strategies, and allocation of resources; and
- develop broader knowledge useful to the field of community development.

Premised on this more idealized version of evaluation, it may be helpful to consider a broad-based framework for describing the purpose of evaluation as a part of community change initiatives. Drawing from the framework presented by Stringer (2007), research is an integral part of the learning and action process. According to Stringer, community-based action research consists of three primary components within a cyclical and dialectic relationship: look, think, and act. At the look stage, research participants are invited to observe the world around them by gathering data, defining issues of importance, and describing them in an effort to construct "pictures" of the community. The think stage calls for exploration, analysis, and interpretation of these pictures for the purpose of explaining the current situation and developing theories to effectively inform action. At the act stage, action may entail reporting research findings as well as planning, implementing, and evaluating programs of social change.

Stoecker (2005) presents a different yet compatible framework that is especially useful for thinking about evaluation research. Stoecker provides a project-driven sequence where investigators move through four stages in an ongoing cyclical process: diagnose the problem, prescribe action, implement the prescription, and evaluate the processes and outcomes. This last step may also involve assessment leading to a new diagnosis.

Considering the multiple reasons for conducting evaluation, and keeping Stringer's and Stoecker's frameworks in mind, the following sections of this chapter address the logic model, the importance of theory in evaluation, types of evaluation, and methods of evaluation research. As a way of bringing these different topics together, the reader is advised to think about building and filling an evaluation tool box for use in a variety of situations.

Logic Model

Much effort has been put into the development of logic-based models to convey the goals and objectives, inputs, activities, outputs, and outcomes of development initiatives. Such models are constructed to illustrate and describe the sequential logic of a project or program (Patton, 2002). Referred to generically as "logic models," there is a wide variety of frameworks in use. Some funding organizations require the development of logic models, including both government agencies and foundations. Logic models are particularly helpful in the evaluation process as they can be used as a guide. Essentially, the relationship between each section of the model (see Figure 8.1) may be evaluated. For instance, an evaluation team may ask, "Given the inputs and subsequent activities, what outcomes were achieved?" "In what

Figure 8.1 Basic Logic Model

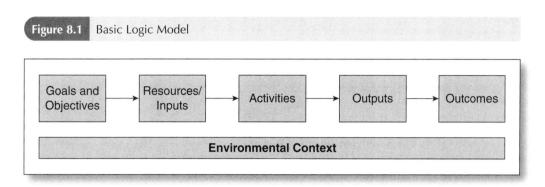

ways did the outcomes relate to the specified goals and objectives?" "Were there any outcomes that were initially unexpected?"

Theory and Evaluation

Moving beyond description, evaluation also entails the development, testing, and elaboration of theories on how groups, communities, and society work, that is, action theories or theories of change. Even when not formally stated, community development efforts are based on assumptions about social structure, interaction, and change. These theories are often found in project, program, and policy models and articulated through project proposals and logic models. Additionally, theories may be drawn from the broader base of knowledge in the social sciences. Attending to an initiative's goals and objectives in combination with social theory has been deemed the multigoal, theory-driven approach to evaluation by Chen and Rossi (1980). This approach entails "defining a set of outcomes as potential effects of a program, some given by the official goals of the program and others derived from social science knowledge and theory concerning the subject matter in question" (p. 108). It is up to the evaluation team to use appropriate evaluation research design, methods, and data analysis tools to further elaborate, test, and even reconfigure theories of change.

Types of Evaluation

Evaluation research takes place in a variety of disciplines and fields related to community development, including education, health, human services, economics, and conservation, among many others. Each area draws on multiple frameworks that may be different in some respects yet share many similarities. There are types of evaluation that cut across disciplinary boundaries. Building upon Fink's (2005) definitions, formative, process, outcome/impact, and cost/benefit evaluations are addressed here (Table 8.1). Additional attention is directed toward the growing and promising areas of participatory and empowerment evaluation.

Table 8.1	Types of Evaluation

Type of Evaluation	Focus of Evaluation
Formative	Activities that take place between the start of a project and before its conclusion, identify and address issues in need of improvement
Process	Implementation, participation, decision making, outputs
Outcome/Impact	Intended and unintended short, moderate, and long-term outcomes
Cost/Benefit and Return on Investment	Financial, material, social, and human resource investment costs of a project relative to the benefits realized through outcomes
Empowerment and Participatory	Engagement of diverse participants in the evaluation process; informing action and building capacity; may include elements of formative, process, outcome, and return on investment evaluations

NOTE: These types of evaluation are not mutually exclusive.

Formative evaluation focuses on the range of activities and outputs that take place between the start of a project and before its conclusion. This is associated with the collection and analysis of data to identify successes and challenges at an interim period. Results from formative evaluation studies are useful to leaders in making decisions about the management of an initiative and determining whether changes are necessary in strategy and/or technique. For example, one of the authors of this chapter conducted a formative evaluation of an organizational capacity development project seeking to improve the services offered to youth in the Mississippi Delta. Between its 6-month and 1-year mark, activity participation data were analyzed, as were results from interviews with participants and a survey of organizational leaders. Findings were shared with the participants, advisory board members, staff, and leaders. This information was then used in planning for the following year.

Process evaluation, sometimes referred to as implementation evaluation, concerns whether and to what extent plans are put into practice, how these are working, who is involved, and recommendations for improvement. Process evaluation overlaps with formative evaluation, yet it is expressly focused on whether and how appropriate decision making and subsequent actions are taking place. To illustrate, consider that one of the authors worked with a regional healthy community project involving in-school activities with teenagers. By conducting process evaluation, special attention was given to the partnerships the organization had developed with schools, the content and delivery of workshops, and the sociodemographic characteristics of the participants in these activities. It was noted that the project had been particularly successful at developing formal working relationships between maternal and child health advocates and schools. Still in need of attention, however, were the curriculum and teaching styles used during in-school workshops.

Outcome and impact evaluation entails research on whether the proposed outcomes from an initiative are achieved. These might be specific short-term outcomes, such as increased knowledge about health risks from pollution, to longer-term impacts, such as improved respiratory health among children. Expected outcomes should be well articulated in the logic model, but evaluators should also seek out and document unexpected outcomes. Overall, outcome/ impact evaluation asks questions about the evidence of the effectiveness of projects, programs, and policies. For many consumers of evaluation research, documented outcomes are the most important element of inquiry. Unfortunately, they are the most difficult to measure, and there are always multiple explanations of what factors external to the project could have influenced the outcome.

It takes resources to implement a project. These might be financial, material, social, and/or human resources. Decision makers are often concerned with the cost of the project relative to the benefits it provides. An evaluator may then ask whether the benefits outweigh the costs. This is a somewhat limited and strict economic logic that has been used to evaluate projects, especially in the public policy context of limited resources and competing demands on them. An expanded and more open approach concerned with return on investment has been gaining ground in recent years. Viewing resources as capital investments in an organizational, community, or social change initiative, evaluation is conducted to determine what returns have been realized from the investment (Phillips & Phillips, 2007).

Each of these evaluation types is reviewed in the existing literature. It is important to note, however, that they are not mutually exclusive. In practice, it is common for multiple types of evaluation to occur simultaneously or in successive stages. Each type of evaluation informs the others. Using multiple types of evaluation provides a useful set of lenses through which to view any particular project.

For all evaluation types, time is a critical factor. To make comparisons between conditions before, during, and after a community development initiative, data must be collected at multiple points in time. Longitudinal analysis in conjunction with control and experimental group comparisons provide for the strongest arguments regarding causality, but it is often the case that consideration of evaluation is deferred to late in the life of the project, meaning that pre-intervention data are not collected as an initial evaluation step. To make up for this, participants may be asked retrospective questions as proxies for longitudinal data. This is a useful yet limited fix. Additionally, depending on the situation, existing administrative and/or secondary data (such as census data) may already exist for across-time comparisons. However, secondary data are often available only for geographic areas such as counties, towns, and census tracts that do not fit neatly with community boundaries. For these reasons, it is strongly recommended that design issues be incorporated in project planning from the start. Planners should consider what type of evaluation is desired, the sources of data to be used, and when data will be collected. In all, evaluation should be incorporated into regular project activities. Evaluation is not an activity that is "tacked on" at the end of a project to please a funding agency.

Empowerment and Participatory Evaluation

Although traditional frameworks, designs, and methods of evaluation have been modeled on the supposed gold standard of experimental designs conducted by neutral, third-party evaluation professionals, there is growing momentum toward using approaches that are more empowerment and participatory in their orientation (Coombe, 1997; Fetterman, 2001; Fetterman, Kaftarian, & Wandersman, 1996; Suarez-Balcazar & Harper, 2003). These approaches to evaluation are focused on engagement and capacity building for action, and they may encompass the other types of evaluation discussed previously (Table 8.1). Within Fetterman's (2001) empowerment evaluation framework, individuals and organizations learn to evaluate their own initiatives by going through a three-step process.

- *Defining the Mission*: This first step in the process asks participants to generate ideas that capture the mission of their project, program, or organization. They then refine these ideas until a collective working mission is developed.
- *Taking Stock*: As the second step in the process, participants identify key activities that take place within their initiative. They rank them in level of importance and then rate the activities in terms of strengths and weaknesses. At this point, participants are to provide justification and evidence to support their ratings.
- *Planning for the Future*: Considering their analysis thus far in the process, participants in the third step establish goals for the future and work to develop strategies to accomplish these goals and subsequent objectives.

This approach to evaluation is action oriented and interactive. It is recommended that the evaluation team use a facilitator to help guide participants. Participants are asked to provide evidence of strengths, weaknesses, and reasons for decisions. In this way, data from the use of evaluation research methods may be particularly helpful.

Participatory approaches to evaluation focus on diverse community members getting directly involved in the process in order to take on greater ownership, leadership, and responsibility for change (Coombe, 1997; Suarez-Balcazar &

Harper, 2003). In these contexts, the professional evaluator moves from being expert to occupying the role of a coach or facilitator. As noted by Flerx (2007) in her writing on self-evaluation, appropriate and culturally competent coaching can help people and organizations to develop greater capacity for evaluation. Using a participatory approach, people from the various groups of stakeholders and constituents of a project, including community residents and organizational staff/leaders, engage in defining the issues, choosing methods, collecting and analyzing data, and reporting and acting on results.

Methods of Data Collection

Among the various types of evaluation, there are numerous research methods that may be used. Covering just a few of the common options, this section provides a practical argument for assembling a set of the most widely used tools and strategies for engaging in effective evaluation research for community development. Rather than prescribe a particular method of data collection for all situations, the assumption here is that evaluators need a tool box filled with methods where they can select the most appropriate methods for the job at hand. This is a pragmatic approach that does not seek to privilege one method over another. For this discussion, specific methods include analysis of project administrative records, observation, interviews, focus groups, and surveys (including use of secondary data).

Administrative Records, Anecdotal Data, Archival Data

Valuable evaluation data are often collected as part of regular record keeping for project administration. These data may include the sociodemographic characteristics of participants, key features of project activities, resources used, outcomes, and stories about successes and challenges. For example, organizations providing direct services typically use intake forms and conduct follow-up case management with corresponding records. Although they are not always obtained for evaluation purposes, if systematically collected and appropriately managed, administrative data may offer the basis for in-depth analysis, especially when used in conjunction with other research methods, such as those discussed below.

Observation

The purpose of observation is to collect information about the world in what is considered its "natural state." Observation is an effort to understand processes and events from the perspective of how they actually take place. It can be used as a key method in qualitative evaluation work (Patton, 2002). This approach to research has a long history in the social sciences.

There are two primary forms of observation.

- Nonparticipant/bystander observation: The researcher is present as a witness but does not actively engage in group activities.
- Participant observation: The researcher does engage in group activities as a way to experience the world.

Situations where one might want to engage in observation include public and semipublic venues such as parks, fairs, markets, stores, restaurants, schools, and farms. For evaluation purposes, observing organizational meetings and project activities may prove especially helpful.

The decision of where to conduct observation should match the research topic, questions, and the other methods being used. If one wants to understand the use of public transportation services, it makes sense to conduct observation on a bus or train and at the location of their stops. If choices regarding the purchase of food are of interest, it would be important to observe at grocery stores, convenience stores, and farmer's markets. One might also want to conduct comparisons between settings. For instance, it is often argued that farmer's markets serve as places for people to engage in more meaningful interaction with one another beyond just buying/selling food when compared to grocery stores. An evaluator could address this through observation in the two settings.

When conducting observation in a public or semipublic venue where activities are occurring at different times of the day, it is critical to develop a sample of observation sessions throughout the applicable time periods. Using the farmer's market versus grocery store example, people shop at different times of day and on different days of the week, and thus researchers should control for this in their work.

Interviews

Interviewing is important for researchers to develop grounding in the field and to obtain a better understanding of the phenomenon being observed (Lofland & Lofland, 1995). In conducting qualitative interviews, the goal is to

- obtain descriptive information concerning people, groups, and institutions;
- document "accounts" or "claims" that the interviewees make about the topic of interest; and
- connect these two types of information to each other.

Part of the appeal of conducting qualitative interviews is the researcher's ability to gain in-depth information (relative to standardized quantitative surveys) and have flexibility in what questions are included and how they are asked. Face-to-face individual and small-group interviews allow the research to move back and forth between a set list of questions and new questions as the conversation proceeds. Knight (2002) points out that a major benefit of qualitative interviews as a form of inquiry is the opportunity to be improvisational. At the same time, it is crucial that the researcher keep in mind the importance of collecting comparable data. Therefore, it is of central importance to make sure similar topics are covered across interviews.

When developing questions for interviews, the researcher should consider the following topical areas:

- *Personal/Background Information About the Interviewee* (note that it may not be necessary to actually ask all of this information): gender, race/ethnicity, age, level of education, places where this person has lived, marital status, occupation, organizational membership.
- *Descriptive Questions*: Ask the interviewee to describe an issue/event/ institution and his or her involvement with the topic of discussion.
- *Interpretive Questions*: Ask the interviewee to interpret or explain his or her understanding of the topic, using questions such as, "Why do you think x is related to y in the way you just identified?"
- *Additional Contacts*: It is a good idea to ask for the names of a few people to contact regarding the topic at hand. This helps to identify more potential interviewees.

Being a good interviewer rests on being a good listener. The researcher conducting the interview needs to hear what someone else has to say. Although he or she wants to keep the interview moving, it is important not to move too fast. Keep the pace steady and relaxed. Remember, this is not an interrogation. A few brief periods of silence are acceptable.

Community research often involves "key-informant" interviews. This entails conducting interviews with people thought to be knowledgeable on a particular subject because of education, profession, expertise, lived experiences, and/or leadership position. Key-informant interviews provide a large amount of data on community conditions and the power structure. Unfortunately, they can also lead to a somewhat narrow perspective on community issues in that those who are often interviewed are community elites.

The concept of key informant can certainly be reformulated to encompass more than community elites. Reconsidering the concept of key informant, a research project focusing on underemployment and workforce development in the Mississippi Delta involved interviews with people perceived to be facing employment-related challenges—underemployed adults. Working collaboratively, a community-based organization, volunteers, and professional researchers chose purposive samples on the basis that underemployed adults represent a hard-to-reach and understudied segment of the broader population. Two frameworks were used for selecting participants. First, a list of people who had been referred to a workforce development agency for services was sampled, and then a snowball technique was used to bring in additional people to interview.

Second, graduate students from other Delta towns selected participants on the basis of their being unemployed; working a part-time job; or working a full-time, low-wage job. Later, these data were compared with results from similar questions asked of area employers (Green, Jones, & Pope, 2004).

Focus Groups

Focus groups use discussion on a set of topics as the primary mode of data collection. They are generally used in situations where researchers want to obtain insight on a fairly well-defined topic of discussion (Morgan & Krueger, 1998). Focus groups are justified as part of the evaluation research tool box for several reasons. They are often effective in facilitating participation in the research process and tapping the views of minority and other often-neglected populations (Baker & Hinton, 1999; Chiu & Knight, 1999). Thus, focus groups provide both rich data and an avenue for public participation in research, planning, and evaluation endeavors (Waterton & Wynne, 1999). Numerous how-to publications are available for practitioners wanting to design and conduct focus group research (Krueger & Casey, 2009; Morgan & Krueger, 1998).

Similar to qualitative interviews, focus groups require a list of topics or questions for discussion. The facilitator should not ask too many questions, because conversation and discussion among a group of people take time. It is also necessary to involve activities in which the focus group participants can engage. In addition to discussing specific topics, activities such as asking participants to write down ideas and report back, create illustrations, and engage in role-playing may be used to enhance participation and generate meaningful data. It is helpful to think of a focus group as an unfolding dramatic performance where people interact based on their roles.

People (or players) in a focus group include

- *Discussion Participants*: These are the people recruited to discuss the issues at hand. The literature on this is mixed, but including 8 to 12 participants appears to be the most effective range.
- *Facilitator(s)*: One or two people should facilitate discussion. They present information, ask questions, probe, and make sure that everyone has the opportunity to participate. If using two facilitators, the backup person can write notes on a flip chart. The facilitator should be someone to whom the participants can relate in some way, while at the same time, he or she should not be viewed as being involved in one particular side of a controversy important to the focus group. This person should have facilitation skills.
- *Documenter*: It is useful to have someone designated to take notes, keep an audio-recorder running (if recordings are being made), and keep focus group documents organized.

Depending on the nature of the topic, the appropriate number of focus groups may vary. In most cases, it is recommended that at least two focus groups be conducted; this allows for some level of comparison and the ability to address issues of reliability/stability. Community-level and multicommunity studies may involve many more. For instance, a research project on health and access to care conducted in the Mississippi Delta involved 12 focus groups with a total of 90 participants from seven counties (Green, Nylander, Harbin, & Edwards, 2003). A similar multicommunity and multi-focus group project was conducted with small-scale farmers wanting to develop alternative markets in Mississippi and Louisiana (Kleiner & Green, 2008). Although conducting more focus groups provides additional data, eventually the rate of return will decline relative to the costs in time and other resources.

If the focus groups will address contentious issues, it is sometimes advisable to plan focus groups around these issues. When using focus groups as part of an evaluation, it may be advisable to conduct one focus group with administrators, one with service providers, and one or two with project participants. A follow-up group session at a later date could bring a sample of these participants back together. If there is reason to believe that a particular group of people will not openly discuss topics because of the presence of other groups, this should be taken into account and additional focus groups planned. Additional caution and planning is needed for focus group projects that will include public officials. It may be necessary to make arrangements to avoid violation of open meeting laws.[1]

Surveys and Secondary Data

Survey research entails asking people a set list of questions, typically with preset response options. Responses are then aggregated and analyzed using statistical tools. Surveys allow for collection of comparable data from members of a sample or population. There are different modes of survey research, including mail and drop-off/pick-up self-completion surveys, group-administered questionnaires, in-person interviews, telephone surveys, and Web-based surveys.

Surveys have become a regular part of life in many cultures, including the United States, and there are several helpful texts on survey research as a data collection tool (Dillman, 2007; Fink, 2003; Fowler, 2009). Such resources are particularly useful in the creation, implementation, and analysis of survey data to be collected from a sample. Questionnaire construction and sampling strategies are of major concern, especially if statistical comparisons are to be made and/or inferences are to be drawn from a sample to a population. An issue pertinent to this chapter is how to fit survey methods into evaluation, including those that are participatory. This can be done by involving community members in the survey design, implementation, and/or the analysis stages of

---

[1]One of the anonymous reviewers of this chapter noted the importance of open meeting laws for evaluation projects, including focus groups.

research. As a middle ground, the authors of this chapter have been involved in numerous projects where project stakeholders participate in focus group-style meetings to engage in dialogue about the types of questions that should be asked in a survey, and then a smaller team works to construct and test the questionnaire. The instrument is then shared again with the larger group, as are subsequent results. This process was used for an annual survey of community residents in Biloxi and Gulfport, Mississippi, following Hurricane Katrina (Bunko, Thomas, Montgomery, Green, & Kleiner, 2008). Sometimes, organizational staff and even community residents can be involved in the process of data collection for a project.

Survey data collected by someone else for a different or broader purpose are referred to as secondary data. Typically, this involves research projects intended to be analyzed by researchers and used to inform policymakers, journalists, and educators. Examples include the U.S. Census, Census of Agriculture, American Housing Survey, General Population Survey, and the Centers for Disease Control's Behavioral Risk Factors and Surveillance Survey. Secondary data may be useful for providing the broader context in which community development projects take place. For instance, investigation of the employment rate; income levels; and poverty of a community, county, and region can be informative for a project that involves interviews and focus groups on a workforce development project. Most of these secondary data are available to the public and accessible through the Internet and printed reports.

Determining the Credibility of Evaluation Research ———

Not all of the tools in the evaluation research tool box are appropriate for all jobs, and it is easy to misuse tools, even unwittingly. Furthermore, work is sometimes performed inadequately. Inappropriate use of research tools may lead to low-quality results and faulty, even misleading conclusions. If members of the evaluation team and their audience are to assess whether the findings are credible, they must be able to determine the soundness of the research process and analysis. Using the standards inherited from traditional quantitative research, evaluation research is generally considered credible if it is judged to be both reliable and valid. Qualitative and participatory-oriented research expand upon the issue by adding other dimensions for judging the soundness of a particular effort, such as the extent to which people who actually participated in the project recognize themselves in the final product, also known as "authenticity." This section of the chapter provides a brief overview of important reliability/stability and validity issues followed by discussion of strategies to help improve soundness in evaluation research projects, including transparency in methods of data collection and analysis, use of multiple methods, and participant validation.

Reliability concerns the extent to which findings occur independently of accidental circumstance (Kirk & Miller, 1986) and/or systematic error. In other words, it is their degree of consistency across space and/or an appropriate period of time. To assess reliability, the researcher must be transparent in describing the research methods used for both data collection and analysis. This allows readers to make important reliability judgments for themselves. The use of research methods that have been shown to have merit also aids in establishing reliability, as does use of multiple methods.

For qualitative research, the concept of stability appears to be more applicable than reliability (Miyata & Kai, 2009). One must ask in what ways and to what extent results are stable across observations. In situations where stability is low, it is critical to address what factors might account for the differences. It could be a matter of differences between participants or change over time, or it could be an artifact of errors in the research process.

Validity is the matter of whether findings are interpreted in a correct or accurate way (Kirk & Miller, 1986). Three basic types of validity are of critical importance. Instrumental validity concerns whether data could have been obtained using other research methods that are generally considered valid. Here, the use of multiple methods is helpful, because there are different schools of thought concerning valid ways of collecting information. Theoretical validity addresses the issue of whether there is acceptable correspondence between the observed data and the constructs used to represent them. This is where it is especially important to make sure that theory, evaluation questions, and methods fit together in a logical manner. Apparent validity focuses on whether the measures used for collecting and assessing information correspond to the phenomenon under study in a commonsense way. Using methods for data collection and coding that are driven by research questions is crucial for achieving some level of this form of validity (Kirk & Miller, 1986).

With advances in the use of qualitative methods in evaluation research and the development of empowerment and participatory-oriented approaches, the use of reliability and validity as the basis for assessing the credibility of research has been questioned (Patton, 2002). Attention has expanded to include concepts such as dependability, confirmability, and transferability (Miyata & Kai, 2009).

The evaluator should also determine the soundness of research by gauging its authenticity in terms of participant involvement—the extent to which there has been meaningful participation in the research process and participants recognize themselves and their efforts in the stories being told about them. Addressing authenticity requires the researcher to spend time interacting with participants before and after initial data have been collected. Sometimes, evaluators may even provide opportunities for participants to review and comment on items such as their own interview transcripts as part of the validation process.

Triangulation

Applying multiple methods of data collection, sources of data, and approaches to analysis (generally referred to as *triangulation*) is one avenue for enhancing the quality of an evaluation study, especially in regard to the credibility of results (Brewer & Hunter, 1989; Patton, 2002; Stoecker, 2005). Triangulation is greatly enhanced by the growing practical interest in mixed-methods research, bringing together multiple forms of qualitative and quantitative research (Creswell & Clark, 2006; Teddlie & Tashakkori, 2009). For example, in the evaluation of the maternal and child health project mentioned earlier, evaluators analyzed administrative records, observed in-class workshops, conducted focus groups, and surveyed participants.

When using multiple research methods, it is important to consider what is to be done in cases where divergence is found. In general, it is assumed that the greater the agreement of results across different research strategies, the more trustworthy the findings. If different results arise from interviews as compared to focus groups and surveys, the researcher must consider why this happened. Is it a technical matter based on the specific methods? Were different samples and/or populations involved with one method compared to another?

In some cases, different methods may be expected to yield different results. According to Knight (2002), it does not make much sense to use multiple methods and then simply ignore differences in results when they arise. In some situations, the use of different methods and analysis techniques might result in different results because of the addition of new people and information. This should not be seen as detracting from the quality of the study, but rather emphasizing the importance of using numerous perspectives.

Ethical Issues in Community Development Evaluation Research

Ethical concerns should be considered when one is planning, conducting, and using results from evaluation research. There are ethical standards in place with social science research and evaluation professional associations. The American Evaluation Association's (2004) guiding principles include, among other topics, competence, integrity/honesty, respect for people, and responsibilities to the welfare of the general public. Of the many issues in need of attention, conflict of interest and informed consent by evaluation participants are particularly important. It is critical to ask whether the research team has conflicts that prevent it from evaluating the project fairly and adequately. To combat potential problems with conflict of interest, funders often require a so-called external evaluator to investigate project outcomes, costs, and benefits. However, as mentioned previously in this chapter, there are many positive reasons for taking a more participatory approach to evaluation that intentionally involves people close to the project. In these cases, it is necessary to be transparent about who was involved with the evaluation and what their connections were to the effort under investigation.

Informed consent is a foundational ethical principle of social science research. It consists of participants (traditionally referred to as research subjects) being informed about the purpose of the research effort and what it will entail, including potential negative impacts. Achieving informed consent also requires that participants understand that their information will be confidential and neither their names nor other identifying information will be made public. Finally, informed consent entails voluntary participation. People should never be required to participate in research. It is their choice.

Given its applied nature, informed consent takes on even greater importance in the realm of evaluation research. Planners should make sure that there is no potential for data to be used against participants, such as through the denial or restriction of services. Additionally, whether or not project participants feel compelled to participate in evaluation must be addressed. It would seem logical that people receiving services from a local nonprofit organization might feel compelled to participate in the organization's evaluation. They might fear retaliation for not participating or saying the wrong thing if they do participate. In these situations, evaluators should spend considerable time and energy working through the issues and possible scenarios.

Conclusion: Evaluation and Development of Knowledge

With their evaluation tool boxes in hand, students and practitioners of community development should now be better prepared to understand and engage in evaluation research. This general overview is, of course, only a starting point. To take the next steps in planning an evaluation for a project, it will be helpful to ask the following types of questions.

- Who will be involved in the evaluation project, and what will be their roles?
- What is the primary purpose of the evaluation?
- Who is the audience, or who are the audiences?
- What are the research questions?
- What is the unit of analysis? In other words, is the focus on individuals, households, organizations, and/or communities?
- How will the study be designed?
- How will data be collected and analyzed?
- Where and in what format will results be disseminated?
- How will evaluation results be used for learning and to inform decision making?

By answering these questions, evaluators are better able to choose the best tools for the job at hand.

Throughout this chapter, evaluation research has been discussed in a manner assuming specific, unified projects that take place in a particular time and place. In cases such as these, each evaluation effort is informative for the organization and its partners. It also informs other organizations or projects addressing similar issues. Expanding this to broader geographical areas and across time, evaluations may be used to develop knowledge in our more general fields of practice in community development. In other words, evaluators can use their tools to build something grand—knowledge.

Box 8.1 Action Research and Evaluation in the Aftermath of Disaster

Many of the ideas presented in this chapter have been put into practice by the authors through their ongoing work with community-based organizations (CBOs) serving residents of the Mississippi Gulf Coast in the aftermath of Hurricane Katrina. Less than 1 month after the hurricane in 2005, CBOs were confronted with the need to systematically assess the challenges being faced by people in their attempt to recover from the immediate disaster and to begin rebuilding their communities. They chose to conduct a needs assessment survey, and through their partnership with Oxfam America were connected to Delta State University's (DSU) Institute for Community-Based Research. Faculty and students from DSU partnered with Southeastern Louisiana University's (SELU) Department of Sociology and Criminal Justice, and the East Biloxi Coordination, Relief, and Redevelopment Agency to assess the needs of more than 1,000 hurricane survivors. Initial results were used to coordinate service delivery and case management for families. Results were used for advocacy as well.

In the fall of 2006, follow-up interviews were conducted with residents to track changes in access to fresh foods, health care, and physical recreation resources and provided analysis to organizations interested in planning for the future. To address the broader action research needs of the region following the hurricane, DSU and SELU organized and facilitated a meeting between representatives from nonprofit organizations, government agencies, and applied researchers. Participants at this October 2005 workshop shared topics of concern and exchanged information on improving disaster recovery and redevelopment. They also shared working principles for ethical action research.

Drawing from a request made by several CBOs, DSU, SELU, and the University of Michigan (UM) School of Public Health conducted interviews with 157 service providers responding to the hurricane and its aftermath in the spring of 2006. UM's Center for Public Health Preparedness published the project report, titled "Voices From the Frontlines: Service Providers Share Their Experiences From Working in the Wake of Hurricane Katrina." It was used in workshops and distributed for the purpose of advocating on behalf of service providers. Following this, a pilot project was created to assist five organizations in building their capacities to better serve the needs of their respective communities. In the spring of 2007, partners conducted case studies of the five groups and assisted them with development of capacity-building initiatives. Mini-grants were provided with funds from the Foundation for the Mid-South. Efforts ranged from social marketing and fundraising to strategic planning.

As part of its capacity-building project, Visions of Hope, Inc. (VOH) realized that although it regularly assessed clients' needs and monitored whether they received services, it lacked a process for evaluating its performance across programs and examining the needs and interests of the wider community. VOH and its research partners decided that its next step would be to survey community residents—to simultaneously evaluate the organization's services and document the needs of the communities it serves. The initial community survey took place in spring 2008, and the second survey was in spring 2009. Results have been used to evaluate existing programs, raise awareness over important issues (health, mold in houses), and inform proposal development for new projects. In the second round of the survey, Coastal Women for Change, another CBO, chose to be a partner in the project. Additionally, activities in 2009 included follow-up focus groups and interviews.

SOURCES: Bunko et al. (2008); Green, Gill, and Kleiner (2006); Green, Kleiner, and Montgomery (2007); Green et al. (2006); Kerstetter, Green, Kleiner, Montgomery, and Edwards (2008); Kleiner, Green, and Nylander (2007).

References

American Evaluation Association. (2004). *Guiding principles for evaluators.* Fairhaven, MA: Author. Retrieved August 4, 2009, from http://www.eval.org/Publications/GuidingPrinciplesPrintable.asp

Baker, R., & Hinton, R. (1999). Do focus groups facilitate meaningful participation in social research? In R. S. Barbour & J. Kitzinger (Eds.), *Developing focus group research: Politics, theory and action* (pp. 79–98). London: Sage.

Battistoni, R. M., & Hudson, W. E. (Eds.). (1997). *Experiencing citizenship concepts and models for service-learning in political science.* Washington, DC: American Association for Higher Education.

Brewer, J., & Hunter, A. (1989). *Multimethod research: A synthesis of styles.* Newbury Park, CA: Sage.

Bunko, A., Thomas, D., Montgomery, J. P., Green, J. J., & Kleiner, A. M. (2008). *Report of evaluation and needs assessment survey for Visions of Hope.* Working paper for Visions of Hope and the Foundation for the Mid South.

Chen, H. T., & Rossi, P. H. (1980). The multi-goal, theory-driven approach to evaluation: A model linking basic and applied social science. *Social Forces, 59,* 106–122.

Chiu, L. F., & Knight, D. (1999). How useful are focus groups for obtaining the views of minority groups? In R. S. Barbour & J. Kitzinger (Eds.), *Developing focus group research: Politics, theory and action* (pp. 99–112). London: Sage.

Coombe, C. M. (1997). Using empowerment evaluation in community organizing and community-based health initiatives. In M. Minkler (Ed.), *Community organizing and community building for health* (pp. 291–307). New Brunswick, NJ: Rutgers University Press.

Creswell, J. W., & Clark, V. L. P. (2006). *Designing and conducting mixed-methods research.* Thousand Oaks, CA: Sage.

Dillman, D. A. (2007). *Mail and Internet surveys: The tailored design method.* Hoboken, NJ: Wiley.

Fetterman, D. M. (2001). *Foundations of empowerment evaluation.* Thousand Oaks, CA: Sage.

Fetterman, D. M., Kaftarian, S. J., & Wandersman, A. (Eds.). (1996). *Empowerment evaluation: Knowledge and tools for self-assessment and accountability.* Thousand Oaks, CA: Sage.

Fink, A. (Ed.). (2003). *The survey kit, volumes 1–10.* Thousand Oaks, CA: Sage.

Fink, A. (2005). *Evaluation fundamentals: Insights into the outcomes, effectiveness and quality of health programs.* Thousand Oaks, CA: Sage.

Flerx, V. C. (2007). Building capacity for self-evaluation among community agencies and organizations. In P. S. Motes & P. M. Hess (Eds.), *Collaborating with community-based organizations through consultation and technical assistance* (pp. 137–187). New York: Columbia University Press.

Fowler, F. J. (2009). *Survey research methods.* Thousand Oaks, CA: Sage.

Green, G. P., & Haines, A. (2008). *Asset building and community development* (2nd ed.). Thousand Oaks, CA: Sage.

Green, J. J., Gill, D. A., & Kleiner, A. M. (2006). From vulnerability to resiliency: Assessing impacts and responses to disaster. *Southern Rural Sociology, 21,* 89–99.

Green, J. J., Jones, A., & Pope, J. C. (2004). Underemployment and workforce development in the Mississippi Delta: Community-based action research for program planning to increase livelihood security. *Southern Rural Sociology, 20,* 80–106.

Green, J. J., Kleiner, A. M., & Montgomery, J. P. (2007). The texture of local disaster response: Service providers' views following Hurricane Katrina. *Southern Rural Sociology, 22,* 28–44.

Green, J. J., Kleiner, A. M., Montgomery, J. P., Bayer, I. S., Kerstetter, K., & Rothney, E. (2006). *Voices from the frontlines: Service providers share their experiences from working in the wake of Hurricane Katrina.* Ann Arbor: University of Michigan School of Public Health, Michigan Center for Public Health Preparedness.

Green, J. J., Nylander, A. B., Harbin, T., & Edwards, A. (2003). *Delta health system assessment: An overview of perceptions obtained from focus groups and key-informant interviews.* Working paper for Mississippi Delta State Rural Development Network, Delta State University, Cleveland, MS.

Hardina, D. (2002). *Analytic skills for community organization practice.* New York: Columbia University Press.

Kerstetter, K., Green, J. J., Kleiner, A. M., Montgomery, J. P., & Edwards, A. (2008). *Enhancing the capacity of nonprofit organizations in the aftermath of disaster: Lessons learned from the field.* Working paper for the Foundation for the Mid South, Delta State University, Cleveland, MS.

Kirk, J., & Miller, M. L. (1986). *Reliability and validity in qualitative research.* Newbury Park, CA: Sage.

Kleiner, A. M., & Green, J. J. (2008). Expanding the marketing opportunities and sustainable production potential for minority and limited resource agricultural producers in Louisiana and Mississippi. *Southern Rural Sociology, 23,* 149–169.

Kleiner, A. M., Green, J. J., & Nylander, A. B., III. (2007). A community study of disaster impacts and redevelopment issues facing East Biloxi, Mississippi. In D. Brunsma, S. Overfelt, & S. Picou (Eds.), *The sociology of Katrina: Perspectives on a modern catastrophe* (pp. 155–171). Lanham, MD: Rowman and Littlefield.

Knight, P. T. (2002). *Small-scale research*. London: Sage.

Krueger, R. A., & Casey, M. A. (2009). *Focus groups: A practical guide for applied research* (4th ed.). Thousand Oaks, CA: Sage.

Lofland, J., & Lofland, L. H. (1995). *Analyzing social settings: A guide to qualitative observation and analysis*. Belmont, CA: Wadsworth.

Miyata, H., & Kai, I. (2009). Reconsidering evaluation criteria for scientific adequacy in health care research: An integrative framework of quantitative and qualitative criteria. *International Journal of Qualitative Methods, 8,* 64–75.

Morgan, D. L., & Krueger, R. A. (1998). *The focus group kit, volumes 1–6.* Thousand Oaks, CA: Sage.

Patton, M. Q. (2002). *Qualitative research and evaluation methods* (3rd ed.). Thousand Oaks, CA: Sage.

Phillips, J. J., & Phillips, P. (2007). *Show me the money: How to determine ROI in people, projects and programs*. San Francisco: Berrett-Koehler.

Stoecker, R. (2005). *Research strategies for community change*. Thousand Oaks, CA: Sage.

Stringer, E. (2007). *Action research*. Thousand Oaks, CA: Sage.

Suarez-Balcazar, Y., & Harper, G. W. (Eds.). (2003). *Empowerment and participatory evaluation of community interventions: Multiple benefits*. Binghamton, NY: Haworth.

Teddlie, C. B., & Tashakkori, A. (Eds.). (2009). *Foundations of mixed methods research: Integrating quantitative and qualitative approaches in the social and behavioral sciences*. Thousand Oaks, CA: Sage.

Voth, D. E. (1979). Problems in the evaluation of community development efforts. In E. J. Blakely (Ed.), *Community development research: Concepts, issues and strategies* (pp. 153–174). New York: Human Sciences Press.

Waterton, C., & Wynne, B. (1999). Can focus groups access community views? In R. S. Barbour & J. Kitzinger (Eds.), *Developing focus group research: Politics, theory and action* (pp. 127–143). London: Sage.

9

The Role of Leadership Behaviors and Structures in Community Development

Josh Stovall, Jerry W. Robinson, Jr., Albert Nylander, and Ralph B. Brown

BEHAVIOR OBJECTIVES

After studying this chapter and completing the online learning activities, students should be able to

1. Recognize the value of competent community leadership.

2. Distinguish between sociological and psychological aspects of leadership.

3. Work effectively to help community residents understand the importance and nature of leadership.

4. Identify leadership challenges that community developers face when seeking change.

5. Explain the primary behavioral characteristics of developmental, directive, and permissive leaders.

6. Evaluate the effectiveness of your behavior as an active listener.

7. Understand how leadership development workshops can help potential leaders view themselves as part of a larger structure so that they and other community leaders can create and maintain network connections.

8. Analyze a community group and determine which leadership role best fits.

9. Identify the primary leadership characteristics of political power actors and economic power actors.

10. Appreciate the dynamic and interdisciplinary nature of leadership in community development organizations.

Separate structures and institutions within the community do not exist in a vacuum. This means that community power is interrelated with the class structure, economic structure, and religious and educational institutions; in short, a community's power structure is interrelated with all the other parts of the community.

—Lyon (1999), pp. 206–207

Introduction

It has become common for community development organizations (CDOs) to emphasize the role of leadership to encourage community change. This is demonstrated by the number of leadership development programs, directly sponsored by either the CDOs or other programs, designed to prepare residents for community leadership. What is often overlooked is the importance of multiple levels of social phenomena involved in leadership development, including the social, psychological, and behavioral characteristics of individuals. Community leaders, regardless of their talents and abilities, must function in the community setting. Consequently, despite their potential or acquired talents, abilities will always be influenced by the larger context—the community itself and the leaders' relationships with one another.

The Goal of This Chapter

This chapter addresses the social, psychological, and behavioral characteristics of leaders and the relationship between leadership roles and behaviors that create effective community development organizations. The personal characteristics of leaders are referred to as their psychological, sociological, and behavioral characteristics. We present concepts that undergird community structure and how it applies to the community, community leadership, and development. Also, a series of online learning activities is presented to help learners better understand, assess, and develop their leadership skills. Through an online case study, we show that concepts originally used to better understand power structures in urban communities are also applicable in rural settings.

Understanding Leadership: Definitions and Its Applications to Community Development

Community leadership requires coordination and interaction among recognized community leaders. This is especially the case in communities characterized by divisions related to wealth, politics, race, and other social characteristics (Nylander, 1998). Coordination and interaction (or lack thereof) can be demonstrated through social and project-based interactions among leaders in the community (Brown, Nylander, King, & Lough, 2000; O'Brien, Hassinger, Brown, & Pinkerton, 1991).

Efforts by CDOs are influenced by differences among people within the organization, the goals of the CDO, and the perceived and actual position of the CDO in the community (see Chapter 10). Coordinating with other groups in a community can become problematic because of traditional differences such as wealth and race (Nylander, 1998).

Defining Leadership

Leadership can be defined as the behavioral process of influencing the activities of an individual or group to accomplish goals in a given situation. This definition is consistent with Rost (1991), who defines leadership as a reciprocal influential relationship between leaders and followers. Leaders, by definition, must have followers who seek specific changes that reflect their shared purposes. Community sociologists and social psychologists, on the other hand, have used variations of the following definition to identify those who wield power within specific community structures: A community leader is a person who has the ability to get people to work together to get things done; or to stop things from getting done (O'Brien et al., 1991; Stovall, 2005).

Leadership can be defined symbolically. Symbolic leadership is derived from the power associated with a particular role and from the accompanying role expectations. Symbolic leadership represents values. For example, the leader chairs committees and sits at the head of the table. The symbolic leader is powerful because people expect him or her to be. The very title gives the leader influence.

Leadership can be defined operationally. Operational leadership refers to the behaviors and roles a leader plays in a group situation or with the staff. It describes the leader's real attempts, successes, and failures to involve and stimulate others. Success is related to real or "operational" power.

Some persons are symbolic *and* operational leaders. For example, the president of the United States must fulfill both symbolic and operational roles. When we see the president on television or as a participant in parades and celebrations, he is a symbolic leader. When he works with his staff or the Cabinet, he is an operational leader.

Leadership Research

Several approaches to the study of leadership are useful in understanding how leaders develop and how relationships are defined. These include the trait approach, the situational approach, and the leader's style or method of interacting. Today, most social psychologists and sociologists believe leadership is expressed as a function of three basic factors: the social situation, an individual's personality, and the leader's behavior. Leadership is not a quality that a person possesses inherently; rather, leadership occurs when people interact in a social situation. A person who is a leader in one situation may not be a leader in another situation.

The Trait Approach. For a long time, scholars searched for the trait or physical characteristics that defined or created leadership. Generally, research shows that leadership is not correlated with a physical trait. One physical trait that is supported by research is that leaders tend to be taller than average, Napoleon notwithstanding. Also, certain psychological traits tend to be correlated with leadership ability. For example, leaders tend to score higher on intelligence tests and score as better adjusted on personality tests. However, the "born leader" or the "great man" theory has been generally discredited (Lieberson & O'Connor, 1972).

The Situational Approach. The situational approach suggests that the leader adjust his or her approach to the group or the situation. Group members may become as important as the leader. And, it is out of the group that the leader emerges, because it is through the group that the leader comes to have authority and exhibit expert power. Thus, the power of facts and figures, as well as the leader's interaction skills, will help the group function in a given situation. As the function of a group changes, leadership roles may be transformed. Sometimes, a leader can be a group maintainer, one who holds the group together; and sometimes, the leader will act as a task specialist, concerned with solving a problem. For example, if a group is lost at sea, and someone knows how to navigate, he or she may become the group leader. The situation calls for an expert, and the expert becomes the group leader. If, however, the group has disagreements about how to proceed, someone with negotiating or listening skills might become the leader. Demands of the group and the situation help to determine the best leadership style and the best leader.

The Role Approach. The most recent approach to studying leadership is to analyze the leadership roles and behavior styles of successful leaders. This approach naturally follows the situational approach. It combines the knowledge that group situations are often very different, requiring a leader to use different leadership styles or behaviors. The basic question is, "How does the leader act?"

By developing a range of behavior skills, leaders increase their options and avoid being typecast as rigid or passive. *The leader's behavior range is his or her repertoire of interaction skills!* The community is the scene where a leader has the opportunity to play many parts with a variety of characters—at home, at work, at play, at worship, or in a community development organization. The following section describes behaviors and roles that a leader may find effective.

Three Types of Leadership Roles

Leadership roles and behaviors can be categorized as developmental, directive, or permissive.

The developmental leader is best described as an involving leader. This type of leader is interested in involving others in the situation or problem. The developmental leader shares the decision-making process, and he or she operates under the principle that people will support projects that they help create (McGregor, 1960). The developmental leader is flexible and actively facilitates group interactions, helping to structure ideas, solidify group decisions, and encourage participation. In summary, the developmental leader (a) stimulates people with relevant information and questions, (b) involves the group in solving problems, (c) assimilates and organizes what has been said, and (d) provides positive psychological reinforcement so that the group feels comfortable in taking action.

The developmental leader is an active listener. More than anything else, a developmental leader does not judge people, perspectives, or ideas. The developmental leader listens attentively and works to understand the speaker's ideas. The leader's eyes follow the speaker, and the leader responds to nonverbal cues as well as verbal cues. In group situations, the developmental leader encourages less vocal members and structures comments for greater task involvement. Finally, the developmental leader seeks feedback after group meetings or counseling sessions. This improves communication and contributes to each team member's knowledge of what to do, when, and why.

The directive leader is best described through a power application role. The directive leader uses power and assumes that creativity is rare and people need direction to accomplish anything. Dependent people may welcome this type of domination because they wish to avoid risks or the responsibility of making decisions. The directive leader (a) regiments others by hiding goals, controlling information, piecemealing work assignments, and isolating functions or people; (b) judges others constantly through voice, stance, and rigid behaviors; and (c) rewards or punishes others depending on whether they follow orders.

The permissive leader uses a pleasure-seeking, nonjudgmental approach. The leader values the support and loyalty of group members, and works to win their support through fun and games. The permissive leader prefers an unstructured and permissive work environment, which provides individual security and pleasure. At times, this leader is so permissive that very little work gets done. The permissive leader (a) sees group approval as a priority, (b) avoids making judgments or decisions that are not popular, (c) meets the security needs of group members, and (d) seeks approval by using positive reinforcement.

Leadership Behaviors Influence Outcomes

Leadership Roles and Communication Networks. Every group develops a communication network that is influenced by the leader's style. Developmental leaders foster a communication network that enhances interaction and establishes communication among group members and leaders (see Figure 9.1). Under a directive leader, communication follows a chain of command, or traditional organizational chart, as illustrated in Figure 9.2. For the permissive leader, the communication system is more like a merry-go-round, with most of the communication among the members of the team and almost none with the leader (Figure 9.3).

Figure 9.1   The Wheel of Interaction

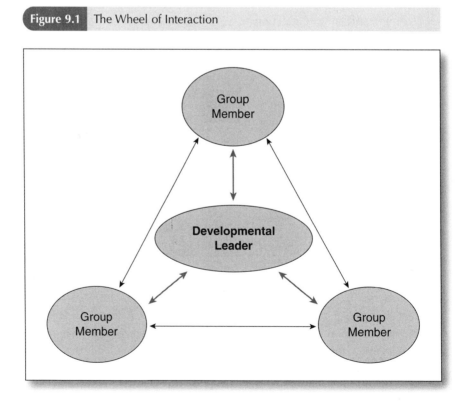

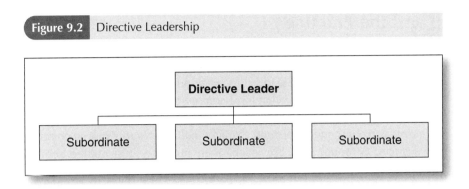

Figure 9.2 Directive Leadership

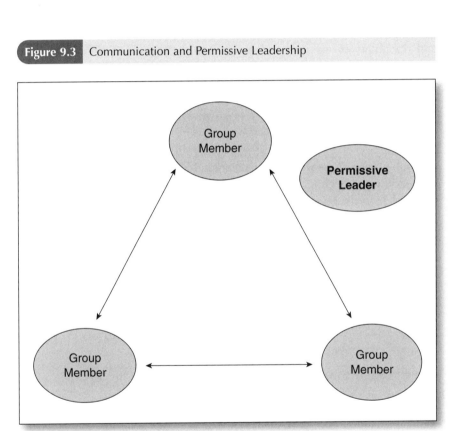

Figure 9.3 Communication and Permissive Leadership

Productivity in the Leader's Absence. When the developmental leader leaves, members of the group tend to continue productive activity because they have a sense of ownership in the outcomes. When a directive leader leaves, activity is likely to stop because no one is there to enforce the rules. Under the permissive leader, group productivity is likely to remain unchanged because group members are already doing what they prefer when the leader is present.

Leadership and the Practice of Community Development

Many of the more than 700 leadership development programs in the United States emphasize the social, behavioral, and psychological aspects of leadership, such as charismatic qualities or personality traits. The intent of such programs is to find and help mold dynamic individuals to work as community leaders. Although this approach often produces outstanding results, problems develop if the sociological aspects of leadership are ignored. The focus must include the structures, specific behaviors, and networks of leaders in a community. A leader must be able to effectively create and tap into resources inside and outside of the community. These resource networks, and the ability to tap into and maintain them, constitute the structure of community leadership.

Widening the Focus to Understand Community Leadership

Effective community leadership requires an understanding of both the psychology and the sociology of community leadership. As the behavioral approach to leadership is more relevant to community development, this chapter has focused on organizational structures that influence leader behavior. Networks become particularly important in creating effective community leaders in rural places with racial diversity, and because a small population requires that leaders network across racial differences. Thus, it is important to examine this structure over and above the personality traits of leaders. Individuals are recognized as community leaders based on different positions they occupy, such as political positions (elected officials), economic positions (wealth), or social positions (family status), *and their behavior!*

Developmental or Directive Organizational Structures?

Directive organizations are more formal, with fixed relationships among leaders or supervisors and their subordinates. The leader is the agent of highest authority. Authority is associated with one's status. The position, not the individual, is of primary importance in directive organizations. Because decisions are made at the top, the directive style may stifle creativity.

In the developmental organization, the work group is a cooperative team. Members identify with organizational goals, communicate openly across status and position, and engage in defining the issues and developing approaches. In development organizations, work is meaningful, and members enjoy working together (Tables 9.1, 9.2, and 9.3).

Table 9.1   Comparing Directive and Developmental Organizations

In Directive Organizations,		In Developmental Organizations,	
People generally are:	*Therefore it is necessary to:*	*People generally are:*	*Therefore it is necessary to:*
1. Lazy	Motivate them	1. Dynamic, self-motivated	Guide and provide guidelines
2. Dependent	Direct them	2. Independent	Provide opportunities for self-direction
3. Irresponsible	Closely supervise them	3. Responsible	Trust them
4. Hostile (enemies)	Mistrust and oppose them	4. Allies	Cooperate, collaborate with them
5. Lacking imagination and creativity	Outline their work in detail	5. Creative	Create conditions that allow them to use their creativity
6. Lacking forethought or vision	Plan their work for them	6. Imaginative, with vision	Allow them to plan their activities or plan with them

SOURCE: Adapted from Robinson and Clifford (1976b) and McGregor (1960).

Table 9.2   Basic Characteristics of Directive and Developmental Organizations

Characteristics	*Directive*	*Developmental*
1. Basic unit	Individual	Team
2. Decisions	Centralized at the top	Decentralized
3. Control	Coercive supervision	Noncoercive involvement
4. Leader/supervisor	Controls and dominates	Activator, involves all group members

SOURCE: Adapted from Robinson and Clifford (1976b).

Table 9.3 Advantages and Disadvantages of Each Organizational Style

	Directive	*Developmental*
Advantages	• Order • Predictability • Control	• Creativity • Flexibility • Cooperation
Disadvantages	• Poor communication • Levels of isolation • Dependency • Revolt	• Lack of leadership • Efficiency • Control • Time requirements

SOURCE: Adapted from Robinson and Clifford (1976a, 1976b).

Consequently, one cannot ignore these positional aspects of leadership. Leadership development workshops must focus on both the psychology and sociology of leadership. When community leaders better understand these structural aspects of leadership, they can use the linkages more effectively to create desired social change. However, to be effective at this level, community leaders need to understand how network linkages and one's relative position to them affect not only their decision making, but also their decision options. Analyzing networks helps leaders understand the dynamics behind many of the community's social, political, and economic problems.

Power and Leadership

Community leadership also revolves around power, or the ability to manipulate existing conditions to create desired outcomes (Allen, 1974). Power is influenced by at least two factors: a leader's own behavior, and the structural connections to resources (Brown & Nylander, 1998). Two generic models of community power structure have dominated the literature—the elite (Hunter, 1953) and the pluralistic (Dahl, 1961) models. These models were developed as a result of research in urban settings.

The elite model depicts a directive community leadership structure as monolithic, controlled by elite business owners who dominate the community's economy through a formal web of interlocking directorships or informal associations. Leaders generally know one another and may gather into cliques collectively coordinated by the most powerful in the group.

The pluralist model is more developmental and includes a variety of groups, some more permanent than others, that wield influence across a broad spectrum of political issues (Dahl, 1961; Domhoff, 1990; Trounstine & Christensen, 1982). Power is widely distributed not only among individuals but also among groups that emerge and later disband across emergent issues. Leadership is often issue-based, and power is fluid and tied to specific issues. Different issues inspire different shifting alliances among interest groups and leaders.

How do community leadership structures develop? Leadership power structures are largely products of the interconnections among leaders—in other words, leaders' intrapersonal networks. Consequently, understanding a community's leadership power structure requires at least two steps: identifying the top echelon of local leaders, and identifying the network connections among them. These points are illustrated with an online case study from two rural communities in the Mississippi Delta.

Case Study 9.1 | **Leadership Skills for Middle School Students**

A political science course at the University of Minnesota uses service-learning to provide leadership skills to middle school students. The project seeks to give middle school students knowledge about the issues seen in their community, and helps the students to apply themselves to these issues. To perform their service hours, undergraduates visit a middle school on a weekly basis, with each college student working with a group of 6-16 younger students. Each group of students has an issue or problem (identified by the student body) for which it is in charge of brainstorming solutions, with the assistance of the undergraduate "coach." Issues that have been addressed by the middle school students range from fighting neighborhood violence to changing the school uniform policy, or from getting a juice machine at school to helping the homeless in the community. The role of the undergraduate coach is to give advice to the students as they plan, teaching them about the politics involved in the practical implementation of ideas and also encouraging the students in leadership skills such as public speaking, negotiating, teamwork, and rule making. The undergraduates all have combined debriefing sessions after their service every week, providing them with an opportunity to discuss their experiences and improve their usefulness to the students with each session.

SOURCE: Battistoni, R. M., & Hudson, W. E. (Eds.). (1997). *Experiencing citizenship concepts and models for service-learning in political science.* Washington, DC: American Association for Higher Education.

Conclusion: Applying Knowledge About Leadership to Community Development

Leadership has inherently sociological aspects that must be considered if we are to effect change in communities during the 21st century. Knowledge of this fact is not enough. We must be willing to share knowledge about the dynamics and skills of leadership with community residents. Providing information to potential community leaders is necessary, but it is not sufficient for creating positive community change. Leaders must understand how existing leadership structures and behaviors are factors in the success or failure of community development efforts. One way to bridge this knowledge gap is to help potential leaders see themselves as part of a larger structure that they and other leaders create through their own connections.

Competencies of Effective Leaders in the 21st Century

For community development organizations to succeed, they must develop a cadre of local leaders that will address the challenges of economic and social change. The following competencies have been adapted from writings by Myrtis Tabb and Christy Montesi (2000).

1. The effective leader in the 21st century will be personally empowered, a lifelong learner, and an educator who values the importance of sharing knowledge and imparting new skills to meet new challenges. As lifelong learners, leaders of the 21st century will possess a natural curiosity and desire to learn new and better approaches toward accomplishing individual and collective goals.

2. The effective leader in the 21st century will work to facilitate a group empowerment process as a developmental leader. Effective leaders will inspire, motivate, and challenge individuals and groups to achieve their highest potential. They will be a catalyst in group settings. They will be effective in helping groups actualize mutual visions and goals.

3. The effective leader of the 21st century will know how to build effective community development organizations and coalitions (see Chapter 10), through designing new structures and processes for achieving individual and collective goals.

4. The effective leader of the 21st century will be able to build and promote healthy communities, understand dimensions of holistic community development, and be effective stewards of resources within their communities and environments. Leaders will see themselves as resources to the broader community and will continually invest in their overall personal and professional development.

5. The effective leader of the 21st century will know how to positively affect public policy and public governance processes. The leader will know and understand relationships between federal, state, county, and municipal levels of policy decisions and actions.

6. The effective leader of the 21st century will understand the larger environment—local, national, and global—within which change is taking place and work to help his or her community deal effectively in the global arena.

Local Problems Are National Problems

Community-building problems exist across the United States in both urban and rural locales. As communities become increasingly diverse, they experience many of the issues found in our online case study. Effective community development requires leaders with a broad set of leadership skills and awareness of the structure that leaders create and perpetuate in the community through their network connections. Consequently, community developers need to recognize and emphasize the behavioral, sociological, and psychological dimensions of leadership. This requires an appreciation of the changing and interdisciplinary nature of community development, as well as an intellectual curiosity that will encourage us to look for useful concepts outside the field of community development. We must realize that all communities have unique characteristics and challenges, and that creating and maintaining strong local leadership is essential for survival.

References

Allen, M. (1974). The structure of interorganizational elite cooperation: Interlocking corporate directorates. *American Sociological Review, 39,* 393–406.

Battistoni, R. M., & Hudson, W. E. (Eds.). (1997). *Experiencing citizenship concepts and models for service-learning in political science.* Washington, DC: American Association for Higher Education.

Brown, R. B., & Nylander, A. B., III. (1998). Community leadership structure: Differences between rural community leaders' and residents' informational networks. *Journal of the Community Development Society, 29,* 71–89.

Brown, R. B., Nylander, A. B., III, King, B. G., & Lough, B. J. (2000). Growth machine attitudes and community development in two racially diverse rural Mississippi Delta communities: A monolithic approach in a complex region. *Journal of the Community Development Society, 31,* 173–195.

Dahl, R. A. (1961). *Who governs?* New Haven, CT: Yale University Press.

Domhoff, W. G. (1990). *The power elite and the state: How policy is made in America.* New York: Aldine De Gruyter.

Hunter, F. (1953). *Community power structure.* Chapel Hill: University of North Carolina Press.

Lieberson, J., & O'Connor, J. (1972). Leadership and organizational performance: A study of large corporations. *American Sociological Review, 37,* 117–130.

Lyon, L. (1999). *The community in urban society.* Prospect Heights, IL: Waveland.

McGregor, D. (1960). *The human side of enterprise.* New York: McGraw Hill.

Nylander, A. B., III. (1998). *Rural community leadership structures in two Delta communities.* Unpublished doctoral dissertation, Mississippi State University.

O'Brien, D. J., Hassinger, E. W., Brown, R. B., & Pinkerton, J. R. (1991). The social networks of leaders in more and less viable rural communities. *Rural Sociology, 56,* 699–716.

Robinson, J. W., & Clifford, R. A. (1976a). *Leadership roles in community groups.* Urbana: University of Illinois, North Central Regional Extension Publication 36-3.

Robinson, J. W., & Clifford, R. A. (1976b). *Organizational styles in community groups*. Urbana: University of Illinois, North Central Regional Extension Publication 36–2.

Rost, J. C. (1991). *Leadership for the twenty-first century*. Westport, CT: Praeger.

Stovall, M. J. (2005). *Stability of and differences in black and white leadership structures over time in two rural Mississippi Delta towns*. Unpublished master's thesis, Delta State University, Cleveland, MS.

Tabb, M., & Montesi, C. R. (2000). A model for long-term leadership development among groups of diverse persons. *Journal of the Community Development Society, 31,* 335.

Trounstine, P. J., & Christensen, T. (1982). *Movers and shakers: The study of community power*. New York: St. Martin's.

10

Principles of Working Together

Developing Relationships That Support Community Development Initiatives

Janet S. Ayres and Anne Heinze Silvis

BEHAVIOR OBJECTIVES

After studying this chapter and completing the online learning activities, students should be able to

1. Understand the importance of people working together in a community to address complex public issues.

2. Understand the challenges of people working together as they work to bring about change in a community.

3. Identify the major changes in community that affect the way people work together in communities.

4. Understand the basic principles of collaborative problem solving.

5. Understand collaborative problem-solving processes and how to apply them in a community.

6. Apply the principles of collaboration to their own initiatives and projects.

7. Use a collaborative process to help individuals, organizations, and government work together in the community.

Introduction

The ability of people to work together is essential to successful community development initiatives. The Pew Partnership for Civic Change conducted more than a decade of research in communities across the country and identified seven key leverage points to create "smart communities" (Morse, 2004). One of these key points is people working together, and how they build trust and relationships to "unleash new talents and resources to address old and new problems and opportunities" (Morse, 2004, p. 51). Yet it is difficult and time-consuming for various segments of the community to work together over time toward a shared goal. Complex, multijurisdictional issues; constantly changing circumstances; vested interests of key stakeholders; and competition over limited resources make working together a challenging endeavor. Such challenges, however, necessitate that communities develop collaborative initiatives that build broad-based involvement and create an effective problem-solving and decision-making process to address important issues.

This chapter suggests that working together, in a collaborative framework, is the most effective way to create equity and ownership in a changing environment, and describes what it means to work together, along with advantages and practical challenges. Principles and major components for successful collaboration are described and illustrated in a case study of an agricultural community that undertook a collaborative effort to identify and address important issues. The chapter concludes with a summary of principles and concepts to build the community's capacity to work together.

Case Study 10.1 Collaborative Design

As part of the architecture program at California State Polytechnic University in Pomona, CA, students can participate in service-learning through design-build architectural studios. The program has developed a direct relationship between the university, a nonprofit housing organization, and disadvantaged communities in Tijuana, Mexico. Students in the architecture program learn about sustainable design and community development by designing and constructing a variety of structures in Tijuana. By collaborating with residents in the impoverished communities, students learn about the impact of physical structures and design on community development and well-being. Corazón, the nonprofit collaborating with the studio work, helps the students involve residents in the design and installation of communication booths for the nonprofit to increase awareness of its events and programs among community residents. Students and residents created spaces for civic gatherings that emphasize landscaping and public art. Students and residents gain practical knowledge in architectural skills as well as a deeper respect for collaborative design and local knowledge. As a result, both groups are empowered by broadening their skill set and contributing to the development of the community.

For more information, contact:

California State Polytechnic University
ieramirez@csupomona.edu

Why Working Together Is Important

The ability of individuals, organizations, and government to work together in a community is essential. Working together allows the community to adapt to a rapidly changing environment and the unpredictable nature of public issues. Working together also changes the community's approach to issues, enhancing its ability to address problems with more creativity and a broader perspective, improving its problem-solving and decision-making ability.

Changing Community Context

Change has been a part of most communities' reality since their founding, but in recent years, the nature of change and subsequent issues are profoundly different. Major technological, economic, political, environmental, and social forces have created issues at the local level that are increasingly complex, interdependent, and controversial. Several key points of the changing community context are worth noting.

Changing Concept of Community. The concept of community itself is being redefined to encompass broad geographic areas. In some areas, urban expansion has created issues around the use of land, provision of services, environmental concerns, and economic opportunities that extend beyond traditional jurisdictional boundaries. Communities are examining ways to pool their limited resources and find creative new ways to provide services, reduce spending, and address multijurisdictional issues.

Changing Volume and Availability of Information. The accessibility of information creates both opportunities and challenges. Information is more available than ever before. It takes time, however, to wade through the myriad of resources and determine credible information on which to base public policy decisions. We benefit from more information that is easily available, but misinformation and conflicting information abound.

Changes in the Stability of Communities and Crisis Situations. Many issues, such as industry closings or natural disasters, can emerge as crises with little forewarning and leave communities in their wake struggling to react as best they can. In an interconnected world, actions external and unknown to the community can have sudden, unexpected local consequences.

Increased Exposure to the Consequences of External Decision Making. National and international events increasingly affect local communities. Federal legislation, the global economy, telecommunications, and corporate mergers or foreclosures are just a few examples of decisions made beyond the local community that have profound local consequences.

Changing Approach to Issues. Communities are changing the way in which local issues are addressed, how decisions are made, and who participates in these processes. Increasingly, special interest groups—those with a narrowly defined, single-issue focus such as "Stop School Consolidation," "Stop the Landfill," or "No More Taxes"—dominate the public decision-making arena. Such advocacy groups are increasingly articulate and powerful in affecting the outcome of issues. Some local advocacy groups have strong ties to well-funded and politically powerful national organizations that often intervene in local decision making. Although advocacy approaches may be effective in bringing about needed change, the adversarial process that is undertaken to address issues often polarizes the community, damaging local relationships and the capacity to work together.

Changing Community Capacity. Another reason for the community to work together is to remain relevant and responsive to an increasingly diverse population. Communities grow and change as their populations grow and change. Populations new to a community bring different perspectives to issues and perhaps different values regarding what is important, what is valued, and how to relate to one another. The ways in which newcomers and groups are brought into community decision-making processes are important in creating more inclusive communities, gaining new perspectives, and creating solutions appropriate to new problems.

Communities often reveal a fluid, dynamic environment in which issues become important and then lose importance, residents organize and then disband, and events change so rapidly that even interested community groups can lose track of situations and strategies (Hyman, Higdon, & Martin, 2001). As communities struggle to deal with rapidly changing issues, it becomes apparent that no one person, organization, or governmental unit has all the knowledge, skills, or resources needed to understand the issues, let alone develop and implement solutions.

Advantages of Working Together

Individuals and organizations with multiple ways of thinking, diverse sets of knowledge and skills, and access to an array of resources are needed to address today's complex community issues. Bringing resources together and building upon assets already in the community not only make good sense, they are essential (Beilharz, 2002). Complex issues such as health care, workforce development, street gangs, job losses, or the environment require more than a small group of people to define the issue and take action. The ability of a community to work together, recognize and then organize its assets, and undertake a collaborative problem-solving process is fundamental to its ability to change and sustain itself. Furthermore, not only is the active participation of the citizenry fundamental to a democratic society, people want to have a voice in and be part of addressing important issues that affect them (Mathews, 2002). From a community development perspective, many benefits can accrue to a community from the active involvement of citizens, civic organizations, and government:

- New leadership to address current and future community issues
- Enhanced leadership capacity through new knowledge and skills gained as people and institutions work together
- Knowledge gained from different perspectives as people discuss issues and inform one another
- An enhanced sense of belonging and commitment to the community
- Enhanced communication and relationships among key players, both internal and external to the community
- A more rapid response to issues as multiple groups or individuals address issues or subsets of an issue simultaneously
- New linkages with outside financial, political, and technical resources
- Synergistic thinking and action that can lead to solutions that address current issues

Challenges of Working Together

Although there are many benefits to be derived from working together, there are challenges to initiate an effort to work together and sustain it over time.

Traditional Mind-Sets. One difficulty in working together may be a traditional mind-set on the part of community residents and elected officials regarding their role in the community. Both Mathews (2002) and Heifetz and Sinder (1988) discuss this problem as twofold. On one hand, the United States is a representative democracy where many Americans expect elected officials to solve public issues on their behalf, but too often, citizens abdicate responsibility for the issues that affect them. At the same time, Americans can be cynical about elected officials and political processes, and they choose not to become involved in public issues because they feel powerless to make a difference, or they feel the decision has already been made (Boyte, 1989; Carpenter & Kennedy, 2001; Chrislip & Larson, 1994). Community residents may be discouraged from participation in change efforts because they are conditioned to accept the status quo and trust that those in power are right and that to question authority is wrong or dangerous. In some communities, citizen involvement may threaten elected officials, who discourage questions and participation. However, the expectation that elected officials can, or even should, solve today's complex public issues without community participation not only is unrealistic, but also sets the foundation for ultimate failure (Heifetz & Sinder, 1988).

High Stakes. Potential collaborators may not want to work together. Most community issues today are complex, with multiple stakeholders who have vested interests in the issue and hold different perspectives and values about solutions. When the stakes are high, as is the case with most community issues, stakeholders may be more interested in winning than in collaborating with others to find solutions. Successful collaboration requires *shared power,* a concept recognized by Bryson and Crosby (1992). They define shared power as "shared capabilities exercised in interaction between or among actors to further achievement of their separate and joint aims" (Bryson & Crosby, 1992, p. 13).

Turf Battles. Many community issues reach beyond jurisdictional boundaries, and traditional leaders may fear working in others' jurisdiction, or they may not see the issue as their responsibility (Bryson & Crosby, 1992; Dukes, 1996; Gray, 1989). A lack of communication between individuals and organizations can further exacerbate misunderstanding about each others' interests (Carpenter & Kennedy, 2001) and foster distrust. Turf battles and the lack of trust may be deeply embedded in a community, making it difficult to bring people together (Beilharz, 2002; Morse, 2004; Putnam, 1993).

Lack of Leadership. Another challenge may be the availability of leadership in the community to initiate a collaborative effort. Not only does working together take time, but it requires courage to take on some issues, especially those that are highly controversial, and skills and knowledge to know how to build a collaborative effort. Some communities may lack the leadership or commitment to do so.

Regardless of the challenges, it is essential for individuals, institutions, and government to work together if they are to address current and future issues. The motivation for collaboration is grounded in the practical efficiencies of working together, and the inspiration for collaboration is embedded in our commitment to a democratic society.

Principles of Working Together

Individuals and organizations working together in a community may take on various forms. Some efforts may be initiated around a short-term, single issue, such as building a new recreational facility, whereas other efforts are focused on long-term, complex issues, such as workforce development or access to health care.

Efforts can be formed at any scale—neighborhood, town, city, county, state, and beyond. And sometimes, collaboration is not necessary. If a decision must be made quickly to avoid danger, or if there are no other options, a decision maker might forgo discussion and take action.

The ways in which individuals and groups organize and structure their efforts can range on a continuum from cooperation to collaboration. Winer and Ray (1997) define *cooperation* as a shorter time, informal relationship without a clearly defined common mission. *Coordination* is a more formal relationship between the entities, requiring planning and division of roles while each individual and organization retains control of its resources and agenda. *Collaboration,* at the far end of the continuum, is a form of working together where partners share goals, resources, decision making, and benefits.

Barbara Gray (1989) defines collaboration in community development work as "a process through which parties who see different aspects of a problem can constructively explore their differences and search for solutions that go beyond their own limited vision of what is possible" (p. 5). In a community context, public issues are usually complex and controversial. People hold different, often conflicting views about the issues and best approaches. A collaborative framework allows people to create a mind-set and set of principles to guide their approach and build consensus, rather than compete with one another. The resulting relationships and actions are the foundation to building a community that is better able to address complex and interrelated issues (Beilharz, 2002; Chrislip & Larson, 1994; Morse, 2004).

Although working together collaboratively is not a new approach and, in fact, was identified in early principles of community development (Biddle & Biddle, 1965; Christenson & Robinson, 1980), the practice of collaboration, and consequently the research, has changed. The major shift has been around the concept of power—who has it and who does not, how to work in a shared power environment, and how to build the power of the community through social capital (Chrislip, 2002; Morse, 2004). Concepts of social capital (Putnam, 1993) define the outcome of processes among people that establish networks, norms, social trust, and cooperation. Communities have a history of who has been involved in decision making and how people work together. Attitudes and actions of citizens and leaders become embedded in the community's culture. To create constructive collaborative approaches to issues, it may be necessary for some communities to evaluate and change their attitudes and behaviors about how residents work together.

Working together in community development requires both a mind-set and a set of skills and knowledge that are based on principles of collaborative problem solving and decision making, including the following six principles.

People are the greatest asset of the community. Community development is about people and their skills, knowledge, and abilities to help themselves. As they claim responsibility for community issues, people develop a sense that they are part of the solution, rather than bystanders or victims of circumstances. When responsibility is shared, power is shared. When people believe they can make a difference, they do.

Relationships are critical. Collaboration is less a matter of familiarity or pleasant associations among people than the ability of people to work together to resolve difficult issues. Mathews (2002) points out that citizen-to-citizen and citizens-to-government relationships are critical. He makes three essential points: (a) Citizens and government officials working together is not only pragmatic, but essential to finding acceptable solutions to community issues; (b) shifting from identifying "the enemy" to building collaborative ties is necessary and is based not on liking others, but on respecting the interests of the other parties; and (c) joining diverse groups of citizens in public relationships requires an openness to divergent views and ways of acting together that may create new relationships and practices.

Mutual respect and a willingness to find shared interests are important aspects of collaborative problem solving. Every perspective is valid. Almost every perspective is developed around a nugget of truth. People must recognize that it is acceptable to disagree, but keep the discussion focused on the issue, not on people or personalities. The shared interests or compatible goals among community residents can provide the basis for mutual learning and collaborative work. Participants must accept responsibility for making the process work. It is important that they express themselves to educate one another about their interests, and seek to understand one another's perspectives. Through this exchange, which becomes a learning process, a common sense of purpose and a more complete understanding of the issue can be developed.

Different points of view can lead to new understanding, new approaches, and effective solutions. When people with diverse viewpoints come together to discuss issues respectfully, it encourages discussions that can lead to new understanding and solutions. To solicit new points of view, people who have not been part of the community's decision making must feel welcome and valued. It may require a special effort to reach out and include those who have been excluded in the past, and to understand the barriers to participation and the issues of importance that might make participation meaningful to groups, including racial or ethnic minority groups, non-English speakers, youth, poor people, newcomers, or even those viewed as "the enemy" based on previous positions.

Shared power can lead to greater community power. In traditional ways of working together, power is seen as zero-sum and one-way. In other words, there is only so much power, and it is used one way—those with power use it over those without. Power may be based upon financial resources, legal authority, information, decision making, or control over people and institutions. In a collaborative model, power is viewed differently. It is regarded as infinite, not scarce, and it can be created. People can grow more powerful without anyone else losing power. In fact, public power tends to increase as it is used. One idea can generate another, one commitment can inspire another, and one relationship can lead to another. When people join together to work on a public issue, they generate power through their knowledge, creativity, and problem solving. Using this collaborative view of power, the role of community leaders becomes more expansive. Community leaders cannot rely on formal authority and the power derived from positions to get things done. Instead, they must rely on networks and influence, with relationships developed through extensive interactions with community residents usually representing many different points of view (Pigg, 1999).

Open communication and shared information are essential to collaborative problem solving. The ability to listen to others; ask questions; understand others' interests; and speak openly and honestly, with emotions in check, is critically important in building relationships and developing solutions. When people are informed and information is shared freely (not to wield power), trust is built. Trust enables people to make decisions and to act.

Collaborative Problem-Solving Framework

To work together, individuals, organizations, and government must have the opportunity to come together, speak openly, and listen to others. The process should enable the group to focus on common issues, explore options, and generate solutions. A collaborative problem-solving process provides a useful framework to address complex community issues. Although a successful effort has many important steps, four major components are discussed here.

Leadership. Successful collaborative initiatives require leaders who have the courage to take on controversial issues and model the use of shared power and mutual respect for all perspectives. Leaders bring people together, encourage and facilitate broad participation, and keep the effort focused on common goals rather than narrowly defined positions. Collaborative mindsets and the leadership skills and knowledge needed to foster successful efforts can be learned and nurtured by people as they work together.

Stakeholders. From the very outset of a collaborative effort, it is important to identify and involve stakeholders. Stakeholders are identified as those individuals or organizations with the formal power to make a decision, those with the power to block a decision, those who will be affected by the decision, and those with relevant information or expertise (Strauss, 2002). It is better to err on the side of being too inclusive than to exclude someone who wants to be involved. There are ways of involving many people in the process without the group becoming large and unwieldy. Strauss identifies different layers of involvement, including a relatively small core problem-solving group, task forces that gather information and study issues, forums and other large group efforts to gain input and feedback, and communications and outreach to reach an even broader community (Strauss, 2002, p. 49).

Process for Problem Solving. Early on, the group needs to identify how it will address issues and make decisions, and how it will involve people in the process. In general, the problem-solving process involves identifying the issues and coming to a common understanding of the issues; identifying alternative solutions; analyzing the alternatives in terms of their consequences, including a cost/benefit analysis; making a decision; and developing and implementing action plans. Some of the group techniques to assist in these processes include nominal group technique, brainstorming, and force field analysis.

Common Goals and Action. People need to feel that their time has been well spent. It is important that the group identify common goals and celebrate milestone accomplishments to keep collaborative efforts moving forward. Acting on short-term, high-visibility projects while more complex issues are being considered will motivate people to continue working together.

Building Community Capacity: A Case Study of Working Together in a Rural Midwestern County ————

The following case study illustrates how a rural community applied a collaborative problem-solving process to address its important issues. It reflects how a traditional community was able to change its mind-set about how community issues are addressed and create an inclusive, collaborative effort to undertake new community development efforts.

Carroll County, Indiana, is a small, rural community in northwestern Indiana with a population of about 20,000. Many immigrants have moved into the county over the past decade to work at the hog processing plant, the largest industry in the county. The economy of the county is based on agriculture—primarily hogs, corn, and soybeans—and several small manufacturing firms. Recently, several large dairies have moved into the community. More than 40% of the population works outside the county. Like many midwestern communities, Carroll County is faced with the structural changes in agriculture and manufacturing, loss of jobs and retail businesses, youth moving away from the community, and environmental issues, especially water quality. People concerned about the environment frequently clash with those who favor the growth of confined animal feeding operations. A major four-lane highway, under construction, will link the county to large urban centers. Public resources are limited and dominate the public agenda. Leaders and residents are concerned about the future of their community.

In 2004, the community foundation board, working with Purdue University Cooperative Extension, initiated a county-wide effort to develop a vision, build consensus on issues, create more community unity, and take action on critical issues. A steering committee of key community leaders was formed to guide the process. The steering committee began by developing a collaborative process and garnering support from county-wide organizations, churches, and schools. The local newspaper devoted extensive coverage to encourage the public's participation in the forums. The community seemed ready and eager to begin the process, and elected officials and other key leaders in the community were ready to participate.

A series of three county-wide forums were held one week apart to provide an opportunity for residents and organizations from across the county to come together to discuss issues. The steering committee tried to involve all segments of the community by geographical areas, organizations, and occupations. Special effort was made to involve youth, senior citizens, and members of the new immigrant community. People were invited in person, through organizations and churches, by letter, and through the news media. Sponsorships from local businesses and the community foundation paid for a meal to be served at each three-hour evening session. The intent was to enable people to talk with one another, build trust and relationships across organizations and small towns, identify areas of common concern, create a shared vision, identify high-priority issues, and develop action steps to address those issues.

The first session focused on engaging activities that enabled people to share their sense of connection with the community and to articulate current strengths and weaknesses, future opportunities, and threats to the county. The second session developed a shared vision through people's dreams for the future, their hopes and nightmares. The third session identified the critical issues to be addressed for the vision to be realized, and what people could do to make the vision a reality. Participants were encouraged to make a commitment to attend all three sessions, as each session built on information generated from the previous session. The discussions took place in small groups, using various techniques to encourage participation. The small groups reported their discussions back to the total group. Everyone had a chance to speak and be heard.

Approximately 220 attended at least one of the three sessions that were held in late August and early September 2004. Many people met others for the first time. The three community forums resulted in a working vision statement and the creation of six taskforces to address the six high-priority issues that were identified. Media coverage of the sessions was extensive.

After the forums, the steering committee was expanded to include the chair from each of the six taskforces. This enabled direct communication between the taskforces and the steering committee to coordinate the entire effort. The steering committee met monthly to ensure that the effort continued to move forward. An e-mail group and a newsletter were established to enable frequent communication among the steering committee members, taskforces, and the broader community.

The forums provided an opportunity to build relationships among community residents as they shared their stories, perceptions, and ideas about the community and its future. The next phase of the collaborative process focused on learning more about the issues while continuing to foster county-wide

relationships. Community seminars were held on topics such as local government and community marketing. Taskforces worked during this time to gather
information regarding their issues by examining studies, talking with experts,
and visiting other communities to develop goals and an action plan.

In the fall of 2005, on the anniversary of the first series of community
forums, a community-wide meeting was held to discuss the goals and action
plans. These goals, strategies, and actions were highlighted in a brochure that
was made available throughout the community.

Several significant actions were taken as a result of this collaborative
effort. The highest priority issue identified was economic development. One
of the strategies was to develop a county-wide Chamber of Commerce. A
group of dedicated people, all with a passion for this idea, met nearly every
week for almost a year to work out details on how this could be accomplished.
The county appropriated funds to launch the Chamber. The Economic
Development Commission, which had been inactive for years, heard the
strong support for economic development initiatives during the forums and
restructured its board to be more representative of the community and more
open in its processes. The commission reallocated funds to create a full-time
director's position.

Another high-priority issue identified during the forums was the need to
build the county's leadership capacity. Another group developed a county-
wide leadership program that helps people learn about the county and builds
collaborative leadership skills. It was launched in January 2006 with a full
class of 30 people and has had full enrollment each year since. The program
has drawn people from across the county to learn more about how they can
be of service to their community.

The collaborative process has been modeled in several of the small towns
in the county as a way to gain community involvement on important issues.
A recent example is the revision of the county's comprehensive land use plan.
A broad representative group of citizens was formed by the County Area Plan
Commission to guide the revision of the county's plan, a process usually
fraught with controversial issues. The committee worked collaboratively with
the community to engage residents in determining future land use. When it
came time for local decision makers to approve the plan, the plan passed
unanimously and with no public dissent. The committee is currently working
on zoning ordinances.

In 2006, a new county-wide organization, Carroll County Focus on the
Future, was formed to continue to foster proactive, collaborative efforts.
When the county reduced funding for county parks, residents came forward
to support the parks. Focus on the Future helped the residents launch another
collaborative effort known as Friends of the Parks.

In August 2009, 5 years after the beginning of the county's collaborative
effort, Focus on the Future, working in collaboration with civic organizations
and local government, launched a revisited collaborative effort to celebrate
successes, identify new issues, and re-engage people.

Conclusions

Francis Moore Lappe and Paul Martin DuBois, in their book *The Quickening of America* (1994), address myths of public life, including the myth that only officials and celebrities have public lives. In fact, each of us has a public life through our involvement in formal and informal organizations. Research in communities has shown that people care about their communities and their quality of life, but they have busy lives and precious little free time, don't know how to get involved, or perhaps have not been allowed access to community decision making. Community residents need opportunities to address community issues collectively. As they become engaged in discussing public issues that are important to them, and building relationships with others who have common concerns, residents become energized and enabled to be part of building a better community. Working together in collaborative ways is essential to make this happen.

A collaborative framework provides a mind-set, a set of principles, and problem-solving and decision-making processes that enable people to work together in ways that build the community's capacity to address its important issues. Processes are based on a set of principles that includes inclusivity, mutual respect, open communication, transparent processes, understanding of others' interests, identification of shared interests, and consensus building. An effective collaborative effort is intentional about its purpose, structure, and processes, but these are defined by the collaborators themselves as they engage in their work together.

During these times of rapid change, and with the complex issues that communities face, collaboration among community residents, civic organizations, institutions, businesses, and government not only makes sense, it is essential. However, it is not an easy job, and it requires courageous leadership to initiate and facilitate such efforts. It requires a broader mind-set about power, as well as skills that may not be developed in some communities that have practiced hierarchical decision making. Collaboration, like community development, is a body of knowledge and set of skills that can be learned, nurtured, and supported.

> The true test of the American ideal is whether we are able to recognize our failings and then rise together to meet the challenges of our time. Whether we allow ourselves to be shaped by events and history, or whether we act to shape them. Whether chance of birth or circumstance decides life's big winners and losers, or whether we build a community where, at the very least, everyone has a chance to work hard, get ahead, and reach their dreams.
>
> —Illinois Senator Barack Obama, Knox College
> Commencement Address, Galesburg, Illinois, June 4, 2005

References

Beilharz, L. (2002). *Building community: The shared action experience.* Bendigo, Australia: St. Luke's Innovative Resources.

Biddle, W. W., & Biddle, L. J. (1965). *The community development process: The rediscovery of local initiative.* New York: Holt, Rinehart and Winston.

Boyte, H. C. (1989). *Commonwealth: A return to citizen politics.* New York: Free Press.

Bryson, J. M., & Crosby, B. C. (1992). *Leadership for the common good: Tackling public problems in a shared-power world.* San Francisco: Jossey-Bass.

Carpenter, S. L., & Kennedy, W. J. D. (2001). *Managing public disputes.* San Francisco: Jossey-Bass.

Chrislip, D. D. (2002). *The collaborative leadership fieldbook: A guide for citizens and civic leaders.* San Francisco: Jossey-Bass.

Chrislip, D. D., & Larson, C. E. (1994). *Collaborative leadership: How citizens and civic leaders can make a difference.* San Francisco: Jossey-Bass.

Christenson, J. A., & Robinson, J. W., Jr. (1980). *Community development in America.* Ames: Iowa State University Press.

Dukes, E. F. (1996). *Resolving public conflict: Transforming community and governance.* New York: St. Martin's.

Gray, B. (1989). *Collaboration: Finding common ground for multiparty problems.* San Francisco: Jossey-Bass.

Heifetz, R. A., & Sinder, R. M. (1988). Political leadership: Managing the public's problem solving. In R. B. Reich (Ed.), *The power of public ideas* (pp. 179–203). Cambridge, MA: Harvard University Press.

Hyman, D., Higdon, F. X., & Martin, K. E. (2001). Reevaluating community power structures in modern communities. *Journal of the Community Development Society, 32,* 199–225.

Lappe, F. M., & DuBois, P. M. (1994). *The quickening of America: Rebuilding our nation, remaking our lives.* San Francisco: Jossey-Bass.

Mathews, D. (2002). *For communities to work.* Dayton, OH: Kettering Foundation.

Morse, S. W. (2004). *Smart communities: How citizens and local leaders can use strategic thinking to build a brighter future.* San Francisco: Jossey-Bass.

Obama, B. (2005, June 4). Knox College commencement address, Galesburg, IL.

Pigg, K. E. (1999). Community leadership and community theory: A practical synthesis. *Journal of the Community Development Society, 30,* 196–212.

Putnam, R. D. (1993). *Making democracy work: Civic traditions in modern Italy.* Princeton, NJ: Princeton University Press.

Strauss, D. (2002). *How to make collaboration work: Powerful ways to build consensus, solve problems, and make decisions.* San Francisco: Berrett-Koehler.

Winer, M., & Ray, K. (1997). *Collaboration handbook.* St. Paul, MN: Amherst H. Wilder Foundation Press.

11

Communities in Rural America

Current Realities and Emerging Strategies

Lionel J. Beaulieu and Glenn D. Israel

BEHAVIOR OBJECTIVES

After studying this chapter and completing the online learning activities, students should be able to

1. Explain and justify the use of the concept—typology.

2. Prepare a list of five beliefs that people may have about why living in rural areas is utopia.

3. Prepare a short essay about rural and urban population trends in the United States since 1950.

4. Prepare a chart or graph describing overall population trends in the reader's home county since 1950.

5. Prepare a table or chart describing major changes in the composition of the workforce by major industries in a state since 1970.

6. Explain why self-employment is a growing trend in rural America.

7. Prepare a short essay about why poverty is increasing in rural America.

8. Select at least one of the strategies that the authors suggest for achieving vitality in rural America, and work with a group of three classmates to prepare a presentation for a group of rural leaders.

Introduction

In its quest to discover the key challenges facing rural areas, a major philanthropic organization engaged the talents of researchers, policy analysts, and communications experts in the hope of getting a better handle on how individuals—be they urban, suburban, or rural residents—viewed the people and issues that are part of rural America. After completing and assessing the contemporary research on rural areas, conducting a national survey of adults, hosting focus group meetings in strategic locations across the United States, and pursuing a content analysis of media reports on rural people and issues, the multifaceted team of professionals concluded that rural America was commonly viewed in two ways—from a "rural utopia" and a "rural dystopia" lens (FrameWorks Institute, 2007).

For those who see rural areas through a rural utopia lens, rural life is simple and wholesome, local residents are hard-working, independent-minded, and compassionate. Most believe that people are living in rural areas willingly, despite the many challenges that a rural existence presents. Even though the difficulties they face are monumental, rural residents want to tackle these problems with limited interference from outsiders. Those who view rural America through a rural dystopia lens, on the other hand, tend to highlight negative features of what they perceive rural life to be about—backward, impoverished, poorly educated, small-minded, and constituted of people with little ambition or interest in making life better for themselves or their communities.

Although simplistic in their treatment of rural America, these images have played out in a variety of venues. In his song "My Little Town," for example, Paul Simon describes a crumbling town, lamenting that only the dead and dying are left behind. John Mellencamp, on the other hand, sings about the virtues of living in a small town—a place with caring networks of family and friends, where one can breathe clean air, and where people have the freedom to be themselves. Even scholars debate the pluses and minuses of living in rural America. More than three decades ago, researchers described rural areas as "left behind" (Whiting, 1974), isolated, and economically unstable, and with limited local services and facilities (Kraenzel, 1980; Warner, 1974). At the same time, classic studies by Wirth (1938) and Simmel (1950) promoted a belief that rural people live in cohesive, peaceful, and harmonious communities. Even today, scholars debate the value of rural places. Recent books by Richard Florida have asserted the vitality of urban and densely populated mega-regions, places that offer a plethora of opportunities and experiences for their residents (Florida, 2002, 2008). For small towns and cities located outside of the mega-areas, prosperity is likely to pass them by. On the other hand, Wood (2008) spotlights stories of rural people who have embraced innovation and are successfully laying the foundation for the long-term prosperity of their communities. No doubt about it, when all is said and done, the notions of rural utopia and rural dystopia remain central tenets of how rural communities are viewed, from both historical and contemporary perspectives.

The Goal of This Chapter

The focus of this chapter is to take stock of what rural communities are all about. Are they areas that are on a downward spiral, or do they remain an important part of the fabric of American life? Do the facts point to a rural utopia, a rural dystopia, or some combination of both? That is what this chapter seeks to explore. We begin by undertaking a general assessment of current conditions in rural areas of America. Before doing so, however, we discuss three major typologies currently in use to define rural areas. We then adopt one of these typologies to help guide us through an analysis and discussion of important features that are likely to have a major impact on rural America's long-term well-being. Next, we detail some of the strategies that rural areas might consider to promote greater economic prosperity. We conclude by assessing the suitability of employing a rural utopia/dystopia lens to frame the current and emerging state of America's rural communities.

Case Study 11.1 Rural Health

Students of medicine are needed in communities of all types, from the largest city to the most sparsely populated town. The unique aspects of service in rural communities are not always considered, but the University of Minnesota Medical School–Duluth has an option for medical students to fill that need. Since 2005, a service-learning program has been in place to bring medical students to rural schools and deliver presentations on the science of the brain for elementary students. Because of its location away from major cities, the Duluth campus Medical School encourages its students to participate in community service in local rural regions. The brain presentations are the most popular choice for students, but other options students have selected include participation in health expos, blood pressure checks at local pharmacies and nursing homes, and volunteer work with Meals on Wheels. The partnership with elementary schools also gives the local teachers the opportunity to engage with the students, as not all elementary school teachers have formal science training.

SOURCE: Fitzakerley, J. L., & Westra, R. (2008). Service-learning in rural communities: Medical students teach children about the brain. Retrieved April 21, 2009, from http://www.minnesotamedicine.com/CurrentIssue/ClinicalServiceDecember2008/tabid/2757/Default.aspx

——— Defining Rural Areas: Exploring Common Typologies

It is not uncommon for individuals to read newspaper articles, government reports, and research articles that spotlight data on urban and rural places, or metropolitan and nonmetropolitan areas. How are these concepts measured? Are they the most commonly accepted approaches for examining rural conditions and trends, or do other typologies exist? Answers to these questions are important because they frame the manner in which assessments of the status of America's rural areas can be conducted.

A good starting point is to clarify the terms most often used in research studies and a host of reports—*urban/rural* and *metropolitan/nonmetropolitan*. Are they the same? The simple answer is no. But the story of how they are measured is more complicated because of changes in the definitions in recent years.

The upper panel in Table 11.1 describes the important features of the two geographic typologies. The first column describes the previous definitions of these concepts, whereas the second column has the current definition. Simply put, rural and urban, as well as metropolitan and nonmetropolitan, are defined differently today, and it is important to be aware of the adjustments that have been made in their measurement.

Urban/Rural Locales

For a number of years, the major building block for determining the rural or urban status of areas was linked to *size of a place*. Specifically, places having a population of 2,500 persons or more were designated "urban." In this context, places were defined as incorporated cities, villages, boroughs, towns, or unincorporated areas having features that the Census Bureau would view as consistent with such places. Rural, on the other hand, applied to places of less than 2,500 persons or areas located outside of incorporated or census-defined places. All told, about 75% of the U.S. population was living in urban areas in 1990, and the remaining 25% was located in areas defined as rural. The nation's total population in 1990 was nearly 249 million.

In 2002, the U.S. Census Bureau adopted a new methodology for defining urban and rural areas and applied this new typology to its 2000 decennial census (i.e., the survey that all households in the United States are required to complete every 10 years). As such, the basis for classifying urban and rural is now tied to *census blocks* rather than places. Census blocks reflect the smallest geographic units established by the Census Bureau.[1] Currently, *urban* refers to all territory, population, and housing units located within an urbanized area (UA) or urban cluster (UC). Both UA and UC boundaries include densely settled territories consisting of (a) core census block groups or blocks having a population density of 1,000 persons or more per square mile, and (b) surrounding census blocks that have an overall population density of at least 500 people per square mile (U.S. Census Bureau, 2008). In most cases, UAs include areas having a nucleus of 50,000 persons or more, whereas UCs represent areas having a minimum of 2,500 but less than 50,000 persons. As for *rural*, it is defined as the territory, population, and housing located outside of a UA

---

[1]According to the U.S. Census, census blocks are generally formed by streets, roads, railroads, streams, and other bodies of water and the legal boundaries shown on census maps. Block groups reflect the next level of geography above census blocks and represent a cluster of census blocks (U.S. Census Bureau, 2005; U.S. Department of Commerce, 1994).

and UC. In most cases, it includes populations of less than 2,500 persons. In 2000, approximately 68% of our nation's 281 million residents lived in UAs, 11% in UCs, and 21% in rural areas.

Metropolitan/Nonmetropolitan Areas

A second geographic typology commonly employed is metropolitan/ nonmetropolitan areas. This typology is based on the *county*. During the 1990s, a metro area was defined as a county having one or more cities of 50,000 people or more, or an urbanized area with a population at or above 50,000, and a total county population of at least 100,000 persons. Contiguous counties having an economic tie to the central county would also be considered part of the metro area (see Table 11.1). Counties not meeting the metro area criteria were labeled nonmetropolitan areas. Nearly three of every four counties in the United States were designated nonmetro in 1990.

In an effort to bring about further refinement to the county classification system, the federal Office of Management and Budget (OMB) released a new county typology in 2003 (called Core-Based Statistical Area, or CBSA), changes that Cromartie (2003) characterized as "far reaching" (Office of Management and Budget, 2003). For one, the definition of a metropolitan area is now different. It refers to central counties with one or more UAs of 50,000 persons or more and outlying counties with strong economic ties to the central counties. How does the OMB determine the strength of the economic links that contiguous counties have with central counties? Simply put, it is based on the commuting patterns of workers. Outlying counties are defined as part of a metro area if they have 25% or more of their employed workforce commuting to the central county, *or* if 25% or more of the outlying county's employed population is made up of commuters from the central county. This is the first time that the OMB has given explicit attention to the flow of commuters to and from the central metro county in determining the status of outlying counties (North Dakota State Data Center, 2009).

A second change associated with the CBSA system is the manner in which nonmetropolitan areas are defined. Nonmetro counties are now divided into two groups—*micropolitan* or *noncore*. Micropolitan counties have one or more urban clusters of 10,000 to 49,999 persons, as well as outlying counties with 25% or more of their employed population commuting (either to the central micro county or from the micro county to the outlying county). The *noncore* label is assigned to nonmetro counties that do not meet the micropolitan definitions and thus have no city, town, or urban cluster of 10,000 residents or more. With the new CBSA system in place, 1,090 counties in the United States are now designated metropolitan, 674 as micropolitan, and 1,378 as noncore (using 2000 census population data).

Table 11.1   Geographic Typology

	Previous	*Current*
Geographic Typology (Census Bureau)		
Urban	Places of 2,500 or more persons incorporated as cities, villages, boroughs, and towns but excluding the rural portions of extended cities. Census-designated places of 2,500 or more persons. Other territory, incorporated or unincorporated, included in urbanized areas.	All territory, population, and housing units located in an urbanized area (UA) or an urban cluster (UC). It involves densely settled territory which consists of: • Core census block groups or blocks that have a population density of at least 1,000 persons per square mile and; • Surrounding census blocks that have an overall density of at least 500 persons per square mile. • Under specific situations, a less densely settled territory may be included as part of a UA or UC. UAs generally involve a nucleus of 50,000 or more people that may or may not contain any cities of 50,000+. UCs represent areas of at least 2,500 but less than 50,000 persons.
Rural	Places of less than 2,500 persons and areas outside of incorporated and census-designated places and the rural portions of extended cities.	All territory, population, and housing units located outside a UA and UC not designated as urban. It typically represents open country and settlements with fewer than 2,500 residents.
Metropolitan/Nonmetropolitan Typology (OMB)		
Metropolitan	Central counties with one or more cities of at least 50,000 residents or an urbanized area of 50,000 or more and a total area population of at least 100,000 persons. Surrounding counties could be included in the metro area if they were economically tied to the central counties (i.e., 15%	Central counties with one or more UAs of 50,000 or more residents and outlying counties that are economically tied to the central counties (i.e., 25% of workers living in the outlying counties commute to the central counties, or 25% or more of the employment in the outlying counties are made up of commuters from the central counties). There is no longer a total area population

	Previous	*Current*
	of their workers commuting, or "metropolitan character" reflected in population density, urbanization, and population growth).	requirement of 100,000 people or more that must be met.
Nonmetropolitan	Any area not located in a metropolitan area.	*Micropolitan Area*: Any nonmetropolitan county with a UC of at least 10,000 but not more than 49,999 persons. An outlying county is included if population commuting to the central micropolitan county for employment is 25% or more, or if 25% or more of the employment in the outlying county is made up of commuters from the central county. *Noncore Area*: Any nonmetro county not meeting the micropolitan designation. Contains no city, town, or urban cluster of at least 10,000 people.
Other Typology (Economic Research Service)		
Rural-Urban Continuum Codes	A nine-item coding system that subdivides metropolitan counties into three levels based on the size of their population, and six levels that differentiate nonmetropolitan areas by their degree of urbanization and adjacency to a metropolitan area(s). Specifically, a code of "1" refers to metropolitan counties having a population of one million persons or more; a "2" represents metropolitan counties with 250,000 to just under 1 million persons; and a "3" is assigned to metro counties with less than 250,000 persons. As for nonmetropolitan areas, a code of "4" represents those counties with an urban population of 20,000 or more persons and located adjacent to a metropolitan area, and a code of "5" is applied to nonmetropolitan counties with the 20,000+ urban population, but not adjacent to a metropolitan area. Nonmetro areas that are assigned a code of "6" have an urban population of 2,500–19,999 and are situated adjacent to a metro area, and those receiving a code of "7" have an urban population between 2,500 and 19,999, but are not adjacent to a metro area. A code of "8" refers to a county with less than 2,500 urban population and geographically adjacent to a metropolitan area of any size. The county code of "9" is assigned to nonmetropolitan areas having an urban population of under 2,500 persons and not located adjacent to a metropolitan county of any size.	

The Rural-Urban Continuum Codes

A third typology that has captured the interest of researchers and policy analysts is the Rural-Urban Continuum Codes, a classification developed by the Economic Research Service of the U.S. Department of Agriculture. The strength of this typology is that it links aspects of the rural/urban classification system with those of the CBSA typology. As such, it allows more detailed assessments to be undertaken of the demographic, economic, and social shifts taking place in U.S. counties.

The Rural-Urban Continuum Codes begins by placing all counties into their appropriate metropolitan and nonmetropolitan categories (using the new measures released by the OMB in 2003).[2] Metro counties are then separated into one of three categories based upon the size of their metro areas (see the lower portion of Table 11.1). Nonmetro areas, on the other hand, are classified into one of six categories based upon their level of urbanization and adjacency to a metropolitan area (Economic Research Service, 2004). For example, the first nonmetro category (code 4) captures counties with an urban population of 20,000 or more that adjoin a metro area (of any population size), whereas the last category (code 9) refers to nonmetro counties having an urban population of under 2,500 and not contiguous to any metro area.

Which Typology to Use?[3]

The classification systems described above can be used to examine conditions and trends in rural America. The typology you use should be guided by at least three considerations: the specific geographic level that you wish to examine, how recent your data must be, and the level of proficiency you have in undertaking data analysis. The rural/urban typology offers a good bit of detail because rural and urban areas are the product of careful analysis of census block data. But the process of defining areas that are urban or rural is complex, and census block-level data are not always up-to-date. The rural-urban continuum classification system has similar features; it provides an excellent mechanism for generating detailed information on rural America, but it requires the user to have excellent skills at mining and analyzing data in order to build the nine groupings that are associated with this typology.

Although it lacks the level of detail offered by other two typologies, the metropolitan/nonmetropolitan (i.e., micro and noncore) classification scheme

---

[2]Whereas the 2003 OMB list divides nonmetropolitan counties into two categories— micropolitan and noncore—the Rural-Urban Continuum Codes does not do so, keeping the counties combined into a single nonmetro grouping.

[3]A variety of other typologies have been developed, most notably by the Economic Research Service. Our intent is not to review all the possible typologies in this chapter, but rather to highlight the concepts that are the most commonplace in the research literature and major government reports.

represents a straightforward and valuable approach for exploring conditions and trends in rural America. Furthermore, a wide array of social, demographic, and economic data is available on a metro/nonmetro basis. With the implementation of the American Community Survey (ACS) in 2005, sample survey data on several key social and economic indicators are available for exploring rural America. The ACS provides annual estimates for larger populations (65,000+ persons), whereas 3-year and 5-year averages are available for areas with 20,000+ persons and areas with smaller populations, respectively (the 5-year data will have its first release in 2010) (U.S. Census Bureau, 2009a). This means that annual ACS data are available for the largest 800 counties and 520 places, and 3-year data are available for 1,882 counties and 2,081 places. But only 5-year averages will be provided for the smallest counties and places (1,337 of the 3,219 counties and 23,211 of the 25,292 places, respectively) in the United States (U.S. Census Bureau, 2009b). One consequence of the sampling procedures used for the ACS is that data for rural communities will be less current and have a larger sampling error than those available for large cities.

Given that one of the main goals of this chapter is to profile some of the issues shaping the well-being of rural communities today, we employ the metro/nonmetro typology to guide our discussion and analysis. As such, whenever we use the terms *rural communities* or *rural areas*, we are typically referring to nonmetro areas, including the micropolitan and noncore counties that together constitute the nation's nonmetropolitan areas.

Key Demographic Trends

A number of articles and reports written in recent years give focus on the state of rural America (Hamilton, Hamilton, Duncan, & Colocousis, 2008; Johnson, 2006). These reports highlight many challenges facing rural areas, but there is a set of factors that is likely to have significant bearing on the well-being of many rural communities for some time to come. These factors include demographic and economic changes occurring in rural America, as well as significant disparities in the income and educational levels of nonmetro residents relative to their metropolitan counterparts. We will highlight these important trends in the next few sections of this chapter.

The Nonmetro Population: Losing Ground

Maintaining a vibrant community depends, in part, on the presence of a stable or expanding population. When people remain in a community and new people migrate into the area, the general assumption is that good things are occurring, such as the availability of good jobs, access to decent schools, or areas with good housing and quality health services. Slow and persistent outflows of people from a county, on the other hand, can be symptomatic of an area that is facing deterioration in its social and economic base.

What has been the nature of the population shifts across the United States? Real gains in population were pervasive in many areas of the United States during the 1990s, with population expansion touching five of every six counties between 1990 and 2000. Those suffering declines tended to be agriculture-dependent counties located in the midsection of the nation. The pattern since 2000, however, has been quite different. Whereas close to 60% of U.S. counties witnessed population increases after 2000, the number of counties suffering population declines between 2000 and 2008 is three times higher than it was during the 1990-2000 period.

More problematic has been the pattern of population gains and losses by metropolitan status. As Figure 11.1 reveals, the lion's share of metropolitan counties (more than 82%) have experienced growth over the span of 2000–2008. The pattern for micropolitan counties, on the other hand, has been mixed—60% have experienced population expansion, 40% have suffered declines. Where the loss of population has been most apparent is among the noncore counties of the United States—nearly two of every three counties lost population between 2000 and 2008.

Despite the high number of noncore counties experiencing population declines in recent years, the aggregate number of people living in the nation's noncore areas has increased slightly since 2000 (+0.6% increase). Of course, this percentage growth is minuscule when contrasted with the

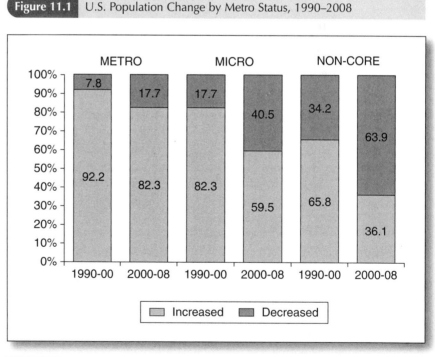

Figure 11.1 U.S. Population Change by Metro Status, 1990–2008

SOURCE: U.S. Census Bureau, Decennial; U.S. Census Bureau, Population Estimates; 2003 OMB Rurality Definitions.

2000–2008 growth pattern of micro (+4.1%) and metro counties (+9.2%). Despite the positive growth in population in micro and noncore areas, America's population is becoming increasingly concentrated in metropolitan counties; 83.5% of the U.S. population now lives in metro counties (up from 82% in 1990). Shares of the population living in micropolitan and noncore counties have been declining gradually since 1990 (see Table 11.2).

Table 11.2 U.S. Population by Metropolitan Status, 1990–2008

County Type	1990		2000		2008		% Change 1990–2000	% Change 2000–2008
	No.	%	No.	%	No.	%		
Metro	204,015,763	82.0	232,579,940	82.6	253,902,396	83.5	14.0	9.2
Micro	26,340,848	10.6	28,955,198	10.3	30,153,791	9.9	9.9	4.1
Noncore	18,429,635	7.4	19,882,479	7.1	20,003,537	6.6	7.9	0.6

SOURCE: U.S. Census Bureau, Decennial Census, 1990 and 2000; Population Estimates, 2008.

NOTE: The 2003 OMB metropolitan classification system is used to define all metro, micro, and noncore counties reported in this table.

Rural Americans: Getting Older, More Diverse

In general, America's population distribution is shifting in important ways. Simply put, nonmetro areas are losing a larger share of their young residents (those under 15 years old) while simultaneously experiencing a growth in their 65+ population. The numbers of youth under 15 years old living in micro and noncore counties have dropped by 4.3% and 10%, respectively, over the 2000–2008 period. At the same time, the 65+ age cohort has swelled by nearly 10% in micropolitan areas and by 6% in noncore areas of the United States.

Moreover, nonmetro areas are becoming more diverse (Saenz, 2008). White residents—be they metro, micro, or noncore in nature—continue to represent the lion's share of people in the United States. But Blacks and Hispanics are increasing their presence across all county types. Of special interest is the relatively high growth of Hispanics in both micropolitan and noncore counties (see Figure 11.2). The expansion of Hispanics was explosive in the nonmetro United States during the course of the 1990s (i.e., increasing by nearly 67% in micro counties and by 58% in noncore areas). Their expansion since 2000 remains high, a stark contrast to the slower pace of growth found among whites and African Americans. Without question, cultural diversity is on the rise in many parts of rural America.

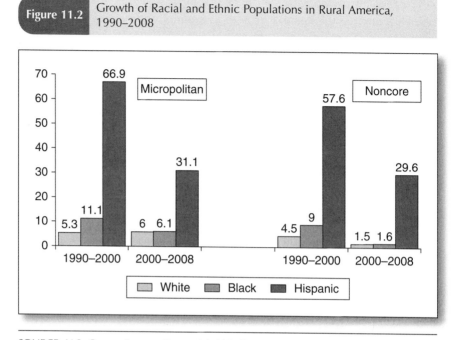

Figure 11.2 Growth of Racial and Ethnic Populations in Rural America, 1990–2008

SOURCE: U.S. Census Bureau, Decennial; U.S. Census Bureau, Population Estimates; 2003 OMB Rurality Definitions.

The Changing Rural Economy

Globalization and technology have brought major changes to rural America (Gibbs, Kusmin, & Cromartie, 2005). Thanks to production-enhancing and labor-saving technologies, U.S. agriculture is more efficient now than at any time in history. Moreover, global competition is accelerating the exportation of low-skilled manufacturing jobs to less developed countries. For manufacturing firms staying put in rural areas, survival has meant shedding low-skilled workers and relying on better technology and/or a smaller pool of better skilled workers to produce their goods (Bartel & Sicherman, 1998; McGranahan, 2001). The long-held image of rural America as the haven for agricultural and low-skilled manufacturing is no longer true (Johnson, 2006). Rural America's historic competitive advantage—lower cost labor and an abundance of natural resources—is less of an asset in today's global marketplace (Munnich & Schrock, 2003).

The declining role of agriculture and manufacturing as key drivers of America's rural economy is highlighted in Figure 11.3. As the chart reveals, only a fraction of the workforce (full- or part-time) living in micropolitan or noncore counties in 1990 were engaged in goods-producing sector jobs (the sector that includes farming, forestry, agricultural services, and manufacturing, as well as mining and construction industries). Furthermore, the proportion of workers employed in this sector has been steadily falling. Service-producing sector jobs (i.e., transportation, utilities, wholesale/retail trade, finance/insurance/real

Figure 11.3 — Employment by Key Sectors in the Nonmetro United States, 1990–2007

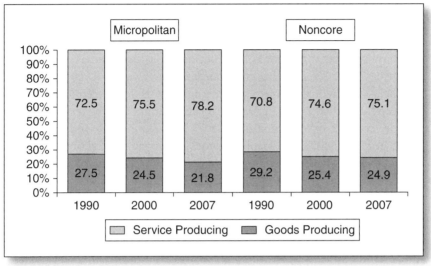

SOURCE: Bureau of Economic Analysis, Regional Economic Information Systems.

estate, government/government enterprises, and services industries), on the other hand, have been on an upward trajectory for some time, now representing better than 78% of all full- and part-time jobs in micropolitan areas and three-fourths of all jobs in the noncore counties of the United States.

Despite these major structural changes in the rural economy, perceptions remain strong that agriculture and manufacturing remain the bedrock of rural America's economy. A 2001 national survey of urban, suburban, and rural residents, for example, found that most respondents identified agriculture, farming, or ranching as the main economic forces in rural America, with a smaller percentage of people selecting factory work as the major driver of the rural economy (W.K. Kellogg Foundation, 2002). Such misperceptions have resulted in ongoing efforts by leaders and economic development organizations to invest time and resources in recruiting and attracting goods-producing sector firms to rural areas, believing that these are the best options for refilling other goods-producing sector jobs that have been lost in past years.

Self-Employment: A Bright Star in the Rural Economy?

One component of the nonmetro economy often overlooked by local leaders is the increasing presence of the self-employed, the one-person operation that is becoming a more dominant part of the economic landscape of rural America. As Low (2004) and Goetz (2005) note, proprietor-owned enterprises are serving as vital sources of new full- and part-time jobs in rural America.

In fact, data show that nonfarm proprietorships have expanded from 3.5 million jobs in 1990 to nearly 5.6 million today (a net increase of nearly 60%). At this pace of growth, it is estimated that one in three nonmetro workers will be self-employed by the year 2015 (Goetz, 2008).

The downside of this pattern, however, is that many of these proprietor-owned businesses are struggling to obtain the level of income needed to thrive in today's competitive marketplace. On average, the earnings garnered by nonfarm proprietors in micro and noncore counties in the United States are well below those of their metro counterparts. With few exceptions, the gap between the self-employed in the metro United States and those in micro and noncore counties has widened since 1990 (see Figure 11.4). Today, nonfarm proprietors in micro and noncore counties are barely making one half of the average incomes being secured by those self-employed in metro areas.

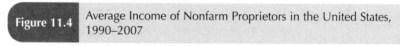

Figure 11.4 Average Income of Nonfarm Proprietors in the United States, 1990–2007

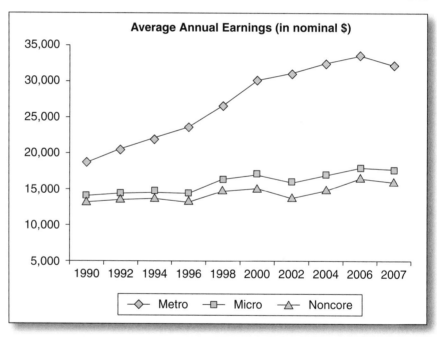

SOURCE: Bureau of Economic Analysis, Regional Economic Information Systems.

Low Income, Low Education, and High Poverty: Continued Realities in Rural America

With the shifting composition of the nonmetro economy, an important question is whether these changes have resulted in any appreciable changes in wages and salaries of workers. In a nutshell, the move from an agriculture- and manufacturing-based economy to one dominated by services, retail trade, and other service sector-producing jobs has not resulted in any substantial improvement in the average earnings of workers in rural America. In fact, the earnings gap between metro and nonmetro workers has worsened in recent years.

As Figure 11.5 indicates, the average income earned by metro workers in 1990 stood at just over $24,000. Micropolitan-based wage and salary earners, on the other hand, made nearly $18,400, or 76% of the earning levels of metro workers. For noncore workers, average earnings were even lower—$16,657—or about 69 cents on the dollar relative to their metro counterparts. Recent figures (for 2007) reveal that micropolitan workers are making 71% of the average earnings of metro-based employees, whereas the noncore wage and salary workers are barely realizing two thirds of the average salaries of their metropolitan peers. Indeed, the types of jobs being created in rural America over the past two decades have paid lower wages/salaries, have often involved less than full-time work, and have come with fewer benefits. Simply put, the expansion of service-producing sector industries in rural areas has resulted in a further weakening in the earnings of many nonmetro workers over the 1990–2007 period.

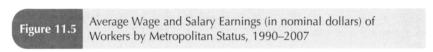

Figure 11.5 Average Wage and Salary Earnings (in nominal dollars) of Workers by Metropolitan Status, 1990–2007

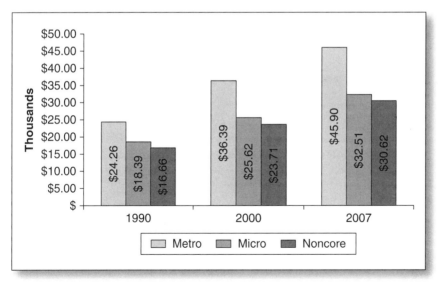

SOURCE: Bureau of Economic Analysis, Regional Economic Information Systems.

Education Credentials Still Weak

Human capital theorists have long ago noted a link between earnings and the human capital attributes of individuals (Becker, 1962; Schultz, 1961).

Simply stated, education matters a lot when it comes to income; the better the level of education, the higher the remuneration the person receives (Provasnik et al., 2007). Recent studies conducted of nonmetropolitan areas arrive at this same finding—higher levels of educational attainment translate into a higher rate of growth in both per capita income and employment (Goetz & Rupasingha, 2003).

Unfortunately, as Figure 11.6 illustrates, micropolitan and noncore counties remain well behind metro areas in terms of the percentage of adults with high levels of education (i.e., baccalaureate degree or higher). The proportion of noncore county-based adults with a college education is nearly 50% lower than in metro areas. Although the gap is less sizable in micropolitan counties, the difference of 11 percentage points is not insignificant. No doubt, the continued absence of a large cadre of well-educated workers is dampening the capacity of micro and noncore counties to make much headway in reducing the earnings gap with metro areas.

Figure 11.6 Percent of Adult Population (25+ years old) With a Bachelor's Degree or Higher

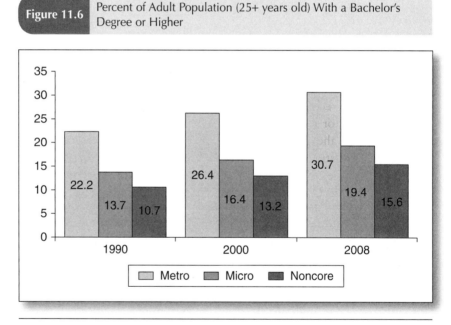

SOURCE: U.S. Census Bureau, Decennial; Economic Modeling Specialists, Inc. (Spring 2009).

Poverty on the Upswing

Given the limited pool of well-educated residents and the lagging salaries and wages associated with jobs in rural America, it is no surprise that nonmetro areas represent the lion's share of our nation's high-poverty counties (i.e., poverty rates of 20% or higher for individuals). It was not too long ago that social scientists were guardedly optimistic about the declining rates of poverty in rural America that seemed to be taking hold during the 1990s (Beale, 2004; Jolliffe, 2004). But the optimism proved short-lived. Since 2000, nonmetro poverty levels have been slowing inching upward (from 13.4% in 2000 to 15.4% in 2007). Drawing on the Small Area Income and Poverty Estimates (SAIPE) from the U.S. Census, we were able to examine county poverty rates (i.e., a 3-year average for the 2005–2007 period) by metro status. We found that 503 counties in the United States are now classified as high-poverty counties. Approximately 13% of them are metropolitan counties, 24% are micro counties, and a sizable 63% are noncore counties. It is these more remote, less populated noncore counties that are facing the greatest challenges in today's economy given their high rates of poverty, the low educational levels of workers, and the limited availability of well-paying jobs.

Achieving Vitality: What Strategies Makes Sense for Rural Areas?

The major demographic and socioeconomic shifts showcased in this chapter illustrate some of the challenges that many rural areas face in an ever-changing global environment. These adjustments mean that new ways for strengthening the economies of nonmetro areas need to be explored, as well as strategies for mobilizing a larger cadre of people to tackle the tough decisions that lie ahead for these communities. Our intent is to describe a series of possible strategies that might make sense for rural areas to consider in light of the conditions and trends that we have highlighted in this chapter. Of course, we fully recognize that these options deserve to be debated and validated by the "on-the-ground" knowledge and insights of local people, organizations, and leaders to ensure that the right mix of strategies that best aligns with their assets, strengths, and hopes for their rural areas are pursued.

- *Expand Civic Engagement*: The capacity of local people, organizations, and institutions to come together for the purpose of acting on opportunities and challenges is critical to the health of any community. But finding the right mechanism for building trust, for deliberating on issues, and acting on key priorities will not be easy in many nonmetro areas. For many of these areas, the process of strengthening civic engagement is going to be complicated by the upswing in racial and ethnic diversity now occurring in more and more micro and noncore counties. Recent research by Putnam (2007, p. 141) suggests that racial and ethnic expansion weakens local social solidarity and trust, at least on a short- and mid-term basis. Despite these difficulties, investing in new forms of civic participation will be important. Models of civic dialogue, deliberation, and engagement—such as those advanced by Everyday Democracy, National Issues Forum, and the Northwest Area Foundation Horizons Project—represent worthy approaches that nonmetro areas might wish to explore. As Putnam notes (2007, p. 164), locally based programs that seek to reach out to new immigrant communities constitute powerful tools for mutual learning. In our view, the civic engagement models we note above can serve as an important process for helping to build a multicultural, broad-based corps of citizens involved in addressing important local issues.

- *Develop Indigenous Leaders and Committed Citizens*: Increasing the capacity for community action requires officials and citizens to enhance their skills in initiating action, organizing groups, and leading others. Having leaders who can build bridges across the historical, cultural, or economic divides that exist in many communities, as well as being able to access resources from outside the community, can make a difference in whether a development project succeeds or not. Many communities also have residents, both young and old, who are hesitant to get involved but can make significant contributions. Young people, for example, have a lot of energy and enthusiasm for serving the community but are often underappreciated and underutilized (see Israel, 2004). Thus, creating opportunities for leaders to enhance their skills and citizens to fully engage in community activities is an important strategy for many rural communities.

- *Build on the Demographic Realities of the County*: The compositional changes that have taken place in rural America make clear that the population is aging and diversifying in terms of racial/ethnic composition. These specific patterns will vary from community to community, but population changes will bring opportunities for developing products and services tailored to the needs of specific groups. This might include adding ethnic foods for a growing Hispanic population or expanding health services in places with an aging population.

- *Explore New Agricultural Markets*: Nonmetro areas with significant dependence on agriculture continue to struggle in their ability to retain their population and to keep their economies vibrant. Rural areas that capture sizable earnings from agriculture can explore opportunities to add value to locally grown agricultural products. These include attracting food-processing plants or finding new uses for such commodities (such as nutriceuticals and functional foods). At the same time, activities such as on-farm recreational enterprises (hunting, fishing, bird watching, and hiking) represent other value-added strategies for stemming the loss of agriculture-related employment in farm-dependent rural communities. For small-scale farmers, expanding the direct marketing of products to consumers or area businesses and institutions (such as restaurants, hospitals, and schools) holds some promise of generating additional revenues. Establishing regionally based small farm cooperatives could provide a mechanism for ensuring that the volume and diversity of products needed to support direct marketing activities are in place.

- *Strengthen the Skills of Those in Low-Wage Jobs*: Low-skill jobs are on the decline in rural America, and the well-being of rural communities is becoming increasingly linked to the capacity of their residents to participate in more skill-intensive sectors of the economy. A case in point is the rural manufacturing sector. Although many manufacturing firms were key employers of low-skill workers in years past, those remaining in rural areas are demanding higher skilled labor that is capable of managing the new technologies and team-oriented production practices being adopted by these firms. Thus, more skilled occupations will be needed to meet the needs of the current mix of industries located in rural communities. Consequently, a key activity is to pursue an upgrading in the skills of workers now employed in the industries located in micro and noncore areas.

- *Give Greater Focus to the Self-Employed*: Be it by design or necessity, the number of self-employed persons in rural America is continuing to expand, representing about one in five nonmetro workers who are now employed. These constitute important economic resources for rural areas. As such, local governments and economic development organizations can help create a seamless system of support for these individuals, one that taps the diversity of local and regional resources (such as local schools, community colleges, land-grant universities, small business development centers, etc.) that can help strengthen the economic viability of these enterprises. Furthermore, creating microloan programs to support the small financial capital needs of these businesses can be part of the services offered to these local proprietors.

- *Identify and Tap Regional Competitive Assets*: A number of rural counties—especially noncore counties—will experience some rough terrain if they continue down the path of "going solo" with regard to their job creation and industrial recruitment activities. Nonmetro counties can benefit from being open to building strong regional alliances with local governments, economic development organizations, and other appropriate entities. The U.S. Economic Development Administration, for example, has taken a lead role in enhancing the use of regional approaches to economic development in rural America (under the banner of "Know Your Region"). Moreover, the Purdue Center for Rural Development, in partnership with the Indiana Business Research Center, offers worthwhile Web-based data resources that rural areas in the United States can use to assess their regional economic competitiveness. Valuable information and resources are available for nonmetro counties that are willing to embrace regional collaboration as one of the components of their economic development plans.

- *Build on the Natural Resource Amenities of the Area*: The physical beauty and amenities that endow many rural areas have brought scores of new residents to natural resource-rich rural communities over the past 2 to 3 decades. In fact, rural communities with recognized natural resource amenities have consistently outperformed less amenity-rich communities in attracting new residents, retaining current residents, and generating quality jobs for local workers (McGranahan, 1999). Research studies have shown how recreation and tourism development often translates into employment growth, higher wage gains, lower poverty rates, and higher education attainment in rural areas. Areas with undervalued or underappreciated scenic amenities might explore the role of recreation and tourism as a possible economic development strategy.
- *Invest in a 21st-Century Information Technology Infrastructure*: Knowledge- and creative-based occupations are emerging as key contributors to the growth and prosperity of many metro areas. Without question, having access to high-quality communication and information technologies is essential if rural communities have any hope of capturing and benefiting from knowledge and creative class-based employers and workers. Although some would suggest that a digital divide no longer exists in the United States, the reality is that high-speed Internet connections remain more of an exception than the rule in many parts of rural America. Recent studies indicate that rural areas are the least likely to have access to high-speed connections (Horrigan, 2008), and rural residents tend to have the lowest uptake in terms of Internet use (Pew Internet and American Life Project, 2008). In instances where broadband is available, the cost service is often prohibitive for rural customers. Building a 21st-century information and communications system will be critical for facilitating entry by existing nonmetro businesses to global markets, attracting high-skilled jobs, expanding access to more sophisticated courses for its school systems, and employing the use of electronic-based advanced health care resources. A tripartite partnership of public, private, and philanthropic sectors is likely to be one of the best options for strengthening the telecommunications infrastructure of most rural areas of the United States.

Closing Comments

In the early stages of this chapter, we made reference to the notion of "rural utopia" and "rural dystopia." Having presented a host of information on nonmetro areas of the United States, the question is, "Which of the two perspectives best captures the state of rural America today?" Certainly, the outmigration of people from nonmetro areas, the topsy-turvy nature of the rural economy, the earnings gap between nonmetro and metro workers, the lower percentage of well-educated nonmetro adults, and the persistent nature of rural poverty could allow one to easily surmise that rural dystopia is alive and well in rural America. On the other hand, there are rural places, such as natural resource-rich locations, where residents enjoy more prosperous conditions. Thus, it is important to recognize that rural American communities are diverse—culturally, socially, and economically, as well as in their natural resource endowments.

In spite of these continuing challenges, however, rural people and leaders in many locations have the capacity to take important steps that can advance the long-term vitality of their communities. Although we suspect that a rural utopia is unlikely ever to be achieved, supporting and enacting a mix of strategies that we have outlined—especially those that align with the assets, needs, hopes, and aspirations of local residents—is likely to set many rural areas on a path of success in the years ahead.

References

Bartel, A. P., & Sicherman, N. (1998). Technological change and the skill acquisition of young workers. *Journal of Labor Economics, 16,* 718–755.

Beale, C. (2004, February). Anatomy of nonmetro high poverty areas: Common in plight, distinctive in nature. *Amber Waves.* Retrieved July 23, 2009, from http://www.ers.usda.gov/Amberwaves/February04/Features/Anatomy.htm

Becker, G. S. (1962). Investment in human capital: A theoretical analysis. *Journal of Political Economy, 70,* 9–49.

Cromartie, J. (2003, September). Defining rural areas based on new county classifications. *Amber Waves.* Retrieved July 23, 2009, from http://www.ers.usda.gov/Amberwaves/September03/Indicators/BehindData.htm

Economic Research Service. (2004). *Measuring rurality: Rural-urban continuum codes.* Retrieved July 13, 2009, from http://www.ers.usda.gov/Briefing/Rurality/RuralUrbCon/

Florida, R. (2002). *The rise of the creative class.* New York: Basic Books.

Florida, R. (2008). *Who's your city? How the creative economy is making where to live the most important decision of your life.* New York: Basic Books.

FrameWorks Institute. (2007). *The rural learning module.* Retrieved July 23, 2009, from http://www.onlinearc.com/frameworks/index.html

Gibbs, R., Kusmin, L., & Cromartie, J. (2005). *Low-skill employment and the changing economy of rural America* (Economic Research Service Report No. 10). Washington, DC: U.S. Department of Agriculture. Retrieved July 23, 2009, from http://explorebrainerdlakes.com/pdf/regional/LowSkillEmployment.pdf

Goetz, S. J. (2005). *Searching for jobs: The growing importance of rural proprietors.* Mississippi State, MS: Southern Rural Development Center. Retrieved July 23, 2009, from http://srdc.msstate.edu/measuring/series/goetz.pdf

Goetz, S. J. (2008). *Self-employment in rural America: The new economic reality.* Columbia, MO: Rural Sociological Society. Retrieved July 23, 2009, from http://ruralsociology.org/pubs/RuralRealities/RuralRealities2-3.pdf

Goetz, S. J., & Rupasingha, A. (2003). The returns to higher education: Estimates for the 48 contiguous states. *Economic Development Quarterly, 17,* 337–351.

Hamilton, L. C., Hamilton, L. R., Duncan, C. M., & Colocousis, C. R. (2008). *Place matters: Challenges and opportunities in four rural Americas.* Durham: University of New Hampshire, The Carsey Institute. Retrieved July 23, 2009, from http://www.carseyinstitute.unh.edu/publications/Report_PlaceMatters.pdf

Horrigan, J. B. (2008). *Home broadband adoption 2008: Adoption stalls for low-income Americans even as many broadband users opt for premium services that give them more speed.* Retrieved January 21, 2009, from http://www.pewInternet.org/pdfs/PIP_Broadband_2008.pdf

Israel, G.D. (2004). Enhancing the rural South's quality of life: Leveraging development through educational institutions. *Southern Rural Sociology, 20,* 1–24.

Johnson, K. (2006). *Demographic trends in rural and small town America.* Durham: University of New Hampshire, The Carsey Institute. Retrieved July 23, 2009, from http://www.carseyinstitute.unh.edu/publications/Report_Demographics.pdf

Jolliffe, D. (2004). *Rural poverty at a glance* (Rural Development Research Report No. 100). Washington, DC: U.S. Department of Agriculture, Economic Research Service. Retrieved July 23, 2009, from http://www.ers.usda.gov/publications/rdrr100/rdrr100.pdf

Kraenzel, C. F. (1980). *The social cost of space in the Youland.* Bozeman, MT: Big Sky Books.

Low, S. (2004). Regional asset indicators: Entrepreneurship breadth and depth. *Main Street Economist.* Retrieved July 23, 2009, from http://www.kc.frb.org/Regional Affairs/Mainstreet/MSE_0904.pdf

McGranahan, D. A. (1999). *Natural amenities drive rural population change* (Agricultural Economic Report No. 781). Washington, DC: U.S. Department of Agriculture, Economic Research Service. Retrieved July 23, 2009, from http://www.ers.usda.gov/publications/aer781/aer781.pdf

McGranahan, D. A. (2001). New economy manufacturing meets old economy education policies in the South. *Rural America, 15,* 19–27.

Munnich, L. W., & Schrock, G. (2003). Rural knowledge clusters: The challenge of rural economic prosperity. In N. Walzer (Ed.), *The American Midwest: Managing change in rural transition.* Armonk, NY: Sharpe.

North Dakota State Data Center. (2009). *Rural/urban/metro/nonmetro and frontier discussion: Definitions and North Dakota maps.* Retrieved July 3, 2009, from http://www.ndsu.nodak.edu/sdc/data/ruralurbanmetrononmetro.htm

Office of Management and Budget. (2003). *Revised definitions of metropolitan statistical areas* (OMB Bulletin No. 03–04). Washington, DC: Author.

Pew Internet and American Life Project. (2008). *Demographics of Internet users: November 19-December 20, 2008 tracking survey.* Retrieved January 21, 2009, from http://www.pewInternet.org/trends/User_Demo_10%2020%2008.htm

Provasnik, S., Kewal Ramani, A., Coleman, M. M., Gilbertson, L., Herring, W., & Xie, Q. (2007). *Status of education in rural America* (NCES 2007–040). Washington, DC: U.S. Department of Education, National Center for Education Statistics, Institute of Education Sciences.

Putnam, R. D. (2007). E pluribus unum: Diversity and community in the twenty-first century. *Scandinavian Political Studies, 30,* 137–174.

Saenz, R. (2008). *A profile of Latinos in rural America.* Durham: University of New Hampshire, The Carsey Institute. Retrieved July 23, 2009, from http://www.carseyinstitute.unh.edu/publications/FS_RuralLatinos_08.pdf

Schultz, T. W. (1961). Investment in human capital. *American Economic Review, 51,* 1–17.

Simmel, G. (1950). The metropolis and mental life. In K. H. Wolff (Ed.), *The sociology of Georg Simmel* (pp. 409–424). New York: Free Press.

U.S. Census Bureau. (2005). *Census block groups: Cartographic boundary files description and metadata.* Retrieved November 23, 2009, from http://www .census.gov/geo/www/cob/bg_metadata.html

U.S. Census Bureau. (2008). *Census 2000 urban and rural classification.* Retrieved June 24, 2009, from http://www.census.gov/geo/www/ua/ua_2k.html

U.S. Census Bureau. (2009a). *Design and methodology: American Community Survey.* Washington, DC: U.S. Government Printing Office. Retrieved July 16, 2009, from http://www.census.gov/acs/www/SBasics/desgn_meth.htm

U.S. Census Bureau. (2009b). *How to use the data: Overview of geographic areas, American Community Survey (ACS).* Retrieved July 17, 2009, from http://www .census.gov/acs/www/UseData/geo.htm

U.S. Department of Commerce. (1994). *Geographic areas reference manual.* Retrieved November 23, 2009, from http://www.census.gov/geo/www/GARM/ GARMcont.pdf

Warner, W. K. (1974). Rural society in a post-industrial age. *Rural Sociology, 39,* 306–318.

Whiting, L. R. (Ed.). (1974). *Communities left behind: Alternatives for development.* Ames: Iowa State University Press.

Wirth, L. (1938). Urbanism as a way of life. *American Journal of Sociology, 44,* 1–24.

W.K. Kellogg Foundation. (2002). *Perceptions of rural America.* Battle Creek, MI: Author.

Wood, R. E. (2008). *Survival of rural America: Small victories and bitter harvests.* Lawrence: University Press of Kansas.

12

Community Development Challenges in Inner-City Neighborhoods

Jeffrey S. Lowe and William M. Harris

BEHAVIOR OBJECTIVES

After studying this chapter and completing the online learning activities, students should be able to

1. Present a summary discussion of the issues that confront African Americans that stimulate the need for community action to improve the quality of life in their neighborhoods.

2. Provide a definition of the African American community that describes the milieu in which community development occurs in inner-city neighborhoods.

3. Summarize the historical development of the African American experience within the context of oppression, discrimination, and racism in the United States.

4. Explain the community development theoretical relations that guide African American inner-city development.

5. Describe the roles of various actors in the African American community development process.

6. Employ community development research methods using the case studies that are presented in the chapter.

7. Identify the broad-ranging community development activities that are most desirable in inner-city neighborhoods.

8. Name four major attributes that help bring about the level of success and/or failure experienced by community leadership in community development.

9. Articulate a middle option to community development processes that offers a clear plan of action for fostering black self-determination and leadership as well as support and assistance from beyond inner-city neighborhoods.

10. Encourage the application of one or more of the community development options that are offered in the chapter.

Introduction

In this chapter, we present the rationale, applicable approaches, and potential consequences of community development applications in African American neighborhoods. Based on more than 50 years of combined experiences in practical application and classroom instruction, we contend that this discussion remains sorely needed to provide guidance to change agents, policy makers, and inner-city residents who commit to purposeful social change in difficult-to-reach and long-oppressed communities. Equally, community development urgently needs to be an expanded activity in black communities that are under dire stress and neglect.

People wish to be free of trouble, major problems, oppression of all kinds, and threats as well as barriers to their future development. In our very complex society, people are nearly always vulnerable to conditions that they believe make them less able to realize their hopes and needs for personal and community development. Awareness of needs may depend upon individual perceptions, observations, and information available about the environment in which the needs arise. Also, the awareness of needs may be heavily influenced by the media or outsiders who either have interest in potential changes in the community or wish to sway the direction and intensity of the sense of needs held by residents (Carpini, 1998). These realities make for a very complex calculus when consideration is given to leadership and support pertaining to problem solving in the most oppressed communities in the United States.

What follows is a discussion of the processes that constitute community development, with a focus upon inner-city or African American neighborhoods. It begins with an overview of history, terminology, and theory regarding community development in inner-city neighborhoods. Case studies follow that offer practical examples and brief descriptions of intent, process, and trade-offs deriving from the respective activities. After proposing a "middle option" for undertaking community development processes that sustains black self-determination as well as support and assistance external from inner-city neighborhoods, the chapter concludes with reflections and lessons for anyone wishing to advance African American community development.

Historical Overview

More than a half-century ago, a study of terms describing community was reported with nearly a hundred definitions in existence. There were common features and significant differences among the variety of meanings for the term (Hillery, 1955). Here, we accept the geographic designation of a neighborhood or collection of contiguous neighborhoods as the definition of community (Ferguson & Stoutland, 1999). However, the multitude of definitions, including this one, does not distract from the present discussion. Our definition for the African American community is that collection of people identifiable as black (racially) residents of areas of the city suffering under the social, political, and economic oppression of a white racist state (Harris, 1976). The term *inner-city neighborhoods* is a typical synonym for poor African American communities. More importantly, this meaning of African American communities holds equally today because the fundamental crisis of race in America has not varied greatly enough to justify another paradigm. The boundaries of former ghettoes may be more elastic than a quarter-century ago, but it is the condition of oppression that produces the need for community development.

Case Study 12.1 Poverty and Service-Learning

Stanford University created a course titled "Poverty and Homelessness in America" to introduce students to service-learning in their local community. Students sign up for a semester-long course, participating in 8 to 10 hours of on-site service-learning per week. Undergraduates are placed in venues serving both homeless families and youth, as well as in winter shelters and schools for homeless children. Students are given partners or placed in teams, and they serve in a variety of functions, including working as assistant case managers, serving as tutors, or providing outreach services for homeless youth. Weekly readings are assigned to supplement the experience, with the students also required to write papers and submit reflections on their service. Students are encouraged to appreciate the multidisciplinary aspects of the course, with a goal of understanding the history and social science of homelessness. The professor for the course, Albert Camarillo, notes that while service-learning courses require a heavy commitment from educators, the feedback given by students indicates a higher level of appreciation for issues of the homeless than would otherwise be possible.

SOURCE: Harkovy, I., & Donovan, B. M. (Eds.). (2000). *Connecting past and present concepts and models for service-learning in history.* Washington, DC: American Association for Higher Education.

African American Experience With Oppression

The 21st century has brought about new language in spelling out the nature and consequences of the oppression put upon some by others. Formally, this negative behavior may have been explicitly referred to as *oppression* rather than the more politically preferred terms of *disadvantage; racial and gender inequality;* and *socially, politically, and economically challenged* far more typical of the past decade or so. Although the new terminology may bring greater comfort in polite company discussion, it fails to relate the reality of those put upon. Clearly then, the implication of the new terminology is to disguise the realities of the calculated behaviors of those who limit the development of others for a variety of reasons. Therefore, here, the more accurate term of *oppression* is employed to present the realities of people who have not earned the station of inferior opportunities for full development; rather, they have been shut out by the more powerful and influential.

Oppression is the willful exercise by some that is calculated to limit or arrest the full development of others. It matters not that individuals participate in the exercise consciously. If the system of laws, administrative practices, and traditions (individual and corporate) serve to the end of denial of full opportunity for development, then oppression exists. In this chapter, the oppression of African Americans is summarized. Of course, other racial, ethnic, and cultural groups have been oppressed in the American context. However, only one racial group has a history of chattel slavery and pervasive discrimination due almost entirely to skin color. It is then the focus upon this group that affords the most challenging demands for redress.

Similarly, it is useful to define racism. Racism requires two fundamental conditions to exist. The concept requires that one group holds another to be inherently inferior for any number of reasons. Such a holding is prejudice. Prejudice may be either positive or negative. For example, the prejudice to fear snakes may be useful in avoiding danger if one were to live in an area of dangerous snakes. A second condition that racism requires is that the prejudiced group possesses and uses its authority, influence, or power to implement policies that institutionalize negative impacts stemming from its prejudices (Carmichael & Hamilton, 1967). Given these required parameters, few African Americans could be racist in America, even if they were prejudiced toward whites. Also, it is important to understand that racism and discrimination are not the same. Discrimination is an outgrowth of racism. Discrimination occurs at the individual, group, and institutional levels. Over a period of time, discrimination based upon racist orientation and promulgated through institutionalization of structural inequalities leads to the superiority of one group over another (Bonilla-Silva, 2006). An additional result is the continued privilege afforded one group at the expense of another (Feagin, 2001).

Community Development Theory

Our effort here is to comment upon theory that explains community development as a process. The reality is that there exists no unique set of principles or theories that fits all aspects of community development. Community development is quite interdisciplinary and borrows themes and propositions from a variety of social sciences. In our imperfect efforts to accurately guess human behavior, we must settle for continued attempts to improve theory building. As a process designed to assist in improving the quality of life for individuals and groups, it is essential to make community development as accurate, effective, and empowering as possible.

The challenge to building a theoretical base for community development is determining its place on a continuum between science and art. Put another way, is community development a science, an art, or a mixture of the two? Although labeled and defined as a process, it would be difficult to justify and convincingly explain community development solely as a science. One would have to demonstrate that the process has a body of postulates, propositions, or theorems that are unique to community development. To qualify as a science, community development would have to be verifiable. To be acceptable as a legitimate science, community development would have to be able to replicate its actions along well-articulated parameters. In turn, to be an art, community development must be able to explain itself within the understanding of participants and observers. As an art, it must represent some state of being, imagined or real, and offer recognizable techniques and application to principles considered legitimate.

The reality, however, is that community development, on a continuum, is a mixture of science and art. In its demands for rigor and discipline, community development becomes a sister to science. In its practice orientation, community development becomes a brother to art. Community development in this respect is not greatly different from the social sciences and professions that employ interdisciplinary relationships with other areas of study and practice that began to emerge during the second half of the 20th century and be influenced by the civil rights movement.

Beginning in the 1950s, urban renewal called for restoration of central business districts by ridding the nation of blight and slum areas mostly inhabited by African Americans; thus, the process was euphemistically called "Negro Removal." Then the civil rights era took hold, and African Americans renewed demands for social justice and full rights as first-class citizens. It is this background of response to citizen needs and the demands of advocates for support that brought community development into full force. Moreover, through advocacy, the voiceless and underrepresented could be brought to a more fair and competitive level in the decision-making process (Davidoff, 1965).

The notion of advocacy (more an art than a science) was not new to the African American community. Always in a challenging mode to white racism and economic and political oppression, blacks were aware that mutual support and outside assistance were necessary when engaging battles for structural change and racial justice. In fact, it was the activity of the civil rights movement that excited Davidoff and other planners to speak to the social ills brought by white racism and societal oppression of blacks (Knowles & Prewitt, 1969). Malcolm X (also known as El-Hajj Malik El-Shabazz), Dr. Martin Luther King, Jr., St. Claire Drake, and many other African American activists, scholars, and organizational leaders were the catalyst to the advancement of the advocacy movement during the mid-20th century. Advocacy planning, however, has not been without critics. For example, Lisa Peattie (1968) offered that the process may co-opt African Americans from the streets to the complex and narrow political actions of decision making;

thus, African American contributions in the social change movement may become less effective. Similarly, other findings support our orientation. Paul Kivel (1969) writes, "Racism affects each and every aspect of our lives (all the time) whether people of color are present or not" (p. 9). Omi and Winant (1994) maintain that race is an intractable and enduring feature of the United States. Finally, Andrew Hacker (1992) posits that the races, African American and white, remain separate and unequal. Within the context presented here, we offer possible scenarios that may be employed by community development agents in finding solutions to inner-city African American problems.

Case Studies of Community Development Activities

An effective method for learning the value and effectiveness of a process is the review of case studies. Case studies are examples of models applied in the solution of a problem, often explaining new standards for improving or describing new approaches. We have found case studies to be useful in classroom instruction and practice for training people to exercise creative, productive methods that may ameliorate the quality of life in their communities. In addition, the specific case studies that follow describe how mutual support and outside assistance aids in the advancement of inner-city community development while also presenting limitations to collective group interests.

Case I: Family-Focused Issues

Some cities have a history of intensive community development activity. Chicago is such a city. O'Donnell and Schumer (1996) reported the process and results of Community Organizing and Family Issues (COFI), a community development effort carried out in Chicago in the early to mid-1990s.

The focus for the application of COFI was a return to problem-solving activities and leadership development for low-income communities on the south side of Chicago. The project coordinators expressed concern about the failure of community development corporations to adequately empower citizens to solve problems that faced the poor. This owed in part, they argued, to the fact that community development corporations had turned away from grassroots leadership in favor of bankers, developers, realtors, and church-based leaders. This was done to attract larger levels of funding from those who were labeled "enemies." As a result, many of the community development corporations no longer reflected the people targeted for uplift. In addition, these organizations had become less democratic, and citizen participation decreased greatly. Finally, they expressed concern that confrontational-style community organizing was used less frequently and defined more narrowly than in the past. Consequently, it was in this institutional context that COFI was involved in strengthening low-income residents in community problem-solving activities.

Box 12.1 **Problem-Solving Models**

Intending to engage in grassroots organizing and leadership development, the problem-solving model employed by COFI consisted of the following five basic steps:

1. Recruiting prospective community leaders explicitly from the ranks of low-income families, primarily mothers

2. Providing leadership training that emphasizes the continuities between family and community leadership and between private and public issues

3. Framing visioning and agenda-setting conversations in terms of what will make the community a better place for families

4. Recognizing that there are many different kinds and levels of leadership—such as personal, family, and community—in family-supportive communities

5. Acknowledging that many of the issues making communities unsafe and unhealthy places for families are rooted in public policies beyond the local level that require leadership training to take on city or statewide policy campaigns.

This model of community development clearly focuses on the poorest individuals in society, African American women and their children. Taking on such a task is both courageous and challenging. The courage is seen in the decision to give priority for leadership development to those who are often held to be expendable. The challenging aspect is seen in the level of readiness of the selected population to move with dispatch in learning and implementing leadership roles.

A very real value to the approach is the tie between individuals and family. Focusing on community improvements from a holistic posture increases the buy-in of the residents. Because children are involved, families will more likely sustain involvement and seek to maximize benefits of resources. Of course, it is necessary to give attention to a broader scope than an inner-city neighborhood. In so doing, the model acknowledges the resources and the barriers experienced by oppressed residents.

A fair criticism of the model and its application rests with the fact that the selected leadership training corps is severely limited. Although poor women and children justify a need of high magnitude, it is not clear why poor men would not be included as a target for leadership development. This is a very serious weakness and falls dangerously close to the public policy of public assistance programs during the middle 20th century, when African American men were not permitted to live with the women and children if benefits were to be received. Similarly, in an oppressed community, there does not seem to be an acceptable reason for the exclusion of anyone, independent of the challenges of reaching those who may be difficult to locate and form working partnerships.

Case II: Faith-Based Organizations

In the African American community, churches have often been the source of leadership in community improvement as well as spiritual guidance. With the creation of national public policy under the second Bush administration, faith-based organizations were invited to take increasing leadership in community improvement efforts. One such effort has been led by the Gamaliel Foundation (Gamaliel Foundation, 2006). The Gamaliel Foundation works in African American, Latino, and South African communities with the hope of creating new and powerful faith-based organizations that would provide an array of leadership training programs, consultations, and research and analysis on issues influencing community development.

Upon inspection, the model takes on a pyramid-like construction regarding leadership development. There does not appear to be any rationalization or justification for the selection of the numbers or magnitude of involvement required in the model. Similarly, the model does not explain why a specific amount of money is required to be raised early in the process. Finally, the model does not appear to take into full consideration how these minimum demands may exclude some very small parishes that may not be able to meet the numbers and fiscal demands. There may also be some concern about the dominant role that ministers in the African American community play and whether this will be a negative force in the democratic expectation of community development practice (Harris, 2005).

In spite of these possible reservations, churches continue to be a very powerful force in the African American community. Churches form the largest membership base of any organization in these communities. They have very diverse organizational styles, arrangements, and, most importantly, leadership postures. Some are very formally tied to national and international religious entities, whereas others are independent as units within themselves. The degree to which outreach for community development is exercised varies greatly. These efforts, where they exist, depend upon the leadership quality, available resources (fiscal and human), location, history of involvement, and readiness of the congregation members to take on community development activities.

Case III: University Community Partnerships

Since the middle of the 20th century, urban universities have been in expansion mode. As these institutions have increased enrollment, expanded research projects, and enlarged sports and recreational facilities, they have moved into adjacent neighborhoods. Moreover, these efforts brought about tensions with the area residents. In urban institutions of higher learning, expansion was nearly always into low-income, mostly African American or poor communities. The consequences of urban university expansion into poor and African American communities brought displacement, property destruction, and town-gown conflict.

Box 12.2 The Gamaliel Foundation

The Gamaliel Foundation community development process employs the following steps:

1. Recruit a minimum of 20 congregations (generally emphasizing those serving low-income communities and communities of color), form a multiracial and ecumenical sponsoring committee, and raise $100,000.

2. Hire in concert with Gamaliel a professional organizer to guide the work.

3. Ensure that the organizer meets with every pastor and 10 laypersons from each congregation to learn about each congregation and identify potential leaders.

4. Bring three to five leaders from each congregation to a weekend retreat to study the basic concepts of organizing.

5. Have each core leader who goes through the retreat recruit 15–100 leaders in his or her congregation.

6. Have this expanded team of 300–800 leaders go through four hours of training in conducting one-on-one interviews with congregation members.

7. Visit anywhere from 150–1,500 people within each congregation over a 6-week period.

8. Hold a large convention in which participants choose four top-priority issues and commit themselves to working on one of them.

9. Engage up to 300 leaders in 4-hour training, this time to learn how to conduct one-on-ones with public officials, professors, agency heads, and business CEOs.

10. Ensure that the leaders spend 8 weeks conducting one-on-ones with public officials.

The University of Pennsylvania engaged in such expansion activities. Moving into University City, the university built this fortress-like environment for its faculty and students in the midst of an inner-city community in West Philadelphia. The tensions that evolved moved the university to begin to address some of the major problems of the community. Creating the Penn Institute for Urban Research, the university embarked upon a community development exercise that is planning and practice-based in an effort to bring about quality-of-life improvements in University City known as the West Philadelphia Initiatives.

Box 12.3 The West Philadelphia Initiatives

The West Philadelphia Initiatives are characterized by the following factors:

1. Making the neighborhood clean, safe, and attractive, with a variety of new interventions

2. Stimulating the housing market

3. Encouraging retail development by attracting new shops, restaurants, and cultural venues that are neighborhood friendly

4. Spurring economic development by directing university contracts and purchases to local businesses

5. Improving the public schools.

To better ensure achievement of these initiatives, the university created the Center for Community Partnerships. The center has a mission that focuses attention upon the targeted community with three fundamental propositions. First, there exists a strong, intertwined future between the university and the West Philadelphia inner-city neighborhood in which it is located. Second, as an important institution to the City of Philadelphia and its place-based status in West Philadelphia, the university can make a significant contribution to improving the quality of life in the community. Third, the university can enhance its overall mission of advancing and transmitting knowledge by helping to improve the quality of life in West Philadelphia.

The community development model employed by the University of Pennsylvania seeks to work with community residents to collaboratively coordinate all university-wide community service programs. While committed to expanding partnerships and positive relationships by changing the nature of town-gown interactions with the community of West Philadelphia, the university offered to work at the national and international levels to learn from other colleges and universities in implementing community development programs (http://www.upenn.edu/ccp/about/). In summary, a very broad range of activities have been established in conjunction with the community that can be considered most typical and desirable in African American neighborhoods more generally. These include activities that attempt to tackle formidable challenges in the areas of education, housing, and health care.

Education

Education has failed the African American in many respects since the founding of the nation. Always seen as less intelligent, more suitable for manual labor and skill instruction, and fundamentally disinterested in intellectual pursuits, blacks have had to overcome these stereotypes and public funding equations that sought to limit their educational achievements. As the education enterprise (public and private) has grown over the years, African Americans continue to lag the academic performance of white Americans in nearly all measured categories.

Housing

Many view housing as a right because it is reasonable and necessary (Bratt, Stone, & Hartman, 2006). Housing is shelter and more. Housing provides protection from the elements and a margin of safety. It is also the investment center for homeowners. Similarly, it is a badge of status, high or low. Many issues abound in the area of housing for the African American community. The most pervasive and persistent barrier to the African American's ability to acquire desired housing is discrimination. In spite of federal, state, and local policies outlawing discrimination in the sale and rental of housing, blacks continue to encounter racial bias in their efforts to secure housing of their choice. In a U.S. Department of Housing and Urban Development–sponsored study conducted in 2000, African Americans were found to experience housing discrimination at significantly high levels (Bratt et al., 2006). The Urban Institute researchers found that black renters receive consistently unfavorable treatment in nearly 22% of their inquiries. They found a somewhat lower percentage (17) for black homebuyers. The practice of racial steering or being told that the property or unit is not available was found to be the primary reason blacks continue to experience discrimination in housing (Turner, Ross, Galster, & Yinger, 2002).

Health Care

The African American community is beset with a myriad of health-related problems. As such, the black community faces diseases that contribute negatively to the quality of life in both urban and rural settings. For purposes here, it is instructive to reflect upon some of the more prevalent diseases that are pervasive in the African American community. Not presented are the related issues of a severe shortage of black physicians and other health care professionals; discriminatory medical practices; lack of adequate funding for research related to diseases that are most common among blacks; high-risk lifestyle practices such as smoking and unprotected sex; and dreadfully insufficient health insurance for women, children, and the poor in African American communities. With these limitations, the following diseases are having an especially negative impact upon African Americans and their quality of life: HIV/AIDS, sickle cell anemia, hypertension, heart disease, and diabetes.

Understandings Essential for Moving Forward ————

The problems mentioned above provide an introduction to the myriad of needs confronting blacks in urban and rural areas. Also, they demonstrate the diversity of issues that an oppressed people face in America. Most important to the intent of this chapter, these problems show the dire need for competent, compassionate intervention within the community development context because the problems are at the critical boundary of those factors that contribute greatly to the quality of life of residents of a community. Moreover, with regard to compassion and competence, citizens, policymakers, and technical experts historically have all played primary roles in responding to the problems besetting the African American community.

Overall, each of the cases describes the emphasis placed on leadership development and empowering the community to be self-determining in problem solving while illustrating the important roles for mutual support and assistance in meeting community needs. In community development, however, citizen leadership is the most essential element in determining the success or failure of any project to improve quality of life, which can be brought about through the convergence of the following four attributes:

1. *Involvement:* African Americans must make an effort to participate in decision-making exercises that afford opportunities for programmatic developments that affect their communities.

2. *Focus:* African Americans must concentrate energy and time toward those targets that are most likely to be productive for their causes.

3. *Media:* African Americans must creatively and forcefully try to change the images and processes used in presenting them negatively in radio, television, movies, newsprint, and media of all types.

4. *Information Sharing:* African Americans must make an intense effort to advise each other of the issues, tactics, resources, barriers, and common interests that influence their community development.

Policymakers, which include council members, alderpersons, and other elected officials at the local level, provide the first line of defense against oppressive policies and practices. In the application of the community development process, local government has a responsibility to ensure that its functions contribute to making a level playing field. Local government may also make adjustments in practices that are known to have adversely affected some in the community, such as exclusionary zoning, police practices, unfair community services, and discriminatory hiring.

Those supportive but outside of the community with technical expertise, such as advocates, liaisons, technicians, historians, and analysts, are discussed in other chapters. One actor deserving attention here who may encompass all of these competencies is the long-range planner. Long-range planners play a central role in proposing systemic change that may mitigate or even rid the oppressed of barriers to community development. Accomplishing this feat will require the planner to avoid elitist orientations that view those in need as unable to handle self-determination activities. Thus, equipped with compassion, consciousness, and savvy, the competence of the planner must be accompanied by courage to remain committed to solving problems that are race-based and highly charged politically.

Some may challenge why a community development process would be appropriate for a group having past and present experiences with white oppression. Some may even argue for revolutionary zeal to bring about radical change in an oppressive system and endure the strong reprisals that may follow. The other pole may suggest an incremental approach to social change that is less threatening to the dominant class and lessens backlash responses. One thing is certain. To do nothing is not an acceptable option.

Given our experiences working with community-based efforts in the field as well as the importance of black self-determination and leadership and outside support and assistance as illuminated by the case studies, we believe that the community development process offers a middle option as a clear plan of action. That middle option must be thought of as having a broad range of approaches. First, the middle option is amendable for broad-based participation by all levels of the community. To this point, it is essential to have as many residents as possible involved in tackling the problems that confront a community. Second, the middle option presents a generalist approach and welcomes a host of skills as presented by various talents in the community. Equally, the approach values this variety and channels it to specific levels of need. Third, the middle option advances the capacity to confront the status quo in a manner that will not appear to be threatening at first glance. A mixture of radical and incremental orientations, the middle option forces the dominant system to consider an effort being entirely legitimate and non-intimidating. Fourth, the middle option holds promise for sustained community involvement. With the welcoming and support of a wide range of skills and talents, the approach encourages citizens to stay the course. This latter point is most critical in maintaining the struggle as it grows and changes in intensity over a long period of time through the continuity and fluidity of the four phases of the middle option described next.

Middle Option—Phase I (Mission and Vision)

The most critical step in the middle option is Phase I. It is here where the reason the group exists and what it finally hopes to achieve over the long term gets articulated. So essential is this phase to the realization of positive outcomes in the community development process, only African American residents may be engaged in carrying out the leadership. For sure, any non-black person of true goodwill would not object to an oppressed people taking the initiative to set the direction and desired community development program activities through self-determination. Alternatively, there may be African Americans who reject the idea of exclusion of non-blacks at the helm of self-determining community development activities, perhaps because of the most damaging results of oppressive white racism: the inferiority complex, insecurity of ability, and low self-esteem that so many blacks harbor.

Middle Option—Phase II (SWOT Analysis)

Determining the strengths, weaknesses, opportunities, and threats (SWOT) of the group is the next phase of the middle option. The SWOT analysis is a planning technique adapted from the business community's forecasting, estimating, and action plan development for products and services. The black community is always confronted by an imbalance of negative forces, and it is these factors that must be well understood. In turn, this particular tool is useful for the African American community because it combines the positive and negative elements that may influence the development of an area or organization. An example for proposed formulation of a process undertaking a SWOT analysis is the effort of a coalition of African American professional organizations and social scientists that suggests using the process of rebuilding New Orleans as a means of securing greater equity (Economic Policy Institute, 2005).

Middle Option—Phase III (Alternative Actions)

The community now must turn its attention to developing options or alternatives that must be designed to ameliorate the problems confronting the residents. There are actually two major activities to be undertaken in this phase. First, the plans of action to be followed are set forth in comprehensive documentation that meets the goals and objectives outlined in Phase I. Second, the plans of action must be readied for implementation. In some planning circles, the latter is thought to be left to those having an expressed management function. However, for the African American community, to be secure from continued exploitation by outsiders, both the action plan development and management must be controlled from within and executed by the residents themselves (staff hired by the community). The establishment of administrative operations is complex and time dependent upon many variables. In addition to listing the potential enterprises, it is important for the community to prepare responsibilities, roles, the allocation of resources, and the location for these activities. In this way, accountability is built into the systems that have been designed as a result of the extensive research and planning afforded by the SWOT analysis and other forms of intelligence identified in Phase II.

Middle Option—Phase IV (Evaluation)

Evaluation is not the last step in the middle option. It is presented in this fashion only for the purpose of facilitating an understanding of the interrelated and various parts of a community development process. In practice, evaluation is most beneficial when carried out continuously and substantially at all phases.

Just as important, assessment must be undertaken solely for the purpose of constantly improving the design, articulation, and management of the community development process. Therefore, evaluation is not for the purpose of punitive action. Instead, it must be exploited as a tool for furthering the growth of the residents toward satisfying the vision set in Phase I. In this fashion, evaluation is nonthreatening and supports all persons involved in the middle option.

Conclusion

Some will differ with a basic premise of this chapter: Only African Americans may advance self-determination through community development activities that improve the quality of life in their own inner-city neighborhoods. The rationale is plain and fundamental. Simply, one would not hire the fox to guard the chickens.

In this presentation, we offer the notion of community that is varied and perhaps more complex than simple analysis can accommodate. The primary consideration of community is people. The physical context is certainly important, but not sufficient to induce purposeful social change. The road map to self-determination for African Americans is cooperative, thorough planning and program management that is vested in goals and objectives that are targeted exclusively to the black community.

Our experiences, coupled with descriptive analysis from the three case studies, lead us to recommend the middle option as the approach for community development in inner-city neighborhoods. In Phase I, we discussed the importance of establishing clearly derived and articulated statements of mission and vision. In Phase II, we suggested that the SWOT analysis can be used to obtain vital data and information, signal positive and negative potential impacts, and identify resources that are available or may be obtained. Phase III presented alternative ways of solving problems that had been identified by the research efforts in the previous two steps. Phase IV identified evaluation at the process and program levels to be ongoing and designed to improve the community development process as needed changes are discovered to meet the goals and objectives.

Finally, three critically important lessons may be gleaned from this chapter. As this chapter is designed for a diverse audience consisting of community residents, change agents, academic faculty and staff, and students, the consequences of proposals made are useful. The three lessons to be taken from the chapter are that African Americans must be the vanguard of self-determination for their inner-city neighborhoods, community development processes are useful tools for planning and executing efforts to solve human development problems, and those from the outside in solidarity with members of the

African American community must have courage and fortitude for the enduring fight in favor of structural change and racial justice.

References

Bonilla-Silva, E. (2006). *Racism without racists: Color-blind racism and the persistence of racial inequality in the United States.* New York: Rowman and Littlefield.

Bratt, R. G., Stone, M. E., & Hartman, C. (2006). *A right to housing: Foundation for a new social agenda.* Philadelphia: Temple University Press.

Carmichael, S., & Hamilton, C. V. (1967). *Black power: The politics of liberation in America.* New York: Random House.

Carpini, M. (1998). *Race and community revitalization: Communication theory and practice.* Washington, DC: Aspen Institute.

Davidoff, P. (1965). Advocacy and pluralism in planners. *Journal of the American Institute of Planning, 31,* 331–337.

Economic Policy Institute. (2005). *Principles and priorities for rebuilding New Orleans: Joint statement by Black social scientists.* Retrieved October 22, 2009, from http://www.epi.org/publications/entry/webfeatures_viewpoints_rebuilding_new_orleans/

Feagin, J. R. (2001). *White racism.* New York: Routledge.

Ferguson, R. F., & Stoutland, S. E. (1999). Reconceiving the community development field. In R. F. Ferguson & W. T. Dickens (Eds.), *Urban problems in community development* (pp. 33–68). Washington, DC: Brookings Institution Press.

Gamaliel Foundation. (2006). *Developing a faith-based CO organization.* Chicago: Author.

Hacker, A. (1992). *Two nations: Black and white, separate, hostile, unequal.* New York: Scribner's.

Harkovy, I., & Donovan, B. M. (Eds.). (2000). *Connecting past and present concepts and models for service-learning in history.* Washington, DC: American Association for Higher Education.

Harris, W. M. (1976). *Black community development.* San Francisco: R&E Press.

Harris, W. M. (2005). Engaging the pervasive: A productive way to discuss racism. *Progressive Planning, 163,* 27–29.

Hillery, G. A. (1955). Definitions of community: Areas of agreement. *Rural Sociology, 20,* 111–123.

Hillery, G. A. (1968). *Communal organizations: A study of local societies.* Chicago: University of Chicago Press.

Kivel, P. (1969). *Uprooting racism: How white people can work for racial justice.* Gabriola Island, British Columbia, Canada: New Society Publishers.

Knowles, L. L., & Prewitt, K. (1969). *Institutional racism in America.* Englewood Cliffs, NJ: Prentice Hall.

O'Donnell, S., & Schumer, E. (1996). *Community building & community organizing: Issues in creating effective models.* Washington, DC: National Housing Institute.

Omi, M., & Winant, H. (1994). *Racial formation in the United States: From the 1960s to the 1990s.* New York: Routledge.

Peattie, L. L. (1968). Reflections on advocacy planning. *Journal of the American Institute of Planners, 34,* 80–89.

Turner, M. A., Ross, S. L., Galster, G., & Yinger, J. (2002). *Discrimination in metropolitan housing markets.* Washington, DC: Urban Institute Press.

13 Engaging Youth in Community Development

Wendy Wheeler and Ana Maria Thomas

BEHAVIOR OBJECTIVES

After studying this chapter and completing the online learning activities, students should be able to

1. Describe the historical shifts in thought regarding the community development field and the youth development field, respectively.

2. Identify four general approaches or attitudes to youth in community development and describe the practical application of each attitude.

3. Define "community youth development." Describe the interaction between youth and communities in this context.

4. Define "youth engagement." Describe its outcomes at four levels of impact.

5. Explain philosophical and practical arguments that may motivate youth engagement work.

6. Identify eight potential methods for delivering youth engagement work.

7. Define "youth leadership." Describe the role of youth leadership development in facilitating pathways to youth engagement.

8. Describe the community youth development framework. Identify and describe its five guiding principles and the four stages of community change. Detail the relationship between the stages and principles.

9. Define "collective leadership" and describe its fundamental characteristics.

10. Distinguish collective leadership from other forms of leadership according to the five guiding principles of community youth development.

11. Identify four challenges to the field of community youth development. Provide methods of meeting these challenges.

An Introduction to Youth and Community Development

Young people are an important but often overlooked element of community development. Actively engaging youth in community development efforts implicitly acknowledges youth as viable and effective members of a community—and has the potential to result in deeper rooted and more sustainable community change.

This pro-youth approach to community development, however, is not a long-standing staple in either the community development or youth development fields. Attitudes and approaches to young people and their involvement in community development have shifted over time and continue to shift to this day. The youth development field has, over the years, recognized that young people need skills, knowledge, and a variety of other personal and social assets to thrive in adulthood. Thus, youth development policies and practices have moved from risk management—attempting to eliminate or limit problems such as substance abuse, adolescent pregnancy, school failure, and involvement with the juvenile justice system—to a more holistic and contextual framework that promotes positive outcomes and helps youth realize their full potential by recognizing the importance and influence that an individual's context has on development (Eccles & Appleton Gootman, 2002). Concurrent to the shift in the youth development field, the community development field began infusing an emphasis on the participation of youth in community building. The fields intersected when community development experts recognized the need to engage young people as partners in community-building efforts, and when the youth development field recognized the strong influence (and opportunity) of context on young people's development.

Despite this large overlap between the fields of community development and youth development, neither experts nor practitioners have yet unified behind a single approach to engaging young people in community change efforts. New research and discoveries, as well as changing societal constructs, keep the attitudes and approaches to the topic in constant flux; from this ever-shifting body of research, four broad perspectives for approaching youth in the context of community development have emerged: youth as objects, youth as recipients, youth as resources, and youth as partners (Innovation Center for Community and Youth Development, 2005).

These four perspectives constitute an entire spectrum of attitudes; manifested in practice, these attitudes dictate one's practical approach to youth in community development. Say, for example, that a community has money to construct a footbridge across a highway. Those who view youth as objects of community development decide to locate the project near a school in the hope that young people will use the bridge. Those who view youth as recipients realize that many of the youth will be skateboarders, and therefore design the bridge with spiral ramps instead of steps. Those who view youth as resources in community development engage young people as occasional advisors to the project—perhaps youth participated in a focus group during the project's planning phase to determine the best location and materials for the bridge. Finally, those who view youth as partners involve young people in every phase of the project, from the earliest stages of idea development to the final stages of actual construction. In this scenario, the bridge reflects not just the interests, but also the values and hard work of the community's young people.

In the "youth as recipients" and "youth as partners" camps, community youth development is the practical approach that marries the goals and strategies of youth development and community development. Community youth development uses youth engagement as a core change strategy, and it has risen to the forefront of youth work as a guiding approach for effective practice. Central to community youth development practices is the belief that young people can be active citizens in their local communities—and that communities should provide youth with support and opportunities to do so. In other words, the community youth development theory posits that youth and communities interact with each other as part of a mutually beneficial relationship. The dynamic of this relationship is bidirectional, thus involving all parties in a situation in which they can make meaningful contributions and from which they can gain meaningful lessons. Communities, for their part, provide the opportunities for young people to develop practical skills; young people, in turn, apply these skills in ways that strengthen the community (Roach, Sullivan, & Wheeler, 1999).

The Goal of This Chapter

This chapter focuses on "youth as partners," specifically on the community youth development approach, to engage young people in community development. A "youth as partners" attitude is the direction in which both the community development and youth development fields are heading; because the "youth as partners" attitude not only values young people, but also builds ownership and catalyzes a deep investment on the part of young people in community issues, it renders sustained success and developmental outcomes for youth. By addressing both theoretical and practical issues, this chapter answers three questions: What is youth engagement? Why do we engage youth in community development? How do we engage youth in community development?

Understanding the Role for
Youth in Community Development

What Is Youth Engagement?

Youth engagement is the sentiment that young people feel toward, and their active investment and involvement in, a particular person, activity, place, group, organization, or outcome. Not to be confused with complacent and/or mandatory participation, true youth engagement harnesses youth's interests and energy for a larger purpose.

Community development offers a definitive platform for youth engagement, an answer to the question so often asked by scholars and practitioners, "Youth engagement for what?" Where youth engagement meets community development, young people have the opportunity to develop a deep investment in and a strong sentiment toward place—their community, and the people, institutions, and efforts that comprise it.

Case Study 13.1 Theater and Service-Learning

Professor Deborah Greer incorporates service-learning into her Secondary Theater Techniques course at Western Washington University (WWU) by pairing student groups with local organizations to direct and coach showcase performances in the local community with at-risk high school youth. The Secondary Theater Techniques course is composed of a mix of students with theater and nontheater majors from WWU who have carried the experiences and skills they gained in service-learning in their community into their careers after college. Greer explains that students who complete her course are more prepared for the communication, organization, and critical thinking requirements of the work world, an observation supported by students' successful placement in respected theater and education positions over the years. At a time when budgets were forcing cutbacks in arts funding in the state, Greer contacted three community organizations—The Martin Center, Sea-Mar Visions, and The Boys and Girls Club of Bellingham—to participate. These organizations work with youth who are disconnected from the community in some way, be it mental or emotional well-being, socioeconomic challenges, or substance abuse-related issues. WWU students worked with youth from the three groups for 3 hours a week over 6 weeks. A fourth hour of class time was required to meet with Greer in order to analyze and troubleshoot challenges that the students faced. At the end of the 6 weeks, both the students and youth participants were surprised and proud of what they had accomplished: a challenging exercise in self-esteem and self-efficacy, and a valuable experience in communication and expression for all involved.

For further information: http://pandora.cii.wwu.edu/showcase2002/greer/portfolio.htm

Because youth engagement in community development entails such hands-on, pointed work, the outcomes of such efforts are similarly specific and focused. The effects of youth engagement play out at four levels: individual, organizational, community, and societal. Thinking through these outcomes to determine desired results is important before delving into deeper project work.

Why Youth Engagement?

Youth engagement is at its best—influencing individuals, organizations, communities, and society—when it is deployed as a strategy tailored to the needs and interests of young people; adapted to support the organizational and community context of the work; focused on measurable outcomes; and meaningful to the young people, the organization, and the larger community. Practically, however, the ideal scenario is not always possible, and one must direct youth engagement toward one of many sets of outcomes. There are countless youth engagement programs, all with a variety of goals and purposes. These goals and purposes, ranging from job training to violence reduction to international development, constitute the "whys?" of youth engagement; they answer the question "Youth engagement for what?" Community development is just one of many possible answers to this question, and youth engagement programs may pursue several goals simultaneously.

Youth Engagement to Strengthen Young People in Their Development. Youth engagement in community development, when combined with intentional learning, reflection, and experience, is a phenomenal strategy for individual youth development because it complements youth's psychological development by building ownership in youth's greater community. It can produce positive cognitive, academic, social, and civic behaviors among young people. Many programs already practice youth engagement to teach young people skills in communication, leadership, problem solving, and decision making, among other areas, and to prepare them to take on further responsibilities as adults. With a little extra intentionality and focused attention to individual youth needs and supports, youth engagement can foster in individuals a sense of belonging, identity development, and caring relationships with adults (Zeldin, Camino, & Calvert, 2003). Research suggests that youth engagement decreases the likelihood that a young person will drop out of high school, abuse drugs, or become pregnant—all factors that jeopardize a young person's development into a thriving, successful, and self-sufficient adult (Zaff & Michelsen, 2002).

Youth Engagement to Strengthen Adults. Although not a common goal, some organizations engage young people in decision making so that the adults learn about young people and their abilities, issues in their communities, and the effect of the organization and its mission on young people. Adults' commitment to the organization increases when youth are involved as their partners (Zeldin, McDaniel, Topitzes, & Calvert, 2000). For adults, the opportunity to engage in partnership with young people to contribute to social justice is a refreshing and rewarding experience that provides new opportunities for personal growth and expression. Thus, youth engagement can be incorporated as a volunteer development and retention strategy for adults by engaging youth coaches and trainers to advise adult community development fellows.

Youth Engagement to Strengthen Organizations. Youth engagement is a strategy to enhance organizational effectiveness and catalyze organizational development and institutional change. Young people influence organizations with their energy, fresh perspectives, knowledge of young people, and sense of community; with young people involved in organizational operations, organizations are able to make better, more informed decisions related to issues that affect youth, and organizational programs are more responsive to youth and communities (Innovation Center for Community and Youth Development, 2001).

For community development organizations, youth engagement builds organizational knowledge for the future while simultaneously building skills among emerging leaders. Youth engagement efforts create an organizational culture that values the skills and knowledge of tomorrow, areas in which young people are already leading the way—multicultural competencies, the use of technology, creativity and innovation, lifelong learning, and understanding of global markets.

Youth participation in organizational operations takes many forms, including a wide range of youth staffing options that include part-time positions, internships, membership in advisory groups or boards, structured employment pathways, opportunities for consulting or contracting at the group or individual level, and volunteer service.

Youth Engagement to Strengthen Community. For some, engaging young people comes from the deep-rooted belief that communities are stronger when they engage the full range of diversity of their residents. With young people providing input, the community is better equipped to create policies that best meet youth's needs; the young people, filled with idealism and energy, are eager to engage in efforts to make change on issues that negatively affect them, their families, and the places and people they care about. Young people may apply their unique skills, knowledge, and talents to solve community problems; create new opportunities; and lead, mobilize, evaluate, and promote diverse efforts aimed at improving all types of social inequalities. Engaging young people in place-based change also often leads to the involvement of other underutilized voices and can create new pathways for civic engagement among marginalized groups. In community change efforts, youth leadership, with its inherent penchant for trying new things and for innovation—and for compelling adults to do the same—builds community capacity to lead social, economic, and cultural change efforts.

Youth Engagement to Improve Society. When taken to scale, youth engagement efforts can affect and change the mores and laws of society. The same energy, enthusiasm, and innovation that young people contribute to individual, organizational, and community projects can build momentum for broad-based social change. Now more than ever, with technology's ability to bridge geographic barriers (and youth's innate ability to use technology), youth movements have the potential to reach and have an impact far beyond local communities.

The civil rights movement in the United States during the 1950s and 1960s, for example, was in large part a youth-led and youth-fueled campaign; more recently, college-aged students successfully pushed for divestment in Darfur, Sudan.

A By-Product of Youth Engagement: Strengthening the Field of Knowledge and Practice. When coupled with the discipline of reflection, youth engagement strategies can inform knowledge and practice on a broad scale. The lessons learned, new models, innovations, and inspiring results catalyzed by youth engagement, when documented and shared, can foster fundamental change in both thinking and practice.

Practically, it is easy to see why one may implement youth engagement strategies: the benefits—for individuals, organizations, communities, and societies—are vast. But these immediate impacts aside, one can make a philosophical case for youth engagement by calling upon the principles of social justice. The United Nations' Convention on the Rights of the Child (CRC) makes the most compelling and concise argument in favor of the authentic participation of young people in organizations and communities. Article 12 of the CRC declares that, as a part of the special rights universally accorded to young people, "the child who is capable of forming his or her own views [has] the right to express those views freely in all matters affecting the child" (United Nations, 1989). With this right to participation in mind, youth engagement is more than simply a program approach; it is an obligation and a right.

Pathways to Youth Engagement

Youth engagement plays out in many different ways in our communities; however, youth engagement efforts tend to fall into at least one of the following modes of delivery: youth service, youth leadership, youth in decision making, youth philanthropy, youth civic and political engagement, youth media, youth research and evaluation, and youth organizing.

Youth working in contribution to the greater good is youth service. Youth service can be as simple as basic volunteerism—young people cleaning up debris from a beach. It also includes more structured, long-term community service activities as well as service-learning activities that link service to classroom lessons and academic outcomes.

There are many definitions of youth leadership, all at least slightly different. According to the Innovation Center, youth leadership occurs when young people, by giving of themselves—their energy, gifts, and beliefs—inspire and propel others to action for the common good. Leaders invest an enormous amount of themselves in their work, and as well possess and use certain competencies—understanding, communication skills, a strong awareness of self, and so on—to catalyze action in others; however, this action must be in service to a larger, shared good.

Youth in decision making focuses on the ways young people are involved in decision-making processes at multiple levels of an initiative, organization, or community. It brings young people "to the table" where decisions are made. Youth in decision making can include advising the individuals or groups that hold decision-making responsibilities, as well as opportunities in which young people are the ultimate decision makers (Search Institute, 2005).

Youth philanthropy is a way for young people to give of their time, talents, and treasures for the common good. Often, this occurs in youth-led grantmaking groups, through which young people perform all of the functions of a large, grantmaking foundation: fundraising, requesting proposals, reviewing proposals, reporting, and so on. Youth may also serve as philanthropic advisors to community organizations (W.K. Kellogg Foundation, 2005).

Through youth civic and political engagement, young people influence community leadership and electoral activities, and they exercise their political voice. Youth civic and political engagement embraces the belief that all individuals can and should meaningfully contribute to the betterment and well-being of their community (Search Institute, 2005). Voting is the classic example of this sort of engagement, but in recent years, we have seen an even deeper and richer involvement as young people play critical roles on political campaigns, advise city planners and local governments, and participate in issue advocacy and activism.

Youth media engage young people in imagining, producing, and distributing their own media, including radio, publications, songs, and videos. In this forum, youth are not passive consumers of television, video, and print media; rather, they are the content creators and are engaged in all aspects of the process (Search Institute, 2005). With the pervasiveness of Internet communications, outlets for youth media have greatly expanded. YouTube, Facebook, MySpace, just to name a few, allow young people to share their media with the world.

Youth research and evaluation engages young people in gathering and analyzing data to address a specific line of inquiry. In many cases, these efforts are linked to program implementation; young people apply research methods to surface practical lessons that can inform or refine their own work or the work of others in their field. At its core, youth engagement in community research and evaluation is a democratic process; it equalizes power between youth and adults, recognizes respective roles and responsibilities, and may be particularly powerful when it places special emphasis on recognizing those youth who are traditionally underrepresented.

Youth organizing is the union of grassroots community organizing and positive youth development, with an explicit commitment to social change and political action. Youth organizing is based on the premise that young people are capable of taking leadership to transform their communities. Young people organize to address community issues and create institutional change.

Engaging Youth in Community Development Practice

To fully and most effectively participate in and lead community development, young people need a skill set that equips them for such activities. Such skills include, but are not limited to, effective communication, organizing, fundraising, teamwork, group process facilitation, and evaluation. Youth leadership development is the process by which young people acquire these attitudes and behaviors. As a precursor to community development work, leadership development prepares youth to be contributing members of their community.

Figure 13.1 illustrates a framework for fostering youth leadership development. Five guiding principles of practice propel work through a four-stage cycle. When fully actualized, the process results in a special form of leadership development: collective leadership. This framework is not exclusive to collective leadership; rather, it informs all good youth leadership development work.

Figure 13.1	Guiding Principles of Youth-Adult Partnerships

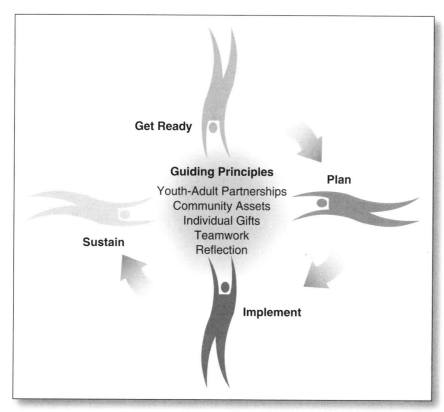

SOURCE: Reprinted with permission from: Innovation Center for Community and Youth Development. (2009). *Browse by Leadership Stages.* Retrieved June 30, 2009, from http://theinnovationcenter.org/activities-toolkits-and-reports/browse-leadership-stages

An emerging practice in leadership development, collective leadership is an approach to leading that occurs when people—youth *and* adults—cross boundaries to come together, commit to mutual learning and leading, and share responsibility and accountability. Collective leadership, by its boundary-crossing nature, is inherently inclusive. It can be practiced in any and all kinds of communities—from communities of interest to place-based, geographic communities. Participants in collective leadership harness the strengths of their differences in age, gender, religion, sexuality, and culture to lead change for the common good. And because collective leadership is both process and outcome oriented, it builds leadership skills, provides a practical outlet for enacting these skills, and creates real results.

Collective leadership seeks transformational change; fosters relational strategies; and embraces fluid, dynamic interventions. These three features interact and combine to create a leadership experience that prepares and enables youth to take action in their communities. First, because collective leadership does not rely on traditional paradigms of leadership, it is a transformational approach to leadership. At the individual, organizational, and societal levels, collective leadership has the capacity to transform. In a collective leadership model, not only the best and the brightest are leaders; rather, collective leadership requires an inclusive group of individuals. This inclusivity inherently addresses, challenges, and transforms issues of power. Also, collective leadership encourages multiple individuals to take leadership roles, making it a relational approach to leadership. Furthermore, while individuals take on leadership within the group, the group itself provides leadership to the community. This dynamic fosters the kinds of interactions that catalyze change at multiple levels of work. Finally, collective leadership is a fluid approach to leadership. Due in part to the diversity of its participants, collective leadership has, and is marked by, the capacity to evolve in response to specific situations and settings. It is an adaptable approach to leadership and can be effective with any group of devoted individuals and in any community (W.K. Kellogg Foundation, 2007).

Stages of Community Change and Principles of Practice

Collective and all leadership development work, as well as youth engagement in community change, cycles through four stages of community development: get ready, plan, implement, and sustain. Getting ready, or building readiness, for community development lays the foundation for all future work. It entails developing deep relationships with community partners and the logistical functions associated with new work. The planning phase is dedicated to visioning—determining desired goals and methods for achieving them; implementation turns plans into action. Sustaining the work uses reflection to identify what changes must be made so that the work's impacts last and continue well into the future.

Uniting these four stages are five guiding principles that inform the hands-on, practical work: youth-adult partnerships, community assets, individual gifts, teamwork, and reflection. It bears repeating that these principles of practice are *not* specific to collective leadership work; rather, they guide all good youth leadership development work. However, in the context of collective leadership, these principles reach an entirely new level of practice, affecting individuals, organizations, and communities in new and deeper ways.

Youth-Adult Partnerships. A youth-adult partnership is the reciprocal and equitable relationship between a young person and an adult that draws on the unique skills of each partner. It is the core relationship in the youth development approach and is characterized by mutual teaching, learning, doing, and trust. In the context of community development, youth-adult partnerships are vehicles for contribution and growth, and they propel the partners toward real outcomes. At a basic level of practice, youth-adult partnerships are a core aspect of youth engagement. Young people and adults come together in a mentoring relationship; youth eventually outgrow the relationship and leave more aware of and concerned with issues confronting their community. But as a guiding practice for collective leadership work, youth-adult partnerships work toward youth leadership development, not just youth engagement. Young people and adults come together in bi-directional mentoring relationships, working together to foster leadership skills within themselves and each other. They support each other and join in shared visioning, and their relationship adapts and evolves as they grow as individuals.

Community Assets. Community strengths and assets are the variety of gifts a community possesses; these strengths and assets can contribute to social change efforts. They may be physical, cultural, or historical and include, but are not limited to, community businesses, local newspapers and radio stations, parks, sports teams, churches, youth groups, and so on. Many times, cultural and historical strengths are overlooked because other community strengths are so obvious; however, cultural and historical strengths are important aspects of both individual and community development. Jointly creating a history wall,[1] a visual representation of a community's past, is just one of many ways to harness lessons from history and culture.

The basic idea that a community itself offers resources for its own development stems from a "strength-based" approach to community development. This approach centers on the process of asset mapping, a capacity-focused process to identify and locate resources, and from that process discover the strengths of a given community. As a core practice of leadership development work, community assets are used for an isolated purpose; individuals analyze a set of predetermined community assets for use in their own work. In the context of collective leadership, community assets serve the common well-being. Collective leadership's facilitative processes encourage youth and adults to think about and identify for themselves their community's strengths (including the

---

[1]You can find directions and resources for the Innovation Center's history wall activity at www.theinnovationcenter.org.

somewhat less visible and often hidden strengths of history and spirit) and how best to unleash these strengths. Using these assets, collective leadership groups effect change that is beyond the individual.

The Gifts of Individuals. Individual gifts are the assets and talents an individual possesses that can contribute to individual or social change. Common skills and attributes that contribute to community development include writing skills, friendship networks, artistic ability, outreach and organizational skills, analytical abilities, courage, media skills, and so on. Basic youth leadership development work develops an individual's gifts for that individual's personal goals and gives young people an outlet for their gifts. Collective leadership takes the notion of individual gifts and does not just find a space to display and exhibit these gifts, but unleashes their full potential. In the context of collective leadership, individual gifts help youth in achieving their personal goals, but are also incorporated into a greater, collective purpose.

Teamwork. Teamwork is an integral aspect of all youth leadership development efforts. It prepares young people to engage with others, a vital skill when working toward community change. As an aspect of basic youth leadership development work, teamwork calls upon team members to work individually to achieve a common goal; participants are responsible for separate aspects of that goal, and their work combines to achieve the desired outcomes. In the collective leadership model, teamwork calls upon team members to work together to achieve a common goal. In this style of teamwork, the entire group assumes responsibility for the results of its work—it is true collaboration.

Reflection. Reflection is the catalyst for improvement and continuation of work. It is also a core aspect of the youth development process—reflecting on one's thoughts, feelings, abilities, and experiences paves the way for future success. As a practice of basic youth leadership development, individuals reflect on and learn from their work. This process occurs at the end of a project as a sort of closing note. In the collective leadership model, reflection does not just happen at the individual level; it is both mutual and shared—youth and adults reflect on and learn from their work and each other's contributions to the process. Furthermore, reflection (and its subsequent learning) as a part of collective leadership is an ongoing process—it can, does, and should occur at all stages of the work.

Case Studies and Lessons Learned

Most successful initiatives practice similar tactics in their efforts to fully involve young people in the work. Youth suffer no fools. They won't return to boring meetings or directionless projects. Thus, the very presence of youth raises the bar for the kind of facilitative processes and tactics employed in youth development and community engagement projects. As a general rule, it is important to remember that youth can and should be a part of the team that leads these facilitative processes. Often, youth and adult teams are especially effective.

This portion of the chapter identifies successful youth engagement tactics and facilitative processes and, with a case study, illustrates their role in deepening youth's connection and commitment to community change initiatives. In many instances, the tactics relate to one of the guiding principles of practice.

Develop Youth's Connections to Their Identity, Culture, and Community

Community youth development has strong ties to identity development. To fully engage in community development work, youth need to understand that they possess strengths and assets to offer their community—who they are, what they believe, where they came from, and what their heritage offers them. This understanding allows young people to appreciate their own identity, understand how historic injustices affect them, and make positive changes. At a collective level, understanding and engaging with the history and identity of a shared place—the geography, physical and cultural, of a community—unites diverse groups of individuals. In many cases, this collective understanding may lead to healing.

Leadership Excellence (LE) is a youth development group in Oakland, California. LE uses identity as a starting point to develop a critical consciousness and cohesion among African American youth.

"I got involved in Leadership Excellence when I was 18," says Ronnell Clayton. Clayton had been arrested during a painful time in his family's life and was trying to get back on track by improving his grades and decisions. LE offered a way to connect the pain and disruption in his own life with the pain of oppression in the African American experience.

Clayton took part in LE's Middle Passage Workshop, which recreates the sights and sounds of capture in Africa and enslavement in the United States. This guided visualization describes the injustice and spiritual erosion African Americans have endured. Clayton remembers his reaction to the workshop. "People in my family had passed; my good friend had passed away at school. Still I didn't cry," he said. "After Middle Passage, I just cried and cried."

There are about 150 youth in LE, ages 5 to 18. They are recruited by word of mouth and sometimes mandated to attend by probation officers or parents. LE offers visualization, role-play, and workshops to encourage understanding of current social and economic issues, all of which have origins in the past. Through programs like Middle Passage Workshop, LE helps youth understand their cultural histories as a source of strength and inspiration.

Recognize That Young People Are Assets to and Experts on Their Community

Young people have perceptive insights about their community and clear ideas about ways to improve it. Often, youth possess a deep passion for equity and a desire to make the world better. Too frequently, adults forget to ask for involvement from young people when they are working on community change. When adults write off youth as apathetic and disengaged, they miss out on some of the richest resources in their community. Just as importantly, young people miss out on a chance to make a real difference, build their own skills, and gain the confidence that comes when others value your work.

"Many times, youth were looked at as the problems, or thought of as 'kids who didn't care,'" says Carolyn Edelbeck, a 16-year-old from Waupaca, Wisconsin, who participated in the town's Healthy Communities-Healthy Youth Initiative. "A lot of activities and groups were planned for youth, but there wasn't anything that involved youth in that planning."

Edelbeck's groups set a new standard when they developed and ran their own projects. Healthy Communities-Healthy Youth worked in partnership with adults, but it was clearly youth-led. Their accomplishments include a new skateboard park for the town, volunteer opportunities at community organizations for sixth graders, a youth-led philanthropy committee (funded by the Kellogg Foundation) to offer local organizations grants in exchange for service projects that involve youth as partners, and seats for young people as voting members of city council.

Edelbeck sees the voting membership on city council as a triumph and a turning point for Waupaca youth. "This was a huge step. It shows that youth are valued and their input is important," she says.

Engage Young People as Community Leaders on Issues That Matter to Them

Through civic activism, young people can channel their frustration with the status quo and devote their energy to social change. Driven by a desire to bring about change, youth are ready and willing to take on leadership roles— and to develop the skills to do the job well. Organizations that capitalize on this interest can help young people develop new skills, confidence, and goals through the experience.

When young members of Youth Ministries for Peace and Justice (YMPJ) in the Bronx, New York, learned that an old cement plant in their neighborhood was slated to be torn down to create a parking lot, they refused to let it happen.

Hernan Melara was 12 when he first joined YMPJ. "I grew up here. I feel safe here. I'll stay here," says Melara. "I see things in the future, how they can be. I don't want a cement plant. I want a park for my children and their children."

He and YMPJ's other 200 members, ages 6 to 21, organized to stop city planners' bid for the parking lot and got the land transferred to the Parks Department. They achieved their goal, but their work is not finished. The city still wants to run a road through the park. YMPJ members have taken action by performing street theater to inform their neighbors, collecting signatures for petitions, meeting with the Department of Transportation, and garnering press attention.

Bring Young People and Adults Together to Work as Equal Partners

True youth-adult partnership requires more than bringing an intergenerational mix of people into a room. Adults must give up the control and leadership that they often view as their right. Young people must give up any distrust of their parents' peers. The process is slow and difficult, but the results are phenomenal.

Adults and youth in Oakland, California, joined forces to improve garment workers' health and working conditions. Together, they changed the lives of women in the garment industry. "Youth had a stake in making sure their moms could come home from work and not feel pain," says Stacy Kono, Project Director of the Youth Build Immigrant Power (YBIP) program at Asian Immigrant Women Advocates (AIWA).

For years, AIWA had mobilized immigrant women on behalf of Asian immigrant families and garment workers. They launched YBIP to engage youth and adults as partners in this effort.

AIWA had offered free medical check-ups to female garment workers and found that 99% of women had injuries related to their work; all experienced regular pain in their back, neck, or arms.

"A lot of youth joined YBIP because their moms are garment workers," says Kono, who hosted drop-in events that attracted mostly young women, ages 14-20. In these informal settings, young people discovered their similar family experiences. One young woman says she began to understand "why it was the humming of sewing machines that put me to sleep as a kid, and not the humming of my mother."

That was enough to spark a movement of YBIP members, adults at AIWA, and the garment workers themselves to negotiate healthier conditions in factories. In collaboration, the young people and adults offered important health and safety training to factory workers, researched options for funding work station changes and raised $33,000 from the county's community grants fund and the city's economic development fund, and successfully installed ergonomically correct chairs in the factory workers' stations.

Teresa Ruan, who joined YBIP when she was 13, says she continues her involvement with AIWA so that other youth "can become leaders like me." Ruan experienced firsthand the inspiring impact of youth-adult partnership in her community and now knows that, in her words, "people together is power."

Inspire Action and Partnership
Among All Members of a Community

True leadership means feeding and inspiring the group, not just lifting up leaders. By involving all parts of their community, organizations can build momentum for social change and begin to reverse patterns of harm and neglect that span generations.

Tohono O'odham Community Action (TOCA), a community organization on the Tohono O'odham Reservation in Arizona, initiated a dramatic turnaround when it tackled a major health issue affecting its community. On top of poverty, drug abuse, trouble with gangs, and high dropout rates, the Tohono O'odham community suffered high rates of diabetes. TOCA zeroed in on a way to improve the health of the community through spiritual, cultural, economic, and physical revitalization. A truly intergenerational organization, TOCA brought community members of all ages together to make it happen.

Leaders traced the rise in diabetes among their people to a loss of the traditional diet, including the absence of tepary beans, once a major staple of the Tohono O'odham diet. Through the Tohono O'odham Food Systems Program, TOCA involved the entire community in a plan to reintroduce tepary beans by growing, harvesting, packaging, and selling the beans themselves.

TOCA rallied community members of all ages to resurrect traditional farming methods and tools; involve elders, who possessed vital knowledge for how to grow and harvest the crop; involve youth, adults, and children, who welcomed the chance to contribute meaningfully—in various aspects and stages of the project—to the health of their families and friends; and host cultural events and celebrations throughout the year to mark seasonal changes and projects, such as planting time and harvesting time.

The beans are once again a part of this community's diet, but the benefits of the project go beyond physical health. The Tohono O'odham Food System Program represents just one facet of this organization's talent for community engagement and impact. The people share goals and priorities in a way they never had before.

Don't Forget the Importance of Food and Fun

The importance of fun in community development work—whether the work is with or without young people—cannot be underestimated. In fact, one of the beauties of engaging young people in community development is that it demands that fun be incorporated into the process. This can be done in meaningful ways; again and again, food presents itself as a fun and engaging activity. Not only is food biologically important for and attractive to young people, but also the sharing of food can serve as a strong community builder, uniting diverse individuals around common and basic needs.

Challenges to Engaging —————————————— Youth in Community Development

Engaging young people in community development is a challenging task—indeed, all good work requires concerted effort. There are challenges associated with the work itself; furthermore, the field of youth engagement faces broad, theoretical challenges pertaining to collaboration. By addressing these challenges, it is our hope that you will be better equipped to meet and overcome them in your work.

Safety and Engaging Minors

In all community engagement work, and especially in community engagement work with young people, it is necessary to ensure that projects, activities, and events are safe for everyone. Working with youth under the age of 18 brings special issues of responsibility. Among the adults in the program, be sure to clearly identify who has responsibility for the young people, and rehearse procedures. Be sure to consider circumstances outstanding to general supervision, such as if a youth becomes sick or can't get a ride home. Established community development organizations often require permission forms, health releases, and contact information for all youth involved in their programs; furthermore, they often secure additional accident insurance to cover minors and boast program staff trained in emergency medical procedures. Consider such measures when planning your work.

Logistical Challenges: Timing and Accessibility

Working with young people poses challenges of timing and accessibility. Typically, youth are not as mobile as adults. Often, they lack access to transportation aside from public transportation (not a reliable or safe option in many communities). As a result, many community development opportunities—group meetings, on-site projects, and so on—are inaccessible to young people. School and employment hours pose another challenge to coordinating meetings and projects, as youth's first commitment is to their education and jobs. Programs designed for after-school hours with transportation from school tend to be most convenient (and, partly because of the convenience, popular) for youth. When financial constraints curtail transportation options, hold meetings and activities in sites centrally located to schools, neighborhoods, and public transportation hubs.

Paradigm Shifts: Changing Opinions and Roles

For many people—youth and adults alike—the idea of adults engaging in partnership with youth is a difficult concept to fully grasp. The equal relationship that is the foundation for youth-adult partnerships challenges social norms. Thus, it is not uncommon for young people and adults to struggle initially when forming a youth-adult partnership. The question we must then ask ourselves is, "How do we help people move forward in their relationships to be comfortable engaging each other in a new and different way?" By beginning the work with an emphasis on knowing the self and identifying individual gifts, people learn to appreciate the gifts of others. This begins to transform the assumed power dynamic of relationships.

Collaboration Across Boundaries

When involving diverse groups of people, all youth engagement and community development faces the common challenge of boundary crossing. There may be boundaries of race, class, gender, age, and sexuality, just to name a few. Often, it is by these boundaries that individuals define themselves; however, although boundaries may constitute self-identity, they also serve to separate individuals. Engaging youth in community development must encourage youth to develop both their identities constituted by these boundaries and a collective community identity that transcends these boundaries—in short, the goal is to both respect and overcome boundaries. Needless to say, this is no simple task. Often, the best approach is to acknowledge differences and then agree on a unifying principle; the value of agreeing to disagree, when appropriate, cannot be overstated.

Conclusions

Youth engagement in community development creates change in a myriad of different ways and at multiple levels of impact. It is so successful because it mirrors and complements the web of connections that constitutes community life. But it is not easy work, nor does it produce results overnight. Preparation—logistical, mental, and spiritual—is vital. Without this foundation of preliminary physical and intellectual infrastructure, the phenomenal results of collective leadership can't reach their full potential. But with proper preparation, young people can lead the world—one community at a time.

References

Eccles, J., & Appleton Gootman, J. (Eds.). (2002). *Community programs to promote youth development*. Washington, DC: National Academy Press.

Innovation Center for Community and Youth Development. (2001). *At the table: Making the case for youth in decision-making.* Takoma Park, MD: Author.

Innovation Center for Community and Youth Development. (2005). *Reflect and improve: A tool kit for engaging youth and adults as partners in program evaluation.* Takoma Park, MD: Author.

Innovation Center for Community and Youth Development. (2009). *Browse by leadership stages.* Retrieved June 30, 2009, from http://theinnovationcenter.org/activities-toolkits-and-reports/browse-leadership-stages

Roach, C., Sullivan, L. Y., & Wheeler, W. (1999). *Youth leadership for development: Civic activism as a component of youth development programming.* Chevy Chase, MD: National 4-H Council's Innovation Center for Community and Youth Development.

Search Institute. (2005). *The power of youth and adult partnerships and change pathways for youth work.* Battle Creek, MI: W.K. Kellogg Foundation.

United Nations' Office of the High Commissioner for Human Rights. (1989). *Convention on the rights of the child.* Geneva, Switzerland: Author.

W.K. Kellogg Foundation. (2005). *Youth engagement: A celebration across time and culture.* Battle Creek, MI: Author.

W.K. Kellogg Foundation. (2007). *The collective leadership framework: A workbook for cultivating and sustaining community change.* Battle Creek, MI: Author.

Zaff, J. F., & Michelsen, E. (2002, October). *Encouraging civic engagement: How teens are (or are not) becoming responsible citizens* [Child Trends Research Brief]. Washington, DC: Author.

Zeldin, S., Camino, L., & Calvert, M. (2003). Toward an understanding of youth in community governance: Policy priorities and research directions. *Social Policy Report, 17*(3). Ann Arbor, MI: Society for Research in Child Development. Retrieved August 4, 2009, from http://www.srcd.org/spr.html

Zeldin, S., McDaniel, A. K., Topitzes, D., & Calvert, M. (2000). *Youth in decision-making: A study on the impacts of youth on adults and organizations.* Takoma Park, MD: Innovation Center for Community and Youth Development.

14

Health

A New Community Development Challenge

Lois Wright Morton and Nina Glasgow

BEHAVIOR OBJECTIVES

After studying this chapter and completing the online learning activities, students should be able to

1. Learn that structural determinants of health and well-being extend beyond medical institutions to the community's social, economic, political, and physical environments.

2. Understand the community development challenge to health.

3. Identify community-level interventions to respond to population health problems and proactively sustain population well-being.

4. Identify the major trends in disparities between and within communities.

5. Provide examples of the different models of community development as they might apply to health.

6. Identify some of the key consequences of the aging baby boom on community health.

7. Describe the key findings of the research on the role of social support on health.

8. Identify the lessons from the case studies that use new community development models to address health concerns.

Introduction

The social and economic conditions of community are fundamental causes of disease and health (Evans, Barer, & Marmor, 1994; Link & Phelan, 2002). A large variety of structural factors influence health and well-being ranging from income distribution, poverty, public safety, workplace conditions, industrial pollutants, the food system, schools, recreation and parks, street and sidewalk layouts, housing and sanitation conditions, water quality, and the overall public health infrastructure (Glasgow, Morton, & Johnson, 2004). Concentration of poverty and income inequality have been correlated to child and adolescent well-being related to infant mortality, low birth weight, child abuse, and adolescent violence as well as health risks to adults affecting all-cause mortality, homicide, cardiovascular disease, and depression (Sampson & Morenoff, 2000). A body of research has linked individual health risk factors such as smoking, overweight, alcohol and drug abuse, and sedentary lifestyles to the environments in which people live, work, and play (Morton, 2001). Local and state responses to health concerns have included no-smoking rules in public places; creation of trails, sidewalks, and public recreation sites; enforcement of driving-while-impaired laws; the return of physical education classes in schools; and efforts to change trans fat and high-calorie menus in public eating places.

Case Study 14.1   The Tioga County Dental Van

In Tioga County, New York, a van is equipped to provide dental care to persons who are not on Medicaid *and* who do not have dental insurance. Fees are charged on a sliding scale of income. The Tioga County Dental Van was the result of a planning process conducted by the Tioga County Health Department. The health department held six focus groups representing 40 agencies and individuals from across Tioga County. Focus group findings were used to identify the county's health/health care priorities, and the health department's advisory committee drafted recommendations to address the priority needs. The lack of health insurance or underinsurance was one of seven top-priority areas of need identified, especially with regard to dental and vision care. Focus group participants identified children and the working poor as being among those most at risk of not having access to primary and preventive health care. The Tioga County Health Department developed the *2005–2010 Tioga County Health Assessment,* using input from the focus groups and the advisory committee to establish the county's health/health care priorities, and the health department now administers and delivers the mobile dental van program.

The dental van parks outside a school at one of 13 designated sites and functions as a school-based clinic during school hours. After school hours, the van's dentists and dental hygienists provide basic dental care to anyone in the community needing care who meets the criteria of not being a Medicaid recipient and being without dental insurance. Appointments are required and are usually scheduled within a 2-week window. During the summer months of school vacation, the dental van is parked outside a school in Owego, the county seat, and service is available to county residents who meet the criteria for receiving services. For some school children, a visit to the dental van was their first ever visit to a dentist or hygienist.

Case Study 14.2   Drinking Vandalia's Water

Vandalia, Missouri, population 2,500, like many small towns in northern Missouri, is reliant upon surface water for its public water supply. The area economy relies heavily on crop and animal agriculture and associated agribusinesses. The primary water source for Vandalia is a 28-acre reservoir supplied by a 3,638-acre watershed. The Environmental Protection Agency, under the Clean Water Act, sets standards and procedures for local waters contaminated with excess nitrogen, phosphorous, fecal coliform, pesticides, and other chemicals. When the reservoir that supplied Vandalia's public drinking water registered atrazine levels in excess of 80 ppb (parts per billion), far above the maximum 3 ppb for finished water health standards, the community mobilized to solve the problem. Atrazine is the herbicide most commonly used in the production of corn and grain sorghum.

A community development specialist and Vandalia's leaders convened several public meetings to identify what farmers and other local residents thought were the issues and to discuss management practices that producers were willing to consider. Community members from both the rural watershed and the town were led through processes in setting goals for their watershed, discovering possible options on what could be done, and what role they were willing to play. The mayor and the water plant manager explained what the city was doing at the water plant to correct the problem. All producers in the watershed signed agreements to participate in changing agricultural practices to reduce atrazine applications and runoff. Farmers talked to Cooperative Extension and other agency technical specialists and to each other across the fence to find effective ways to produce their crops while protecting the watershed. Since the establishment of the watershed management committee—a group of local citizens—and the writing and implementation of a watershed plan, the levels of atrazine in the reservoir went from a peak of 85 parts per billion in the untreated water to averaging less than 6 parts per billion in the raw water.

Understanding How Health
Is a Community Development Challenge

The community perspective on health and well-being argues that a population develops the wherewithal to avoid disease and death because it has "resources of knowledge, money, power, prestige, and beneficial social connections" (Link & Phelan, 2002, p. 730). The community development challenge is to make the best use of existing resources and leverage them to build not just a strong medical infrastructure but also an environment that ensures the health and well-being of all community members. Health is more than low death rates and increased longevity; it is also reduction of unnecessary pain and suffering, illness, and disability (U.S. Department of Health and Human Services [USDHHS], 1990). Health comes from an improved quality of life, which is measured by citizens' sense of well-being as well as objective measures such as infant mortality, all-cause mortality, and morbidity rates (USDHHS, 1990).

Not only does good health benefit individuals, a healthy population is able to contribute to community development goals. Healthy children learn better in school; a healthy workforce is more productive; and healthy older people contribute expertise and experience in paid work, volunteer roles, and civil society activities. Good health has intrinsic value to individuals, and communities have a vested interest in promoting the health of local populations.

Case Study 14.3   Homelessness and Service-Learning

East Tennessee State University established a relationship with the Johnson City Downtown Clinic for Homeless (JCDTC), creating a solid model for the health care field to utilize service-learning. Nursing students were given the opportunity to apply their knowledge of health care to the issue of homelessness. Students became involved in the course work with students from other nearby campuses to provide services to the JCDTC. All students are asked to complete at least 30 hours of service, aside from assigned readings, required journaling, papers, and presentations. One activity involved using students to provide weekly screening programs for diabetes, hypertension, anemia, and foot problems. This program was advertised for people in need at local shelters and clinics. Students run the entire activity, from setting up equipment and organizing the venue to filling out forms and charts for the patients. Another aspect of the course involved rotating two students at a time into the more formal work of the JCDTC. Students in this position are able to provide basic care for needy people in a positive environment. This incorporation of students into a non-university organization provides valuable experience for the students, while giving the JCDTC extra help in achieving its goals.

Source: Norbeck, J. S., Connolly, C., & Koerner, J. (Eds.). (1998). *Caring and community concepts and models for service learning in nursing.* Grand Rapids, MI: Stylus.

The Role of the Federal Government

The U.S. Department of Health and Human Services (USDHHS) is the primary agency with responsibility for the health of the national population.

State and county health departments financed by local, state, and national taxes provide the necessary infrastructure for gathering health data (birth and death certificates, disease prevalence, and morbidity); monitoring infectious diseases; developing disease prevention strategies; and implementing wellness programs for targeted disadvantaged populations based on income, age, and disabilities (Morton, 2001).

Broad population health goals set by USDHHS in *Healthy People 2000* and *Healthy People 2010* are as follows: (a) increased longevity, (b) reduction in health disparities among populations, and (c) access to preventive services for all (Morton, 2001). The accomplishment of these goals requires that local communities assess their own population's health and develop a variety of funding mechanisms and strategies for achieving better health. Responsibility for getting to better health outcomes goes beyond government agencies to private sector businesses and voluntary organizations. Communities that build partnerships among their local institutions and connect their community to regional and state organizations and agencies increase the resources available to meet healthy population goals.

Differences in socioeconomic resources among and within communities affect their capacity to protect, intervene, and advance health and well-being. For example, the effects of income inequality on poor health persist at many levels in both rural and urban contexts (Lynch et al., 2004; McLaughlin, Stokes, & Nonoyama, 2001; Ram, 2005; Wilkinson, 1997). Those living in counties in a state with higher income inequality and a higher percentage of blacks will, on average, have higher age-adjusted mortality.

The Role of Communities

Communities that wish to create a health advantage must go beyond documenting the health problems experienced by their population to seeking the underlying causes and implementing interventions that can solve these concerns. This means finding ways to interpret the growing medical and life sciences knowledge base, adapting new and old technologies to the needs of their populations, and developing the political will to discover solutions and make difficult public policy and intervention decisions. The search for population health solutions often overlooks the importance of "politics, ideologies, states, and institutions in producing the kind of societies that distribute their material wealth, food and living standards in a health-enhancing way" (Szreter, 2002, p. 724).

The role of community development in achieving better population health is complex, conflictual, and messy, but essential if improvements are to continue. The myriad of relationships among the state, local government infrastructure, private market-based services, civic organizations, and citizens are key factors in whether the health of the people in a community remains status quo, declines, or improves. In this chapter, we document the health disparities within and between communities that are targets of change. Then we discuss the structural components of creating a local health infrastructure with attention to models of community development and offer examples of community strategies. The community development focus is on wellness, not disease management. The new challenge to communities is not to respond with more medical infrastructure, but to reinvent the community so it is a healthy place to live. Finally, we identify the challenges of the future that community development efforts must address.

National Trends in Health Disparities Within and Between Communities

The U.S. Department of Health and Human Services reports annually on the overall health status of the U.S. population as well as by sociodemographic characteristics. In recent years, life expectancy for men and women has continued to increase, and mortality from heart disease, stroke, and cancer, as well as infant mortality, has declined (National Center for Health Statistics [NCHS], 2007). This progress, however, is not shared equally across geography, income, race, ethnicity, and education. Furthermore, longevity is accompanied by increases in the prevalence of chronic conditions and associated disability and pain (NCHS, 2007). Insufficient exercise and overweight risk factors contribute to current chronic medical problems related to heart disease, diabetes, hypertension, and back pain. Increasing numbers of overweight children and adults suggest increased morbidity and mortality in future years (NCHS, 2007). In addition, unacceptable levels of risky behaviors in children and young adults such as binge drinking of alcohol, illegal drug use, and suicide attempts are of great concern.

An aging nation and more racially and ethnically diverse communities are challenges that local leaders and their citizens must address. The portion of the U.S. population over age 75 is projected to be 12% by 2050. The aging population is concentrated by region (South, upper Midwest), in rural areas, and by places with retirement amenities (Brown & Glasgow, 2008). Although all communities will need to respond to an aging population, those communities in which chronic diseases and limitations in usual activities are more pronounced will experience a greater burden or opportunity. Changes in vision, hearing, and musculoskeletal systems (e.g., joint pain) are individual health problems that can be ameliorated by community infrastructure changes such as signage with larger letters, crosswalks with sound, and gently sloped and obstacle-free walkways.

Although the black and white population life expectancy gap is narrowing, it persists (NCHS, 2007). Major disparities in health exist by race, ethnicity, socioeconomic status, and insurance status. More than 50% of non-Hispanic black women over 20 years of age were obese in 2001–2004 compared with 39% of Mexican-origin women and 31% of non-Hispanic white women (NCHS, 2007). Noncitizen foreign-born persons, both legal and undocumented, represent more than 7% of the U.S. civilian non-institutional population, and they are disproportionately low income and uninsured (NCHS, 2007).

Social Support Is a Valuable Resource

Human health and well-being are partially contingent on the social relationships among people. A large body of research has found that people who are socially integrated have better health and greater longevity than similarly placed individuals who are socially isolated (Berkman, 1983; Moen, Dempster-McClain, & Williams, 1989; Pillemer, Moen, Wethington, & Glasgow, 2000). Humans appear to be hardwired to need and flourish on the company and social support of others. Moreover, informal social networks are instrumental in providing hands-on caregiving and services, such as rides to doctors' offices, which contribute to individuals' health and well-being. Studies of caregiving in the United States estimate that as much as 80% of the care that persons receive when they are ill is provided informally by families, especially, but also friends and neighbors (Brody, 2006). Communities that shore up the ability of informal network members to care for children, spouses, disabled individuals, and elders who need care benefit not only individuals and their families but also the community in which those individuals live. Informally provided care relieves communities and society from having to finance some formal services that would otherwise be required.

It is often the formal respite care provided to persons with long-term illnesses that gives informal caregivers a break so that they are able to return to duties as primary or secondary caregivers. Communities and informal caregivers have, in a sense, formed partnerships in providing health care. It should be recognized, however, that formally provided long-term health care is necessary in instances where workers need to continue in their jobs to keep their families financially solvent.

Baby Boomers and Our Aging Population: Prospects for the Future

The leading edge of the baby boom generation turned 62 in 2008, and as baby boomers continue to advance in age, certain of their characteristics portend less availability of informal caregivers (Pillemer & Glasgow, 2000). Fertility rates were lower among baby boom women than the previous generation, leaving them with fewer adult children who will be available as informal caregivers during baby boomers' old age. Moreover, baby boomers have been more likely to divorce than previous generations, and even though remarriage is common, intergenerational relationships become strained and informal caregiving is less likely to be forthcoming, even when aging parents have one or more adult offspring (Pezzin & Schone, 1999). Adequate provision of long-term health care may be one of the greatest challenges to community development between now and 2050, at which point the size of the aging population is projected to peak.

Implementing Health Projects in a Community ———————

Models of Community Development

The infrastructure of a community is frequently conceptualized as bricks and mortar, and in the health arena often limited to the medical infrastructure: hospitals, nursing homes, clinics, doctors, nurses, public health, pharmacies, and physical and mental health therapy practices. However, the community structure influencing health goes beyond medical services to the daily physical and social environment experienced by residents. With growing empirical evidence of the effects of the social and economic environment on health, models of individual well-being are being revised to incorporate three overarching factors: social environment, physical environment, and genetic endowment (Evans et al., 1994; Lichtenstein et al., 2000; Morton, 2001). The community development process must link health assessments and health and well-being goals and interventions to all three of these factors.

Models of community development traditionally have been categorized as social action, social planning, and locality development (Rothman et al., 1995). To address community health, each of these models has a place depending on the health concern, community resources, known science, and current state of political will to act on issues.

Social Action. Social action is frequently citizen-led and the result of human experiences (anger, frustration, conflict, strong emotions, and violent actions based on perceptions of injustice and unfairness) that become catalysts for action. Goals of social action emphasize legislative outcomes, legal redress, and/or empowering minority groups and victims of health disparities (Rothman, Erlich, & Tropman, 1995). Social action is one of the precursors to social change in public policies related to health. Seat belt regulations, toxic waste cleanup rules and financing, clean water and air legislation, and the creation of agencies such as the Food and Drug Administration and the Occupational Safety and Health Administration have their origins in citizen outrage and activism (Brobeck, Mayer, & Herrmann, 1997; Harper, 2007; Meier, Garman, & Keiser, 2003).

Health care institutions are heavily regulated, from insurance and public payment systems, to certification of health professionals, hospitals and nursing homes, to capital improvements and the construction of new health care facilities. Although regulations and rules abound in protecting health against water, air, and land contaminants from industry, agriculture, and construction, monitoring and enforcement can be weak or nonexistent. Social action may target rule development and/or monitoring and enforcement of existing regulations. Thus, current and future social actions may build on past social actions to ensure safety and protect human health.

Citizens can mobilize around unsafe conditions, citing existing laws that need to be enforced or insisting that new ones be enacted. The classic example is Love Canal and the 4-year battle that three community activists, a research scientist, and the New York community fought in order to have the entire community evacuated from the toxic chemical site that was causing miscarriages, birth deformities, and unexplained resident illnesses (Harper, 2007; Meier et al., 2003). State and local smoking bans in public places are an example of community action that has made a big difference in cancer mortality and morbidity rates. Science clearly links smoking (and secondhand smoke) to cancer, yet for many years the economic clout of the tobacco industry was unchallenged (Morton, 2001). In recent years, more than 30 states and hundreds of U.S. cities have passed local ordinances banning indoor smoking in public places, even though this is a heated, highly conflictual issue (Carlton, 2007). Despite the link between high smoking and cancer rates (24% of Alaska adults smoke compared to the U.S. average of 21%), Anchorage's July 1, 2007, smoking ban in bars and bingo halls faced stiff opposition requiring persistence from citizens and legislators to enact and enforce. Community action was required to initiate these smoking bans and in some places may be necessary to retain them.

Social action depends on high levels of media exposure, mobilization of mass support, and charismatic leadership. The goals of public communication are to create public awareness, challenge existing institutional hegemony, and incite structural and institutional change. The sustainability of social action lies in the laws and regulations it motivates as well as the organizational capacities that are built when groups mobilize to address public issues of concern. In some instances, legal mandates lead to social planning as health objectives and activities become institutionalized forms of responding and solving issues that social action brought to public attention.

Social Planning. Social planning is expert-led and data-driven (see Chapter 4 on technical assistance) with a focus on tasks and activities that lead to solutions (Rothman et al., 1995). Health social planning is the result of legislative mandates and the creation of public agencies charged with health. Many of the public and private medical institutions of a community/region are the product of social planning ranging from 1950s funding and creation of local rural hospitals across the United States through the Hill Burton Act, to designated medical shortage areas, to community health centers in urban disadvantaged neighborhoods, to Medicaid and Medicare reimbursement rules. Public health departments, quasi-public and private hospitals, emergency medical services, and private health services are the community's cornerstone for responding to current health conditions (infectious disease, accidents, noninfectious disease, disease prevention and wellness) and planning for community health emergencies.

Social planning that influences health extends beyond the medical infrastructure to highway departments' responsibility for street and road repairs and safe driving conditions, street signs, and traffic control. Police and fire departments also engage in social planning, making decisions about monitoring and enforcing speed limits, illegal drug production and use, and fire hydrant and detector locations and emergency services. Local zoning, building permits, and housing standards are designed to protect the quality of life from overcrowding and unsafe buildings and to assure the orderly development of businesses and residential housing. Parks and recreation services create trail systems and recreational programs for physical exercise and socialization as well as visual green space for mental relaxation. Many of the government organizations in a community have a health and safety component to their mandates.

Locality Development. Locality development is characterized by local initiatives and shared decision making, with efforts to engage diverse members of the community (Rothman et al., 1995). Problem solving occurs through extensive communication and public dialogues. Although national and local health organizations and groups have existed for a very long time, it is only recently that these organizations are linking together and engaging local citizens in proactive as well as response modes (Morton, 2001). Constructing social networks and assuring space for citizen politics are important in solving local health care and assuring population health and well-being. A number of community groups ranging from individual disease-focused organizations (e.g., American Heart Association, American Cancer Society, La Leche League, and other local support groups) to the United Way to Chamber of Commerce economic development and employment projects are engaging citizens in local development.

The foundation of locality development is social capital—the connections and relationships among people to discover and act on common goals. These grassroots projects undertaken by community organizations specifically link perceived gaps and needs in the health care and community infrastructure to targeted programs.

Building Community Capacity to Increase and Sustain Health Care

A New Community Development Model

The categorization of community development intervention models overlooks the reality that social action, social planning, and locality development happen concurrently. Furthermore, the synergy produced when all are present creates a new and exciting dynamic. When the facts and data collected by public agencies charged with social planning are shared with citizens, social action often emerges and in turn spurs locality development.

One goal of the new community development model is to create citizen scientists, people who question and probe accepted practices and current infrastructure and search for local data and ways to apply new science and technologies to solve community problems (Morton & Miller, 2007). Health solutions come from the integration of three points of a triangle: the science of disease and well-being, which is continually being advanced; the technological expertise that is built as new science and knowledge are applied; and the political will of the community, region, state, and nation to *act* on what is known. Each of these areas is fraught with conflict, special interests, economic challenges, and divergent social goals that community development must resolve. It is further complicated by science, which is a moving target. As we learn more about the human body and its responses to the environment, known facts become myth and new facts seem tenuous, making community decisions even more difficult. To respond adequately to these dynamics and uncertainties, the community development process must develop citizens and leaders in public and private organizations who will accept that equilibrium and balance are elusive and yet are willing to act on the best available science.

Case Studies of New Community Development

Fight the Fat. In Dyersville, Iowa, everyone is into fighting fat. Here, the national diabetes and overweight epidemic is local and personal. Using a buddy system, this town lost 3,998 pounds in 2 years. Organizers said:

> Fight the Fat started as a way for people to get together with their friends or to make new friends who could help them in their struggle. . . . It is about being able to turn to people who can help you—and to help yourself by helping others. (Clemen, Kirkwood, & Schell, 2002, p. 3)

The process of creating teams to help each other lose weight affected the whole community food system and changed how people thought about their sidewalks, exercise, and recreational programs. The Cardinal Lounge now serves broiled fish; LeRoy's Pizza offers a low-fat pizza; the Ritz Restaurant has a low-fat special, locally raised ostrich; McDonald's posts nutrition tips and an alternative menu of low-fat and healthy foods (Clemen et al., 2002). Much of the pressure for changing the food system came from employees and store owners who joined Fight the Fat for personal reasons. The catalyst for this initiative originated in a focus group of six people who told their local health care provider that weight was their biggest problem and they needed help with daily changes. Three colleagues from Dyersville Mercy Medical Center listened: the director of nutrition, the supervisor of rehabilitation outreach services, and the director of marketing. The result was a 10-week Fight the Fat program in 1998 that did not end after 10 weeks. It became a contagious movement that changed community norms about eating and exercise.

The program reinforced that the best food value is no longer buying the biggest portion; that it is OK to take extra food home; that as a customer they can ask for changes in food preparation and have sauces and salad dressing put on the side (Sagario, 2002). Power walking around town in good weather also became a community norm, using up calories and building social connections and a sense of purpose among community members.

Northeast Iowa Food & Fitness Initiative. The five-county Northeast Iowa Food & Fitness Initiative grew out of a food and farm coalition whose goal was marketing local crops and preserving small- and medium-sized farms. A strategic plan among producers, processors, and food storage businesses to strengthen the local food and farm economy became the foundation for expanding into local health and fitness. Led by Iowa State University Extension, the group competed for and won a $500,000 Kellogg Food and Fitness grant to "fund a two-year community planning effort to increase access to local healthy foods and promote physical activity and play" (www.extension.iastate .edu/news/2007/apr/121907.htm). The planning process includes mapping availability of local foods in schools, restaurants, and grocery stores; improving opportunities for residents to incorporate physical activity into daily lives; and strengthening public understanding of the economy, health, and environment.

This regional community development process includes five county planning teams that assess local conditions, develop priorities, and initiate activities in support of the region's vision: "vibrant communities that support families and their children by promoting a way of life focused on healthy food and physical activity and play." County teams consist of health departments, human service agencies, volunteer organizations, farmers, elected officials, community businesses, and school leaders. A regional team, drawn from each county team, searched for common concerns and developed a list of top priorities on which the region should focus: establishment of a local food system; assessment and building of a fitness infrastructure; education and awareness; and creation of policy and wellness change within organizations, across communities and counties, and within the region.

Ithaca Health Alliance and the Ithaca Free Clinic. Federal government programs such as Medicaid and Medicare provide health insurance and health care for many Americans. Still, more than 45 million Americans currently have no health insurance, putting them in peril of not having access to health care when they need it. This has prompted initiatives at local and state levels to provide health care for the uninsured who do not qualify for Medicaid. In 2006, the State of Massachusetts passed legislation to implement a system of universal health care for its residents—the first state to do so. New York State has not passed similar legislation, but the state's rural health networks and various other groups are strong advocates for passage of state legislation to develop a system of universal health care in New York (Community and Rural Development Institute, 2006).

Some localities in New York have established programs designed to address the needs of the uninsured. In Ithaca, New York, the Ithaca Health Alliance and the Ithaca Free Clinic were founded for the purpose of providing access to health care based on need, not ability to pay (http://www.ithacahealth.org). The Ithaca Health Alliance was founded in 1997 and has since provided low-cost loans and grants to uninsured individuals who need health care they could not afford. The Alliance also provides nutrition and general health education programs. The Ithaca Health Alliance is financed through donations, grants, and community fundraising, and after 8 years of saving money and putting plans into place, the Alliance opened the Ithaca Free Clinic on January 23, 2006. The clinic offers free integrative health and wellness services to uninsured residents of New York, not just residents of Ithaca and surrounding areas of Tompkins County. The clinic is staffed by doctors, nurses, herbalists, acupuncturists, and other health care workers who volunteer their time and labor. The talent and generosity of the health care community come together to provide mainstream medical services, complementary alternative medicine, and social advocacy. The clinic is not equipped to provide all medical tests and procedures, but the volunteer health care workers and the clinic coordinator broker services in hospitals and other facilities at discounted rates for individuals who need them. The Ithaca Health Alliance helps pay for outside services through grants and low-cost loans. The Ithaca Free Clinic is open 2 days per week during regularly scheduled hours for drop-in visits and immediate care. One day per month, by appointment, clinic doctors and nurse practitioners provide free physical examinations for adults.

Other Examples of Change About How Communities View Health. It may be tempting to say changes could not happen in other communities because they are too big or too small, or they do not have the right resources. However, communities are changing how they think about health and are taking bold actions. In late 2006, New York City banned trans fat from restaurant menus, turning the food system upside down ("New York City Passes Trans Fat Ban," 2006). The New York City Board of Health voted unanimously to phase in over an 18-month period the removal of artificial trans fat from restaurants throughout the city, with final phase-in to occur by July 1, 2008. Trans fat used in cooking has been linked to increases in heart disease, stroke, and bad cholesterol, but customers cannot see restaurants' use of trans fat in food preparation, and this ban was intended to protect public health.

Wegmans, an upscale leading supermarket chain in the northeastern United States with more than 70 stores, announced in December 2007 they would no longer sell cigarette and tobacco products. This is a risky business decision, but corporate leaders say they are in the business of selling good health. This suggests that when businesses and community leaders recognize the seriousness of health risks to their communities, they can make difficult political and economic decisions if so motivated.

Helping Communities
Achieve the Health Advantage —————————————————————

The health care industry is a leader in the buzzwords of disease and well-being indicators and outcomes, evaluation, accountability report cards, protocols, and managed efficiencies and effectiveness. Communities that want to make a difference in health must learn the buzzwords while looking beyond their medical infrastructure to their whole community infrastructure to achieve health outcomes that Americans have set for themselves: reduced health inequality among populations, increased longevity, and access to health care services for all. Community indicators of progress will include changes in social and environmental conditions that are underlying causes of poor health. Although the focus in recent years has been on individual health, an emerging body of science on root causes of disease, morbidity, and mortality reveals that the structure of place—the environment in which people live and work—affects physical and mental well-being.

Mortality rates during the past few decades are down for heart disease, stroke, atherosclerosis, and cancers—all of which are leading causes of death. New health challenges have arisen, however, in climbing obesity rates and diabetes morbidity and mortality. Solving health issues is a concern that must be shared by the community and solved by the combined efforts of citizens, private businesses, voluntary organizations, and the governmental bodies they have created. The community development approach to health is not an option but a necessity if gains in population health are to continue.

It is becoming increasingly evident that many risk factors are beyond the ability of any one individual to control or change (Israel, Checkoway, Schulz, & Zimmerman, 1994). Thus, there are two opportunities for community development: the first is to address health risks to individuals through a communal process (e.g., buddy systems, support groups, coalitions and alliances to develop education and intervention programs), and the second is investments in the community infrastructure that change the social and physical environment (e.g., transportation, medical services, recreation/exercise, smoking bans, calorie and nutrient counts on menu items).

Conclusion —————————————————————————————————

Future challenges for communities include creating environments that make public and private services available and easily accessible to an aging and chronically ill population. This will mean solving the transportation issue to accomplish routine, everyday needs such as traveling to work and social activities, shopping for food and other consumer needs, as well as accessing medical services. Good transportation and an array of home care services will enable members of the community to retain their independence as long as possible and reduce the burden and cost of care to the community.

In addition to an aging population, many communities are experiencing in-migration of younger populations, such as Hispanics, with quite different health needs, experiences, and knowledge of the medical infrastructure. These in-migrants bring different concepts of community and have different family, social cultures, and networks that the community development process can use to build a healthy community. Persistent health inequalities of African Americans compared to other races and ethnicities will continue to challenge communities to invest their resources in ways that reduce these disparities. Many communities have pockets of poverty as well as social, environmental, and economic concerns that are barriers to achieving health and well-being. The solution to these problems includes community-based participation, public discussions, and actions that are linked to the public and private institutions whose missions include health, safety, and well-being.

The challenge to community leaders is to build and sustain the health advantage. The science of disease, gene mapping, and medical technologies will continue to grow and increase what we know about the human body and the process of staying healthy. Communities that create a health advantage are those that leverage this knowledge and technology along with their diverse human and financial capital.

References

Berkman, L. F. (1983). The assessment of social networks and social support in the elderly. *Journal of the American Geriatrics Society, 3,* 743–749.

Brobeck, S., Mayer, R. N., & Herrmann, R. O. (1997). *Encyclopedia of the consumer movement.* Santa Barbara, CA: ABC-CLIO.

Brody, E. M. (2006). *Women in the middle: Their parent care years* (2nd ed.). New York: Springer.

Brown, D. L., & Glasgow, N. (2008). *Rural retirement migration.* Dordrecht, The Netherlands: Springer.

Carlton, J. (2007, Dec. 27). Smoking ban leaves Alaskans out in the cold. *Wall Street Journal,* pp. A1, A8.

Clemen, J., Kirkwood, D., & Schell, B., with Myerson, C. (2002). *The town that lost a ton.* Naperville, IL: Sourcebooks.

Community and Rural Development Institute, Rural New York Initiative, New York State Legislative Commission on Rural Resources and Cornell Cooperative Extension. (2006). *A vision for rural New York.* Ithaca, NY: Cornell University and New York State Legislative Commission for Rural Resources.

Evans, R. G., Barer, M. L., & Marmor, T. R.. (1994). *Why are some people healthy and others not? The determinants of health of populations.* New York: Aldine de Gruyter.

Glasgow, N., Morton, L. W., & Johnson, N. E. (2004). *Critical issues in rural health.* Ames, IA: Blackwell.

Harper, C. L. (2007). *Environment and society: Human perspectives on environmental issue* (4th ed.). Upper Saddle River, NJ: Prentice Hall.

Israel, B. A., Checkoway, B., Schulz, A., & Zimmerman, M. (1994). Health education and community empowerment: Conceptualizing and measuring perceptions of individual, organizational and community control. *Health Education Quarterly, 21,* 149–170.

Lichtenstein, P., Holm, N. W., Verkasalo, P. K., Iliadou, A., Kaprio, J., Koskenvuo, M., Pukkala, E., Skytthe, A., & Hemminki, A. (2000). Environmental and heritable factors in the causation of cancer. *New England Journal of Medicine, 343,* 78–85.

Link, B. G., & Phelan, J. C. (2002). McKeown and the idea that social conditions are fundamental causes of disease. *American Journal of Public Health, 92,* 730–732.

Lynch, J. W., Smith, G. D., Harper, S., Hillemier, M., Ross, N., Kaplan, G. A., & Wolfson, M. (2004). Is income inequality a determinant of population health? *Milbank Quarterly, 82,* 5–99.

McLaughlin, D. K., Stokes, C. S., & Nonoyama, A. (2001). Residence and income inequality: Effects on mortality among U.S. counties. *Rural Sociology, 66,* 579–598.

Meier, K. J., Garman, E. T., & Keiser, L. R. (2003). *Regulation and consumer protection* (4th ed.). Houston, TX: Thomson.

Moen, P., Dempster-McClain, D., & Williams, R. M. (1989). Social integration and longevity: An event history analysis of women's roles and resilience. *American Sociological Review, 54,* 635–647.

Morton, L. W. (2001). *Health care restructuring: Market theory vs. civil society.* Westport, CT: Auburn House.

Morton, L. W., & Miller, L. W. (2007). Connecting sustainable agriculture to rural development: The case of pasture-based dairy grazing. *Journal of Community Development Society, 38,* 23–38.

National Center for Health Statistics. (2007). *Health, United States, 2007 with chartbook on trends in the health of Americans.* Hyattsville, MD: Author.

New York City passes trans fat ban. (2006, Dec. 5). Retrieved from http://www.msnbc.msn.com/id/16051436/

Norbeck, J. S., Connolly, C., & Koerner, J. (Eds.). (1998). *Caring and community concepts and models for service learning in nursing.* Grand Rapids, MI: Stylus.

Pezzin, L. E., & Schone, B. S. (1999). Parental marital disruption and intergenerational transfers: An analysis of lone elderly parents and their children. *Demography, 36,* 287–297.

Pillemer, K., & Glasgow, N. (2000). Social integration and aging: Background and trends. In K. Pillemer, P. Moen, E. Wethington, & N. Glasgow (Eds.), *Social integration in the second half of life* (pp. 19–47). Baltimore, MD: Johns Hopkins University Press.

Pillemer, K., Moen, P., Wethington, E., & Glasgow, N. (Eds.). (2000) *Social integration in the second half of life.* Baltimore, MD: Johns Hopkins University Press.

Ram, R. (2005). Income inequality, poverty, and population health: Evidence from recent data for the United States. *Social Science and Medicine, 61,* 2568–2576.

Rothman, J., Erlich, J. L., & Tropman, J. E. (1995). *Strategies of community intervention* (5th ed.). Itasca, IL: F. E. Peacock.

Sagario, D. (2002, Feb. 17). Small town shares big losses. *Des Moines Register,* p. 1E.

Sampson, R. J., & Morenoff, J. D. (2000). Public health and safety in context: Lessons from community-level theory on social capital. In *Promoting health: Intervention strategies from social and behavioral research* (pp. 366–389). Washington, DC: National Academies Press.

Szreter, S. (2002). Rethinking McKeown: The relationship between public health and social change. *American Journal of Public Health, 92,* 722–725.

U.S. Department of Health and Human Services. (1990). *Healthy people 2000.* Washington, DC: Author.

Wilkinson, R. G. (1997). Socioeconomic determinants of health: Health inequalities: Relative or absolute material standards? *British Medical Journal, 314,* 591–595.

15

Schools and Community Development

Kai A. Schafft and Hobart L. Harmon

BEHAVIOR OBJECTIVES

After studying this chapter and completing the online learning activities, students should be able to

1. Identify the key reasons why schools are critical institutions in the community development process.

2. Explain how schools define the boundaries of communities and why.

3. Understand the implications of the No Child Left Behind Act for community action.

4. Analyze the ways in which service-learning and place-based education connect schools to communities.

5. Understand some of the consequences of school consolidation for rural and urban communities.

6. Identify the barriers that community development organizations might face in developing partnerships with schools.

7. Explain the benefits of place-based education.

8. Identify the key lessons learned from the case studies about school-community interactions.

Introduction

This chapter discusses the role of schools in community development, the process of making communities stronger by creating conditions that enable local residents to improve their social and economic well-being. Although global cultural and economic forces challenge the boundaries of community and the identity of community members, people still live in localities and interact with others within those localities. It is the quality of this social interaction that defines community through the resulting associations, formation of local identity, attachment to place, and capacity for collective action (Wilkinson, 1991).

The fates of schools and the communities they serve are closely entwined. Because of this, community development is in the best interests of schools, although school leaders may be hesitant to assume community development roles if they fear that this may interfere with students reaching a level of achievement required by the current high-stakes testing and accountability system enacted by the federal No Child Left Behind Act. However, the goals of community betterment and academic achievement in a global era can be mutually reinforcing in multiple respects. All things being equal, students who live in distressed communities and fragmented home environments cannot reasonably be expected to perform at the same academic level as their peers from healthy home and community environments. For this reason alone, community well-being is in the best interests of schools.

Similarly, the health of a neighborhood or community can be significantly enhanced by the presence of a strong, well-functioning school that provides a context for community interaction, a sense of collective identity, and an attachment to place. Alternately, as one commentator has observed, "the link between schools and neighborhood quality is often a precarious balance, and when one is trapped in the downward spiral of disinvestment, the other indubitably follows" (Chung, 2002, p. 8). In short, vibrant schools require vibrant communities, and vice versa.

Of all local institutions, schools may be best placed to catalyze community development because of their capacity to mobilize community members and create new linkages between educators, parents, community members, and community-based developers (Dodd & Konzal, 2002; Longo, 2007; Warren, 2001, 2005). This insight is important because many communities in the United States are changing in ways that often present new opportunities, but may also entail serious challenges. These challenges include economic decline, as well as changing demographics in both rural and central city locations, aging and/or shrinking populations, and/or diversifying populations. High residential mobility of students and their families, especially mobility associated with poverty and housing insecurity, may weaken connection to place and undermine school attachment (Killeen & Schafft, 2008). School consolidation, one of the most consistent educational reform policies in rural areas over the past 100 years, has also damaged the school-community connection by closing local schools, increasing the distances required to travel to school, and reducing opportunities for parental and extracurricular involvement.

Many schools often experience high turnover rates among administrators and teachers, and they are beleaguered by high-need student populations, limited resources, aging infrastructure, and overcrowded conditions. Large, over-populated urban and rural schools reduce the once-prevalent personal contact between teachers and students that facilitated effective teaching and learning, particularly in schools with a high percentage of impoverished students. Addressing these challenges will require innovative approaches and flexibility by local leaders in all facets of political, economic, and educational decision making.

Case Study 15.1   Tutoring and Service-Learning

The Hikone-Angell School After-School Tutoring Project was initiated by sociology students at the University of Michigan in Ann Arbor. Connections were first made with social workers from the Hikone housing project, who believed that tutoring would help improve the achievement of elementary-age students who were falling behind in their studies. Children living in Hikone were from low-income families, and there was a high level of racial and ethnic diversity. Initiative was then taken by Joan Scott to create a service-learning course, established in partnership with volunteers from a dormitory on campus. The course was created to allow approximately 14 students per semester to receive credit for participating in a twice-weekly tutoring program. Students in the course were given course readings related to the sociology of education to supplement the weekly tutoring. University students provided educational help in spelling, math, history, and English skills. Early problems included too many children seeking assistance, a lack of supplies and space, and transportation from campus to Hikone. The project has dealt with many changes over the years. The tutoring program was moved to Angell School from Hikone, and new partnerships were created with the Community Action Network after the partnership with the initial social workers was dissolved.

SOURCE: Galura, J., Meiland, R., Ross, R., Callan, M. J., & Smith, R. (Eds.). (1993). *Praxis II: Service-learning resources for university students, staff, and faculty.* Ann Arbor, MI: OCLS Press.

Understanding School-Community Development Linkages

In the United States, schools have historically served as the backbone of neighborhoods and communities (Theobald, 1997). In a variety of ways, both formal and informal, schools help to shape the local boundaries of communities and the identity of community members. Schools also often provide a focal point for community social organization, providing residents with a place and a context to assemble and address local issues, fostering local democracy and civic engagement.

Because of their essentially *integrative and interactive* nature, schools naturally tend to have socially developmental outcomes (Longo, 2007; Lyson, 2002). If we consider that the core of any community development process is building increased community solidarity and the capacity of community members to take action for collective best interests (Hustedde & Ganowicz, 2002), then schools have the potential to be essential institutions in bringing diverse elements of a community together within a shared context for achieving important community development goals.

Beyond socially integrative functions, schools play distinct local economic roles as well. In addition to providing a significant source of local employment, schools produce human capital by educating cohorts of young people and providing them with skills and knowledge to become economically productive adults. Data show that the value of education to the economic status of individuals has increased steadily over time. In 1979, a male with a bachelor's degree could expect to make 51% more in lifetime earnings than a peer with only a high school diploma. By 2004, that difference had jumped to 96%. Between 1984 and 2000, about two thirds of job growth in the United States was accounted for by positions requiring a bachelor's degree or more, whereas the economic prospects dimmed considerably for those with high school diplomas or less (Glasmeier & Salant, 2006; Kirsch, Braun, Yamamoto, & Sum, 2007; Webster & Alemayehu, 2006).

Clearly, the economic value of education to individuals is substantial and is increasing. However, these individual-level effects have both local and regional spillover effects. By educating the future workforce, public schools help make states and localities more economically competitive. A strong local labor force represents a distinct asset to local businesses requiring a well-educated workforce, and the quality of public schools can directly influence business site selection, labor location decision making, and residential property values (Gibbs, 2005).

In Oklahoma City, planners noted that the renovation of an elementary school resulted in local property values increasing anywhere from 30% to 100% (Finucan, 2000). These same relationships hold true in rural areas. Lyson (2002), for example, found that municipalities containing schools in rural upstate New York had higher housing values; higher percentages of professional, managerial, and executive workers; greater entrepreneurial activity; higher percentages of residents working locally; and lower commuting times.

Conversely, because of the strong relationship between school quality and community well-being, a local mortgage lender in Madison, Wisconsin, went so far as to spearhead a collaborative initiative called "A Home in Madison." Organized in conjunction with the school district, the city planning department, local businesses, and neighborhood associations, the initiative was designed to boost sagging enrollments by providing prospective home buyers with information about the strengths of Madison's schools and neighborhoods (Finucan, 2000).

Clearly, there are many intrinsic connections between schools and communities. These connections may be further leveraged for community mobilization and improvement efforts. The way in which this happens—and the outcomes that result—is shaped by local needs, resources, community types, and the capacity of local people to develop effective collaborations. In the section that follows, examples of school-community partnerships for community development are described in both urban and rural settings. We then conclude the chapter with some reflection on the factors that may either weaken or enhance the possibilities for schools partnering in community development efforts, suggesting what this means for both policy and practice.

————————————— Building School-Community Partnerships

The Logan Square Neighborhood Association: A Case Study of Urban School-Community Collaboration[1]

Logan Square, a neighborhood in Chicago's west side, has historically been a home to immigrants. Its residents are currently made up overwhelmingly of Latinos, mainly from Mexico, but also with some families from Puerto Rico and Central America. Although the area has a mix of middle-class families, 90% of students in the local schools come from Latino and low-income, working-class backgrounds.

The Logan Square Neighborhood Association (LSNA), a nonprofit, grass-roots community organization, has been an active part of the Logan Square area since the early 1960s, engaging in economic development efforts, community housing issues, living-wage jobs, and neighborhood safety, as well as the training of local community leaders. The LSNA has 40 member organizations, including churches, schools, social service agencies, and other local groups. Its collaborative efforts with local schools began in the early 1990s as a consequence of legislation that granted new local-level decision-making power to elected parent majority local school councils. Among other things, the councils would have responsibility for hiring building principals on 4-year contracts. The LSNA believed that an organized community would be far better positioned to effectively work with schools and make informed hiring decisions.

The LSNA's school-community collaborations also developed out of earlier efforts by the LSNA to lobby the city of Chicago to address the problems of growing enrollments and school overcrowding. Initial efforts, spearheaded by a coalition of parents, teachers, and principals, and organized by the LSNA, established strong working relationships with local educational leaders. The coalition's work resulted in new facility additions to five existing elementary schools and the construction of two additional middle schools in response to needs within the schools. The coalition further convinced the city to complete the construction in such a way that the new space could be used in the evenings for community education.

Working from this original connection, the LSNA created a Parent Mentor Program and hired parents to work within classrooms for 2 hours a day, supporting teachers and assisting with educational activities. From the beginning, Latina mothers, most of whom had not worked outside the home, had limited previous contact with the school, and often were culturally and linguistically

---

[1]The material for this section was drawn from Brown (2007), Warren (2005), and the Logan Square Neighborhood Association Web site at http://lsna.net.

isolated, occupied nearly all of the mentor positions. Parents additionally took part in weekly workshops to develop their capacity to assist within the classroom and also to become better informed on a range of local social and educational issues. As Brown (2007) writes, "At the core of the parent mentor experience is a personal transformation from a private, often isolated immigrant or welfare mother to a person who sees herself as a school or community leader" (p. 32). As of 2007, more than 1,300 parents have completed the program, often going on to assume teaching positions at local schools, run in local school council elections, and take part in other community betterment initiatives. On any given school day, about 170 parent mentors and parent tutors assist teachers in local elementary school classrooms and work directly with students.

The development of the Parent Mentor Program led to discussions among the mentors about actions that could be taken through the school that might result in broader community improvement. Out of these discussions, a plan was developed to start school-based community learning centers for both adults and children. A community learning center offering night classes was started at one elementary school in the neighborhood, and it eventually expanded into seven area schools. The learning centers offer English as a Second Language (ESL) instruction, GED and adult education, and citizenship classes, as well as a range of cultural enrichment programs. Managed by local parents, about 700 families participate weekly in evening classes and activities run through the community learning centers.

The Parent Mentor Program was so successful that the LSNA partnered with Chicago State University to develop a program that would train local residents to become bilingual teachers in Logan Square area schools. Through a federal grant paying all program costs, Chicago State faculty members offered instruction out of the local community learning centers as part of a college degree program resulting in certification as bilingual and ESL teachers. Fifty students participated in this program, a group almost entirely composed of Latina parent mentors and/or parents of children in Logan Square schools. The success of the program led to it serving as a model for the state-funded Grow Your Own Teacher program.

Although the LSNA's efforts have been explicitly community oriented, using local schools as resources and partners in community betterment efforts, the outcomes for schools have been notable as well. In addition to a markedly improved school climate—much more welcoming and inclusive of community members than previously—standardized test scores have tripled, and parent engagement is now a hallmark of Logan Square schools. The working assumption behind the LSNA's parental outreach and collaborative work with the schools has been that by treating parents as "partners and welcoming what they have to offer into the classroom, we can create schools that engage students and increase student achievement" (Brown, 2007, p. 34). This again suggests how academic improvement and community engagement can be mutually beneficial to schools and their communities.

A High-Tech Rural District: A Case Study

Unlike the Logan Square neighborhood area of Chicago, the Ridgemont School district is located in a mountainous, isolated area in central Pennsylvania.[2] A former coal mining region, the area's local economy is now largely dependent upon revenue brought in by nearby outdoor recreation opportunities. The district's largest employer is the school itself, which serves about 850 students. Local residents not employed by the school district mainly rely upon low-paid local service sector work, or they must commute long distances. The small communities located within the school district (which covers about 100 square miles) have steadily lost population over the years, and school district administrative records show similar enrollment drops.

One of the distinguishing features of the district is its geographic isolation. The nearest major highway is a 45-minute drive from the school over winding mountain roads, a trip that can take considerably longer in inclement weather. There is no local police force, cell phone coverage is spotty at best, and landline telephone calls out of the immediate area are charged long distance, causing concerns for public safety as well as basic communication challenges.

In the late 1990s, a new superintendent was hired who began to steer the district in some radically different directions. The new superintendent's vision for the district was shaped by a few basic observations. First, although the school's mission was first and foremost educational, the superintendent believed that educational goals could not be addressed effectively without confronting geographic isolation and economic decline, both of which affected the vitality and sustainability of not only the townships served by the school, but also the school itself. In short, in order to fulfill the district's educational mission, community issues would also have to be meaningfully addressed. The superintendent decided that under the circumstances, this might best be accomplished through the introduction of broadband Internet and information technology.

Over a 10-year period, the superintendent began efforts to transform the district from one that had only 24 Apple IIe computers, no Internet access, and some classrooms without telephone lines, to a cutting-edge, high-tech district with the latest in instructional technology based within a completely wireless broadband environment. Mobilizing community support and aggressively seeking and securing private and public grants as well as corporate donations from information technology and software development firms,[3] the superintendent was able to secure more than 850 computers, including four mobile wireless laptop labs. The school campus itself was turned into a wireless environment housing eight 80-gigabyte servers.

---

[2]The following discussion is based upon Schafft, Alter, and Bridger (2006). The place name is a pseudonym.

[3]From 1998–2003 alone, the district secured almost $3.8 million in funding and resources. One of the major selling points for the community was that none of the initiatives drained local resources.

The district then acquired the resources to build a network of microwave antennae towers providing Internet connectivity to households within a 10-mile radius, a service provided by a private vendor for about $11 per month to more than 500 area households. A portion of the subscription fee is funneled back into the Ridgemont Education Foundation, which funds mini-grants to teachers, supports residential wireless broadband access to area low-income households, and provides an annual scholarship award to senior projects exploring the theme of "school and community."

These efforts blur the distinction between educational improvement and community development in several respects. As part of the established curriculum, students in the high school provide valuable community services by working directly with area businesses to develop and maintain business Web sites, hosted on the district's servers. Students consequently develop Web design and information technology skills while engaging in a community-based project, and local businesses benefit from increased exposure to potential customers in the community. Second, as a way of ensuring that low-income community members have access to computer hardware, as aging computers in the schools are phased out and replaced, they are sold at minimal cost to district residents. Finally, the district is in the process of expanding the initiative regionally, working to expand the range of broadband access across multiple districts and communities within the region.

School and community leaders point out that the district's information technology initiatives also increase the likelihood of economic benefits, not only through educating cohorts of technologically skilled young people, but also through job start-ups and firm relocations. The superintendent explained,

> I'd like to develop . . . an economic development incubator-type business for this area, because when you look at Harrisburg and all these places that have Internet high-speed bandwidth and they're charging really large sums of money, we have the workforce here. So all we'd have to do is get people to understand that rural Pennsylvania has a workforce, and all we have to do is have the jobs. Yeah, instead of outsourcing we should be insourcing. We should be bringing the jobs into . . . communities like this that have the workers who are displaced and can't find jobs or have to work at $5.00 an hour. (Schafft et al., 2006, p. 6)

The Ridgemont case is an excellent example of school-community collaboration spearheaded by educational leadership strategies embracing educational improvement and community betterment as fundamentally complementary and mutually reinforcing goals. Several things are worth noting regarding these efforts. First, the superintendent was astute in his ability to identify and mobilize local resources, in particular local community groups with whom the school could form effective partnerships. This was coupled with strong efforts to build ties outside of the local community to acquire material and financial support for the school-led community development efforts. Finally, the efforts were characterized by a broad, inclusive orientation toward community development that encompassed the whole community. Although the district's collaborative efforts with the community cannot alone solve all of the problems of local economic decline, these efforts have nonetheless yielded valuable community development outcomes, providing new opportunities and possibilities for local residents.

The examples of the Logan Square Neighborhood Association and the Ridgemont School District are an interesting study of contrasts. One is based within inner-city Chicago, and the other is based in a highly isolated rural area. The Logan Square initiatives were led by a grassroots civic organization that partnered with local schools, whereas the Ridgemont effort was school-led and strongly dependent upon partnerships with local groups. And yet there are also striking parallels between the two efforts.

Like the example of Chicago's Logan Square Neighborhood Association, the Ridgemont effort was based upon several basic assumptions by local leadership. First, educational improvement and community building are not mutually exclusive efforts, but rather can be deeply complementary and mutually reinforcing. Students can provide important community services while also applying valuable knowledge and skills learned in the classroom setting. Second, schools are uniquely positioned to leverage resources, create coalitions, and work with local groups to identify local assets and take advantage of potential opportunities. Finally, local leaders in both the urban Logan Square neighborhood and rural Ridgemont each understood the importance of building ties and new collaborative connections across diverse segments of the community. This cross-cutting connection and capacity for collective action is what Wilkinson (1991) and others have referred to as the community field: locality-based social networks that cut across diverse subgroups within a community, facilitating the interaction of diverse local actors and, in turn, building awareness of local concerns as well as the capacity to address those concerns.

Several lessons can be drawn from these two examples. First, community development and school-community partnerships are most effective when shaped by local needs and contexts—and through effectively identifying local human, institutional, and other resources. That is, customized rather than one-size-fits-all approaches may be most effective across communities with widely varying needs, resources, and capacities. Second, local leadership in each case worked carefully to build a bottom-up, broad-based effort, increasing community ownership of the effort and, likely, the sustainability of the initiatives.

Some cautions are in order as well. Bureaucratic organization and the narrowed mission of schools mitigate against broad-based collaboration and make partnering with schools more difficult. To do so effectively requires enlightened educational leadership with a commitment to fostering mutually beneficial partnerships with parents, organizations, and groups. As well, entrenched power structures within communities can easily create mistrust and derail collaborative efforts (Schafft & Greenwood, 2003). These are not insurmountable challenges, but they are significant and cannot be discounted. Ultimately, both school district and community leaders must recognize how student participation in "service to community" builds essential skills for success in a democratic society and global economy.

Enlightened local leadership helps schools become significant developmental assets, as illustrated in each of our two examples. And, in the past few years, community engagement has been promoted through educational initiatives such as service-learning and place-based education. But although opportunities for engagement may exist, numerous factors undermine the effective use of schools as catalysts for community development. In this final section, we discuss some of the factors that may mitigate for and/or against school-community engagement, and what this may mean for both policy and practice.

Enhancing the Role of Schools in Community Development

Given the strong roles that schools have historically played in the cohesion of neighborhoods and communities, schools should be natural players in local community development efforts. And yet schools "often see themselves in the business of education and not community development" (Chung, 2002, p. 31). Educational leaders are increasingly faced with state and federal mandates that have radically narrowed the community role of schools and the scope of educational provision. For many teachers and administrators, this creates conditions that place civic education, community engagement, and place-based learning at direct odds with the goal of raising test scores.

Signed into law in early 2002, the No Child Left Behind Act requires states to develop K–12 academic achievement standards in mathematics and reading, and administer annual assessments in grades 3–8, and once in high school. States are required to develop annual proficiency goals for Adequate Yearly Progress (AYP) to attain 100% student proficiency by the academic year 2013–2014. Proficiency applies across all student subgroups, including racial and ethnic groups, economically disadvantaged students, special education students, and those with limited English proficiency (McGuinn, 2006; Nichols & Berliner, 2007).

It is difficult to overstate what high-stakes educational reform has meant for the way in which schools are organized, curricula are developed and taught, and, ultimately, for the relationship between schools and communities and the community development role that schools may assume. The pursuit of AYP vis-à-vis standardized test scores effectively sidetracks a deeper philosophical discussion concerning the ultimate purpose of education, much less how schooling might provide valuable lessons about learning to live and work collaboratively in one's home community or elsewhere. It is because of this that many commentators have argued that No Child Left Behind has undermined the capacity of local communities to determine what constitutes an appropriate education, and the capacity of schools to engage meaningfully with community needs (Gruenewald, 2006; Nichols & Berliner, 2007).

And yet there are numerous (although often unrecognized) examples of educational leadership keenly responsive to community development opportunities, and schools that take on active developmental roles, catalyzing community mobilization and change. This approach to educational leadership would appear to be supported by the newly revised standards for preparing school administrators, released by the Council of Chief State School Officers (CCSSO) in 2008. The Interstate School Leaders Licensure Council (ISLLC) standards are "the first step towards creating comprehensive, locally tailored practice standards and other approaches for developing and retaining high-quality school leaders" (CCSSO, 2008, p. 3). As standards and expectations for school leaders, they include

- Setting a widely shared vision for learning;
- Collaborating with faculty and community members, responding to diverse community interests and needs, and mobilizing community resources, and;
- Understanding, responding to, and influencing the political, social, legal, and cultural context. (CCSSO, 2008, p. 6)

These standards are clearly consistent with community engagement by educational leaders (Harmon & Schafft, 2009). However, community engagement is often underemphasized in teacher and educational leadership preparation programs (Lawson, Claiborne, Hardiman, Austin, & Surko, 2007), and the institutional realities of educational reforms such as NCLB further mitigate against an understanding of educational improvement and community betterment as interconnected goals (Longo, 2007).

Similarly, community-based developers often do not automatically partner with schools in community development initiatives. As Tompkins (2008) notes,

Community development activists find school officials unapproachable, bound by too many bureaucratic rules and practices; educators often do not believe they have the time or skill to engage students in place-based work and are worried that such work will distract from the push for higher test scores. Neither side has had much experience or training in developing cooperative relationships. And so each waits for the other to initiate the conversations and provide the energy and leadership to connect and plan together. (pp. 179–180)

However, there are strong precedents of schools and community organizations working together, notably social service agencies and youth development organizations. As we have argued, there are clear reasons for community-based developers, local organizations, and citizens groups to develop partnerships with local schools. An effective initial strategy for civic groups and community-based developers hoping to partner with schools may be to frame the benefits of partnership in terms of mutual benefit to school and community, especially if community mobilization is focused on issues that have direct impacts on the school district, such as community economic decline, affordable housing options, "brain drain," and/or youth development.

Examples of this type of partnership include service-learning and a range of different practices associated with integration of academic and vocational (career and technical) training, resulting in collaborations between schools and local businesses, apprenticeships, job-shadowing, and mentoring—all with the aim of extending classroom learning into real-world contexts (Green, 2005). School-business partnerships may play an important role in enhancing youth developmental assets, better preparing a local workforce, and providing new local opportunities for young people (Harmon, 2000; Scales et al., 2005). Although these partnerships in career-oriented programs tend to assist young people in aligning educational goals with potential career paths, service-learning is oriented more toward students performing community service work in non-profit organizations and public entities (Hengel & Shumer, 1997).

Similar to service-learning, place-based education is in part a reaction against patterns of development connected to economic globalization that have had disruptive rather than developmental effects on community, and it has also gained momentum as an approach to school-community engagement. In this sense, it is most directly concerned with relocalizing education and reconnecting education to community well-being and betterment. Place-based educators do this by drawing heavily upon local history, culture, and environment as the focus of study, using local issues to introduce students not only to core academic topics, but also to the inclination and skills needed to live well within any community in which they happen to reside. Advocates of place-based education argue that not only are there developmental outcomes for community, but that learning grounded in local context and experience has the best chance of engaging students intellectually, academically, and civically. Place-based education is not driven by a nostalgia for place, but rather by an acknowledgment of the interdependence among all people in all places. Acquiring the skills to analyze and understand local issues affecting communities leads to an enhanced capacity to understand similar issues at a global level. Therefore, although local in its orientation, place-based education is simultaneously global in its scope (Gruenewald & Smith, 2008).

Conclusion

Considering the role of schools in community development is more than simply a matter of identifying an additional resource to enlist in community betterment efforts and empower community members to enact local change more effectively on their own behalf. It really is also a consideration of the role of education itself. Numerous commentators have observed that public education has drifted increasingly toward business models of management, stressing standardized curricula and assessment of quantitatively measured indexes of individual-level achievement. These changes in the way education is structured have had the effect of removing education from the community sphere, disembedding it from place and local context. Worse yet are circumstances in local neighborhoods and communities where community development leaders view education as a drain upon scarce local tax revenues and educators see the schools only as supporting the prosperity of individual students without regard for service to community. Without more collaborative engagement by education and community development leaders, urban and rural places alike will both likely face enormous challenges in the global era.

Recent school reforms have used the concept of "accountability" as a centerpiece. Yet, under circumstances imposed by No Child Left Behind and other similar educational reforms, "accountability" does not meaningfully refer to one's family or one's community, but rather to the distanced and abstracted mandates of a removed bureaucratic other (Corbett, 2007)—often in the form of a standardized test score! This has disturbing implications for the health of our civic sphere. As Budge (2006) argues, however, local leaders "exercising a critical leadership of place may serve as a springboard for future generations of citizens that are accountable to each other and to the community they inhabit" (p. 9). That is, educational leadership that takes community development seriously is not simply an act of accountability for educational improvement, or even for economic development, but for democracy itself.

References

Brown, J. (2007). Parents building communities in schools. *Voices in Urban Education, 17*, 26–34.

Budge, K. (2006). Rural leaders, rural places: Problem, privilege, and possibility. *Journal of Research in Rural Education, 21*, 1–10. Retrieved March 10, 2009, from http://jrre.psu.edu/articles/21-13.pdf

Chung, C. (2002). *Using public schools as community-development tools: Strategies for community-based developers.* Cambridge, MA: Joint Center for Housing Studies of Harvard University.

Corbett, M. (2007). *Learning to leave: The irony of schooling in a coastal community.* Halifax, Nova Scotia: Fernwood.

Council of Chief State School Officers (CCSSO). (2008). *Educational leadership policy standards, 2008.* Washington, DC: Author.

Dodd, A. W., & Konzal, J. L. (2002). *How communities build stronger schools: Stories, strategies, and promising practices for educating every child.* New York: Palgrave Macmillan.

Finucan, K. (2000). Reading, writing and real estate. *Planning, 66*, 4–9.

Galura, J., Meiland, R., Ross, R., Callan, M. J., & Smith, R. (Eds.). (1993). *Praxis II: Service-learning resources for university students, staff, and faculty.* Ann Arbor, MI: OCLS Press.

Gibbs, R. (2005). Education as a rural development strategy. *Amber Waves, 3,* 20–25.

Glasmeier, A., & Salant, P. (2006). *Low-skill workers in rural America face permanent job loss.* Carsey Institute Policy Brief No. 2. Durham, NH: Carsey Institute. Retrieved July 26, 2009 from http://www.carseyinstitute.unh.edu/publications/PB_displacedworkers_06.pdf

Green, G. P. (2005). Work-based learning in rural America: Employer participation in school-to-work programs and apprenticeships. *Journal of Research in Rural Education, 20,* 1–10. Retrieved March 10, 2009, from http://jrre.psu.edu/articles/20-16.pdf

Gruenewald, D. (2006). Resistance, reinhabitation, and regime change. *Journal of Research in Rural Education, 21,* 1–7. Retrieved March 10, 2009, from http://jrre.psu.edu/articles/21-9.pdf

Gruenewald, D. A., & Smith, G. A. (2008). *Place-based education in the global age.* New York: Lawrence Erlbaum.

Harmon, H. L. (2000). Linking school-to-work and rural development. *FORUM for applied research and public policy, 15,* 97–100.

Harmon, H., & Schafft, K. A. (2009). Rural school leadership for collaborative community development. *Rural Educator, 30*(3), 4–9.

Hengel, M. S., & Shumer, R. (1997). *School-to-work and service learning.* Scotts Valley, CA: National Service-Learning Clearinghouse.

Hustedde, R. J., & Ganowicz, J. (2002). The basics: What's essential about theory for community development practice? *Journal of the Community Development Society, 33,* 1–19.

Killeen, K., & Schafft, K. A. (2008). The organizational and fiscal implications of transient student populations in urban and rural areas. In H. F. Ladd & E. B. Fiske (Eds.), *Handbook of research in education finance and policy* (pp. 631–650). New York: Routledge.

Kirsch, I., Braun, H., Yamamoto, K., & Sum, A. (2007). *America's perfect storm: Three forces changing our nation's future.* Princeton, NJ: Educational Testing Service.

Lawson, H. A., Claiborne, N., Hardiman, E., Austin, S., & Surko, M. (2007). Deriving theories of change from successful community development partnerships for youth: Implications for school improvement. *American Journal of Education, 114,* 1–40.

Longo, N. V. (2007). *Why community matters: Connecting education with civic life.* Albany: State University of New York Press.

Lyson, T. A. (2002). What does a school mean to a community? Assessing the social and economic benefits of schools to rural villages in New York. *Journal of Research in Rural Education, 17,* 131–137. Retrieved March 10, 2009, from http://jrre.psu.edu/articles/17-3.pdf

McGuinn, P. J. (2006). *No Child Left Behind and the transformation of federal education policy, 1965–2005.* Lawrence: University of Kansas Press.

Nichols, S. L., & Berliner, D. C. (2007). *Collateral damage: How high stakes testing corrupts America's schools.* Cambridge, MA: Harvard University Press.

Scales, P. C., Foster, K. C., Mannes, M., Horst, M. A., Pinto, K. C., & Rutherford, A. (2005). School-business partnerships, developmental assets, and positive outcomes among urban high school students: A mixed methods study. *Urban Education, 40,* 144–189.

Schafft, K. A., & Greenwood, D. J. (2003). The promises and dilemmas of participation: Action research, search conference methodology and community development. *Journal of the Community Development Society, 34,* 18–35.

Schafft, K. A., Alter, T. R., & Bridger, J. (2006). Bringing the community along: A case study of a school district's information technology rural development initiative. *Journal of Research in Rural Education, 21,* 1–10. Retrieved March 10, 2009, from http://jrre.psu.edu/articles/21-8.pdf

Theobald, P. (1997). *Teaching the commons.* Boulder, CO: Westview.

Tompkins, R. (2008). Overlooked opportunity: Students, educators, and education advocates contributing to community and economic development. In D. A. Gruenewald & G. A. Smith (Eds.), *Place-based education in the global age* (pp. 173–195). New York: Lawrence Erlbaum.

Warren, M. R. (2001). *Dry bones rattling.* Princeton, NJ: Princeton University Press.

Warren, M. R. (2005). Communities and schools: A new view of urban education reform. *Harvard Educational Review, 75,* 133–173.

Webster, B. H., & Alemayehu, B. (2006). *Income, earnings, and poverty data from the 2005 American community survey* (U.S. Census American Community Survey Reports). Washington, DC: U.S. Census Bureau.

Wilkinson, K. P. (1991). *The community in rural America.* New York: Greenwood.

16

Sustainable Communities

Sustainability and Community Development

Jerry Hembd and Jane Silberstein

BEHAVIOR OBJECTIVES

After studying this chapter and completing the online learning activities, students should be able to

1. Define sustainability and sustainable community development.

2. Discuss the IPAT identity and the three variables it employs to quantify the human impact on the environment.

3. Discuss the implications of a systems approach to community development.

4. Explain the evolving views of community and community economic development from the 1950s to present within a community capitals context.

5. Discuss The Natural Step (TNS) sustainability framework.

6. Discuss the five interrelated system levels that comprise the TNS framework.

7. Describe the ABCD planning process.

8. Explain backcasting from principles and how it incorporates sustainability into the ABCD planning process.

9. Define the seven steps to change (signposts for the journey to sustainability) as set forth in the TNS context.

10. Discuss the four challenges posed by the transition to sustainability and give examples of each.

Introduction ───

Sustainable was added to the postwar development lexicon in the 1980s—joining economic, urban, rural, industrial, agricultural, technological, and other types of development, including community. It remains a contested concept in terms of definition. More recently, the global triple crisis of peak oil, climate change, and natural resource depletion has created a contemporary imperative around sustainability and heightened interest in pursuing it through sustainable development.

The most commonly cited definition of sustainable development is contained in the Brundtland Report (The World Commission on Environment and Development, 1987, p. 43):

> Sustainable development is development that meets the needs of the present without compromising the ability of future generations to meet their own needs.

This definition emphasizes the meeting of needs, as opposed to wants, and places a clear focus on intergenerational equity. It implies the need for making development decisions on behalf of those not yet born and unable to participate in the process but who will nonetheless be affected by the outcomes of the process. What remains subject to interpretation is how this type of equity might be met and what it would entail.

The balance of the definition provides a measure of clarity, as well as introduces two fundamental parameters, but is cited much less often and remains less well-known.

> It [sustainable development] contains two key concepts:
>
> - the concept of "needs," in particular the needs of the world's poor, to which overriding priority should be given; and
> - the idea of limitations imposed by the state of technology and social organization on the environment's ability to meet present and future needs.

This expands the equity focus to include an intragenerational dimension through prioritization of the current needs of the poor. Limitations are explicitly invoked as directly related to the technological and organizational characteristics of the human enterprise and "the ability of the biosphere to absorb the effects of human activities" (The World Commission on Environment and Development, 1987, p. 8).

Development of all types requires reconsideration and transformation in light of the sustainability imperative. Community development is no exception. New approaches and models are emerging around the world. Evidence indicates that this is less a movement than a scientific revolution and, as such, represents a paradigm shift (Edwards, 2005). Traditional science, with its "reductionist" focus on individual parts of broader systems, is giving way to systems thinking, which expands the focus to include the interactions and relationships between the parts of these complex systems. Understanding the relationships between nature and society—between the biosphere and the human enterprise—is a fundamental aspect of this shift.

Communities pursuing sustainability are using science- and systems-based approaches as frameworks for their participatory planning and decision-making processes. This chapter anchors sustainability and community development within a broader global context and provides an overview of a sustainability framework and strategies that are coming to typify such communities.

Case Study 16.1   Living Routes Service-Learning

Living Routes develops accredited, college-level programs based in ecovillages around the world that help students gain the knowledge, skills, and inspiration to build sustainable lifestyles for themselves, their communities, and the planet. Living Routes is an independent, nonprofit educational organization with academic programs accredited by the University of Massachusetts Amherst. Living Routes programs are both academic and experiential. They challenge you to grow on academic, professional, and personal levels. Programs are taught by faculty with international experience and expertise across a wide range of fields. Students and faculty together create a learning community within the living community of the ecovillage. These remarkable educational environments facilitate real, transformative intellectual and personal development.

Program Basics: http://www.livingroutes.org/programs/p_basics.htm

Weblogs and pictures: http://www.livingroutes.org/weblogs/weblog.php

Programs: http://www.livingroutes.org/programs/specificmajors.htm

Contact: http://www.livingroutes.org/forms/contact.htm

A Global, Science-Based, Systems View

Sustainability refers to the ability of humans and human society to continue indefinitely within a finite natural world and its underlying natural cycles. At the center of this dynamic is human economic activity and its relationship with and impacts on the natural environment. It is no longer possible to think of the world as so big that the human enterprise has no impact on the planet's climate and the functioning of its ecosystems. The challenge is to move this relationship toward sustainability. The century-old expression "Think Globally, Act Locally" is appropriate. Sustainability strategies at the community level need to reflect a global view and understanding.

Science-based analyses are increasingly shaping and underpinning contemporary global discussions on sustainability and related policy considerations. The fourth assessment report of the Intergovernmental Panel on Climate Change (IPCC, 2007) had a profound effect. Two settled areas of science emerged—that the Earth is warming, and that humans are playing a significant role in that warming. The report goes on to offer mitigation and adaptation options. The Millennium Ecosystem Assessment (2005) is an international scientific consensus report that focuses on ecosystem services. It concludes that two thirds of ecosystems and their services are degraded or being used unsustainably, and it also outlines the changes necessary to reverse this degradation.

The IPAT identity (Ehrlich & Holdren, 1971), which is described below, provides a useful starting point for framing and working with sustainability issues. It was used to structure early debates about human factors affecting the environment and remains a popular framework today. IPAT deconstructs the human impact on the environment [I] into the product of three variables: total population [P]; affluence (per capita consumption or income) [A]; and the level of technology [T], which reflects the environmental impact of each unit of consumption—yielding the I = PAT equation.

When the IPAT identity was introduced, the world's population totaled 3.7 billion, was growing around 2% annually, and was characterized by an exponential growth curve. Population growth has since slowed to a current rate of 1.2% annually. World population is projected to stabilize at around 9.1 billion in 2050. Nonetheless, this represents a fairly significant increase over the current figure of 6.7 billion. This growth will occur primarily in developing countries, and primarily within the urban areas of those countries. Population growth has been and continues to be a variable that adds to the human impact on the global environment.

Regarding the affluence part of the relationship, the global consumption playing field is getting noticeably more crowded. The size of the world economy increased tenfold between 1950 and 2000. China has grown at around 10% per year for the past two decades, doubling in size economically every 7 years. India's growth rate, although lower than China's, still allows it to double in size economically every 8 to 9 years. China and India both have emerging middle classes that are estimated to number around 300 million—equivalent to the current total population of the United States—and, at present, they seem to be using U.S. consumers as their consumption role models. Economic growth has consistently exceeded population growth and is projected to continue to do so. This means that not only are there more and more people, but that each person, on average, consumes more and more each year.

This leaves only technology as a potentially mitigating variable. In order to reduce environmental impacts faster than the combined growth rates in population and consumption, the implication is rapid technological change. There is considerable debate regarding the merits of technological optimism and the belief that answers to the sustainability question lie solely with technological change. A countervailing view acknowledges the scientific uncertainty inherent in the release and widespread application of new technologies and recommends use of the precautionary principle. This principle is folk wisdom—look before you leap. It has been defined as follows: "When an activity raises threats of harm to human health or the environment, precautionary measures should be taken even if some cause-and-effect relationships are not fully established scientifically."[1]

The affluence variable, in particular, embodies the current structure of the human enterprise and its emphasis on economic growth. (This has interrelated production dimensions that bring the technology variable into play.) The evidence that more is better, however, or that higher levels of consumption yield higher levels of happiness is less than compelling. A new field of research, happiness studies, has been exploring this question. The correlation between absolute income and happiness appears to extend only up to some threshold of "sufficiency," and the importance of nonmonetary and nonmaterial sources of human well-being is being recognized and documented.

No single element of the IPAT identity fully captures or explains the growing human impact on the environment. The same is true in terms of implications for human well-being. It is the interrelationships and implied trade-offs between the variables that point to the need for a broader context. In order to make this analytical step, a systems-based definition of sustainability is needed—one that emphasizes key relationships among economy, society, and the environment. The properties of systems depend on the relationships between the parts as much as on the parts themselves. This systems view is important and applicable at all levels—from global to local.

Community Sustainability in Context

A standard economic model can be used to demonstrate and link global and community-level analytical frameworks as well as underscore the importance of systems thinking. The building block of this model is capital. Capital, as an economic concept, is a stock of anything (such as land, machines, and money) that has the capacity to generate a flow of benefits valued by humans.

The standard model views total capital stock as composed of three types of capital:

- Natural capital—nonrenewable and renewable resources including the atmosphere, sources (of raw materials) and sinks (for storing or recycling waste products) of the planet, and other ecological resources and ecosystem services;

---

[1]This definition was agreed upon at the Wingspread Conference on the Precautionary Principle, which took place in January 1998 (http://www.sehn.org/wing.html).

- Physical (built) capital—based on manufacturing or related economic activities and including machinery, buildings, houses, roads, railways, and infrastructure; and
- Human capital—knowledge, technical know-how, and health.

This is a simplified model, by design. More nuanced models can be expanded to treat financial and built capital separately and to include other types of capital such as cultural, social, and political. Nonetheless, the standard model remains the basis for the commonly used tripartite representation of the components of a community as economy (built capital), society (human capital), and environment (natural capital) as shown in Figure 16.1.

Figure 16.1   Evolving Views of the Community

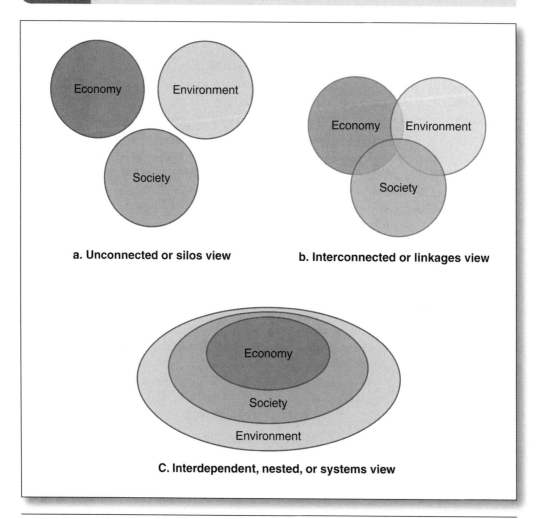

SOURCE: Copyright © 1999 Maureen Hart. Reprinted with permission. Available at http://www.sustainable measures.com.

These Venn diagram depictions can be interpreted at other levels, such as global or national, but in this case, they represent a simplified community-level analysis and associated visual framework. They are used here to demonstrate the evolving views of the community and economic development in the postwar period, with an emphasis on the perceived relationships among the three types of capital. These changing views are highlighted because they reflect the historical movement in thinking that has led to the emerging systems view. This analytical approach links directly to the community capitals frameworks currently in vogue.[2]

Figure 16.1a depicts economy, society, and environment as unconnected to each other and representing a "silos" view of capitals within the community. This typified the industrial recruiting wave of economic development that prevailed from the 1950s to the early 1980s.[3] This approach drew its inspiration from export base models, and it was a time when environmental impacts and potential limits were not well recognized. The focus was on economic development, and industrial development in particular, and the environment (natural capital) was seen as a relatively unlimited resource to be exploited, as needed, to support industrial development. Economic concerns were accorded primacy over environmental and societal considerations.

Figure 16.1b is representative of both the cost competition and regional competitiveness waves of community economic development; the former gained strength from the early 1980s through the early 1990s, and the latter dates from the early 1990s and continues today. Economic concerns were no longer viewed as fully independent of and primary to social and environmental considerations, with the economy, society, and environment seen as linked or interconnected. Although this implies that all three need to be considered for development decisions in light of these links, note that large portions of each circle remain outside of the interconnected areas. This depiction does not reflect, in a meaningful way, the environmental impacts of the human enterprise that have become increasingly apparent over the past few decades. Notably, this type of diagram is often used to depict a sustainable development point of view.

The depiction in Figure 16.1c is fundamentally different from the other two. It shifts attention to a central aspect of the sustainability revolution and what can be termed the fourth wave of community and economic development. With its nested and interdependent circles, the emphasis is on a systems view of the community and the interrelationships between its parts.

---

[2]See Flora, Flora, and Fey (2004) as a basic reference for the community capitals model.

[3]The three waves of community economic development provide a useful historical context for the emergence of sustainable community development as a "fourth-wave" phenomenon. A synthesis of the literature related to these three well-documented, postwar waves of development can be found in Shaffer, Deller, and Marcouiller (2006).

Specifically, it shows that the economy exists and functions *within* society, and together they exist and function *within* a finite environment and are totally dependent on it. A growing economy implies that the size of its circle changes—gets larger—relative to the unchanging size of the environment circle. The longer-term environmental implications of continued economic growth are made readily apparent. In terms of sustainability, this changes how community development decisions must be considered.

The contrast between Figures 16.1b and 16.1c illustrates the differences between the concepts of weak and strong sustainability. Proponents of weak sustainability maintain that natural and built capital are substitutable in the long term. This view places considerable reliance on anticipated technological change and its ability to create built capital solutions to compensate for environmental degradation and a decreasing stock of natural capital. This reflects the technological optimism noted earlier. The strong sustainability view, on the other hand, maintains that certain functions that the environment and ecosystems perform cannot be duplicated by humans and/or built capital, and that the existing stock of natural capital must be maintained and enhanced.

The interconnections and links in Figure 16.1b, while invoking relationships between economy, society, and environment, are significantly different from the interrelationships inherent in the systems view shown in Figure 16.1c. The systems view provides a simple way of perceiving the implications of scale—in this case, scale of the human enterprise relative to the finite environment or global ecosystem. These sustainability constraints can be viewed as system boundaries or boundary conditions (Ny, MacDonald, Broman, Yamamoto, & Robèrt, 2006). These boundary conditions have relevance at the community level and are clearly reflected in emerging approaches to community sustainability.

Community Sustainability in Practice

The explicit consideration of sustainability represents a growing but often controversial approach or theme within community development. There are differing definitions of sustainability, which create obvious difficulties in terms of mutually agreed-upon approaches. There are numerous examples of strategies that have sustainability components—such as industrial ecology, triple bottom-line business development, green jobs, renewable energy, and so on—but far fewer cases of community-based and comprehensive approaches to development that are framed conceptually around sustainability. This is changing. Among these latter approaches, The Natural Step[4]

---

[4]TNS is an international nonprofit research, education, and advisory organization. Its international Web portal (www.thenaturalstep.org) provides links to 11 country-specific TNS organizations and a wide array of resources, case studies, and research about application of the TNS framework

(TNS) provides an emblematic example of a sustainability framework that is being applied in communities around the world. It is given emphasis here because it is the most fully developed framework of its type, it reflects the global science-based and systems view outlined previously, and it has an accompanying track record of community-based application and success.

TNS Framework

TNS is a framework to help communities, businesses, organizations, and individuals take meaningful steps toward sustainability. It is nonproprietary and nonprescriptive. It includes a decision-making framework and process as well as a shared language that communities can use to plan and implement for sustainability.

The TNS planning approach is framed within five hierarchically different yet interrelated levels:

1. *System*—the overall principles of the functioning of the system, in this case, the biosphere and the human enterprise

2. *Success*—sustainability principles for a favorable outcome of planning within the system

3. *Strategic*—a systematic, step-by-step approach for sustainable development to reach the favorable outcome

4. *Actions*—every concrete step and action in the transition to sustainability

5. *Tools*—tools to systematically monitor the (4) actions to ensure that they are (3) strategic to arrive at (2) success in the (1) system.

Robèrt et al. (2002) use this systems approach to show that familiar sustainability tools and approaches are complementary, rather than contradictory, and can be used in parallel for strategic sustainable development. The tools they use as examples include life cycle assessment, ecological footprinting, Factor 4, Factor 10, sustainable technology development, natural capitalism, and the TNS framework. They emphasize the importance of a systems perspective to guide the selection of relevant tools, policies, and actions.

The TNS framework identifies four system conditions for sustainability. They are premised on the scientific understanding of basic biological and geological cycles and the laws of thermodynamics, which constitute the overall principles at the system level. The system conditions provide principles for success to guide subsequent planning and actions and are stated as follows:

In the sustainable society, nature is not subject to systematically increasing:

1. concentrations of substances extracted from the Earth's crust;

2. concentrations of substances produced by society;

3. degradation by physical means; and, in that society;

4. people are not subject to conditions that systematically undermine their capacity to meet their needs.

The first system condition focuses on stored deposits of minerals in the Earth's crust and rests on the first and second laws of thermodynamics, which hold that nothing disappears and everything disperses. The Earth is a closed system with respect to matter. The amount of matter has not changed and will not change. The first law states that total mass is conserved. It does not disappear, it just changes form. For example, the burning of fossil fuels simply creates gases in the atmosphere. The second law states that matter and energy tend to break down over time. For example, a car will eventually turn into rust. The second law also states that as matter breaks down, it tends to disperse and bioaccumulate. Examples range from mercury and lead poisoning to water pollution and toxic waste. All versions of the second law have the idea of irreversibility in nature in common. If this first system condition is not met, concentrations of substances in the environment will increase and eventually reach limits—many of which are unknown—beyond which irreversible changes occur.

The second system condition focuses on synthetic compounds and other man-made substances and materials. More than 100,000 substances fall into this category, and reliable and established toxicity information is available for only around 15% of them. The two laws of thermodynamics apply here as well. Matter changes form but does not disappear. These substances tend to break down, disperse, and bioaccumulate. Persistent man-made compounds— those that are not easily broken down by nature or through natural processes—are of concern worldwide because of their toxicity, their tendency to accumulate in human and animal tissue, and their persistence in the environment. If this system condition is not met, as was the case for the first system condition, the concentration of substances in the environment will increase and eventually reach limits beyond which irreversible changes occur.

The third system condition focuses on what can be termed *ecosystem manipulation*. This condition underscores the need to maintain the integrity of ecosystems, including biodiversity, and to place value on the functions of living systems such as water and air purification; pollination and climate regulation; oxygen production; protection against cosmic and ultraviolet radiation; solar energy; and the storage, detoxification, and recycling of human waste—all examples of ecosystem services. This implies drawing resources from only well-managed ecosystems and using them efficiently and exercising general caution in all kinds of manipulation of nature. For this system condition to be met, human activities need to work in harmony with the cyclic ecological principles of nature.

The fourth system condition addresses the necessity of equity and provides an ethical aspect to TNS. One way to think of this is that the types of large-scale changes implied by the first three system conditions will necessitate high levels of social stability and cooperation. This condition has been framed within a human needs context based on the work of Manfred Max-Neef. Max-Neef (1992) postulates that "basic needs are finite, few and classifiable" (p. 199), and that they "are the same in all cultures and all historical periods" (p. 200). In contrast to Maslow's hierarchy of needs, Max-Neef believes that these needs are always present. "What changes, both over time and through cultures, is the way or means by which the needs are satisfied" (p. 200). He does not believe needs are substitutable—you can fulfill one need to a great extent, but that does nothing about the other needs. You can, however, depending on the choice of need satisfiers, fulfill more than one need at a time. The lack of any one of these needs suggests poverty of some type. The nine basic needs are subsistence, protection/security, affection, understanding, participation, leisure, creation, identity/meaning, and freedom. Unless basic human needs are met worldwide through fair and efficient use of resources, it will be difficult to meet the other three system conditions on a global scale.

The first three system conditions are grounded in the physical and natural sciences and represent a clear departure from most existing community development frameworks and approaches. They provide the needed systems framework within which to reconsider and transform community development. The fourth system condition covers more familiar social science territory. In some ways, this is also the least fully integrated part of the framework. The nexus between the two, where natural and social sciences meet, remains to be more fully established and elaborated. The community development field clearly has much to bring to the community sustainability equation.

The planning and decision-making process associated with TNS builds on a generic strategic planning model that is similar in many ways to existing processes used by community developers. But it is the differences that make it come alive in terms of sustainability at the community level, and these differences flow directly from the four system conditions. The TNS strategic planning framework uses "backcasting from principles" and what is referred to as an ABCD methodology.

Backcasting is a way of planning in which a successful outcome is imagined in the future and used to help decide which actions need to be taken today to reach that outcome. Forecasting, by contrast, projects current trends (and problems) into the future, which may limit the range of options and inhibit creativity. TNS applies backcasting from the four system conditions or principles as a means to achieving sustainability. These science-based principles represent something that can be agreed upon at the system level. As the community frames its success level, which includes its compelling vision of the future, it is with the understanding that contravention of system-level principles will make the community unsustainable. At the strategic level, the community identifies concrete steps and actions that serve as flexible stepping stones to move it in the right direction. Transitions and next steps are continuously reevaluated along the way.

Backcasting from principles is integrated into the ABCD planning process. The four steps of this continuous process are as follows:

- *Step A—Awareness*: The TNS framework is shared to create a common understanding of what sustainability means and how it can provide a model for community building. Participating community members are able to approach planning and implementing for sustainability by collectively agreeing upon and trusting the same rules. The community starts the process with a shared sustainability language.

- *Step B—Baseline Analysis*: This is an assessment to see where the community is today using the four system conditions as a lens. For example, the community identifies the ways it is increasing dependence on fossil fuels, scarce metals, and other substances extracted from the biosphere. This assessment can proceed from a meta-analysis level to the listing of all current flows and practices that are problematic, from a sustainability perspective, for each sector of the community. These would include transportation, food, housing, land use, and so on. Similarly, this is the time to determine all of the community assets that are currently in place to deal with these problems and serve as building blocks for the transition to the future. In this step, the current reality is assessed using the same principles that define success in the future, which is an essential element of backcasting. Communities learn to assess and reassess the course they are taking after each action in relation to the four principles of sustainability.

- *Step C—Compelling Vision (and Creative Solutions)*: This is the brainstorming step of the process. A positive vision of the desired future is developed that specifies agreed-upon and desirable community characteristics. These are compared with the baseline evaluation and four system conditions to ensure they describe an actual sustainable outcome. Using the systemic limits of the sustainability principles to generate creativity, possible solutions and actions that would lead to success in the future are listed. At this point, the community can begin to identify early action steps that could create the conditions for future possibilities.

- *Step D—Down to Action*: The creative solutions generated during Step C are both scrutinized and prioritized through the use of three questions. Measures that generate positive responses to the following questions pass scrutiny and become candidates for prioritization.

  1. Does this action or solution proceed in the right direction with respect to all four principles of sustainability?

  2. Does this action or solution provide a stepping stone or flexible platform for future actions?

  3. Will this action or solution provide sufficient return on investment and add impetus to the process?

How This Process Differs

To summarize, this planning process differs from most models in two fundamental ways. First, backcasting from principles entails the development of a community vision that clearly complies with the four system conditions. Success, in this case, is defined at the principle level, where sustainability principles have been agreed upon at the beginning of the process. Second, the prioritization process for actions and solutions includes the use of three focused questions (as part of Step D) to determine which ideas pass muster with respect to sustainability, flexibility, and return on investment. This strategically winnows the set of possibilities for subsequent prioritization.

Sustainability Practice and Principles

In Sweden, where this framework originated in 1989, there are more than 70 "eco-municipalities," and they comprise a quarter of all local governments. An eco-municipality attempts to develop an ecologically, economically, and socially healthy community using the TNS framework as a guide. The largest concentration of local governments and communities in North America that have adopted this framework is in the state of Wisconsin.

Seven Steps Toward Sustainability

James and Lahti (2004) provide an extensive analysis of the use of TNS in Sweden. They focus on changes at the community level that led to sustainable practices in the areas of renewable energy, transportation and mobility, housing, business, buildings, schools and education, agriculture, waste, natural resources, and land use and planning. All of these specific areas of practice were approached within the systems context provided by TNS. A range of specific examples of strategies, actions, and plans are provided for each area—with accompanying North American examples. But the emphasis remains on the principles and steps essential to successful community adoption of change proposals rather than on a compendium of sustainable development practices.

The analysis identified seven steps to change as signposts for the journey to sustainability:

1. Finding the fire souls—"fire souls are community citizens who have a burning interest in sustainable development and community change" (p. 204)

2. Education and raising awareness—this coincides with Step A of the planning process

3. Official endorsement of sustainability operating principles—gaining the support of local political leadership as a beginning of the institutionalization of community change

4. Involving the implementers—enlisting local officials, community members, households, and businesses

5. Applying the sustainability framework—using the shared sustainability language of TNS and the associated steps of the planning process

6. Whole plan endorsement—achieving official adoption of the sustainability plan

7. Keep it going—continued use of the framework combined with sustainability indicators and measurement of progress toward the system conditions.

The Natural Step in North America

The first community to adopt the TNS framework in North America was Whistler, British Columbia, Canada, in 2004. It took a decade of work for the community to develop an understanding of what sustainability meant within their specific context as a resort community facing the growth challenges associated with hosting the 2010 Winter Olympic and Paralympic Games. Whistler subsequently created an award-winning, comprehensive, community sustainability plan guided by local values and TNS's sustainability principles.[5] Other Canadian communities using TNS are District of North Vancouver, British Columbia; Canmore, Olds, and Airdrie, Alberta; and Wolfville, Nova Scotia.

The Alliance for Sustainability in the Chequamegon Bay area of northwest Wisconsin, inspired by the story of Sweden's eco-municipalities, held an international conference in 2005 to explore the principles and concepts of TNS and the potential for eco-municipalities in the region. Local governments began adopting eco-municipality resolutions, starting with the City of Washburn, later that year.[6] Washburn was the first community to take such a step in the United States. Since then, more than 25 towns, cities, and counties in Wisconsin have become eco-municipalities, passing resolutions adopting the TNS framework as a guide for planning and decision making.[7] Additional

[5]The TNS Web site provides background information and links related to the Whistler experience (www.thenaturalstep.org/en/resort-municipality-whistler-bc).

[6]Gruder, Haines, Hembd, MacKinnon, and Silberstein (2007), in response to statewide interest, developed a tool kit for local governments interested in pursuing sustainability and leading by example.

[7]The University of Wisconsin–Extension Sustainability Team maintains a Web-based Sustainable Communities Capacity Center (www.capacitycenter.org) that features an eco-municipality section. This section includes information on all eco-municipalities in the state and related TNS and community sustainability resources.

communities in Wisconsin and other states are using TNS both with and without passing formal resolutions. Examples are Corvallis, Oregon; Hanover and Portsmouth, New Hampshire; and Lawrence Township, New Jersey.

TNS is not the only framework being used to guide efforts aimed at community sustainability. It does, however, fully incorporate the science-based and systems approach outlined at the beginning of the chapter. It is being applied by communities around the world and is generating a significant knowledge base at the conceptual, practical, and case study levels. The American Planning Association adopted a "Policy Guide on Planning for Sustainability" in 2000 that delineates four basic objectives guided by the four system conditions of TNS (American Planning Association, 2000). And, although the focus here has been on communities, TNS has a strong history of use and application by the business and nonprofit sectors, as well as at the household level.

Shared Principles

The types of changes in thinking, understanding, and decision making outlined in this chapter and represented by TNS, along with other models, portray elements of an ongoing paradigm shift and sustainability revolution.[8] At this juncture, it is less a matter of identifying the top 10 things a community can do to be more sustainable and more one of rethinking the nature of the entire human enterprise and its relationship to a finite global ecosystem. Edwards (2005) analyzes this ongoing sustainability revolution and assesses existing sets of principles that characterize a range of approaches with emphases on community, commerce, natural resources, ecological design, and the biosphere. He identifies seven common themes: stewardship, respect for limits, interdependence, economic restructuring, fair distribution, intergenerational perspective, and nature as a model and teacher. Similarly, Assadourian (2008), in an overview including TNS, lists these key areas of community engagement (practices): modeling sustainability through physical design, cultivating community connections, localizing economic production, mobilizing community funds, and mobilizing society using community members' energy and resources for broader sustainability efforts. These shared principles provide a first sketch of the emerging sustainability paradigm.

---

[8]Another community-based approach that is expanding its reach and application internationally is the Transition Towns model. Also known as the Transition Network and Transition Movement, it was founded in Ireland in 2005, spread to England in 2006, and has since grown to include 150 communities worldwide. Boulder County, Colorado, was the first Transition Town in the United States, and it has since been joined by 48 others. The transition concept focuses on reducing the impacts of industrial society and an "elegant descent" from the peak of human production and consumption. Rob Hopkins is the founder of this movement and has authored a detailed transition handbook (Hopkins, 2008).

Conclusion

The transition to sustainability poses significant challenges. A revolutionary process and attendant paradigm change of this type will require considerable effort at the community level before the tipping point is reached. As traditional models and approaches lose their explanatory power and applicability, viable new models and approaches will take their place. Systems thinking—and an explicit focus on the interactions and relationships between nature and society—enables us to reconsider and transform development of all types in light of the sustainability imperative.

Orr (2004) lists four challenges posed by the transition to sustainability:

- "We need more accurate models, metaphors, and measures to describe the human enterprise relative to the biosphere" (p. 60).
- It "will require a marked improvement and creativity in the arts of citizenship and governance" (p. 61).
- The public's discretion will need to be informed through greatly improved education (p. 62).
- It "will require learning how to recognize and solve divergent problems, which is to say a higher level of spiritual awareness" (p. 63).

This chapter describes fundamental responses to these challenges. Science- and systems-based frameworks are enabling communities to move from incremental to transformational approaches to sustainability. Community-based approaches to sustainability firmly point to the importance of decision making and control at the local level whenever possible and practical. Although not covered in this chapter, all sustainability efforts will be made more potent through a commitment to public education. Finally, to quote Orr (2004), the ability to recognize and resolve divergent problems "must be founded on a higher order of awareness that honors mystery, science, life, and death" (p. 64). Examples abound at the community level of ongoing change and capacity building in response to each of these challenges. They provide reasons to be optimistic and hopeful for the future. Community developers, with their strong sense of place and tradition of purposive change, are poised to play key roles in the ongoing sustainability revolution.

References

American Planning Association (2000). *Policy guide on planning for sustainability*. Available: www.planning.org/policy/guides/adopted/sustainability.htm

Assadourian, E. (2008). Engaging communities for a sustainable world. In G. Gardner & T. Prugh (Project Directors), *2008 state of the world: Innovations for a sustainable economy* (pp. 151–165). New York: Norton.

Edwards, A. R. (2005). *The sustainability revolution: Portrait of a paradigm shift*. Gabriola Island, BC, Canada: New Society Publishers.

Ehrlich, P., & Holdren, J. (1971). Impact of population growth. *Science, 171,* 1212–1219.

Flora, C., Flora, J., & Fey, S. (2004). *Rural communities: Legacy and change* (2nd ed.). Boulder, CO: Westview.

Gruder, S., Haines, A., Hembd, J., MacKinnon, L., & Silberstein, J. (2007). *Toward a sustainable community: A toolkit for local government.* Available: http://www4.uwm.edu/shwec/publications/cabinet/reductionreuse/SustainabilityToolkit.pdf

Hopkins, R. (2008). *The transition handbook: From oil dependency to local resilience.* Totnes, Devon, UK: Green Books Ltd.

IPCC. (2007). *Climate change 2007: Synthesis report. Contribution of working groups I, II and III to the fourth assessment report of the Intergovernmental Panel on Climate Change.* Geneva, Switzerland: Author.

James, S., & Lahti, T. (2004). *The natural step for communities: How cities and towns can change to sustainable practices.* Gabriola Island, BC, Canada: New Society Publishers.

Max-Neef, M. (1992). Development and human needs. In P. Ekins & M. Max-Neef (Eds.), *Real-life economics* (pp. 197–214). London: Routledge.

Millennium Ecosystem Assessment. (2005). *Ecosystems and human well-being: Synthesis.* Washington, DC: Island Press.

Ny, H., MacDonald, J. P., Broman, G., Yamamoto, R., & Robèrt, K.-H. (2006). Sustainability constraints as system boundaries. *Journal of Industrial Ecology, 10,* 61–77.

Orr, D. (2004). *The last refuge: Patriotism, politics, and the environment in an age of terror.* Washington, DC: Island Press.

Robèrt, K.-H., Schmidt-Bleek, J., Aloisi de Larderie, J., Basile, G., Jansen, J. L., Kuehr, R., Price Thomas, P., Suzuki, M., Hawken, P., & Wackernagel, M. (2002). Strategic sustainable development—Selection, design and synergies of applied tools. *Journal of Cleaner Production, 10,* 197–214.

Shaffer, R., Deller, S., & Marcouiller, D. (2006). Rethinking community economic development. *Economic Development Quarterly, 20,* 59–74.

The World Commission on Environment and Development. (1987). *Our common future.* Oxford, UK: Oxford University Press.

17

Globalization and Community Development

Synergy or Disintegration

Paulette Meikle and Gary Paul Green

BEHAVIOR OBJECTIVES

After studying this chapter and completing the online learning activities, students should be able to

1. Define the four processes of globalization.

2. Identify the alleged benefits and costs of globalization to communities.

3. Understand the effects of trade liberalization on developing countries.

4. Provide examples of dilemmas created through linking environmental and economic policies on the global level.

5. Describe what is meant by "globalization from below."

6. Explain several strategies for relocalizing economies in the context of globalization.

7. Explain some of the lessons from the case of the United States banning imports of tuna from Mexico.

8. Understand the implications of the antiglobalization efforts on the role of social movements.

Introduction

The new era of globalization has contributed to the increased mobility of people, cultures, ideas, goods, and services. Anthony Giddens (1990) defines globalization as a decoupling of space and time. He notes that with instantaneous communications, knowledge and culture can be shared globally simultaneously. Thus, social scientists are increasingly endorsing the view that globalization encompasses changes in the spatial, environmental, and economic contours of communities (Conroy & Glasmeier, 1992; Gill, 1992; Hodges, 2005; Meikle-Yaw, 2005; Stiglitz, 2002).[1] Globalization has four inherent processes:

a. *Economic*—the deepening integration of markets as a result of heightened trade and investment, as well as enhanced capital mobility. These economic structural developments are embedded in technological and spatial changes in the movement of capital and the organization of production.

b. *Political*—the restructuring of power relations associated with new supranational centers of political authority. The declining influence of national governments and the rising power of transnational corporations is critical to this restructuring.

c. *Cultural*—diffusion of values, tastes, and norms driven by communications technology.

d. *Ideological*—growing emphasis of ideas associated with market liberalism, deregulation, and privatization (Skogstad, 2000).

Proponents claim that globalization as a contemporary social change phenomenon will generate unprecedented economic prosperity; promote greater competitiveness; and encourage good governance, transparency, and accountability. These changes are seen as contributing to the economic advancement for poor countries. Globalization, it is argued, will provide poor countries with access to overseas markets so that they can sell their goods; allow foreign investment that will make new products at cheaper prices; and open borders so that people can travel abroad to be educated, work, and send home earnings to help their families and fund new businesses (Stiglitz, 2006). However, the ratio of income of the richest 10% of countries to the poorest 10% of countries rose from 10.5 in 1975 to 18.5 in 2005. Countries (and, by extension, their local communities) that do not possess comparative advantage in the world economy have inherent difficulties. For example, the World Bank (2004) points out that between 1965 and 1995, the gap between developed countries and most developing countries widened vastly. Asia was the only region to realize considerable convergence toward the developed countries' level of GNP per capita (The World Bank Group, 2004). A country like China, however, has decidedly benefited from trade openness. For example, per-capita income in China has nearly quadrupled in

---

[1]We argue that local economies have always been a part of the globalization process, beginning with the advent of colonialism through the era of the internalization of world economies in the 17th to 19th centuries, but the globalizing effect on local communities, cultures, peoples, and politics has accelerated dramatically since the 20th century, particularly during the past five decades or so (we refer to this as the new era of globalization).

the past 15 or so years. This growth rate compares favorably to that of the "Asian tigers"—Hong Kong, Korea, Singapore, and Taiwan—which had an average growth rate of 7%–8% in the 1980s and 1990s (Hu & Mohsin, 1997). The World Bank further points out that per-capita income in the newly industrialized Asian economies such as Hong Kong (China), the Republic of Korea, Singapore, and Taiwan (China) increased from 18% of the developed countries' average in 1965 to 66% in 1995. Over this same period, African countries became poorer, in that the average per-capita income in African countries equaled 14% of the developed country level in 1965 and just 7% in 1995 (The World Bank Group, 2004).

Market-oriented, corporate-led globalization has major implications for localities. There is increasing apprehension that local communities in developed countries may lose farm and nonfarm livelihoods to global competition and that globalization may threaten their sustainable development paths. In addition, addressing global environmental problems at the local level has taken on new dimensions. The ability of local governments to protect the quality of life of residents may be impaired by global processes. Social scientists are seeking to fully understand, explain, and predict the comprehensive set of environmental and economic factors that affect communities, regions, and nation-states, and the consequences of their connections to the global system.

Case Study 17.1	International Development and Service-Learning

The University of Technology in Kingston, Jamaica, created a service-learning program in 1995. The program was adapted from a mandatory community service program created by the university. A goal of the program is to present students with some of the unfortunate and formidable social conditions seen in Jamaica, and help them address these problems in a tangible way. The service-learning program is run directly through the University of Technology, and an advisory board of faculty and local representatives involved with the projects oversees implementation. The program, which is required for all students in their first year at the university, requires completion of 45 service-learning hours in the field. Students are allowed to work as individuals or in groups. There are a number of partnerships with schools and organizations in the communities near the university. Effort is made to expose students to issues of class, race, and poverty in their service-learning projects. An example partnership is with Papine High School, where the university staff and students work with high school staff and students to provide resources for enhancing education and elevating the school in the ability it has to educate students well.

SOURCE: Chisholm, L. A. (Ed.). (2005). *Knowing and doing the theory and practice of service-learning.* New York: International Partnership for Service-Learning and Leadership.

Understanding Globalization and Community Development

The effects of globalization, although increasingly ubiquitous, are not homogeneous in benefits or in threats for communities. Pertinent issues surround the question of how globalization fuels change in the substance of social relations and in the livelihood and environmental foundations of communities in different geographic milieus. Several questions arise: How has globalization produced unequal environmental costs and livelihood benefits in local communities in developing countries? What are the economic, political, and social differences between developed countries and developing countries in the way they partake in the benefits of globalization and respond to the risks of globalization?

Social scientists are now, more than ever before, challenged to examine the global nature of community change as they grapple with people, boundaries, and interactions in diverse economic, environmental, and social spheres. For example, how has globalization produced unequal economic and environmental costs and benefits among individuals, communities, and nation-states? This is particularly important for understanding community change, where social and economic relations continue to be embedded in space and place. Yet different communities experience the disembedding of local economic and environmental activities through accelerated infiltration of shared lifestyles via fluid and unbounded cultures, infiltration of services, innovations, economic activities, and even political persuasions.

The purpose of this chapter is to discuss the effects of globalization on livelihoods and the environment at the local level. It examines how global trade may adversely affect the economy and the environment at the local level. It makes the link between trade policies and environmental policies in promoting sustainable development. The core of the chapter places particular attention on the policies governing the issues of trade liberalization, economic growth, and cross-border externality. Most important, it investigates whether the promise that globalization will bring greater prosperity to local communities in diverse places is making such a mark. The chapter ends by evaluating conflicting trade and environmental policy issues, and how they might be resolved at the local level in the interest of sustainable community development. What kinds of justice and social equality movement and strategies can we employ to address the ramifications of the ravishing effects of globalizing forces on the environment and local livelihoods and social organization? Is the bottom-up social movement viable in these regards? Such movements are locally grounded, nationally networked, and globally connected. Other pertinent issues are the emergence of the "global justice movement," the "antiglobalization movement," and "globalization from below" (Katz-Fishman & Scott, 2008).

Trade Liberalization

The international trading system is based on the principles of free trade, which began in the 1940s as an alternative to the protectionist global trade regime. Trade liberalization and globalization have led to a tremendous expansion of world trade over the past few decades and are anchored in the belief that markets are self-regulating. Lower tariffs and other trade barriers over the past five decades have facilitated free trade and the closer integration of national economies. Free trade is rooted in the logic of comparative advantage. Theoretically, communities and nation-states trade to exploit the comparative advantage they derive from differing factor endowments, such as available resources, the quality and price of labor, the policy environment, the costs of inputs, and proximity to markets (Hart & Sushma, 1992). The principle of comparative advantage refers to the idea that the gains from trade are achieved as an economy specializes. For example, if the United States can produce a set of goods at a lower cost than a foreign country can, and if the foreign country can produce some other set of goods at a lower cost than the United States can, then clearly it would be best for the United States to trade its relatively cheaper goods for the foreign country's relatively cheaper goods. In this way, both countries may gain from trade.

The interaction between international trade and the environment is increasingly becoming a major community issue (Goodman & Howarth, 1997; Kirmani, 1994a). The United Nations Conference on Environment and Development (UNCED) held in Rio in 1992 belabored the value of integrating international environmental and economic policies. Trade policy measures for environmental purposes, it was argued, should not constitute only a means of arbitrary or unjustifiable discrimination or a disguised restriction on international trade. Environmental measures addressing global environmental problems should, as far as possible, be based on an international consensus.

Increasing world trade and severe global environmental pressures bring trade and environmental protection interests into tension. The trade-environment debate took on widespread prominence in 1991 when the General Agreement on Tariffs and Trade (GATT) dispute settlement panel ruled that import restrictions placed by the United States against tuna imports from Mexico were inconsistent with GATT rules. The conflict arose when Mexico contested the ban, which was imposed under the U.S. Marine Mammal Protection Act. The conflict was one where a GATT panel ruled that trade restriction applied by the United States against tuna imports from Mexico contravened GATT rules. The restrictions were defended on the ground that Mexican tuna fishing practices resulted in the killing of more dolphins than prescribed under the U.S. law (Kirmani 1994a; Trachtman, 1991). GATT ruled in favor of Mexico.

This ruling sparked wider deliberation on the extent to which trade and environmental objectives were compatible and on the consequent need to change existing international rules to take greater account of environmental concerns. In its concluding remarks on the issue, the GATT panel emphasized that a party is not permitted to restrict imports of a product because it originates from a country with environmental policies that differ from those of the importer (Runge, 1993). The ruling represented a watershed event for the linkage of environmental issues to global trade (Kirmani, 1994b; Trachtman, 1991).

In addition to raising environmental concerns, the tuna restriction conflict also raised some technical issues, such as the extent to which U.S. regulation could be applied to activities in communities outside the United States in connection with the production of goods imported into the country. To what extent may the United States use the fact of importation as a basis for prescriptive jurisdiction to apply its law to activities abroad? Also, to what extent may import restrictions be used as a penalty to enforce that law (Trachtman, 1991)? The conflict brought to the fore the failure of the international community to legislate comprehensive rules in the area of regulatory jurisdiction as well as its failure to legislate rules regarding environmental protection at the local level (Trachtman, 1991).

The North American Free Trade Agreement (NAFTA) is a regional trade agreement among the governments of the United States, Canada (the two core countries), and Mexico (a semi-periphery country). NAFTA has been a reality since 1993 and was fully implemented in 2008. The chief objectives of NAFTA include the elimination of barriers to trade, promotion of conditions of fair competition, and increased investment opportunities (Runge, 1993). NAFTA has been criticized by many policy scholars as contributing to environmental degradation in the United States by encouraging the government to lower standards and motivating business to lobby against environmental policies that make the country less competitive with regard to lower environmental standards existing in Mexico (Steel, Clinton, & Lovrich, 2003). On the other hand, NAFTA has been touted as the "greenest-ever" international trade agreement (Allison, 1997).

Ties between trade and the environment in the world economy gained the attention of researchers and policymakers only in the 1990s, as disputes over the environmental impacts of NAFTA and GATT converged in international negotiations. The recent recognition of environmental quality as a global concern has highlighted the extensive interface among environmental degradation, pollution control, and international trade (Goodman & Howarth, 1997). Whether trade measures have primary environmental impact at the local level at home, abroad, or in the "global commons," a decision must first be made to take action in response (Runge, 1993).

Antiglobalization Disputes

Despite global flows of labor, jobs, and capital, globalization continues to create unbalanced, skewed wage structures in communities as well as ecological and social disruptions. Recent organized riots and protests against the policies and actions of globalization bodies such as the World Trade Organization (WTO), the International Monetary Fund (IMF), and the World Bank point to the ills of globalization. The infamous WTO 1999 antiglobalization protests among diverse constituents disputing environmental, labor, and human rights issues not only call attention to the cons of globalization processes, but also reflect the bottom-up drive for greater equality and consideration for desperate local places. These antiglobalization protests (globalization from below) are signs of the time reflecting a new form of connectedness (that local communities can take advantage of), linking people and communities across borders. Globalization from below is now being touted as an alternative for local communities in the new global era.

What is the connection between a protesting upper-class male teenager in the United States and a working-class male working in inhumane factory conditions in Taiwan? Or a small farmer in Jamaica who has had to dump his milk because he cannot compete with imported powdered milk that has flooded the local market? The connection is clear. Community-based, citizen-driven, local stewardship-oriented groups network with global environmental watchdog groups and powerful international allies, such as World Social Forum, and are reinventing social movements and connecting diverse voices in distant places. In this way, local communities can harness the energy, connectedness, and resources of these global social movement groups. Globalization from below suggests that social movements are pivotal in protecting and advocating for the economic and environmental well-being of marginalized people even in the remotest of communities. The aim is to manage the regulatory systems of international environmental and economic organizations in such a way that regard is given to local ecosystem contexts and local livelihoods, as well as social systems.

Nobel Prize-winning economist Joseph Stiglitz (2002) points out that the recent wave of protests accompanying meetings of the IMF, the World Bank, and the WTO have provoked an enormous amount of soul-searching by those with global power. Stiglitz notes that he witnessed firsthand, while working with the World Bank, the devastating effect that globalization can have on developing countries, particularly the poor in those peripheral countries. He further notes that globalization today is not working for many of the world's poor, the environment, or the stability of the global economy. Stiglitz argues that globalization can have a positive impact on developing countries only when the IMF, the World Bank, and the WTO reform the way that they operate. All of these organizations need to become more transparent and reexamine their flawed policies. He also criticizes the "one-size-fits-all" policies of the IMF, which show little regard for national differences.

Practicing Community Development at the Local Level

The benefits of globalization wrapped in capitalist production and distribution systems leave little room for players like small farmers, who are a major part of the social organizations on the periphery that help to fuel the global market system. They are often treated as oblivious players, yet they are doing the hands-on jobs that shape the quality of primary produce and environmental degradation. Within the context of globalization, this is the main issue for rural communities that cannot compete effectively. Thus, accelerated poverty in marginalized communities is one of the greatest threats of globalization; this threat is often superseded by the immutable economic rationalism of global capitalism.

Not many people consider the real effect that globalization has on small communities, and not much attention is given to local people whose livelihoods are intimately tied up with natural resources and the trading of their traditional crops. The fact that the small farmer or the small itinerant trader buys and sells little is not evidence, as it is sometimes thought, of his or her absence from and unconcern for the market. Rather, the world market affects him or her directly and deeply, although adversely. Furthermore, farmers and traders are important entities in their fragile local economies—entities that are often displaced in the global economy.

The Effect of Globalization on Local Communities in Developing Countries

In the case of a developing country like Jamaica, small (and large) banana farmers now operate under the imposition of an arbitrary power mechanism that no longer allows them to relate to the land the way their ancestors did. The price for retail bananas (produced in Jamaica) in the overseas market does not necessarily reflect negative externalities such as the cost of inefficient use of resources, the loss of biodiversity from the clearing of forests for cultivation, deforestation, soil erosion, water contamination by agro-chemicals, nor the social and economic dislocations that occur in rural communities of producing countries.

"One-size-fits-all" policies of the WTO, the World Bank, and the IMF do not work well in rural communities. Policies geared toward agricultural sustainability should be cognizant of the different value systems, cultural attitudes, and sociocultural dynamics of communities before implementing new agricultural programs.

In the context of the globalization of agriculture, advocates claim that closer economic integration, especially trade and financial liberalization, will increase economic prosperity in developing countries and encourage good governance, transparency, and accountability. The responses of critics are far more pertinent, in the case of poor communities. Critics acknowledge that globalization imposes difficult and perhaps counterproductive policies on struggling economies. This is one of the key foundations of globalization. They also charge that globalization undermines workers' rights and encourages environmental degradation. Moreover, they say that most of the benefits of globalization have gone to those countries that were already developed. Recent developments in economic theory show that whenever information is imperfect and markets are incomplete, which is to say always, and especially in developing countries, then the "invisible hand" works most imperfectly (Stiglitz, 2002). In this context, there are desirable government interventions that can improve upon the efficiency of the market. These restrictions on the conditions under which markets result in efficiency are important—many of the key activities of government can be understood as responses to the resulting market failures (Stiglitz, 2002).

Where does this leave local communities on the periphery? Can government improve the outcome by well-chosen interventions as implied by Stiglitz? Is the globalization of agriculture simply "modern colonization"? Globalization proponents downplay economic and political control of the core nations over former colonies under the guise of economic and cultural integration and progress. For globalization to work, the same variables of the old system are necessary: global division of labor, export orientation, and increased spread of multinational corporations.

Should rural communities in poor countries limit their participation? Perhaps not as they face the realities of a globalized world. In the globalization equation, local livelihoods will continue to be marginalized if people cannot have some control over their own long-term socioeconomic development and garner benefits for the families living in their communities.

The idea here is not pure endogenous development, which is a complex task, but complexity does not negate the fact that the international organization of space negatively affects local socioeconomic relationships. Rural communities can surely benefit from having trade and other economic relations with the world, but they should have some control and voice in decision making over this relationship. Distant exogenous factors should not dominate. Overreliance on the world market for staple goods should be curbed. Furthermore, many local communities have little or no comparative advantage in the global economy and should be reoriented toward pro-protectionist policies.

The ethic of externality (hidden costs) should be upheld in distant producing places. Any extraction from, use of, or disruption of the land comes with a cost. Who should pay for the unaccounted costs of land degradation and social disruption? Even though the environmental problem is in "someone else's backyard," it can be rationalized or simply dismissed in terms of its implications either for ecosystem change and degradation or for the human experiences involved. Who should pay for the loss of biodiversity from the clearing of forests for cultivation, deforestation, water contamination by agro-chemicals, and social and economic dislocations that occur in local communities of the producing countries? The price of ripe bananas in core countries such as the United States has remained basically stable over the past 10 years, whereas the small farmers in Jamaica, the Dominican Republic, Ecuador, Costa Rica, Honduras, and other peripheral countries have had to pay increasingly more for farm implements, agro-chemicals, and other farm inputs because of price inflation, not to mention the declining soil fertility and land degradation that their local communities must endure.

Balanced Trade Pattern

In terms of a proposal for change, the key is achieving balanced trade patterns. At the community level, it means improving the quality of local decision making and balancing the use of imported agro-chemicals with indigenous means of controlling pests and maintaining soil fertility. In addition, a balance between local crops and imported crops in the local markets should improve food security within local communities. The capitalization of food production and trade has its place, but small farmers still have a role to play in local food security. The local economy must be stimulated and given the opportunity for self-determination, reduced dependence on foreign economies, and strengthening of local community action. For example, indigenous local crops should be given a deliberate boost. Efforts should be made by the tourism sector to have backward linkages to the small farmers. When the comparative position of the country's local economy has reached a stage where it can be tied successfully into the world market, then different countries can profit mutually and equally.

Free trade weakens communities by freeing multinational corporations to exhaust the local natural-resource base. It is glaringly evident that the way small farmers in Jamaica, for example, participate in the international banana trade (with its homogenized, rationalized structure) is not viable for the long run. The cheap retail price of ripe bananas in the developed world is provided at a cost of socioeconomic dislocation and environmental damage in the producing countries. For sustainability, prices in the international banana economy should reflect the real costs at the various stages of the production process.

As a parallel, the influx of imported vegetables in local markets threatens local food security and quality of life in small farming communities. Beyond the issue of food security, structural changes in the global capitalist system are clearly essential if we are to protect vulnerable local social and natural systems. Rural farmers, merchants, and consumers in developing countries testify that imported foods are cheaper than locally produced foods, which negatively affects local production and trade. Extensive and prolonged availability of cheaper imported foods will undermine local production. McMichael (2000) believes that this process destabilizes rural communities by displacing the small farmer and compromises local food security. Based on the accounts of the small farmers in Jamaica, their livelihoods and the food security of the country are threatened from imported foods (Meikle-Yaw, 2005).

The less powerful peripheral countries should have a part in policy determination or form a collective alternative. How do we achieve this redistribution of power? This is the question that looms. One alternative is implied in the concept of "glocalization," which is the integration of global and local (Ritzer, 2004). The glocalization of agriculture would see the merging of global opportunities and local interests, giving local communities new avenues by which to carve out livelihood opportunities and maintain some local socioeconomic traditions, crops, and sociocultural autonomy.

Making Globalization —————————————————— Work in Developing Countries

On the positive side, free trade and the globalization of food consumption patterns can provide new opportunities in the global marketplace for communities. Nevertheless, structural changes in the global capitalist system are clearly essential if vulnerable livelihoods, and social and natural systems are to be preserved. The influx of imported produce in local markets threatens local food security and quality of life in local communities. Many have little or no comparative advantage in the context of the global production and marketing system. Beyond the issue of food security, structural changes in the global-national capitalist system are clearly essential if we are to protect vulnerable local social and economic systems. Efforts should be made continuously at the community level to advance a balance between the economic profits and ecological stewardship. Globalization needs a pragmatic monitoring system to control further disruption and displacement of rural societies. Less powerful communities should have a part in policy determination or form a collective alternative (regional integration).

Local communities and their inhabitants are forced to respond to exogenous shocks and their new livelihood vulnerability by finding innovative alternative survival strategies and social networks. Sustainability and survival are linked by a wide spectrum of alternative strategies, some of which are ironically linked to global connections and yet rooted in the horizontal networks and character of rural community relations.

Globalization has drafted remote rural communities in to the global competition, even though the social organization of their livelihood systems has unique historical contexts, natural resources management, and financial and marketing strategies that inherently relegate them to a competitive disadvantage in the global marketplace. Nevertheless, agriculture, although small scale and often unmechanized, is a major part of the livelihood structure of such communities. In comparison to the U.S. agricultural system, agriculture has some natural and economic disadvantages such as hilly topography, small acreage, low density of population, high costs of transportation, poor roads, irregular and/or expensive water supply, and inadequate community management. In addition, the kinds of jobs available in rural communities rely heavily on the extraction of natural resources, contributing to and/or intensifying environmental degradation.

There is a need to bring into intellectual discourse how globalization affects the livelihood and environment of small rural communities and their inhabitants in distant places. What are some environmental consequences, and what are farmers' environmental responses to increasing second-wave globalization on agricultural systems? We argue that small farmers in rural communities should be integrated in the analytic and globalization theorization agendas of social scientists. As Sassen (2007) notes, "Capturing the specificity and variability of global formations makes for richer and more complex findings" (p. 12).

As the global organization and integration of agricultural markets ensue, serious community and economic shocks and displacement occur (Flora & Bendini, 2007).

> As the integration of the global food economy deepens, with comparative advantage heavily conditioned by vast disparities in the scale, technology, and subsidization of production, and the enormous influence of transnational corporations (TNCs) on consumers and producers, profound concerns have arisen about the future of peasants in developing countries in the face of rising competitive pressures. (Weis, 2004, p. 461)

Going Local

Although much of the current research emphasizes the dominance of global forces, other literature points to opportunities to relocalize economies (Shuman, 2000). There are alternative strategies that resist the processes of economic globalization. Rather than considering these factors of production (land, labor, and capital) as commodities, these strategies tend to decommodify them. This means that land, labor, and capital are allocated not solely on the basis of their exchange value, but also on their contribution to community sustainability. A couple of examples will help illustrate these differences.

Capital markets across the globe have become much more integrated, allowing capital to flow to the most profitable outlet. In many communities, community development financial institutions have been established to benefit businesses in the area. These credit institutions are for-profit organizations, but rather than maximizing profits, they seek to find profitable loans in the region.

In the next section, we review several models for communities seeking alternative approaches to economic development in a global era. We focus on institutional arrangements that attempt to relocalize key factors of production—capital and labor.

Sources of Capital

Financial markets have undergone a significant transformation since the 1980s. Many of the regulations that created a separation between banking and other industries have been eliminated. Restrictions on the ability of large banks to own and control small banks across state lines have disappeared. As a result, local financial markets have become more tightly integrated into national and international markets. Also, there has been considerable consolidation and centralization of financial markets as a result of deregulation.

Globalization of financial markets presents a variety of challenges for community development. Increased capital mobility makes it much more likely that poorer and minority communities will experience a drain in financial capital. Capital will flow to places that can provide a higher return, and possibly less risk. Local financial institutions seeking to maximize their profits will be less inclined to invest in community projects.

In response to these changes in the financial sector, many communities have sought to relocalize their financial resources by building community development financial institutions. These financial institutions limit their geographic range to a specific region or territory. Most of these institutions continue to be profit-oriented, but they limit their loan activity to businesses and residents in the community. Below, we discuss some of the most common types of community development financial institutions.

Revolving Loan Funds. Most revolving loan funds provide loan funds to existing businesses in a community to remain in the area or to expand. Many of the revolving loan funds in the United States have been established through federal and state loans to businesses to help them expand or locate in a community. When the loans are repaid (with interest), they are recirculated in the community to more businesses. Revolving funds are often restricted to existing businesses and rarely support new business start-ups. They are, however, often directed to small businesses. A chief characteristic of these funds is that the credit is available only to businesses in the area.

Community Development Banks. Community development loan funds are privately owned, nonprofit organizations that make loans to residents in poor neighborhoods. Many of these funds are part of a larger social investment fund that seeks to find socially attractive investments. Community development loan funds have been used to help revitalize some of the most distressed neighborhoods in large cities and depressed rural areas.

Community Development Credit Unions. Community development credit unions (CDCUs) operate like a regular credit union but have a geographic or associational bond in a limited area. Most CDCUs are organized to meet the needs of local residents by providing personal loans or home rehabilitation loans that might not be available through other financial institutions (Green & Haines, 2007).

Microenterprise Loan Funds. Microenterprise loan funds provide very small amounts of start-up funds (debt capital) for businesses. Many of the funds have been established by foundations or local governments as a way to promote entrepreneurship, especially among the poor and underemployed. Some microenterprise loan funds use a method of rotating funds among a group of entrepreneurs. Once one loan is repaid, the next person receives a loan. The use of these social mechanisms provides support and improves the likelihood of repayment. Most microenterprise loan funds are limited to neighborhoods, villages, tribes, or some relatively small geographic area.

Labor

Worker and Community-Owned Firms. One of the basic features of economic globalization over the past quarter century has been the shift in production from high-wage to low-wage areas. Corporations seeking to lower their production costs have moved factories and other economic activities to low-cost areas such as Mexico and, more recently, China. This process has led to the deindustrialization of many regions, especially the Rust Belt, which has historically relied heavily on manufacturing as its economic base. This process has not only led to higher rates of unemployment and poverty in many communities, it has also put downward pressure on wages and benefits for workers who remain employed.

In many cases, firms are not moving to these low-cost areas because they are not making a profit, but because the profit rates are higher elsewhere. In response, many communities have attempted to decommodify their labor by promoting community or worker ownership. This strategy does not remove the profit motive from the business. Instead, the option of capital mobility is set aside and firms seek other strategies for competing.

Many small towns choose this strategy because they are often dependent on a few businesses. Community ownership may provide more stability for employment and support other firms that provide goods and services in the region. One of the major obstacles to both community and worker ownership is access to capital. There are a few financial institutions that specialize in support of worker-owned firms. Community-owned firms normally raise funds through selling stock and leveraging the funds to obtain external financing (Green, Flora, Flora, & Schmidt, 1990).

Community Unionism. Unionism refers to the organizing activities of workers in a specific industry. Community unionism refers to the practice of unions collaborating and reaching out to community-based organizations to enhance the benefits to both unions and communities. The concept of community unionism emerged in the 1990s as support for unions continued to decline. Community unionism is part of a strategy to gain broader support for the union movement.

Conclusions

Globalization is typically viewed as a process that presents new opportunities for development, but places significant constraints on governments at all levels. This is often interpreted to mean that localities have few choices, but attempt to become more competitive and provide inducements to capital investment. This approach has been heavily criticized in the literature on community economic development. What is the appropriate response to the increased mobility of capital and labor in a global economy?

Shuman (2000) argues that one strategy many communities are using in response to these economic changes is to promote self-reliance and community control. Reducing dependencies on outside investments generates not only economic benefits, but environmental and social benefits as well. Establishing small worker-owned firms, community development corporations, and community financial institutions creates more sustainable local economies that resist some of the negative consequences of globalization. This does not mean that communities become more insular and do not participate in global markets. Relocalizing institutions does reduce some of the vulnerability and dependency that have been built into globalization strategies over the past two decades.

The ultimate outcome of globalization, then, may not be greater synergy, but increased fragmentation or even disintegration. These processes may ultimately portend a greater role for communities and regions. Communities may take a wide variety of options in response to economic globalization. The ultimate outcome may be greater diversity in local economies and potentially more sustainable policies and practices.

References

Allison, J. (1997). Trade liberalization and the natural environment: Conflict or opportunity? In S. Kamieniecki, G. A. Gonzalez, & R. O. Vos (Eds.), *Flashpoints in environmental policymaking* (pp. 229–256). Albany: SUNY Press.

Chisholm, L. A. (Ed.). (2005). *Knowing and doing the theory and practice of service-learning.* New York: International Partnership for Service-Learning and Leadership.

Conroy, M., & Glasmeier, A. (1992). Unprecedented disparities, unparalleled adjustment needs: Winners and losers on the NAFTA "fast track." *Journal of Inter-American Studies and World Affairs, 34,* 1–37.

Flora, C., & Bendini, M. (2007). Globalization and changing relations among market, state and civil society: A comparative analysis of Patagonia and Iowa. *International Journal of Sociology of Food and Agriculture, 15,* 1–21.

Giddens, A. (1990). *The consequences of modernity.* Stanford, CA: Stanford University Press.

Gill, S. (1992). Economic globalization and the internationalization of authority: Limits and contradictions. *Geoforum, 23,* 269–283.

Goodman, D., & Howarth, R. (1997). International trade and sustainable development. In S. Kamieniecki, G. A. Gonzalez, & R. O. Vos (Eds.), *Flashpoints in environmental policymaking* (pp. 257–277). Albany: SUNY Press.

Green, G. P., Flora, J. L., Flora, C. B., & Schmidt, F. E. (1990). Local self-development strategies: National survey results. *Journal of the Community Development Society, 21,* 55–73.

Green, G. P., & Haines, A. (2007). *Asset building and community development* (2nd ed.). Thousand Oaks, CA: Sage.

Hart, M., & Sushma, C. (1992). Trade and the environment: Dialogue of the deaf or scope for cooperation. *Canada-United States Law Journal, 18,* 207–228.

Hodges, J. (2005). Cheap food and feeding the world sustainably. *Livestock Production Science, 92,* 1–16.

Hu, Z., & Mohsin, S. (1997). *Why is China growing so fast?* Retrieved July 15, 2009, from http://www.imf.org/external/pubs/ft/issues8/issue8.pdf

Katz-Fishman, W., & Scott, J. (2008). Twenty-first century globalization and the social forum process: Building today's global justice and equality movement. In A. Hattery, D. Embrick, & E. Smith (Eds.), *Globalization and America: Race, human rights and inequality* (pp. 231–245). Lanham, MD: Rowman & Littlefield.

Kirmani, N. (1994a). *International trade policies: The Uruguay round and beyond, volume I: Principal issues.* Washington, DC: International Monetary Fund.

Kirmani, N. (1994b). *International trade policies: The Uruguay round and beyond, volume II: Background papers.* Washington, DC: International Monetary Fund.

McMichael, P. (2000). *Development and social change: A global perspective.* Thousand Oaks, CA: Pine Forge.

Meikle-Yaw, P. (2005). Globalization of agriculture: Effects on social and natural systems in rural communities in Jamaica. *Caribbean Geography, 14,* 40–53.

Ritzer, G. (2004). *The McDonaldization of society* (Rev. new century ed.). Thousand Oaks, CA: Pine Forge.

Runge, C. F. (1993). *Freer trade, protected environment: Balancing trade liberalization and environmental interests.* New York: Council on Foreign Relations Press.

Sassen, S. (2007). *A sociology of globalization.* New York: Norton.

Shuman, M. H. (2000). *Going local: Creating self-reliant communities in a global age.* New York: Routledge.

Skogstad, G. (2000). Globalization and public policy: Situating Canadian analyses. *Canadian Journal of Political Science, 33,* 805–828.

Steel, B., Clinton, R., & Lovrich, N. (2003). *Environmental politics and policy: A comparative approach.* Boston: McGraw Hill.

Stiglitz, J. (2002). *Globalization and its discontents.* New York: Norton.

Stiglitz, J. (2006). *Making globalization work.* New York: Norton.

Trachtman, J. (1991). United States—Restrictions on imports of tuna. *American Journal of International Law, 86,* 142–151.

Weis, T. (2004). Restructuring and redundancy: The impacts and illogic of neoliberal agricultural reforms in Jamaica. *Journal of Agrarian Change, 4,* 461–491.

The World Bank Group. (2004). *Economic growth rates.* Retrieved October 17, 2009, from http://www.worldbank.org/depweb/english/beyond/global/chapter4.html

18

Emerging Issues in Community Development

Gary Paul Green and
Jerry W. Robinson, Jr.

BEHAVIOR OBJECTIVES

After studying this chapter and completing the online learning activities, students should be able to

1. Understand the significance of regionalism to the community development field and some of the obstacles practitioners face in promoting community collaboration.

2. Describe how community informatics can influence community development practice.

3. Be aware of how homeownership affects community interaction.

4. Understand how local food systems address the problems associated with the corporate food system.

5. Understand how local food systems emphasize the role of community in markets.

6. Identify some of the basic challenges that practitioners face in building local food systems.

Introduction

In this final chapter, we identify some of the emerging issues in the field of community development. Many of the key issues facing community development practitioners, such as sustainability and globalization, have already received some attention in this volume. In this chapter, topics that have received less attention will be discussed. Special attention is paid to the influences of regionalism, technology (community informatics), housing, and local food systems. Many other issues could be discussed, but these represent a wide variety of opportunities and challenges for community development practitioners.

Regionalism

The concept of regionalism has received attention on and off during the past half-century. Many regional economic development initiatives were established during the Depression. During the 1960s, the federal government made substantial investments in regional development programs. These investments included infrastructure projects and regional planning organizations. Emphasis on regional strategies waned after the 1960s but re-emerged in the 1990s, primarily through the interest in growth management and economic development. During the 1990s, statewide and regional coalitions were established to promote rural development. Over the past decade, interest in regionalism has focused on economic development, housing, and education. The central idea of regionalism is that the economic, environmental, and social issues facing communities transcend political boundaries (Dreier, Mollenkopf, & Swanstrom, 2004). Local governments, especially counties and municipalities, contribute to fragmentation that exacerbates community development problems (Orfield, 1997). In many cases, localities compete for resources, which makes it more difficult to address social and economic problems. Hypercompetition may produce fewer benefits for local residents. It also generates more duplication of effort and inefficient use of resources. Regional solutions seek to overcome fragmentation by organizing localities and counties around common interests that accentuate the development of local resources. Regional efforts take a variety of forms, from intergovernmental coordination to separate regional institutions.

The significance of regionalism can be illustrated in several examples. Economic markets are not limited geographically to local communities. Today, people often live in one place, work in another, and consume in yet another place. Such a situation can present some challenges for community development practitioners. Jobs created in one community may benefit workers in another community. The local government in which workers live may not see increases in tax revenues because the employer is located elsewhere. And many of the costs of providing education and infrastructure may be borne by other communities not benefiting from the job creation. Regional approaches to economic development have attempted, in some places, to provide innovative tax structures that spread the benefits of economic development across all communities in a region. This does not mean that all communities will bear the same costs, but it does balance out the costs and benefits to a greater extent. In other states, regional economic development organizations have been created to help avoid some of the competition between communities over economic development. In a few situations, regional governments have been established that have the ability to tax and to distribute services (and benefits of economic development) across a region.

Another illustration of the importance of regionalism is the environment. Many times, the source of an environmental problem may not be in the community that is being affected, but in neighboring localities. In the case of water pollution, farmers upstream may contribute to the problems in lakes and rivers downstream. Watersheds cross political boundaries and can make it difficult to regulate or to develop collaborative solutions. In some states, community development practitioners have been working at the level of watersheds to help people collaborate across these regions to address environmental issues. Local residents are being trained to monitor environmental conditions and be able to recognize changes in their local environment.

Both of these examples demonstrate how many of the issues facing communities are regional in nature. Institutional structures in many communities often do not match the scale of the problem. Innovative community development strategies are being used at the regional level to build collaborative strategies that promote community collaboration (see Chapter 10). Regionalism represents a broader definition of community that fits the changing nature of communities. Many of the same principles of defining community can be applied to regional efforts. Additional strategies may be needed, however, because of the need for collaboration across communities. Practitioners are dealing with not only individual interests, but also multiple collective interests as well. Neighborhoods and communities have collective identities as well that generate obstacles to collaboration. These identities can be supported through schools, churches, and other organizations and institutions. So, for example, it may be difficult for two communities to collaborate because their schools have been sports rivals for years. The issues of multicommunity collaboration and coordination undoubtedly will be of greater concern in the future.

There are many obstacles to collaboration across communities. In most metropolitan areas, racial and income segregation make it difficult to mobilize residents across neighborhoods or communities. For example, wealthier neighborhoods may not see it in their interest to collaborate with poor neighborhoods with respect to housing, education, and so on. Mark Warren (2001) describes a successful effort to mobilize across racial and ethnic groups in San Antonio around educational issues. It is not clear that the same strategies would work for economic or environmental issues. One might assume that there are fewer challenges to regionalism in rural areas. Resistance to collaborating across school districts can present difficult challenges for mobilizing residents in nonmetropolitan areas. Conflicts between urban and rural communities in these areas can be major obstacles as well. This is especially the case for transportation, environmental, and economic development issues.

Community Informatics

Community informatics refers to the growing practice of using information and communication technology within communities to promote interaction and collaboration (Gurstein, 2007). Community informatics and community development have essentially the same goals—to enhance community processes and self-development. Community informatics emphasizes dispersed network structures that permit autonomous (almost individualized) action. The concept of community tends to stress the importance of common values and norms that are the basis of collective action. The two concepts potentially overlap in the field of community development.

There is a great deal of potential in increasing communication and interaction through community informatics. One of the chief benefits of community informatics is that it is built from the ground up and minimizes centralized control over community processes. There is concern that community informatics creates individualized networks that do not build social capital or support consensus building. Is face-to-face interaction necessary for the development of community? Much of the community development literature emphasizes the important role that social institutions play in bringing together people to promote interaction, which ultimately facilitates trust and the flow of information (Wilkinson, 1991). There is growing evidence, however, that new technology can promote social networks (Wellman, 2001). Many people prefer to interact with others through this medium, and it is possible that this interaction achieves many of the same goals that more conventional social institutions have played in the past.

It is unclear how this emerging area of community informatics will influence the practice of community development. What role does the community development practitioner play in community informatics? One possible role is to moderate or facilitate discussion. This would be a very limited role, but may be closest to the self-help model of community development (Chapter 5). Clearly, there is an educational role for practitioners to play here by introducing new technology to communities and helping residents learn how to use new information technology. Finally, community informatics can be used as part of a participatory process to engage residents who are unable to participate through other venues. Youth and the elderly may be able to use new technology to overcome barriers to participation.

Service-learning can play a critical role in promoting and facilitating community informatics. Communities and nonprofit organizations have a need for technical assistance in establishing information networks and providing education to residents. This is an excellent opportunity for students to gain experience, apply their classroom knowledge in the community, and provide benefits to local residents.

The Housing Crisis

Housing is a "bread-and-butter" issue for community development practitioners. Nothing is more place-based than housing. In surveys of community development corporations, housing typically is identified as the top category among the various activities in which these organizations are involved (National Congress for Community Economic Development, 1995). Community development corporations and intermediary institutions, such as the local initiative support corporations, have become the primary sources for low-income housing in the United States. Most of the work in the community development field has been to provide affordable housing in poor neighborhoods. Although there have been significant achievements in this area, there is a recognition that the demand for affordable housing continues to far exceed the supply.

The subprime housing crisis has reinserted the issue of affordable housing in the public's eye. In 2008, there were approximately 3 million housing foreclosure filings. Banks repossessed about 800,000 homes during that year. This crisis has created a rising rate of homelessness. Community development practitioners have been active in organizing residents to ensure that homeowners receive their rights and to seek new strategies for alleviating these problems in low-income neighborhoods. Much of the subprime housing crisis was concentrated in poor neighborhoods, but it eventually spilled over into many upper middle-class neighborhoods as well. The crisis raised some important issues about our financial system and our emphasis on homeownership.

The focus of most community development efforts has been on homeownership. This is the American dream. The housing crisis that began in 2007 may mark the shift in focus to rentals. Changes in banking regulations have made it more difficult for low-income families to purchase homes. The depressed housing market also may make it more difficult to sell houses in the future. Younger families may be reluctant to purchase a home if they are uncertain about staying in the community. Older families may face more difficulty moving closer to family because of the housing market. Some workers may not be able to take advantage of job opportunities. Many young families may put off purchasing homes and rely more on rentals.

All of these changes may contribute to real shifts in community attachment. Research has consistently shown that homeownership has been a major factor contributing to community attachment and local collective action. Homeowners have a major investment in the place and have a more long-term commitment to the quality of life in the community (Davis, 1991). This may present new challenges to community organizers because it may be more difficult to mobilize residents who are not homeowners.

These changes may also mean that community development practitioners will focus more on promoting rental housing rather than homeownership. Most community development corporations focus most of their effort on building or refurbishing housing for the poor. This shift to rentals may generate some new policy and practical challenges because most of the housing system is set up to promote ownership.

Again, these changes offer many opportunities for service-learning. Many nonprofit organizations providing support to tenants use students to educate the public about tenant rights and to examine instances of housing discrimination. Law students often provide legal assistance to tenants as well.

Local Food Systems

The local food movement offers new economic opportunities for small- and medium-sized farms, reduces their environmental footprints, and promotes good nutrition among consumers (Kloppenburg, Lezberg, DeMaster, Stevenson, & Hendrickson, 2000). Local food systems take a variety of forms, including farm-to-school programs, farmers' markets, community-supported agriculture, and others. Many of these community programs to support local food systems have been initiated as part of a critique of the corporate food system, which includes environmental, social, and economic concerns (Shuman, 2000). The corporate food system has been criticized for relying on chemical inputs that degrade the environment, eliminating small farm operations, and contributing to global warming through centralizing production (Pollan, 2006).

Community-supported agriculture (CSA) originated in the 1960s in Switzerland and Japan. Today, CSA farms are concentrated in the Northeast, Midwest, and West Coast in the United States. Most CSA farms are relatively small and practice organic farming techniques. CSA farms are normally within 2 to 3 hours' drive of an urban area. Consumers in the region purchase a share of the farmer's crop or product. Normally, consumers receive a box of produce each week. Through this investment, consumers take on some of the risk usually borne by producers. If production is low, consumers receive less produce. If it is higher, they receive more.

Another approach to promoting local food systems is through farm-to-school programs. These programs connect schools with local farms with the objectives of serving healthy meals in school cafeterias, improving student nutrition, providing health and nutrition education opportunities that will last a lifetime, and supporting local small farmers. More than 8,000 schools in the United States now participate in these programs.

Finally, farmers' markets offer another approach to community development. A farmers' market is one in which farmers, growers, or producers from a defined local area are present in person to sell their own produce, direct to the public. All products sold should have been grown, reared, caught, brewed, pickled, baked, smoked, or processed by the stallholder. These markets usually benefit small producers, who are most likely to participate in these direct-marketing strategies.

These three different forms of local food systems represent attempts to re-establish the importance of community in the local economy. They do this in several ways. First, market transactions are not based solely on cost, but also consider other factors (including proximity). Purchasing food from regional producers enhances the regional economy and has many indirect benefits that are not considered in solely economic transactions. Second, local food systems are good examples of asset-based development. They seek to mobilize local institutions, such as schools and hospitals, to enhance the quality of life. These institutions purchase food and can help support local farmers and ranches.

What is the role of community development practitioners in building local food systems? Probably the most serious challenge that practitioners face in developing local food systems is matching the level of demand by institutions, organizations, and consumers. Most local producers are relatively small and would have a difficult time meeting the demand for local food. In order to increase the supply, it may be necessary to promote a collaborative effort among producers to satisfy demand. Community development practitioners can play a critical role in facilitating this process.

Local food systems face other institutional challenges. In the farm-to-school programs that have been established, one of the major difficulties is that many of the school systems purchase only processed foods. Most small producers do not have the equipment or facilities to process local produce. In some cases, producers have helped establish community kitchens or community-owned facilities that provide the necessary equipment. All of these efforts require facilitators who can provide evidence of the need, pull together community resources, and promote collective action to achieve the objectives.

There are numerous opportunities available for service-learning related to local food systems. Many universities are engaged in outreach to provide mechanisms to link producers with institutional buyers. This may involve developing Web sites, publications, or social networking efforts. Similarly, there are many opportunities for students to become more engaged in farm-to-school programs and develop educational programs for primary and secondary students on the food system. Finally, practitioners/students can help organize farmers to meet the growing demand for local food.

Conclusions

The field of community development is undergoing a fundamental transformation in theory and practice. Technology, culture, and economics have interacted to create new opportunities and constraints for collective identity and action in communities of place. In many respects, the scale of community interactions has increased, as has the range of issues affecting residents. Theoretically, our conceptual understanding of community is continually in flux and varies considerably across individuals. A major premise of this book is that the concept of community is growing in relevance, even as economic and social changes have integrated localities into the larger global system. We no longer conceive of communities as medieval places that were self-sufficient and isolated. Recognizing the greater interdependence and linkages between places does not necessarily diminish the role of local social relationships and the significance of issues that apply to specific places.

For much of its history, the practice of community development has been based in face-to-face interaction and rooted in social relationships. It is unclear how technology will reshape practice. Emphasis on new technology and community informatics opens up the possibilities of promoting community interaction in new ways. These methods, however, are inherently individualistic and may be less successful at promoting collective behavior. At the same time, these practices may open up new forms of dialogue and ultimately be more democratic than what we typically think of as community participation.

Community development will continue to address some of the basic needs of localities, such as housing, education, jobs, and environmental issues. These are all considered issues that affect people in specific places. One of the continuing challenges for the community development field is organizing across communities to gain greater power and influence. Ultimately, the greatest gains for communities will be to develop larger social movements that can address the needs of social, political, and economic inequalities that persist in our society.

References

Davis, J. E. (1991). *Contested ground: Collective action and the urban neighborhood*. Ithaca, NY: Cornell University Press.

Dreier, P., Mollenkopf, J., & Swanstrom, T. (2004). *Place matters: Metropolitics for the twenty-first century* (2nd ed.). Lawrence: University of Kansas Press.

Gurstein, M. (2007). *What is community informatics? (And why does it matter?)* Milan: Polimetrica.

Kloppenburg, J., Lezberg, S., DeMaster, K., Stevenson, G. W., & Hendrickson, J. (2000). Tasting food, tasting sustainability: Defining the attributes of an alternative food system with competent, ordinary people. *Human Organization, 59,* 177–186.

National Congress for Community Economic Development. (1995). *Tying it all together: The comprehensive achievements of community-based development organizations*. Washington, DC: Author.

Orfield, M. (1997). *Metropolitics: A regional agenda for community and stability*. Washington, DC: Brookings Institution Press.

Pollan, M. (2006). *The omnivore's dilemma*. New York: Penguin.

Shuman, M. H. (2000). *Going local: Creating self-reliant communities in a global age*. New York: Routledge.

Warren, M. R. (2001). *Dry bones rattling: Community building to revitalize American democracy*. Princeton, NJ: Princeton University Press.

Wellman, B. (2001). Computer networks as social networks. *Science, 293,* 2031–2034.

Wilkinson, K. P. (1991). *The community in rural America*. New York: Greenwood.

Index ——————————————————

About the Editors ──────

Jerry W. Robinson, Jr., is Distinguished Professor of Rural Sociology, Emeritus, at the University of Illinois, Urbana-Champaign, and Delta State University, Cleveland, MS. He has written more than a dozen other books and 125 learning modules. With James A. Christenson, he co-edited *Community Development in America* (1989) and *Community Development in Perspective* (1989), which were published by Iowa State University Press. Also, he served as Editor of the *Journal of the Community Development Society*, 1976–1979, and in 2002. At Illinois, Professor Robinson led the effort to create Rural Partners: The Illinois Coalition for Community and Economic Development, which spread throughout the Midwest. At Delta State, he served as B.F. Smith Chair for Economic and Community Development and founding director of the Center for Community and Economic Development. In 1995, he led the effort to create the Master of Science in Community Development program at Delta State.

Gary Paul Green is a Professor in the Department of Community & Environmental Sociology at the University of Wisconsin–Madison and a community development specialist in the Center for Community & Economic Development at the University of Wisconsin–Extension. His applied research, teaching, and outreach interests focus on community, economic, and workforce development. His recent books include *Amenities and Rural Development, Asset Building and Community Development* (2nd ed.), *Workforce Development Networks in Rural Areas,* and *Mobilizing Communities: Asset Building as a Community Development Strategy.* Also, he served 3 years as editor of *Rural Sociology.*

About the Authors ———

Janet S. Ayres is Professor and Extension Specialist in the Department of Agricultural Economics at Purdue University. She has worked in more than 200 communities in Indiana conducting studies, developing statewide programs, and training staff in extension and many state and federal agencies. Her work focuses on building leadership capacity to address change, stimulate collaborative efforts, and create a shared vision and strategic direction.

Alan W. Barton is Associate Professor of Sociology and Community Development and Faculty Associate at the Center for Community and Economic Development at Delta State University in Cleveland, Mississippi. He teaches courses on sustainable development, rural sociology, demography, and environmental sociology. His research focuses on heritage tourism, environmental education, and protected area management in the Mississippi Delta region. He earned a BA in Sociology and Spanish from the University of California, an MS in Forest Management from the University of Washington, and a PhD in Development Sociology from Cornell University.

Lionel J. Beaulieu is Director of the Southern Rural Development Center and Professor of Rural Sociology in the Department of Agricultural Economics at Mississippi State University. He is the author of numerous publications, including edited book volumes, book chapters, and articles that address rural development, education, and labor force issues in America. Dr. Beaulieu received his MS and PhD degrees in Sociology from Purdue University. He completed his term as president of the Rural Sociological Society (RSS) in August 2004. He recently completed a 4-year term as Editor of the *Rural Realities* policy/information series sponsored by the RSS.

M. A. Brennan is Associate Professor in the Department of Community and Leadership Development at Penn State University. Dr. Brennan's teaching, research, and program development concentrates on the role of local citizen action in the community development process. He has more than 15 years of experience in designing, conducting, and analyzing social science research related to community and development. He has served as chair/co-chair on a variety of national committees and guest editor of journal special issues focusing on a variety of community and related topics.

J. C. Bridger is Senior Research Associate in the Department of Agricultural Economics and Rural Sociology at Penn State University. His research and teaching interests include community theory, research methods, rural development, university-community engagement, and the human dimensions of natural resources.

Ralph B. Brown is a Professor in the Department of Sociology at Brigham Young University and Director of the International Development minor at BYU. He is a rural sociologist by training with expertise in rural, agricultural, and community development and social change. His PhD is from the University of Missouri–Columbia. His research publications have focused on community satisfaction and attachment, community leadership networks, and subsistence lifestyles. Recently, he has begun a new project that focuses on the social and economic impacts of motorcycle adoption as a primary transportation option in many Southeast Asian countries.

Frank Fear is Senior Associate Dean in the College of Agriculture and Natural Resources at Michigan State University. He is also an MSU Senior Fellow in Outreach and Engagement. A sociologist by education, Fear's work focuses on organization and community development with emphasis on change in higher education. Examples of his work include serving as the founding director of the Liberty Hyde Bailey Scholars program, an interdisciplinary program that enables undergraduate students' character development; and writing (as lead author) *Coming to Critical Engagement,* a volume that depicts the evolution of four scholars' work in university outreach and engagement.

Lorraine E. Garkovich holds a PhD in Sociology from the University of Missouri–Columbia. Dr. Garkovich joined the faculty of the University of Kentucky in 1976. She is coordinator of the Public Service and Leadership specialization in the Community Communications and Leadership Development undergraduate degree and is a community development extension specialist. Dr. Garkovich's extension specialty areas include leadership development, strategic planning, community/economic development, and sociodemographic trend analyses. She has been recognized as a 2009 Provost Distinguished Service Professor, and she was the 2008 recipient of the Bonnie Teater Community Development Educator Lifetime Achievement Award presented by the Southern Rural Development Center, and the 2004 recipient of the Excellence in Extension and Outreach Award from the Southern Rural Sociological Society.

Nina Glasgow is a Senior Research Associate in the Department of Development Sociology at Cornell University. Her research focuses primarily on the sociology of aging, especially aging in rural environments. She has co-edited two books, *Social Integration in the Second Half of Life* and *Critical Issues in Rural Health,* and she is co-author of *Rural Retirement Migration* (2008). She co-leads the Rural Learning Network of Central and Western New York, which delivers activities designed to facilitate community and economic development in the region.

John J. Green is an Associate Professor of Sociology and Community Development at Delta State University in Cleveland, Mississippi. He is the interim chair of the Division of Social Sciences and founding Director of the Institute for Community-Based Research. He regularly teaches courses on community development, applied research, and statistics. His research interests include topics such as health, agri-food systems, workforce development, social dimensions of disaster, and organizational development.

Hobart L. Harmon, an independent consultant, is one of the nation's leading experts on public education in rural America. Previously, he was director of the National Rural Education Specialty, associate director of the ERIC Clearinghouse on Rural Education and Small Schools, and vice-chair of a state rural development council. He specializes in educational planning, research, and evaluation. Dr. Harmon has served as an external evaluator for several rural education projects funded by the National Science Foundation and the U.S. Department of Education. In 2000, he co-edited the book *Small High Schools That Flourish: Rural Context, Case Studies, and Resources*. He serves on the editorial boards of *The Rural Educator* and the *Journal of Research in Rural Education*. He earned doctoral and master's degrees from Penn State University. He also holds an MS degree from The Ohio State University, a BS degree from West Virginia University (magna cum laude), and an associate's degree from Potomac State College of West Virginia University.

William M. Harris is Martin Luther King, Jr. Visiting Professor Emeritus of Urban Studies and Planning at the Massachusetts Institute of Technology. He has published widely in the areas of planning, inner-city community development, and professional ethics. He is a member of the College of the Fellows of the American Institute of Certified Planners. He currently consults in community development, land use planning, and higher education. Harris holds a PhD in Urban Planning from the University of Washington.

Jerry Hembd is an Associate Professor of Economics at the University of Wisconsin–Superior; a State Specialist in Community and Economic Development with the University of Wisconsin–Extension (UWEX); and Director of the Northern Center for Community and Economic Development, which is a joint venture of both institutions. He co-chairs the UWEX Sustainability Team, which includes a statewide roster of more than 30 county-based educators and state specialists. He earned a PhD in Applied Economics from Stanford University and has degrees in agricultural economics and urban planning. He has been working, writing, and teaching in the area of community development—domestically and internationally—for more than 25 years and is currently focusing on community sustainability. He is a co-editor of the recently released book *Renewing the Countryside—Wisconsin*, which features stories of sustainable living, working, and playing in Wisconsin. He is a past editor of *Community Development: Journal of the Community Development Society* and recently rejoined the journal as CD Cases Editor.

Glenn D. Israel is Professor in the Department of Agricultural Education and Communication at the University of Florida. His primary responsibilities are in extension program development, program evaluation, and organizational accountability. He also collaborates on projects that involve youth in community service-learning, develop leadership in rural communities, and assist local leaders in identifying assets and needs. His research focuses on community influences on educational achievement and survey design and implementation.

Anna M. Kleiner is Assistant Professor of Sociology at Southeastern Louisiana University. She has extensive experience in developing and implementing strategies to enhance collaborative efforts to assist community groups with identifying and answering questions affecting their quality of life. She uses community-based research methodologies to understand and address the social implications of disasters and the local impacts of the globalization of agriculture and food, which are her primary research interests.

Jeffrey S. Lowe is Visiting Associate Professor/Associate Director of the Mid-Sized Cities Policy Institute, Graduate Program in City and Regional Planning, at the University of Memphis. He is past chair of Planning and the Black Community Division of the American Planning Association. His research about equity, community planning, and policy development focuses on Gulf Coast revitalization efforts post-Hurricane Katrina, community development corporations, university-community partnerships, and philanthropy. He is the author of *Rebuilding Communities the Public Trust Way: Community Foundation Assistance to CDCs, 1980–2000*. Dr. Lowe holds a bachelor degree in Business Administration from Howard University; a master's degree in City and Regional Planning from Morgan State University; and a PhD in Urban Planning and Policy Development from Rutgers, The State University of New Jersey.

A. E. Luloff is Professor of Rural Sociology at Penn State University. He teaches, conducts research, and writes about the impacts of social change on sociodemographic shifts and on the natural and human resource bases of the community. Changes in land cover and use, particularly at the rural-urban fringe, and the impact of rural development policy on small and rural communities are central features of his work.

Paulette Meikle is Assistant Professor of Sociology and Community Development at Delta State University. Her research interests include sociology of community, civic engagement, globalization and its impact on rural and marginalized communities, livelihood, global stratification, gender, and grassroots natural resource management. She completed her PhD at Mississippi State University and the Master of Philosophy degree at the University of the West Indies. Her primary teaching interests are in community development, social theory, social research methods, and leading study abroad programs. She has published in *Caribbean Geography, The*

Journal of Extension, Journal of the Community Development Society, and other sources.

Lois Wright Morton is Associate Professor in the Department of Sociology at Iowa State University. Her research examines the civic structure of places, the social organization of communities, and how their people join together to solve the problems of the public commons. She is the author of *Health Care Restructuring: Market Theory vs. Civil Society* and co-editor of *Critical Issues in Rural Health*. A third book, *The Citizen Effect: Pathways for Getting to Better Water Quality Outcomes* (in press), applies the concepts of civic structure, leadership, and community development to watershed management.

Albert Nylander is Dean of Graduate Studies and Continuing Education and Professor of Sociology and Community Development at Delta State University. Dr. Nylander's recent research has focused on areas related to leadership, especially the role of school board members in education. He also has research and teaching interests in the sociology of education, the sociology of leadership, community studies, and Asian studies. He has published in *Community Development Journal* and *Sociological Spectrum*.

Kai A. Schafft is Assistant Professor in the Department of Education Policy Studies at Penn State University, where he directs the Penn State Center on Rural Education and Communities and edits the *Journal of Research in Rural Education*. Trained as a rural sociologist, Dr. Schafft's research foci include rural community development and rural poverty.

Theresa Selfa is an Assistant Professor of Sociology at Kansas State University. She has expertise in rural, environmental, and development sociology, with research experience in Brazil, the Philippines, Europe, and the United States. Her recent research has focused on consumer-producer networks in local food systems, and on farmer environmental attitudes and land management practices in Devon, England, and in central Kansas. She is the principal investigator on a Department of Energy-funded study on the impact of biofuels production on rural communities in Kansas and Iowa. Her work has been published in *Society and Natural Resources, Environment and Planning A, Journal of Rural Studies, Agriculture and Human Values*, and *Environmental Science and Policy*.

Jane Silberstein has more than 20 years of experience in community development as a consultant, city planner, facilitator, author, and teacher. Currently, she is Associate Dean at the Bainbridge Graduate Institute—the nation's first Green MBA program (Bainbridge Island, WA). Prior to moving to Washington, she served as a faculty member for the University of Wisconsin–Extension as a community, natural resource, and economic development educator. As a planner and community development professional, she has acquired extensive experience in community visioning, eco-municipality advancement, comprehensive plan, and local coastal program development; waterfront, downtown, bikeway, open space/environmental, and neighborhood plans; and ordinance and policy development, growth management, environmental review, and economic improvement/diversification plans. She co-authored a book (with Chris Maser) titled *Land Use Planning for Sustainable Development* in 2000.

Anne Heinze Silvis is an Extension Specialist in Program Development for the University of Illinois Extension and is Director of the Laboratory for Community and Economic Development, Department of Human and Community Development at the University of Illinois at Urbana-Champaign. She also serves on the community and economic development team for University of Illinois Extension. Her work focuses on topics including leadership development, community leadership, sustainable agriculture, and group process skills. She chairs the planning committee and hosts the annual Illinois Leadership Conference, and she also directs funded projects in leadership development, community planning, and sustainable agriculture.

L. Steven Smutko is a Policy Specialist in the Department of Agricultural and Resource Economics at North Carolina State University, and Director of the North Carolina Natural Resources Leadership Institute. He conducts training and research in decision making and negotiation on issues related to natural resource management and environmental policy. Since joining the North Carolina State University faculty in 1995, he has designed, convened, and facilitated stakeholder engagement projects on major regulatory issues in North Carolina and the southeastern United States. He conducts negotiation training programs for local, state, and federal agencies, private industry, and nonprofit organizations; teaches an annual negotiation course for environmental professionals; and teaches negotiation analysis to North Carolina State graduate students.

Josh Stovall is a PhD student, Instructor, and Research Assistant in Sociology at Brigham Young University. He is a native Mississippi Deltan and earned a Master of Science in Community Development from Delta State University (2005), where he completed longitudinal research on leadership and community development in the Delta. His research publications have focused mainly on rural sociology and community development, including research methods, community satisfaction and attachment, and social change. He is currently working on his dissertation, which compares attitudes of rural residents and leaders on community development issues over time.

Ana Maria Thomas coordinates the Innovation Center for Community and Youth Development's communications work, using a combination of high-tech and high-touch strategies to actualize the organization's tagline in a real way: connecting people and ideas to create change. Ana graduated cum laude from Georgetown University in 2008, where she studied government and English. She is especially interested in the intersection of education, youth engagement, and public policy.

Wendy Wheeler is the President and Founder of the Innovation Center for Community and Youth Development. She seeks out, nurtures, and brings to scale exceptional strategies to support young people, strengthen communities, and promote social justice. An expert in training and organizational, youth, community, and leadership development, she consults for organizations, universities, and philanthropic institutions to increase youth engagement in communities and adult partnerships with youth. Prior to founding the Innovation Center, she held leadership posts at the YMCA, YWCA, and Girl Scouts of the USA, and was a Senior Vice President at National 4-H Council. She serves on advisory boards for the Center for Information and Research on Civic Learning and Engagement (CIRCLE) at Tufts University, the Center for Advancement of Informal Science Education (CAISE), and the *Encyclopedia of Youth Activism*. She is also the Howland Endowed Chair in Youth Leadership at the University of Minnesota.

Supporting researchers for more than 40 years

Research methods have always been at the core of SAGE's publishing program. Founder Sara Miller McCune published SAGE's first methods book, *Public Policy Evaluation*, in 1970. Soon after, she launched the *Quantitative Applications in the Social Sciences* series—affectionately known as the "little green books."

Always at the forefront of developing and supporting new approaches in methods, SAGE published early groundbreaking texts and journals in the fields of qualitative methods and evaluation.

Today, more than 40 years and two million little green books later, SAGE continues to push the boundaries with a growing list of more than 1,200 research methods books, journals, and reference works across the social, behavioral, and health sciences. Its imprints—Pine Forge Press, home of innovative textbooks in sociology, and Corwin, publisher of PreK–12 resources for teachers and administrators—broaden SAGE's range of offerings in methods. SAGE further extended its impact in 2008 when it acquired CQ Press and its best-selling and highly respected political science research methods list.

From qualitative, quantitative, and mixed methods to evaluation, SAGE is the essential resource for academics and practitioners looking for the latest methods by leading scholars.

For more information, visit **www.sagepub.com**.